Where Great Powers Meet

Where Great Powers Meet

America & China in Southeast Asia

DAVID SHAMBAUGH

OXFORD

UNIVERSITY PRESS

OXFORD
UNIVERSITY PRESS

Oxford University Press is a department of the University of Oxford. It furthers
the University's objective of excellence in research, scholarship, and education
by publishing worldwide. Oxford is a registered trademark of Oxford University
Press in the UK and certain other countries.

Published in the United States of America by Oxford University Press
198 Madison Avenue, New York, NY 10016, United States of America.

© Oxford University Press 2021

Library of Congress Cataloging-in-Publication Data
Names: Shambaugh, David L., author.
Title: Where great powers meet : America and China in Southeast Asia / David Shambaugh.
Description: New York : Oxford University Press, 2020. | Includes index. |
Identifiers: LCCN 2020022184 (print) | LCCN 2020022185 (ebook) | ISBN 9780190914974 (hardback) |
ISBN 9780190914998 (epub) | ISBN 9780190091132
Subjects: LCSH: Southeast Asia—Foreign relations—21st century. | United States—Foreign relations—
China. | China—Foreign relations—United States. | United States—Foreign relations—Southeast Asia. |
Southeast Asia—Foreign relations—United States. | China—Foreign relations—Southeast Asia. |
Southeast Asia—Foreign relations—China. | United States—Foreign relations—21st century. |
China—Foreign relations—21st century.
Classification: LCC DS525.8 .S674 2020 (print) | LCC DS525.8 (ebook) | DDC 327.59051—dc23
LC record available at https://lccn.loc.gov/2020022184
LC ebook record available at https://lccn.loc.gov/2020022185

1 3 5 7 9 8 6 4 2

Printed by LSC Communications, United States of America

Dedicated with Great Admiration to

Professor Wang Gungwu

Exceptional Scholar, Gentleman, Colleague, Friend, and, Inspiration

OTHER BOOKS BY DAVID SHAMBAUGH

China's Leaders: From Mao to Now (2021)

China & the World (edited, 2020)

The China Reader: Rising Power (edited, 2016)

China's Future (2016)

International Relations of Asia (co-edited, 2008 and 2014)

China Goes Global: The Partial Power (2013)

Tangled Titans: The United States and China (edited, 2012)

Charting China's Future: Domestic & International Challenges (edited, 2011)

China's Communist Party: Atrophy & Adaptation (2008)

China-Europe Relations: Perceptions, Policies, and Prospects (co-edited, 2008)

China Watching: Perspectives from Europe, Japan, and the United States
(co-edited, 2007)

Power Shift: China & Asia's New Dynamics (edited, 2005)

The Odyssey of China's Imperial Art Treasures
(co-authored, 2005)

Modernizing China's Military: Progress, Problems, and Prospects (2002)

Making China Policy: Lessons from the Bush and Clinton Administrations
(co-edited, 2001)

The Modern Chinese State (edited, 2000)

Is China Unstable? (edited, 2000)

The China Reader: The Reform Era (co-edited, 1999)

China's Military Faces the Future (co-edited, 1999)

Contemporary Taiwan (edited, 1998)

China's Military in Transition (co-edited, 1997)

China and Europe: 1949–1995 (1996)

Greater China: The Next Superpower? (edited, 1995)

Deng Xiaoping: Portrait of a Chinese Statesman (edited, 1995)

Chinese Foreign Policy: Theory & Practice (co-edited, 1994)

American Studies of Contemporary China (edited, 1993)

Beautiful Imperialist: China Perceives America, 1972–1990 (1991)

The Making of a Premier: Zhao Ziyang's Provincial Career (1984)

Contents

List of Figures

List of Tables

Preface

Being on the deck of an American aircraft carrier is an awe-inspiring experience. In a different way, so too is witnessing a land reclamation construction project as far as the eye can see. These two experiences that I had within a month during 2017 encapsulated and brought home to me the respective differences between the United States and China in Southeast Asia.

I first visited the Changi Naval Base in Singapore and went aboard the massive aircraft carrier USS *Carl Vinson* (Fig. 0.1)—the 101,300-ton Nimitz-class flagship of Carrier Strike Group 1 of the US Third Fleet (home-ported in San Diego but part of the Pacific Fleet).

With its accompanying carrier battle group of guided missile destroyers, cruisers, submarines, and supply ships, the *Carl Vinson* had docked at Changi following back-to-back exercises near North Korea in the Sea of Japan and Chinese-occupied islands in the South China Sea—sending powerful deterrent signals in each case. Walking the massive deck of the supercarrier past an array of F-18 Super Hornet fighters, anti-submarine warfare planes, electronic attack and

Figure 0.1 USS *Carl Vinson*
Source: US Navy photo by Mass Communication Specialist 3rd Class Eric Coffer

early warning aircraft, and helicopters, with more planes and lethal munitions below deck (Fig. 0.2), and speaking with the dedicated sea and air men and women onboard was a moving and memorable experience.

The carrier visit was a potent reminder of America's unrivaled military power—which has been projected throughout East Asia and the western Pacific for more than seven decades. Quietly but firmly, every day of the year, the US Navy and other military forces contribute to securing and stabilizing this dynamic and strategically important region of the world, supporting America's five allies and many partners in the region, and giving daily credence to the century-long presence of the United States as an Asian and Pacific power.

Subsequently, two weeks later, I crossed the causeway that connects Singapore to Malaysia and traveled up to the scenic port city of Malacca (Melaka in Malay). First, 20 miles or so into the southern Malaysian state of Johor, one

Figure 0.2 The author aboard USS *Carl Vinson*
Source: Author's photo

encounters the massive Chinese residential development of Forest City—a joint project between Johor and a Chinese company. A sprawling multipurpose complex encompassing 20 square kilometers and four separate islands, Forest City bills itself as the "largest residential complex in the world" and as an "Exclusive Island Living Paradise."[1] It is still in the early stages of construction (Figure 0.3), while Figure 0.4 is a scale model of what the whole project will look like upon completion by 2025.

Forest City's developer, the Guangzhou-based developer Country Garden Group, is building enough residential housing for as many as 700,000 people. It will be a complete self-contained "eco city"—with schools, hospitals, entertainment, three 18-hole golf courses, and other amenities. Although within commuting distance of Singapore, most of the residents are intended to live there or use it as weekend getaways from China. The apartments were selling quickly to mainland Chinese citizens prior to 2018, when the Chinese government slapped stricter controls on the movement of private capital out of the country. For a while, the developer was offering Shanghai residents a "two for one" opportunity—buy a flat in Shanghai and get one free in Forest City. While PRC capital controls slowed sales somewhat, the young saleswoman

Figure 0.3 Forest City development
Source: Author's photo

Figure 0.4 Scale model of Forest City
Source: Author's photo

I met ("Charlotte," an information technology graduate from Beijing Normal University) maintained that 40 percent of all planned units had been bought.

As one walks into the sales gallery you are greeted with the soothing background music of John Denver's "Country Roads," and the sprawling gallery opens out on to idyllic pools and a beach with Bali-style umbrellas (although no swimming is permitted). I toured several model apartments, pretending to be a potential buyer (speaking Chinese with her may have helped my credibility). A three-bedroom, 635-square-foot flat was going for $198,200, while a 1,141-square-foot three-bedroom with small yard was going for $450,000. I thanked Charlotte and told her I would get back to her. While an ambitious development, Forest City has also encountered scathing criticism for the size of the footprint of the project, the environmental damage that it has caused, lack of consultation with the local community, around-the-clock construction, and the imported labor from China.[2]

Several hours beyond Forest City one reaches the ancient seaside city of Malacca. The somewhat sleepy fifteenth-century enclave occupies an incredibly important strategic location astride the Malacca Strait (see Fig. 0.5).[3] The strait—which runs between Malaysia, Indonesia, and Singapore—is one of the busiest shipping lanes and trade routes in the world, with approximately 50,000 vessels ferrying 40 percent of the world's merchandise trade and 25 percent of all oil shipments carried by sea annually.[4] At its narrowest point near Singapore, the strait is only 1.5 miles wide, making it a strategic chokepoint in times of conflict. The Chinese refer to their "Malacca dilemma"—a reference to the potential that, in wartime, the US Navy could close the strait and thus inhibit China's energy imports and merchandise exports. Dozens of massive ships—oil supertankers, vehicle carriers, container ships, naval vessels—all ply this narrow isthmus at close proximity with each other daily.

Given their dependence on imported energy supplies, all Asian states—particularly those in Northeast Asia—would be profoundly affected if a blockade or naval conflict shut down this strategic passageway.

As one leaves the charming central quarter of Malacca City—which is filled with quaint "shop houses," open-air food stalls, vibrant markets, and old-world architecture—one drives across a causeway to a connecting islet where one is greeted with a massive billboard announcing the entrance to the multipurpose "Melaka Gateway" project being built by the Chinese in cooperation with Malaysian partners.[5] It is a somewhat typical example of China's vaunted "Belt and Road" Initiative. When I visited the Melaka Gateway project in 2017, I was stunned by its potential scale. Sitting directly adjacent to the strategically sensitive Malacca Strait, Malacca Gateway spans 750 acres and will encompass four distinct islands (mainly reclaimed land).

Figure 0.5 The Malacca Straits near Singapore
Source: Author's photo

Figure 0.6 Melaka Gateway
Source: Author's photo

The project includes a large residential district with hotels and condominiums, hospitals and schools, a Ferris wheel, a marina for 600 private yachts, and a major terminal that can berth up to four Royal Caribbean cruise ships at once. Next door will be a high-rise financial center and free trade zone see Fig. 0.6). Melaka Gateway, which is due for completion in 2025, also includes a mammoth deep-water port (that can handle vessels up to 12,000 TEUs, a measure essentially equal to a cargo container). The port will be 25–30 meters deep with a 3-kilometer-long wharf that can accommodate huge container vessels and tankers carrying oil and liquefied natural gas, and is projected to accommodate more shipping traffic than Singapore. Next to the port will be a storage facility with capacity for 5 million containers. Finally, Melaka Gateway will include a Maritime Natural Park.

Melaka Gateway is one of the largest "One Belt, One Road" infrastructure projects that China is building across Malaysia. As chapter 5 describes in more detail, OBOR—or the Belt & Road Initiative (BRI) as it has been officially rebranded by Beijing—is a gargantuan $1.2 trillion megaproject that spans the globe; it connects Asia to Europe through an overland route across Eurasia (the "Silk Road Economic Belt"), and a second one spanning the South China Sea through the Indian Ocean and Red Sea to the Mediterranean (the "21st

Century Maritime Silk Road"). Numerous commercial infrastructure projects—including construction of ports, power plants, electricity grids, railroads, highways, industrial parks, commercial and financial centers, telecommunications facilities, and residential housing—are already under way, with many more on the drawing board.

***

These two respective experiences—one highlighting America's hard military power and the other China's soft economic power—are emblematic of the respective roles of the two competing powers where they meet in Southeast Asia today. While illustrative, they both are somewhat stereotypical and misleading. That is, both the United States and China use a much broader range of mechanisms and have established much deeper footprints across the region than their respective military and economic presence would suggest. While each power has its own comparative advantages, both possess and deploy an array of instruments in a range of sectors—diplomatic, commercial, cultural, military, technological, and other spheres—and they bring these comprehensive capabilities to bear both vis-à-vis regional countries and in their incipient competition with each other.

In this book I examine these instruments in Beijing's and Washington's "toolboxes," the legacies of each power's historical interactions with the region, how the ten different Association of Southeast Asian Nations (ASEAN) states in the region all interact with—and navigate between—the United States and China, and I peer into the future to anticipate how their incipient rivalry may play out. As comprehensive rivalry between the United States and China is now *the* major defining feature of international relations, indefinitely into the future, it is of global significance and consequence how this strategic competition evolves out in Southeast Asia. The region is extremely important in its own right, but it is also a microcosm of many of the features of US-China great power rivalry that is taking place worldwide.

For many decades I have written about US-China relations and Chinese foreign policy, publishing numerous books and articles about various aspects of these subjects. But Southeast Asia had never attracted my close attention. I regret this, as I have come to "discover" it late in my career. But better late than never, as they say. Having now done so, I find myself absolutely fascinated by the rich cultures and complexities of the societies and states in the region—and this is a new love affair that will continue for the rest of my life. In my scholarship, I also very much like to research and write about things that are new and about which I do not know much. Thus, book writing for me has always been a true educational exploration. Some scholars, indeed most, spend their entire careers working on one or two relatively narrowly defined subfields. I have never been this way. I like new puzzles. And this volume has been a particularly challenging—but rewarding—experience.

However, precisely because I am not an expert and do not have a long career of working on Southeast Asia, I am hyperconscious of what I do *not* know about the region (a great deal). I thus must offer a sincere apology to those many specialists in the field of Southeast Asian studies for the "overview" nature of this study, and any errors contained herein. Both China's and America's relations with the region, and the histories of the individual countries themselves, are all exceedingly complex. It is indeed a daunting and impossible task—indeed probably a superfluous undertaking—to try and capture these complex histories (particularly in chapters 2 and 4). I can hear many readers asking, "What about this or that?" There is, therefore, an inevitable degree of generalization in this study. I am also not an historian by training—but I have tried my best to capture these histories accurately and to provide readers with a broad sense of how the past has shaped the present. With these caveats, I have done my best to explore and capture the multilayered chessboard of interactions by the United States and China with the nations by Southeast Asia.

1

Sino-American Competition in Southeast Asia

"Everything in Southeast Asia now has to do with U.S.-China relations."

—Professor Wang Gungwu, National University of Singapore[1]

"We do not wish to choose between China and the United States. Any competition between these two is not beneficial to us or the region."

—Desra Percaya, Director-General for Asia-Pacific, Indonesian Ministry of Foreign Affairs[2]

"Great Power competition isn't all bad for Southeast Asia since it can provide opportunities to hedge and secure benefits from rival camps."

—Jonathan Stromseth, Brookings Institution[3]

Great power rivalry is back. On the complicated landscape of international relations today one predominant factor is rising to the fore: *comprehensive competition* between the United States and People's Republic of China. This competition is now playing out across all functional domains—diplomacy, commerce, security, intelligence, ideology and values, science and technology, and others—as well as across all continents and many countries.[4] This book is about how the two powers are competing in one geostrategically important part of the world: Southeast Asia.

For the United States, the shift from "engagement" to "competition" and rivalry with China has been the product of a seismic shift in American thinking about China in recent years. Over the past decade a variety of constituencies became progressively more frustrated with Chinese behavior in their respective professional spheres: the US military, diplomats, educators, members of Congress, media and journalists, NGOs of a wide variety, intelligence and law enforcement agencies, and the business community. As a result of

these growing frustrations with trying to carry on what should be normal cooperative interactions with Chinese counterparts, a progressive groundswell in an-
tipathy and shift in attitudes about China occurred among these constituencies
and across the United States.

The consequence of this national *gestalt* has been a sea change in American
thinking about China.[5] In many publications, and particularly on Capitol Hill,
there has been an evident and widely shared shift toward advocating a "tougher"
and more "competitive" strategy. Today's competition between the United States
and China affects multiple realms: military/security; political systems; diplomacy; economic/commercial; ideology; values; media; culture and soft power;
governance practices; public diplomacy and "influence operations"; espionage;
technology; innovation; Indo-Pacific regional and global competition in all of
the aforementioned areas; and in some international institutions and areas of
"global governance." In *every one* of these areas the United States and China find
themselves in disagreement and competition for advantages vis-à-vis the other.
Two-thirds of Americans now view China unfavorably,[6] while politicians and
pundits alike now call for full-blown "competition" with China.[7] The Trump
administration's *National Security Strategy of the United States* and *United States
Strategic Approach to the People's Republic of China* both reflect and drive this
hardened perspective.[8] China policy seems to be the one policy area where there
is also considerable bipartisan consensus and a shared approach between the
Congress and executive branch in the administration.[9] This is also reflected in
an apparent overall shift in public opinion which, according to a 2019 Chicago
Council on Global Affairs survey, has shown a sharp uptick in the number of
Americans who now view China as a "rival."[10]

The new great power rivalry bears some similarities to Cold War 1.0, but
it also has significant dissimilarities. One is that China, unlike the Soviet
Union, is thoroughly integrated into the international institutional order
and has a multidimensional presence in most countries around the world.
A second obvious difference is China's domestic economic success and its
international influence. China's science and technology base is also more
diversified than the Soviet Union's (which was dominated by the military-
industrial complex). While the United States and China possess antithetical
political systems and ideologies, the PRC is just beginning to actively export
its ideology and create political client states (economic client states as well)
as the Soviet Union did. As Kurt Campbell and Jake Sullivan have astutely
observed: "China today is a peer competitor that is more formidable economically, more sophisticated diplomatically, and more flexible ideologically
than the Soviet Union ever was."[11]

There are other differences, as well as similarities, in the emerging superpower struggle. One other is that it has not—yet—become an action-reaction,

zero-sum, type of geostrategic contest. During the Cold War, Moscow and Washington carefully gauged their actions in *response* to what the other was doing in different domains. While this has been occurring in the military procurement sphere between the American and Chinese militaries for a number of years, it has not yet spread to an explicit contest for influence and clients around the world. Nor are there clearly defined spheres of influence, as was the case in Europe and Latin America during the Cold War—today the United States has a long-standing and deep presence throughout Asia, while Beijing is building a significant presence throughout the western hemisphere, in Europe, Africa, and elsewhere.

This said, we *are* witnessing during the Trump administration, for the first time, American strategy and actions being taken intentionally to *counter* China. We have seen this in critical speeches by the US secretary of state concerning China's presence in Africa and Latin America as well as China's Belt and Road Initiative; we have seen it in the public diplomacy (PD) realm (the State Department's Global Engagement Center as well as tailored PD programs to counter Chinese propaganda around the world); we are seeing it in the economic area with the rollout of the BUILD Act (an explicit counter-action to Belt and Road) and the Asia Reassurance Act; we are seeing it in the intelligence and espionage domain (especially cyber); we see it in exposure of Chinese influence and united front operations abroad; and we are seeing it in a number of US military actions to counter the rapidly growing capabilities of the People's Liberation Army (PLA). So, for the first time, under Donald Trump, a presidential administration has *gone on offense* against China.

****

Since comprehensive competition between the United States and China is *the* most distinguishing feature of international relations at present and indefinitely into the future, it is affecting all regions and most countries in the world, including in Southeast Asia. This book is about both the comprehensive Sino-American competition, as well as the individual elements of each power's respective positions, using that region as a case study of the global contest. Both scholarly analyses and public opinion polls indicate that the Sino-American competition in the region is intensifying. One 2019 poll, conducted by the ISEAS-Yusof Ishak Institute ASEAN Studies Center in Singapore, surveyed over 1,000 Southeast Asia experts and officials and asked: "Do you think the US and China are on a collision course in Southeast Asia?" Fully two-thirds of respondents (68.4 percent) answered "yes."[12] Some observers see not only rivalry (which suggests a kind of balanced competition), but actually a *shift* in relative power and influence—from America to China.[13]

In this book I will examine the competition broadly, their respective capabilities more narrowly, and will assess the relative balance of power between the two. However, some cautionary caveats are in order at the outset.

First, the US-China competition is not merely dyadic, as if no other actors matter. Quite to the contrary, the superpower competition is ameliorated and adjudicated by the ten member states of the Association of Southeast Asian Nations (ASEAN). Indeed, other regional "middle powers"—notably Japan, India, Australia, and the European Union, and to a lesser extent Russia—are also involved on the strategic chessboard of Southeast Asia.[14] Each of these actors has its own interests and possesses its own agency in the complex and fluid environment—thus buffering the Sino-US rivalry to some extent. ASEAN states also exercise their own agency, as is explored in chapter 6. Indeed, born out of their colonial histories, ASEAN states have a long history of protecting their independence and warding off interference and great power competition. Southeast Asia is not like Europe and other regions during the Cold War where each major power had its sphere of influence and client states. Today, Beijing and Washington compete *within* and *among* the same states. Moreover, these states and societies do their best to maximize gains from each big power, not wishing to become beholden to either one. Yet, as China is increasingly able to pre-empt Southeast Asian states—individually or collectively—from issuing public statements or undertaking certain actions, it reveals compromised independence and "agency" on their parts. So, the strategic contest between the United States and China in Southeast Asia is complicated.

The second caveat flows from the first. Thus far, as noted earlier, the US-China competition is not (yet) a Cold War–style one—either in Southeast Asia or elsewhere in the world. During the Cold War, the United States and Soviet Union largely engaged in an *action-reaction direct competitive contest*—whereby each side calculated its moves based on what the other was doing. While China is certainly taking its own initiatives that affect American interests across many spheres, and some are covert or opaque, I only see Beijing taking minimal actions specifically to counter the United States. Beijing takes actions more to advance its own position than to counter and undermine the US. Thus, there is not yet a real tit-for-tat dynamic in the US-China global competition. This is what I call *soft rivalry* or *soft competition* rather than *hard rivalry* or *hard competition*. That is, the two powers are kind of shadow-boxing with each other. It also reflects the fact that the two powers have very different toolboxes of instruments that they use in pursuit of their international goals. The most apparent difference lies in China's economic strengths versus America's military strengths. This dichotomy is quite apparent in Southeast Asia.

Thus, in the new twenty-firstcentury great power environment, both Beijing and Washington—but particularly China—are operating mainly on their own without calibrating their global moves vis-à-vis the other. For the United States, there has been a large element of "autopilot"—whereby Washington has based its global activities around its allies and traditional friends. But, as noted earlier, this has changed under the Trump administration—which has taken a much more explicit approach to competing with and confronting China. This is a result of a sea change in American strategic thinking about China and is highly likely to last well beyond Trump's time in office.

For its part, China constantly and stealthily maneuvers in "grey zone" regions and with countries neglected by the Americans. This is notably the case in Central Asia, Africa, and Central Europe. But China is also attempting to peel off traditional US allies and partners in Asia, Europe, and Latin America. Southeast Asia must be viewed in this broader context—as there is enormous fluidity across the region.

In this context, and with these two caveats, this book has several principal findings. First, China is intensively beavering away to broaden and deepen its presence in all Southeast Asian countries, while the United States remains much more neglectful in its attention and static in its actions. Second and relatedly, there is a resulting pervasive and predominant narrative across the region that China is the "inevitable" dominant power, while the United States is in inexorable eclipse and decline. Third, when examined empirically, however, this book finds that this narrative (meme) is not accurate. That is, I counterintuitively find that the United States still has *deep roots* and possesses far more *comprehensive* power in the region than China. The United States is hence an "underappreciated power," whereas China is an overestimated one.[15]

I find this to be the case certainly with respect to relative *capabilities*, but not necessarily with respect to power as defined by *influence*. American influence has definitely waned—notably among its traditional allies Thailand and the Philippines—while China now casts a long shadow across Southeast Asia, which has resulted in Beijing having a virtual "veto power" over *every* ASEAN state. That is, no Southeast Asian government is willing to openly criticize or stand up to China or premise its foreign and security policies on countering China's expanding reach into the region. Yet, precisely because of the United States, the "middle powers" noted above, and the independent agency of each Southeast Asian state, Southeast Asia can by no means be considered China's sphere of influence.

Because ASEAN states have their own "agency" (as described in chapter 6) domestic politics in these countries actually have a significant influence on a nation's orientation vis-à-vis China and the United States (witness the Philippines under Duterte, Malaysia under Najib and subsequently Mahathir, Indonesia under Jokowi, and Thailand under Prayut).

As a result, the game will go on and the strategic contest between China and the United States will be protracted. My guess is that the ultimate "winner" will be *Southeast Asia*—not Washington and not Beijing—as ASEAN states and societies will be able to maximize benefits from *both* powers while success-fully adapting their traditional "hedging" strategies to keep both powers at bay. However, I can also envision the region succumbing to China *if* the United States does not pay it appropriate attention. This said, I further can also envision China stumbling as it maneuvers to expand its position and influence in the region. Beijing will overreach, overstep, and aggravate its Southeast Asian neighbors (we are already seeing signs of it with the Belt and Road Initiative and South China Sea). This is more of a prediction than a conclusion. The implication, however, is that the United States needs to play the long game, be patient, and fashion a sustainable strategy to be present and to offer Southeast Asian states a reasonable (and hopefully dependable) alternative when China trips up.

The Importance of Southeast Asia

Southeast Asia is a dynamic and sprawling region, spanning 1.7 million square miles (more than 3,000 miles from east to west and over 2,000 miles from north to south) between Australasia to the southeast, South Asia to the west, and northeast Asia. The region is composed of eleven nation-states, ten of which are members of ASEAN.[16] With a combined population of 636 million people, Southeast Asia is one of the most heavily and densely populated regions of the world. Indonesia alone has the fourth-largest national population in the world (255 million), and the largest Muslim population worldwide (205 million). The Asian Development Bank projects a combined regional population of 700 mil-lion by 2030.[17] Demographic size is matched by religious diversity, as Southeast Asia has 240 million Muslims, 140 million Buddhists, 130 million Christians, and 7 million Hindus.

Diversity defines everything about Southeast Asia—ethnicity, cultures, re-ligion, geography, economies, politics, and external influences—and it is one reason ASEAN has such difficulty acting with coherence and common purpose. The region's diversity has historical roots. As Kishore Mahbubani and Jeffery Sng describe well in their excellent book *The ASEAN Miracle*, Southeast Asia was forged by four successive "waves" of immigrants: Indian, Chinese, Muslim, and Western.[18] The Western wave spanned the sixteenth to twentieth centuries, with different European maritime powers establishing a trading presence and series of colonies (Dutch, Portuguese, British, and French). Following World War II, Southeast Asian societies broke free of colonialism and established independent nation-states. These nationalist struggles against colonialism, and the prized autonomy that accompanied independence, did much to define the region's collective identity. This history remains vitally important to understanding international relations in the region to this day. Southeast Asians chafe against all forms of external intervention and manipulation—a mindset that intrinsically makes them wary of both China and the United States.

Geographically, Southeast Asia is of vital strategic importance, particularly the South China Sea and the Straits of Malacca. Southeast Asia is the nexus of the Indo-Pacific region—lying at the intersection of South Asia, East Asia, and Australasia.

In economic terms, Southeast Asia has become the fastest growing region in the world since the global financial crisis of 2008–2009. According to the Asian Development Bank, in 2016 ASEAN collectively averaged 4.6 percent growth, with Vietnam leading the way at 6.7 percent, while no country averaged less than 3 percent growth.[19] The ASEAN economies collectively constitute the sixth-largest economy in the world (behind the United States, China, Japan, Germany, and the United Kingdom, and just ahead of France), with an aggregate nominal gross domestic product of $2.6 trillion ($7.92 trillion purchasing power parity) in 2017.[20] As China's economy begins to slow, and in response to rising operating costs and bureaucratic obstacles, many multinational companies have begun to practice the "China Plus Strategy"—maintaining, but lowering, their exposure in China while relocating some of their investments, production facilities, and supply chains from China to ASEAN countries. This process has only accelerated in the wake of the 2020 coronavirus pandemic.

Southeast Asia is also a politically diverse environment. The region includes five distinct types of political systems. Communist Vietnam and Laos are classic Leninist-type party-states—two of the five remaining ruling communist parties in the world today (China, Cuba, and North Korea being the others). Cambodia, Malaysia, and Singapore may all best be described as "authoritarian democracies," where the government permits multiple parties to exist and contest elections; but in reality, a single ruling party has dominated politics (respectively, the Cambodian People's Party, United Malays National Organization, and the People's Action Party in Singapore).[21] All three are centralized, patronage-based, hegemonic ruling parties that operate in ostensibly pluralistic polities. Singapore's world-class technocratic civil service is an important element that distinguishes it (among many other differences) from Cambodia and Malaysia. Indonesia and the Philippines are full-fledged democracies, where multiparty parliamentary systems genuinely exist. Both, however, are marred by weak civic institutions, patronage politics, and corruption. Brunei and Thailand are monarchical states, led, respectively, by a sultan and a king. Brunei is a complete monarchical sultanate, whereas Thailand has a long tradition of monarchy and democracy paired with interventionist military politics. Myanmar is an emerging democracy after decades of military rule.

In the diplomatic realm, the Association of Southeast Asian Nations cele-brated its fiftieth anniversary on August 8, 2017. Although frequently criticized for its shortcomings, ASEAN nonetheless has much to be proud of in its half-century of existence,[22] not least of which has been the absence of interstate war since the end of the Cambodia-Vietnam conflict in the mid-1990s.

The organization also prides itself for what it describes as the "ASEAN Way"—a descriptor for the priority placed on decisions reached by consensus, non-interference in each other's internal affairs, and voluntary cooperation. These norms have bonded the group together but, at the same time, have severely impeded the organization's ability to tackle tough issues and take concerted action when needed. ASEAN has, however, been quite successful in addressing transnational nontraditional security challenges such as piracy, human trafficking, smuggling, organized crime, public health pandemics, and transboundary environmental pol-lution. Still, its inability to mediate the South China Sea territorial disputes or to stop China's island-building has been a glaring weakness. Nonetheless, after sev-eral years of negotiation, the reaching of a Framework Agreement on a Code of Conduct in August 2017 was an encouraging step in the right direction. The procla-mation in 2009 of "three pillar communities"—the ASEAN Economic Community, the Political-Security Community, and the Socio-Cultural Community—remains a laudable goal and a blueprint for further regional integration.

ASEAN has also spawned a wide variety of multilateral mechanisms with other countries in Asia, the Americas, and Europe. To the extent that regional institutionalism exists in the Asia-Pacific region, it is the organization's signature contribution. This is known as "ASEAN Centrality."

Finally, regionwide military modernization is increasing Southeast Asia's strategic importance. All ASEAN states—except Cambodia and Laos—have been spending growing amounts on defense and procuring new equipment. In 2016, Singapore led the region in defense spending with a budget of $9.7 billion, followed by Indonesia ($6.9 billion), Thailand ($5.3 billion), Malaysia ($4.7 bil-lion), Vietnam ($3.3 billion), the Philippines ($3 billion), Myanmar ($2.4 bil-lion), Cambodia ($192 million), and Laos ($18.5 million).[23]

Although these are not enormous amounts when viewed globally, they are in-dicative of the region's increasing economic development, as well as the growing list of nontraditional security threats and territorial disputes in the South China Sea. These security challenges have placed a premium on procuring littoral coast guard and naval capacities, as well as ground force and air force capaci-ties. Counterinsurgency operations require the acquisition of helicopters and other special operation forces capabilities. Attack fighters are also in particular demand, and the appetite for submarines is growing. Drones, radars, and other reconnaissance systems are also on regional states' shopping lists.

Because Southeast Asian countries possess minimal indigenous defense production capacities they must purchase the vast majority of their equipment from foreign suppliers. The United States and Europe have long dominated the market, with China, Japan, and Russia all gradually beginning to establish a foothold (particularly in Malaysia, Myanmar, the Philippines, and Thailand—markets previously dominated by US and European suppliers).[24] Vietnam has long bought its weapons from Russia.

For all of these reasons, Southeast Asia is no backwater. It possesses significant strategic attributes and opportunities coveted by major powers.

Navigating among the Powers

Southeast Asia is no stranger to great power competition.[25] As a consequence, it is practiced at the art (perhaps the inventor) of "strategic hedging," with a predisposition towards neutralism and non-alignment. Yet, on the other hand, several Southeast Asian states have also adopted policies of alignment, "bandwagoning," and alliance formation. Thus, while independent neutralism may be a preference, many have practiced traditional defensive realist tactics of strategic alignment with larger powers.

The region endured a lengthy colonial encounter with European powers from the fifteenth through the mid-nineteenth centuries, as well as the invasion and occupation by Japan from 1941 to 1945. Following Japan's surrender and the end of the Pacific War, one Southeast Asian country after another gained its independence: the Philippines (1946), Burma (1948), Indonesia (1949), North and South Vietnam (1954), Laos (1954), Cambodia (1954), Malaysia (1957), Brunei (1959), and Singapore (1965). Thereafter, as a product of their colonial histories, the new Southeast Asian states fashioned a neutralist, independent tradition that began at the 1955 Bandung Conference. The Non-Aligned Movement, established in 1956, grew out of that conference; today it counts all Southeast Asian states among its 120 members. ASEAN itself was founded in 1967, in considerable part to more effectively stave off intervention and manipulation by external powers. Since its founding, ASEAN has wrestled with different strategies and tactics of how best to manage the roles of external powers in Southeast Asia. In 1971, ASEAN proclaimed the "Zone of Peace, Freedom, and Neutrality" (ZOPFAN), which was an explicit attempt to achieve regional security by excluding external powers from the region. ZOPFAN was never realistic given the Cold War, although it symbolized the sentiment of neutralism. In 1994, ASEAN created the ASEAN Regional Forum (ARF), which in many ways took the opposite approach of ZOPFAN by trying to bind external powers *into* a multilateral security framework.

Since the mid-1990s, ASEAN has thus adopted a proactive and inclusive approach of engaging external powers—by tying Australia, Canada, China, the European Union, India, Japan, and the United States into a plethora of multilateral dialogue arrangements and groupings. It holds lots of meetings and issues numerous communiqués; insofar as these mechanisms are intended to be confidence-building measures that bind the powers into the region, they must be deemed at least formally successful. At the same time, however, they are criticized for being empty "talk shops" that accomplish little of substance and whose agreements are largely non-binding.

Over time, Southeast Asian states have been masters of hedging and shifting alignments. These are not the same phenomena, however. Hedging behavior is more neutralist, ambiguous, and flexible. The whole purpose of hedging is to avoid becoming too close—and hence too dependent—on any single external power. Alignment behavior, by contrast, willingly accepts some degree of dependency and seeks to align a smaller country with a larger power.

Scholars—most notably Professors Cheng-Chwee Kuik of the University of Malaysia and Evelyn Goh of the Australian National University—have written many astute studies about Southeast Asian hedging behavior. Kuik defines hedging as "insurance-seeking behavior under high-stakes and uncertain situations, where a sovereign actor pursues a bundle of opposite and deliberately ambiguous policies vis-à-vis competing powers to prepare a fallback position should circumstances change. The aim of these contradictory acts is to acquire as many returns from different powers as possible when relations are positive, while simultaneously seeking to offset longer-term risks that might arise."[26] Whereas Kuik describes hedging as a conscious, proactive, and deliberate choice that Southeast Asian states make, Goh describes hedging as more of an unconscious, reactive, and default option given the inability of ASEAN states to make more concerted strategic decisions. She writes: "Hedging is a set of strategies aimed at avoiding (or planning for) contingencies in a situation in which states cannot decide upon more straightforward alternatives such as balancing, bandwagoning, or neutrality. Instead they cultivate a middle position that forestalls or avoids having to choose one side at the obvious expense of another."[27] Whatever the motivation, hedging behavior buys Southeast Asian states flexibility and time, and it plays to the neutralist impulses of the postcolonial era.

In contrast, University of Michigan scholar John Ciorciari argues that Southeast Asian states have long demonstrated shifting alignments toward the major powers over the past half-century. He views Southeast Asian states as demonstrating alignment behavior by decisively tilting toward external powers, and he thus rejects the neutralist assumptions of the hedging literature. Ciorciari demonstrates how, with few exceptions, Southeast Asian states have all consistently opted for "limited alignments" with external powers. The only exceptions came during the pre-1996 period, when Vietnam allied with the Soviet Union (1978–1985), and the long-standing alliances that the Philippines and Thailand have had with the United States.[28]

What has not been apparent in Southeast Asia since the Cold War is any *explicit balancing* behavior against either Beijing or Washington. Balancing occurs when states explicitly view another state as a potential adversary and coordinate their policies and actions against that country. No ASEAN state has sought to explicitly balance *against* (not between) either China or the United States. Even Vietnam, the nation most suspicious of China, has consistently maintained ongoing relations with Beijing in a wide variety of areas.

Shifting Sands in Southeast Asia

Although the nascent strategic competition between China and the United States has been brewing for some time worldwide and in Southeast Asia,[29] the maneuvering between Beijing and Washington intensified significantly after President Obama launched his "pivot" policy toward Asia in 2012.[30] The pivot (or "rebalance") included many functional components, but Southeast Asia was a central geographic focus of the policy. The US initiative was initially welcomed across the region. Over time, however, it came to be viewed as more rhetoric than reality—particularly as the Obama administration failed to confront China over its building of islands in the South China Sea or to support the Philippines in the wake of the landmark Hague Tribunal ruling invalidating China's claims during Obama's last year in office. This failure fueled the "empty cannon" perception of Washington seen by some in the region. Nonetheless, overall, by the time Obama left office in January 2017, the United States' position in Southeast Asia may never have been stronger any previous time.[31]

The pivot surprised Beijing and stimulated it to increase China's presence across multiple spheres and countries in the region. This new priority was first noticeable when the Chinese Communist Party (CCP) Central Committee convened the "Peripheral Diplomacy Work Conference" on October 24–25, 2013.[32] It is highly unusual that such a topic should be considered at the Central Committee level, thus indicating its importance. China's President and CCP General-Secretary Xi Jinping chaired the conference and gave an important speech to the conclave.[33] This was not the first time that China's leaders had decided to emphasize the country's Asian periphery in its diplomacy—such was the case following the 1997 Asian financial crisis. This decade-long period (1998–2008) of Chinese cultivation of Southeast Asia has been described as the "golden decade" of China-ASEAN ties.[34] Thereafter, however, Beijing severely undermined its successful efforts with its own heavy-handed behavior during its "year of assertiveness" (2009–2010),[35] when it began to bully many of its neighbors, before attempting to improve regional relations in 2011–2012. The Peripheral Diplomacy Work Conference signaled a renewed prioritization toward the region. Since the work conference, China took a wide-ranging set of regional initiatives not only in the diplomatic domain, but also in the security, cultural, and especially economic spheres in order to try and recoup its damaged reputation and relationships.[36]

The "One Belt, One Road" (OBOR) initiative is, by far, the most noteworthy of these proactive steps. OBOR (rebranded the "Belt and Road Initiative," or BRI) is a gargantuan project unprecedented in history. Although first signaled by Xi Jinping in twin speeches in Kazakhstan and Indonesia in September and October 2013, respectively, President Xi formally launched BRI by receiving twenty-nine heads of state and other officials from 130 countries and seventy international organizations to Beijing for the inaugural Belt and Road Forum on May 14–15, 2017. A follow-up summit took place in Beijing April 27, 2019.

The BRI plan envisions an expansive array of infrastructure projects that will connect Asia to Europe through an overland route across Eurasia (the "Silk Road Economic Belt"), and a second route spanning the South China Sea through the Indian Ocean and Red Sea to the Mediterranean (the "21st Century Maritime Silk Road"). Numerous commercial projects—including construction of ports, power plants, electricity grids, railroads, highways, industrial parks, commercial and financial centers, telecommunications facilities, and residential housing—are already under way, with many more on the drawing board. Given the pressing need for this kind of infrastructure in countries along these twin tracks, the BRI has been generally welcomed by most countries. In connection with researching this book, I have personally visited a number of these projects and have interviewed a number of government officials (central and local) involved, and most view BRI as a positive development. At present, China claims that more than sixty countries are involved in the $1 trillion multiyear initiative. Southeast Asia figures prominently in it, with every ASEAN country involved to some extent.[37]

Despite the grandiosity of the initiative, it will be at least five years before analysts can fully assess the degree of success or failure of China's initiative. Some Southeast Asians are skeptical. As one Vietnamese scholar-official described it to me: "China intends to use OBOR to expand its influence—but these other countries don't trust China."[38] India is also noticeably cool to the idea and has refused to participate. Although the initiative will likely encounter significant challenges and some failures along the way, there will surely be successes.

Notwithstanding the skeptics, the BRI is indicative of the new activeness of China on its Asian periphery. By 2017, there was thus an unmistakable *push* by most Southeast Asian states, as well as the *pull* by Beijing, to bring these countries more into China's geoeconomic, geopolitical, and increasingly geostrategic orbit. To be sure, this shift did not occur overnight, but has been building incrementally as Southeast Asians began to judge the Obama pivot as more hype than reality. As Singaporean Ambassador-at-Large Chan Heng Chee observed, "In reality some ASEAN states have been realigning toward China in differing degrees for quite some time. Cambodia, Laos, and to some extent Thailand, Brunei, and Malaysia have all moved into the Chinese orbit without fanfare."[39] Leading Thai scholar Thitinan Pongsudhirak echoes this perspective: "China has been gaining ground in Southeast Asia by picking off ASEAN member states one-by-one. No Southeast Asian state can now afford to stand up to Beijing on its own."[40]

Most Southeast Asian states see practical utility in moving closer to China, and thus far they have experienced no counter-consequences from Washington for doing so. As one senior official in Malaysia's Ministry of Foreign Affairs told me, "We do not have an ideological approach to China, just pragmatic and transactional. China needs friends and we are in a position to be friends. What are the costs for us of getting close to China? What can America do about it?"[41] Another senior Malaysian Foreign Ministry official elaborated, "On the question of why ASEAN and Malaysia are tilting towards China, the crude and simple answer is money. Money talks. China offers huge investments and markets."[42]

****

Although several Southeast Asian states appear to be "bandwagoning" and establishing closer alignments with Beijing, and many officials in the region describe a shift in the "balance of influence" between China and the United States, observers should not overstate this trend or expect it to continue indefinitely. Several factors could contribute to a distancing of Southeast Asian states from China in the future.

One key consideration is the United States. While many observers see US power and influence to be diminishing in the region, I argue this is a misperception. As detailed in chapters 3 and 6, the cultural, diplomatic, economic, and security footprint of the United States across Southeast Asia remains unprecedented. In most dimensions it is, in fact, *greater* than China's. I know that this assertion seems counter-intuitive and will surprise readers, but with the exception of the realms of trade and diplomacy, it is empirically true (and even in these two spheres the US is hardly absent). The breadth and depth of America's presence throughout Southeast Asia is one of the central arguments and principal findings of this study. Seen and measured *comprehensively,* the United States holds comparative advantages and the upper hand (although, as Trump has demonstrated, it can be squandered). In addition, public opinion surveys reveal a reservoir of positive perceptions of the United States among many Southeast Asian publics, although there has been significant drop-off since Trump became president (paralleling a global trend).[43] More deeply, however, as of 2020 many Southeast Asians are viewing the United States to be in a deep and prolonged state of malaise and decline. Years of bitter political partisanship and deadlock in Congress have badly tarnished respect for American democracy. The dysfunctional mishandling by the national government of the coronavirus pandemic shocked many in the region (and around the world), revealing a real breakdown of governance. The nationwide demonstrations and civil unrest to protest police brutality and systemic racism revealed deep social inequalities and fissures in American society. The Trump administration's "America First" foreign policy of harassing and neglecting allies and partners simultaneously has further undermined faith in the United States.

Taken together, these factors all contributed to deepened critical perceptions of the US throughout much of Southeast Asia (as elsewhere). So, subjective perceptions definitely matter—and oftentimes they matter more than objective realities. I would still argue, though, that despite the declining perceptions of the United States in the region in recent years, the US still has a broad and deep presence as well as a thick web of ties in Southeast Asia (I return to this theme in chapters 3, 6 and 7).

A second factor is China. Beijing is quite capable of overplaying its hand, becoming too demanding and even dictatorial toward Southeast Asian states. Evidence of this behavior already can be found in Chinese interactions with Cambodia, Laos, Malaysia, Myanmar, Thailand, and Vietnam. Southeast Asians have deeply ingrained postcolonial identities, and they are quick to react to larger powers seeking to establish asymmetrical relationships and acting with arrogance. Southeast Asians also still have fresh memories of China's subversive policies and actions in the region during the 1960s and 1970s, when Beijing actively supported communist party insurgencies in every single country throughout the region (see chapter 4). This wariness of China is especially apparent in Indonesia, the Philippines, and Vietnam, although it remains in the subconscious of most Southeast Asians. Thus, their challenge is to navigate increasingly close relations with China while not becoming overly dependent. As a senior Thai diplomat described it to me, "It is too late for us Thais to escape China's embrace—we are just trying to keep from being smothered by it."[44]

A third factor is ASEAN itself. The association and its individual member states are not without their own agency and capacity to recalibrate, to some extent, their external linkages. I say "to some extent" because the degree of their economic dependence on China is already high and is only going to grow over time. Southeast Asians can, at best, only modulate their economic relationships with China; they cannot escape their dependence. Nor is their geographic proximity to China going to change. Bilahari Kausikan, the deeply experienced, respected, and candid former Ambassador-at-Large of Singapore, puts it this way: "China understands ASEAN better than the U.S. and knows far better how to work with ASEAN, which is a polite way of saying manipulate our weaknesses."[45] Nonetheless, ASEAN is not a completely passive party; it has proven itself adroit at flexible maneuvering and hedging behavior. The question is, with China's increasing strength and influence in the region, combined with Washington's episodic attention, will ASEAN be able to maintain its flexibility and hedging—or will Beijing progressively erode its agency?

Fourth, other regional "middle powers" help ASEAN from being caught in a pincer between China and the United States.[46] Japan, in particular, is an important player in Southeast Asia—certainly economically, but increasingly diplomatically and culturally as well. Japan possesses more soft power in Southeast Asia than China, by some measure. Tokyo is even stepping up its security cooperation with several ASEAN states. India is also rapidly expanding its position in Southeast Asia, commensurate with Prime Minister Narendra Modi's "Act East" policy. South Korean President Moon Jae-in has also unveiled his country's "southward policy" (I was in the audience in Singapore when he did so in July 2018). For reasons of geographic proximity, security, and commerce, Australia considers itself to have a special relationship with Southeast Asia. Even Russia is attempting to play a greater role in the region. These actors further complicate the regional chessboard.

Thus, despite Southeast Asia's apparent gravitational shift toward China, it would be wise not to view the die as cast. The four factors described above, individually or in conjunction, could alter the region's current gravitation toward China.

The current American and Chinese competition in Southeast Asia is also conditioned by the past. While the contemporary interactions of the United States and China with Southeast Asia are the subject of this study, and they contain various new dynamics, for both powers as well as for Southeast Asia there is important historical context that shapes contemporary relations. Both powers have their own distinct histories in the region—and both have left their respective imprints on the regional psyche. We turn to this dimension in chapters 2 and 4.

PART I
THE AMERICAN ENCOUNTER
WITH SOUTHEAST ASIA

2

America's Legacies in Southeast Asia

"The Pacific Ocean, its shores, its islands, and the vast regions beyond, will become the chief theatre of events in the world's Great Hereafter. Who does not see that this movement must affect our own complete emancipation from what remains of European influence and prejudice, and in turn develop the American opinion and influence?"
—Senator William Seward, Speech in the US Senate,
July 29, 1852[1]

"No Western power can go to Asia militarily, except as one of a concert of powers. To contemplate anything else is to lay ourselves open to the charge of imperialism and colonialism or at the very least—of objectionable paternalism."
—President Dwight D. Eisenhower, April 26, 1954[2]

"Around the globe—from Berlin to Thailand—are people whose well-being rests, in part, on the belief that they can count on us if they are attacked. To leave Vietnam to its fate would shake the confidence of these people in the value of the American commitment and in the value of America's word."
—President Lyndon Johnson, Johns Hopkins University,
April 7, 1965[3]

The American presence in Southeast Asia dates to the early nineteenth century.[4] Prior to that it was largely confined—as in China—to commercial trade and missionary activity. As in China, commerce and religion led the way. The flag followed traders and missionaries. US diplomats arrived in the region in the early 1800s and by mid-century US Navy ships sailed the seas as well.

Early Encounters

The American presence in Asia is usually dated to the arrival of the trading ship *Empress of China* in the southern Chinese port city of Canton (Guangzhou) in 1784. Similar commercial sailings put into ports in northern Borneo, Java, Sumatra, and along the Malacca Straits en route to India.[5] An American consul was sent to the Dutch East Indies as early as 1802, although the Dutch did not recognize his status. The first officially recognized American consul was in the British colonial city of Singapore in 1833. This step was part of a broader effort to establish an American presence in the region under President Andrew Jackson. In 1832, Jackson commissioned Edmund Roberts (Fig. 2.1), a New Hampshire merchant, to undertake a mission to East Asia to conclude a series of amity and cooperation treaties. Roberts was rebuffed by the Chinese in Guangzhou, who refused to recognize his official status (it would not be until 1844 that the United States successfully negotiated such a treaty with the Chinese, the Treaty of Wangxia, a consequence of the Opium Wars).

Following this failure, Roberts headed south aboard the US warship *Peacock* to Annam (present day southern Vietnam, also known at the time by its French colonial name Cochin China)—but he was spurned a second time. Undeterred, the Roberts Mission next headed to Siam (Thailand), where they arrived on February 18, 1833 and were more warmly received. The Roberts party was lodged for a month at a government guest house inside the King's compound.[6] On March 20 Roberts was given an audience with King Rama III, who presented the King with several gifts on behalf of President Andrew Jackson (including a gilded ceremonial sword embossed with an eagle (for the United States) and an elephant (for Siam). Thereafter, the Roberts Mission successfully negotiated the first US bilateral treaty with a Southeast Asian country: the Siamese-American Treaty of Amity and Commerce (a.k.a. the "Roberts Treaty").[7] The treaty was approved by, and received the blessing of, the Thai King. It is to this event that the United States and Thailand date their nearly two hundred year long relationship.

With the conclusion of the treaty the Americans established an initial foot-hold in Southeast Asia. In 1859 President James Buchanan sent a gift of 102 books to King Mongkut of Siam—for which the king reciprocated with a gift of a sword, a pair of elephant tusks, and an offer to send elephants to the United States.[8] This was supplemented by a further US-Thai treaty in 1856, negotiated by the American diplomatic emissary Townsend Harris (Fig. 2.2).

US industry enjoyed a shipbuilding boom in mid-century, quintupling the tonnage of American vessels between 1830 and 1860.[9] Thereafter, American trading vessels plied the seas of East, Southeast, and South Asia—putting into ports in Malaya, Singapore, Sabah, Sarawak, and across the East Indies (Indonesia)—trading in a range of primary products. Trade boomed, bringing many American companies and entrepreneurs to the region.

The other early aspect of the American imprint in Southeast Asia was the missionary presence. Protestant and Baptist missionaries arrived in Burma (from India) in 1813. While Dutch, Portuguese, and British missionaries

Figure 2.1 Edmund Roberts
Source: Library of Congress

Figure 2.2 Townsend Harris
Source: *The Elephant & the Eagle*

dominated the foreign religious presence in Malaya and the East Indies, the Americans confined themselves to Burma and Siam (and later the Philippines). Much of this American effort—in commerce and religion—was focused primarily on China, secondarily on Korea and Japan, but to a significantly lesser extent in Southeast Asia.[10]

The "missionary impulse" was motivated by a strong sense of paternalism. "The White Man's Burden" to "lift up" and "civilize" the "lesser races" was widespread among white Americans at the time, and the missionaries went forth under this self-convinced mantle.[11] Future Secretary of State William Seward opined in 1849 that the "exhausted civilizations of Asia" needed to be infused with "renewal" through "the Bible, the printing press, the ballot box, and the steam engine."[12] As historian John Curtis Perry says of Seward, "[he] was one of the first to articulate a grand, comprehensive view of America's place in the world. He saw global politics in simple moral terms as a struggle between forces of right and wrong, a battle between freedom and despotism."[13] Later, President McKinley similarly told his supporters that the United States had "no choice" but to "uplift, civilianize and Christianize" the Filipinos.[14] The discriminatory 1882 Chinese Exclusion Act was another manifestation of these racist tendencies, which came about as a result of the influx of Chinese workers ("coolies") who came to build the transcontinental railroad and mine for gold—which produced a xenophobic backlash in America (against the "yellow peril").[15]

As American traders and missionaries established their presence in East Asia during the nineteenth century, so too did the US Navy. The Pacific Squadron was established as in 1821, based on the West Coast and Hawaii. The Pacific Squadron was reconfigured in 1835, renamed the East Indies (or "East India") Squadron, and established an in-region presence operating out of Canton (Guangzhou),

China. Beginning in 1842 it maintained a constant presence along the China coast. In 1832 it had its first military engagement in Southeast Asia—an assault by 300 marines aboard the USS *Potomac* on a village on Sumatra where a number of seamen aboard the American merchant vessel *Enterprise* had been seized (and their ship) and massacred the previous year. President Andrew Jackson ordered the retaliation. A second "Sumatran incident" occurred in 1838 when another American trading vessel, the *Eclipse*, was similarly attacked and looted by Malays. "Retaliation" came in January 1839, when the US frigates *Columbia* and *John Adams* were diverted from circumnavigating the globe (they were in the Indian Ocean) to attack two coastal villages.[16]

The American projection and use of force in the Pacific and Southeast Asia thus has a long history. Following the Opium Wars, in 1853 under the command of Commodore Matthew Perry, the squadron was ordered by President Millard Fillmore to sail north to "open" Japan.[17] By 1860 the Asiatic Squadron had grown to thirty-one vessels and assumed region-wide responsibilities throughout the western Pacific and Southeast Asia.[18] In 1902 the Asiatic Squadron was renamed the Asiatic Fleet.

Becoming an Imperial Power

At the turn of the twentieth century, America took on new roles internationally (as an imperial power) and regionally in Southeast Asia (as a colonial state). It was not merely the Spanish-American War that precipitated these new twin roles (although this was the facilitating event), deeper intellectual underpinnings were developing in the American intellectual class and in the US military (the Navy in particular) which justified America's transition from a continental to a maritime power and from an essentially insular nation to a more expansionist one. Individuals such as Senator Henry Cabot Lodge and Secretary of State John Hay made the case that America's future economic development now depended on supplies of raw materials from abroad (although the United States certainly had no shortage of such at home and in the newly acquired territory of Alaska) and expanded international commercial links. When the United States seized the Philippines from Spain in 1898, domestic debates erupted over the value of the island nation.[19] Lodge, then an influential senator, argued: "It has been my firm belief that the Philippine islands would not only become an important supplier of raw materials and market for us . . . but still more importantly would furnish a large opportunity for the investment of surplus capital."[20] Indeed, the second half of the nineteenth century witnessed an enormous explosion of American commercial activity throughout East Asia, culminating in the proclamation of the "Open Door" policy in 1899. This policy, proclaimed in a series of "Open Door

Figure 2.3 Alfred Thayer Mahan
Source: Library of Congress

Notes" by US Secretary of State John Hay in 1899-1900, called for equal trading rights by all countries (as distinct from the exclusive rights claimed, mainly in Chinese "treaty ports" by European colonial powers).[21]

In parallel with the economic justifications for America's ascent as an imperial power, there was a second school that argued the military rationale. By far the most influential figure here was Alfred Thayer Mahan (Fig. 2.3).

Mahan was a Union naval officer during the Civil War and he went on to gain an appointment at the newly established Naval War College in Newport, Rhode Island. There he taught, wrote prolifically, and served two terms as president of the college. His 1890 treatise *The Influence of Sea Power upon History, 1660–1783* had an enormous impact on the Navy, US government, and intellectual class.[22] He made the unabashed case that national greatness was indivisibly tied to the sea.

One individual who was particularly drawn to Mahan's writings and theories was Theodore Roosevelt, who had been a young lecturer at the Naval War College before being appointed assistant secretary of the Navy under President William McKinley. In this position Roosevelt ordered Admiral George Dewey to deploy ships of the Asiatic Squadron to Hong Kong and prepare for offensive operations against the Spanish in the Philippines. After the outbreak of the Spanish-American War in 1898, Roosevelt resigned from this position to join a cavalry unit (the "Rough Riders") in Cuba, which earned him considerable fame—so

Figure 2.4 The *Olympia* leads the Asiatic Squadron in Manila Bay (1898)
Source: "Battle of Manila" lithograph published in 1898 by Butler, Thomas & Co.

much so that McKinley selected him as his running mate in the 1900 presidential election. When McKinley was assassinated the following year, Roosevelt succeeded him as president—and immediately began drawing on Mahan's vision to undergird a turn toward an imperial America in the world and in Asia. This centrally involved the expansion of the US Navy.[23]

This is all relevant to Southeast Asia, as it became one of the first theaters to "test" the new American imperial ascendency.[24] The Asiatic Squadron, under the command of Commodore Dewey, undertook the first major naval engagement of the Spanish-American War by sinking the Spanish Pacific Fleet in Manila Bay on May 1, 1898 (Fig. 2.4).

By December 1898, with Spain's defeat, the Spanish ceded the Philippines to the United States in the Treaty of Paris (the annexation was confirmed by the Senate on February 6, 1899). America was suddenly thrust into empire, becoming an imperial power and—in the single case of the Philippines—a colonial one too.

The Filipinos did not acquiesce to their new status smoothly or peacefully— they resisted violently in what became known as the "Philippine-American War" of 1899–1902. An intense insurgency and counterinsurgency conflict ensued. Other than fighting against Native American tribes, this was the first foreign counterinsurgency operation for the American military. By the summer of

1900 fully *two-thirds* of the US Army were deployed in the Philippines to sup-press the "insurrection."[25] As the conflict dragged on, domestic opposition grew at home—led by essayist Mark Twain.[26] Altogether, the brutal three-year sup-pression involved 125,000 American troops (5000 killed in action), cost the United States $160 million, and resulted in the deaths of 16,000 Filipino fighters and 200,000 civilians.[27] While brute military force eventually prevailed, and US colonial administration ensued, the population of the Philippines—notably the Muslim population on the southern island of Mindanao—never fully acqui-esced to their secondary status. There were persistent entreaties to Washington to grant the country its independence. In 1900 a presidential commission recommended to President McKinley a series of steps for self-rule and William Howard Taft, the first civilian governor-general of the Philippines, began to enact some steps beginning in 1901.[28]

President Woodrow Wilson (1913–1921) was more amenable to the demands and, for the first time, acknowledged independence as an ultimate objective. Wilson also invited Thailand to the Versailles Conference in 1919, where he championed the country's appeal for an end to the "unequal treaties." Although Wilson's ideal of the League of Nations collapsed on the floor of the US Senate, which failed to ratify it, a year later in 1920 Wilson ordered the unilateral end to extraterritoriality and restored tariff autonomy to Thailand.[29]

The interwar period in Southeast Asia saw progressive American economic expansion. With the exception of the post-Depression dip in trade and in-vestment from 1930 to 1934, the US commercial foothold steadily expanded throughout much of the region. By the 1920s, American companies were en-gaged in rubber production and petroleum extraction across these territo-ries, and by 1940 Standard Oil and Mobil Oil operated over 500 oil wells across the East Indies (Indonesia).[30] The Americans exported a variety of goods and imported diverse raw materials. By the 1930s, Southeast Asia supplied about 90 percent of America's crude rubber and about 75 percent of its tin.[31] The vast bulk of these imports were sourced from British Malaya and the Dutch East Indies—dominating those colonies' exports. American oil companies also sunk wells throughout the region. By 1929, American investment in Southeast Asia totaled $165 million ($2.48 billion today).

Thus, for the United States, the interwar period in Southeast Asia was charac-terized by growing direct commercial interest—but otherwise was disengaged from the region. Domestically, American society was enduring economic con-traction following the Great Depression, with substantial unemployment in cities and across the Great Plains. Externally, Washington withdrew into an iso-lationist foreign policy following Wilson's failure with the League of Nations (the Senate's rejection was itself indicative of rising isolationist sentiment) and the impotent aftermath of the Washington Naval Conference of 1921–1922. In this environment, distant regions of the world such as Southeast Asia held no interest to America.

The exception, of course, was the Philippines—where the US government continually wrestled with how to manage its colonial rule while simultaneously mapping out a pathway toward self-rule and eventual independence. In 1902 the US Congress passed the Philippines Organic Act, which created a National Assembly. This was further formalized with the 1916 Philippines' Autonomy Act (a.k.a. Jones Act), which provided a formal commitment to independence. Toward this end, Wilson instructed that Filipinos were to be put in charge of most governmental institutions.[32] This was followed in 1934 by the Philippines Independence Act (a.k.a. the Tydings-McDuffie Act), which designated the Philippines as a commonwealth and provided a road map to full independence. This situation lasted tenuously until Japan invaded the Philippines right after attacking the US Pacific Fleet at Pearl Harbor.

War Draws America In

The outbreak of the Pacific War (World War II in Asia), Japan's aggressive invasions throughout Asia, and attack on Pearl Harbor fundamentally changed the dynamics of the American role in the region. Once the United States entered the war, American forces fought on three fronts: the China-India-Burma (CBI) theater to harass and dislodge Japanese forces in mainland China, the maritime Southeast Asian theater, and in the southwest Pacific against the Japanese fleet.

The Japanese sweep through Southeast Asia was stunningly swift. With the December 7, 1941 devastating attack on Pearl Harbor, Japan launched a multi-directional offensive in Southeast Asia. The following day, December 8, Japanese forces thrust down the Malay peninsula and began bombing Singapore. On December 17 the strategic Malay port of Penang fell to Japanese forces, and the capital Kuala Lumpur succumbed three weeks later on January 11. From there Japanese forces moved swiftly down the peninsula, overrunning British, Australian, and Indian troops, before reaching Singapore on February 1. After two weeks of resistance and grotesque atrocities against Singaporean citizens and British soldiers, Japanese forces prevailed and Singapore formally surrendered on February 15, 1942. Further atrocities and looting ensued for weeks. The Japanese occupation of Singapore was particularly brutal (particularly against ethnic Chinese), with many drowned or machine-gunned to death. Estimates range from 25,000 to 100,000 killed during the homicidal frenzy. With the fall of Singapore, Britain's "impregnable fortress" had fallen.

Japan's thrust down the Malay peninsula was matched by simultaneous lightning strikes into Thailand and the Dutch East Indies. Both succumbed quickly.

Thailand mounted no real resistance and was occupied within days. In Indonesia, the Dutch military contingent was incapable of resisting the onslaught and the colonial government capitulated by March 1942.

The other pincer was Japan's assault on the Philippines, which—like Malaya—commenced in a coordinated fashion the day after Pearl Harbor. Between December 10 and 24, 50,000 Japanese forces landed on the main island of Luzon. The American B-17 bombers and fighters based at Clark and Iba airfields were quickly incapacitated and put out of action. Manila quickly fell to Japanese forces on January 2, 1942. General Douglas MacArthur, the commander of US forces, ordered a retreat 30 miles south to the island of Corregidor. There 12,000 American troops and 40,000 Filipinos held out in tenacious combat with Japanese forces, which bombed the island relentlessly. By March, after three months of bombardment, MacArthur decided to personally leave the island—ordering his men to stay and fight, while famously promising "I shall return" (Fig. 2.5).

It wasn't long until the remaining forces were overrun by Japanese troops. On May 6, General Jonathan Wainwright surrendered all American and Allied forces. Thereafter 70,000 soldiers (including 14,000 Americans) were force-marched on the infamous Bataan Death March. At least 11,000 perished due to the heat, lack of food and water, disease, brutality, and executions at the hands of the Japanese.

Figure 2.5 General Douglas MacArthur promises: "I shall return"
Source: US National Archives

With the conquest of the Philippines complete, Japan now controlled all of Southeast Asia. It had been a stunning military offensive, perhaps unparalleled in modern history.

The US and Allied counterattack began with the Battles of the Coral Sea and Midway in May–June 1942, which devastated Japan's carrier and surface combatant fleet, sinking five of Japan's six aircraft carriers. These were pivotal encounters, turned the tide in the Pacific, and allowed US forces under the command of General Douglas MacArthur and Admiral Chester Nimitz to subsequently pursue a protracted and arduous "island-hopping" campaign against Japanese forces over the next two years (Fig. 2.6).

Progressing from the Gilbert Islands, Caroline Islands, and Marshall Islands to New Guinea, the Dutch East Indies, and the Philippines—including the famous Guadalcanal and Corregidor campaigns—American forces progressively

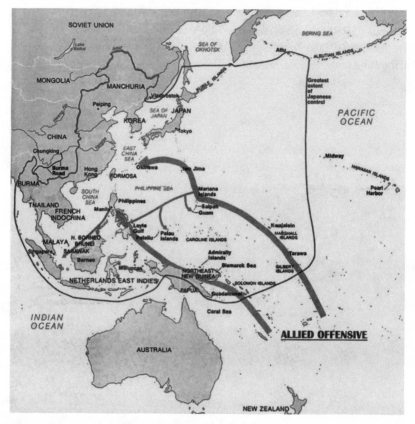

Figure 2.6 MacArthur's "island-hopping" campaign
Source: Content available under CC-BY-SA license through Wikia.org

worked their way north to within striking distance of the main home islands of Japan. Following the capture of the Mariana Islands and Iwo Jima in March 1945, American bombers started to pummel mainland Japan, including the industrial centers of Nagoya, Osaka, and Kobe on the main island of Honshu. At sea, American submarines also took a toll on Japan's Imperial Navy and support ships. By the summer of 1944, nearly 700 Japanese vessels had been sunk. Yet the Japanese High Command refused to capitulate and surrender. This, of course, led to the dropping of atomic bombs on Hiroshima and Nagasaki on August 6 and 9, and the final Japanese surrender on September 2, 1945.

Thus, the American role in the Southeast Asian theater of the Pacific War was concentrated in Burma, the Philippines, and western Pacific. Other than in the Philippines, the United States did not have a physical presence that was dislodged by Japan's onslaught. But the US role was critical in turning the tide of the war in the Pacific naval engagements and island-hopping campaign.

Postwar Transitions

For Southeast Asia, the immediate postwar period was consumed by the question of recolonization vs. decolonization. The essence of the matter lay in the European colonial powers' desire to return to their territorial holdings across the region (which were also deemed crucial to European reconstruction efforts after the war, notably in the Netherlands but also Britain and France).[33] But the Americans—notably President Franklin Delano Roosevelt—had other ideas. Roosevelt was adamantly opposed to recolonization, as FDR held deep beliefs about the right of self-determination and reflected the anti-imperialist strain of Woodrow Wilson, Walter Lippmann, and other liberals in American thinking. Roosevelt was explicit about his anti-colonial convictions at a press conference in March 1941: "There never has been, there is not now, and there never will be any race on earth fit to serve as master of their fellow men. . . . We believe that any nationality, no matter how small, has the inherent right to its own neighborhood."[34]

With this conviction, FDR opposed the return of Great Britain, France, the Netherlands, and Portugal to reclaim their Southeast Asian colonies (and elsewhere in the world) after the war. His strong preference was for *trusteeships* to be put in place as a transitional mechanism to full independence and self-determination for former colonies. In January 1942—merely three weeks after declaring war on Japan following the Pearl Harbor attack and with three years of war still to come—Roosevelt instructed his close foreign policy advisor and Under Secretary of State Sumner Welles to set up the Advisory Committee on Postwar Foreign Policy. The Advisory Committee had several subcommittees, including the Subcommittee on Territorial Problems and Subcommittee on

Political Problems. The latter was mainly responsible to think through the process of decolonization, independence, and restoration of sovereignty—while the former would adjudicate the redrawing of colonial boundaries where necessary in order to restore appropriate sovereignty to newly independent states after the war. These State Department committees continued their work throughout the war, and they increasingly began to work in close collaboration with the Division of Far Eastern Affairs and other regional bureaus. As the war progressed and victory came into view, the Roosevelt administration more assertively pressed its trusteeship plans. This brought FDR into direct disagreement with British Prime Minister Winston Churchill at the November 1943 Cairo and Tehran Conferences, as well as at Yalta in February 1945. Roosevelt's insistence on a trusteeship arrangement for Indochina caused further significant strains with the French. Interestingly and fatefully, the one East Asian territory for which Roosevelt did not advocate trusteeship status was Taiwan, which had been a full Japanese colony since 1895. Unlike former European colonies in Asia, Roosevelt believed that China's sovereignty included Taiwan, despite Japanese colonization, and therefore that the island should revert to the Republic of China following Japan's defeat.[35]

At the time of FDR's death on April 12, 1945, the situation in Southeast Asia was anything but clear. It would take years to sort out. The Japanese surrender in August 1945 opened more questions than it answered. Who was to take the surrender in Japanese occupied and former colonial states in Southeast Asia? Could the Allied forces restore stability and enforce rule? And, most important, *whose rule*? Would the British, Dutch, and French be permitted to reinstate their colonial rule? If not as directly administered entities, then under what auspices? Limited sovereignty? Transitional periods to self-rule and full independence? Would they follow the American example of granting independence to the Philippines? What role would the newly formed United Nations play? A full gamut of policy options were on the table. Additionally, but importantly, the Japanese occupation emboldened indigenous nationalist and insurgent movements and sowed the seeds of postwar independence movements. Subsequent memoirs of former Japanese officers even reveal that Japanese forces themselves were involved in arming some of these movements.[36]

The answers to these questions, of course, varied by country and by colonial power. The French were still deeply entrenched in Indochina, British forces were in a position to take the Japanese surrender, but the Dutch were in a weak position. British forces crossed over from liberated Malaya and Singapore to take the Japanese surrender in Sumatra, central Java, and the capital of Batavia (Jakarta), but the size of the British contingent was nowhere near sufficient to occupy the 5,120-kilometer long archipelago and 17,500 islands. By November 30, 1946, the British withdrew and handed over security to a 92,000-person Dutch contingent.[37] But the core issue was not one of security and disarming remnant Japanese forces—it was that Indonesians sought independent sovereign statehood. The local resistance against Japan built upon years of anti-colonial resentment, and by the end of the war Southeast Asians (as those in colonial dependent territories in South Asia, the Middle East, Africa, and Latin America) grabbed for control of their own futures. This was a pattern to be played out across Southeast Asia from the immediate postwar years for more than a decade. The paths to independence varied by country—some were granted, some were seized, some were negotiated, and some were fought for.

The Cold War Comes to Southeast Asia

At first, the United States adopted a more accommodating position toward the former colonial powers, but following the proclamation of the "Truman Doctrine" in 1947—which linked domestic political movements to Soviet expansionism worldwide—Washington adopted a more activist policy toward blunting perceived Soviet advances. This was particularly the case following the conquest of China by the Chinese Communists in 1949 and the North Korean invasion of the south in 1950. With these events, the dynamics in Asia changed entirely. But even before these traumatic events in China and Korea, for the senior members of the Truman administration, the prospects of "Asiatic communism" paralleled their concerns of Kremlin advances on the postwar European front.

Consequently, Washington adopted a more supportive view of Britain's return to Burma and Malaya, the Dutch to Indonesia, the French to Cambodia and Vietnam, and the Portuguese to East Timor. But when it became clear that the independence movements in these countries had developed substantial momentum of their own, American policy shifted abruptly in favor of full independence for these former colonial areas. Burma gained its independence from Britain in July 1947. Independence for the Malayan states was a more protracted process—Britain continued to rule them as protectorates until full independence was granted and sovereignty restored on August 31, 1957. Indonesia proclaimed its independence on August 17, 1945—but this really only kicked off the final armed resistance movement against the Dutch, which finally capitulated and recognized Indonesian independence on December 27, 1949. Thailand, which had never been colonized and had been independent since 1238, presented an unusual case. Britain had predatory designs on the Thai kingdom at the end of the war, but Washington staunchly resisted, and Thailand was admitted to the United Nations as a sovereign state in December 1946. The United States granted the Philippines its independence on July 4, 1946.

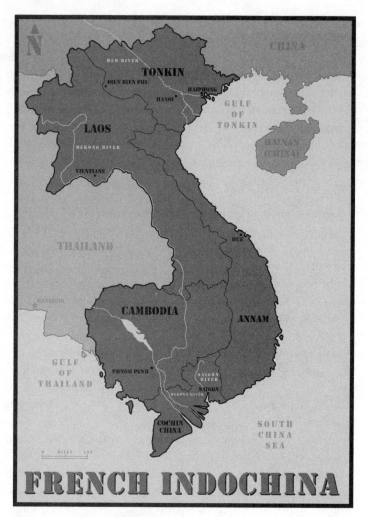

Figure 2.7 French Indochina
Source: ©CPA Media Pte Ltd/Alamy

By far, the most complicated case was French Indochina (Cambodia, Laos, Vietnam).

The French Vichy administration was not ready to vacate its colonial possessions and continued to administer the three Indochinese territories after the war (Fig. 2.7). All three territories seethed under French rule, and armed resistance grew in each. By the summer of 1953, Cambodian King Sihanouk had forced Paris into independence negotiations. France capitulated to reality and independence was proclaimed on November 9, 1953.[38] Next door in Laos the situation was similar but more complicated. In 1947 France granted Laos semi-autonomy as an "associated state" within the French Indochina Union, giving the monarchy control over most internal affairs. In February 1950, however, the United States and Britain forced France's hand and recognized the Kingdom of Laos as an independent state. The French government had no choice but to recognize the same in October 1953.

The third—and by far most complicated piece of the postwar Indochina puzzle—was the "Vietnam Question." As in other Southeast Asian countries, the anti-Japanese resistance movement in Vietnam morphed into a pro-independence (communist) insurgency. The Viet Minh, led by the charismatic nationalist-communist Ho Chi Minh, enjoyed remarkable social and political support in much of the country while building its guerrilla military network. Ironically, Ho even lived briefly in Boston and New York during his eight years traveling the world as a seaman (1911–1919), where he grew fond of Boston cream pie and also was admiring of the American struggle for independence.

In 1947 full-scale war broke out with French forces. Military engagements between the two sides raged for several years. The situation became increasingly untenable politically and militarily. The end of French colonial rule was in sight and would play out until the catastrophic collapse of French forces at Điện Biên Phủ in 1954.

For the United States during these key transitional years, it has to be said that Southeast Asia was not a high priority. The postwar order in Europe, North Africa, the Middle East, and Northeast Asia all took precedence. Even within Asia the postwar challenges of occupying Japan, the civil war in China, and a divided Korea were all befuddling for Washington. Speaking in October 1945, John Carter Vincent, a senior State Department diplomat and Director of the Bureau of Far Eastern Affairs, listed "Southeast Asian colonies" last among "Far Eastern problems."[39] Moreover, the orientation and disposition of senior US officials back in Washington was profoundly Eurocentric. As diplomatic historian Paul Heer's superb study of George Kennan (the father of the postwar "containment" policy) makes clear, Kennan had a general ignorance of Asia, lacked knowledge, and had a condescending approach toward Southeast Asia in particular. He was similarly dismissive of the rising forces of nationalism and postcolonial peoples seeking independence.[40] Compounding the general dismissiveness toward Southeast Asia was the Truman administration's preoccupation with the unfolding and deteriorating situation in China. Efforts by George Marshall and Alfred Wedemeyer to broker a coalition government and civil war truce all came to naught, as the Chinese Communists pressed ahead on the battlefield against their far less competent Nationalist adversaries.[41] With its long-standing support for the Kuomintang, the regime of Chiang Kai-shek, and the "democratic"

Republic of China, the increasing prospect of "losing China" to the Chinese Communists hung heavy over decision makers in Washington. Comparatively speaking, Southeast Asia was indeed a sideshow.

While Southeast Asia was deemed "marginal" by Kennan and other Eurocentric and Soviet-centric policymakers in the Truman administration, some had greater experience and exposure to Asia. John Paton Davies was one. Being one of the State Department's senior Asia hands, Davies had spent many years in the region—particularly China. He had been a member of the "Dixie Mission" that was sent behind enemy lines to Yan'an to observe Mao and the Chinese Communist forces there. This experience gave Davies and his colleagues a deep understanding of the intersection of popular nationalism, anti-Japanese resistance, and appeal of communism.[42] These three elements were just as important in understanding Southeast Asia as in China at the end of the war.

During the immediate postwar years, 1945–1946, the more sympathetic views of the Asia and China hands dueled with the more dismissive views of the Europeanists within the Truman administration. The former faction followed in Roosevelt's footsteps and advocated for trusteeship and transitions toward independence for the former colonies, while the latter cohort indulged European powers' desire to reassert their rule across the world.

By 1947–1948, though, a new phenomenon was arising—and particularly in Europe: communism. Stalin's Soviet Union had refused to withdraw the Red Army from Central Europe, where the Kremlin installed one communist client state after another. With the situation in Greece and Turkey quickly deteriorating and pro-communist forces poised to seize power, President Truman addressed a Joint Session of Congress on March 12, 1947, where he, in essence, fused together national independence struggles with Moscow-inspired expansion—which needed to be countered by the United States and its allies with the twin policies of supporting non-communist elements within societies and ringing the Soviet Union with anti-communist states. This became known as the "Truman Doctrine." At its core was the guiding doctrine of *containment* (as formulated by senior diplomat George Kennan) and the *domino theory* (as later articulated by Secretary of State Dean Acheson). The latter posited that, unaided by the United States and other Western powers, country after country (like Greece and Turkey) would fall like dominoes into the communist camp. The former was premised on the assumption of the Soviet Union as an aggressively expansionist power that had to be "contained." Kennan first put forward his strategic argument in a classified cable (known as the "long telegram") from the US embassy in Moscow to the State Department in Washington in February 1946, which was subsequently and famously published under the title "The Sources of Soviet Conduct" and the pseudonym "X" in the prestigious journal *Foreign Affairs* in July 1947.

After a brief tour in the US embassy in Moscow, John Paton Davies found himself back in Foggy Bottom in 1947 working under George Kennan as the Asia specialist on the State Department's Policy Planning staff (PPS). Under Kennan's direction this bureau was the brain trust that thought through and worked out comprehensive strategies for US foreign and strategic policy in the early years of the Cold War. Kennan himself was a Eurocentric strategist, albeit one who focused on the growing Soviet threat. But he was quite unknowledgeable about and dismissive of Asia. In a general overview of the situation confronting the United States, Kennan wrote in Policy Planning Study No. 23 (PPS-23) in February 1948 that the United States was "greatly overextended in [its] whole thinking about what we can accomplish, and should try to accomplish, in Asia."[43]

In June 1948, Kennan charged Davies with drafting an assessment of the situation specifically in Southeast Asia. This document, "United States Policy Towards Southeast Asia," was labeled PPS-51 and went through multiple drafts. But, throughout, there was a tension—on the one hand between Kennan's own dismissiveness of the region and tendency to view it through the prism of Soviet expansionism, and on the other hand the view held by many career Foreign Service officers with long experience in Asia who took the growing forces of nationalism more seriously and viewed the popular appeal of communism in this context. This was a key divide. The final product revealed both orientations and—like many such government policy papers—sought to accommodate both perspectives. If anything, the perspectives of Davies and the Asia hands gave way to Kennan and those who viewed the region mainly through the prism of the Soviet Union. In the end, PPS-51 concluded Southeast Asia was to be deemed "a vital segment on the line of containment" from Japan to India and that the American objective should be "the denial of Southeast Asia to the Kremlin."[44] PPS-51 thus advocated a multifaceted and multilateral approach to blunting Moscow's advances all around the eastern and southern flanks of the Soviet Union. As events were moving quickly in China while the Nationalist government was collapsing and in retreat to Taiwan, Secretary of State Acheson finally officially approved PPS-51 for intergovernmental dissemination as a "policy guidance document" on July 1, 1949. In other words, it was transmitted throughout the government and to embassies in the region without authorization to implement its findings. Yet, a blueprint had been written, and it simply required subsequent events to fulfill its prophecies and put flesh on the bones of a containment policy for East (and Southeast) Asia.[45]

Nearly six months later, on December 30, the main thrust of PPS-51 was reconfirmed in the National Security Council policy paper "The Position of the United States with Respect to Asia" (NSC-48/2). The intervening period between the adoption of PPS-51 and NSC-48/2 included the final military sweep to power by the Chinese Communist Red Army and the proclamation of the establishment of the People's Republic of China on October 1, 1949. Whatever ambiguity was apparent in PPS-51 was hardened into a firm anti-Soviet and anti-communist blueprint in NSC-48/2, which proclaimed that the "immediate objective [in East Asia] was to contain and, where feasible, reduce the power and influence of the USSR in Asia."[46] Other operative sections of NSC-48/2 stipulated:[47]

- Development of sufficient military power in selected non-Communist nations of Asia to maintain internal security and to prevent further encroachment by communism.
- Scrutinize closely the development of threats from Communist aggression, direct or indirect, and be prepared to help within our means to meet such threats by providing political, economic, and military assistance and advice where clearly needed to supplement the resistance of the other governments in and out of the area which are more directly concerned.
- Gradual reduction and eventual elimination of the preponderant power and influence of the USSR in Asia to such a degree that the Soviet Union will not be capable of threatening from that area the security of the United States or its friends and that the Soviet Union would encounter serious obstacles should it attempt to threaten the peace, national independence, and stability of the Asiatic nations.

This document mandated a range of initiatives including military assistance to Indonesia, the Philippines, Thailand, and the French in Vietnam, as well as the maintenance of forward-deployed US forces sufficient to blunt any "future Soviet aggression." These forces would be deployed along the island chains running from Japan down through the Ryukyus to the Philippines. This became known as the US "defense perimeter" in the Far East. Not included in this "first line of defense" was the island of Taiwan, where the remnant Nationalist Chinese regime had retreated. Nor were any mainland Asian territories—notably the Korean peninsula and Indochina—included.

The North Korean attack on South Korea in June 1950 changed everything. Historians debate to this day whether the exclusion of the Korean peninsula from America's "defense perimeter" invited the North Korean aggression. Regardless, it solidified the Cold War perspectives in Washington and directly tested the Truman Doctrine and Kennan's Soviet containment policies. Not only did the Korean conflict result in the dispatch of American soldiers, under United Nations authorization and command, but Washington also strengthened its defense commitments to the Republic of China on Taiwan (culminating in the 1954–1979 Mutual Defense Treaty) and throughout the region.

Southeast Asia was no longer the peripheral concern that Kennan and others in Washington had assumed—it was now thrust forward to the frontline of the

Cold War.[48] Even *before* the outbreak of the Korean War, another Top Secret National Security Council document (NSC-64) issued on February 27, 1950 proclaimed:[49]

> It is important to United States security interests that all practicable measures be taken to prevent further Communist expansion in Southeast Asia. Indochina is a key area of Southeast Asia and is under immediate threat. The neighboring countries of Thailand and Burma could be expected to fall under Communist domination if Indochina were controlled by a Communist-dominated government. The balance of Southeast Asia would then be in grave hazard. Accordingly, the Departments of State and Defense should prepare as a matter of priority a program of all practicable measures designed to protect United States security interests in Indochina.

Similarly, but perhaps more important, NSC-68 was adopted by President Truman on April 7, 1950. The Top Secret sixty-six-page blueprint for "containment" and rollback of Soviet expansionism worldwide was authored by a nine-member team of elite State and Defense Department planners (chaired by Paul H. Nitze but also including Dean Acheson, Charles "Chip" Bohlen, and Robert Lovett), and is considered the template document of American strategy in the Cold War.

The North Korean attack on South Korea only served to starkly reinforce these judgments and the view that communist aggression throughout Asia emanated from Moscow and had to be countered by the United States and its allies. After three years of horrendous war in Korea the battle lines stalemated near the 38th Parallel, and an armistice was signed in 1953.

Thereafter, the major powers convened in Geneva, Switzerland, to adjudicate the division of the Korean peninsula as well as the future of Indochina. These questions were treated separately: the two Korean regimes, the People's Republic of China, the Soviet Union, and the United States dealt with the Korean issue—while they were joined by France, the UK, and the Viet Minh to resolve the Indochina dilemmas. The template for adjudicating both cases was the same: division of the countries into two zones with respective provisional governments, pending national elections under international supervision. The former occurred in each case (Korea was divided at the 38th Parallel and Vietnam at the 17th Parallel), but the latter never took place. Additionally, the sovereign independence and neutrality of the kingdoms of Cambodia and Laos were guaranteed. This was important because it stipulated that neither country could host foreign military personnel or bases, lest they lose their neutral status. (Vietnam was divided into the two zones controlled by the Democratic Republic of Vietnam in the north and the State of Vietnam government in the south). Even before the French defeat at Điện Biên Phủ, the United States was progressively expanding military assistance to French forces as well as the remnant Bảo Đại government forces in the south.

The new Eisenhower administration in Washington was agnostic at best concerning the prospect of national elections across Vietnam, as it feared (probably correctly) that the communist Viet Minh would win . . . and the dominoes would begin to fall one after the other across Southeast Asia. The American objective was therefore to perpetuate the division of the country.[50] Sustaining the South Vietnamese regime (now the Republic of Vietnam) thus became Washington's *sine qua non* of the Cold War in Southeast Asia.

Washington's fusing together of its Cold War struggle against Moscow and its client states (of which the new Chinese Communist regime was seen as one) and the civil war in Vietnam led to two decades of bloody and costly struggle that directly pitted the United States against the Soviet Union and People's Republic of China during the Kennedy, Johnson, and Nixon administrations. The quagmire dragged on until Saigon fell to communist North Vietnamese forces on April 30, 1975. It cost the United States nearly 59,000 service deaths and an estimated $155 billion.[51] It ripped apart the American polity and society. There were many other costly consequences. There are many excellent studies of the American war in Vietnam and this history is well known.[52] The "Pentagon Papers" clearly document the escalation of US commitment through 1967.[53] The basic error in the American approach was to misconstrue a civil war for Sino-Soviet expansionism. Throughout this period, Southeast Asia was elevated from a secondary- or lower-level global concern to a level of commitment commensurate with confronting and deterring the Soviet Union and Warsaw Pact forces in central Europe. The legacy of China's civil war and the seizure of power by the Chinese Communists also haunted policymakers in Washington. In November 1963, President Lyndon Johnson proclaimed: "I am not going to lose Vietnam. I am not going to be the president who saw Southeast Asia go the way China went."[54]

US Relations with Non-Indochina Countries during the Vietnam War

What the Vietnam War meant for US relations with other countries in Southeast Asia varied. To be sure, relations with each were seen by Washington through the prism of the conflict in Vietnam (a kind of "with us or against us" mentality), although the United States had genuine concerns about the spread of communist appeal and activities in each country. Either way, the anti-communist metric was the dominant feature that structured America's approach to every Southeast Asian state.

Throughout this period the United States cultivated the Philippines and Thailand as allies. Both countries were instrumental for US military operations in Vietnam, Laos, and Cambodia. Thailand was designated a "frontline state." The enormous American military facilities at Subic Bay Naval Base and Clark Air Base in the Philippines were instrumental in the war effort. At the height of the war more than 200 US Navy ships put into Subic every month. Clark was a major staging area for US Air Force bombing runs over North Vietnam. Both bases offered crucial repair facilities for US military equipment, hospitals, and housing for forward-deployed troops. Thailand was even more crucial to the US war effort. The Thais permitted US forces to operate out of a number of air bases, notably Udorn and Utapao; over 80 percent of US Air Force strikes against North Vietnam originated from bases in Thailand. The Thai bases were so important that the United States regarded them as an "unsinkable aircraft carrier." The total number of flights (bombing raids, reconnaissance missions, air drops, covert action missions) from bases in Thailand skyrocketed from approximately 4000 in 1964 to 90,000 by 1969.[55] Given its contiguous borders with both Laos and Cambodia, Thailand was also crucial for the US "secret wars" in those countries. As the "Ho Chi Minh Trail" supply corridor snaked through the border regions of both countries, it permitted the North Vietnamese to ferry personnel and provisions southward to resupply their regular forces and the Viet Cong. American aircraft regularly bombed this vital supply route from bases in Thailand. In Laos the bombing extended to the Plain of Jars, where more ordnance was dropped on the country than in the *entirety* of World War II.[56]

Both the Philippines and Thailand had their own treaties and military agreements with the United States that predated the Vietnam War. Both also became signatories to the September 1954 Southeast Asia Collective Defense Treaty (SEACDT), more commonly known as the Manila Pact, which morphed into the Southeast Asia Treaty Organization (SEATO) in February 1955.[57] But they were the only Southeast Asian states to join. The four Indochina states (Cambodia, Laos, North and South Vietnam) were not eligible owing to the 1954 Geneva Conference agreements. Burma and Indonesia cherished their neutral non-aligned status and both strongly opposed the formation of SEATO,[58] while Malaya (including the Borneo territories and Singapore) chose not to join, as they were parties to the 1957 Anglo-Malay Defense Agreement, which became the Five Power Defense Arrangement in 1971. While SEATO was intended by Washington as one of a series of collective security structures to ring the Soviet Union (along with NATO and CENTO), it was doomed from the outset given its limited appeal to Southeast Asian states, and it was finally formally dissolved on June 30, 1977.

The Enigma of Indonesia

Throughout the years of the Vietnam War, American relations with the Republic of Indonesia were generally quite positive. President Sukarno's foreign policy of nationalist neutralism and non-alignment was seen by Presidents Eisenhower, Kennedy, and Johnson as a preferable alternative to communism, and all three presidents sought to cultivate Sukarno (Fig. 2.8). His visit to Washington in May 1956 included a rare address to a joint session of Congress. All three presidents lavished military assistance and civilian aid on Indonesia in an attempt to counter the growing appeal of the Indonesian Communist Party (PKI) and keep Indonesia neutral if not pro-Western. For his part, Sukarno maintained an ambivalent relationship with the PKI. In August 1948 he ordered the Indonesian armed forces (TNI) to crush a PKI uprising in eastern Java, killing 8,000 rebels and decimating the PKI as a political force.[59]

At this early juncture, the US government thought they had found in Sukarno what they sought across Southeast Asia: an anti-communist nationalist. Yet, by the mid-1950s the PKI had resurrected itself and Sukarno sought to incorporate it in his "guided democracy" coalition. For the PKI this offered a classic Leninist

Figure 2.8 Official portrait of President Sukarno (1949)
Source: Indonesian Government photo in public domain

tactical opportunity to build a "bloc within"—which the Chinese Communist Party (with which the PKI had close ties) countenanced. The CCP had, on orders from the Comintern in Moscow, practiced exactly this tactic vis-à-vis the Kuomintang during the 1920s. Not only was Sukarno increasingly courting the PKI, but he was actively building state-to-state ties with the new government in Beijing. Indonesia was one of the first governments to recognize the new PRC government, and diplomatic ties were established on April 13, 1950. By 1955, relations had developed to the point where China was invited to send a senior delegation (headed by Premier Zhou Enlai) to the Bandung Conference of Afro-Asian Countries. Twenty-nine countries sent delegations and the Non-Aligned Movement was born. Bilateral ties with China continued to grow stronger thereafter, as did China's party-to-party linkages to the PKI.

As Sukarno drifted increasingly to the left and assertively cultivated ties with Beijing, the United States grew progressively more alarmed. This precipitated the Eisenhower administration to set in motion a CIA operation dubbed "Project Haik" in the fall of 1957 and spring of 1958. CIA operations veteran Frank Wisner was put in charge and was sent to Manila to coordinate the operation.[60] Almost an identical forerunner of the failed Bay of Pigs operation in Cuba in 1960, Project Haik was intended to arm a group of dissident Indonesian officers on the island of Sulawesi to gain a foothold and mount an offensive against Sukarno's troops. How this was supposed to happen was never worked out. Wishful thinking and ineptitude plagued the operation from the beginning. The rebel officers' would-be uprising collapsed almost as it began. Sukarno's military got wind of the plot and deployed its own air force and marines to suppress the rebels. The operation was a complete fiasco and failure. When questioned about it, both President Eisenhower and Secretary of State John Foster Dulles denied any US involvement, dismissing the abortive uprising as the undertaking by "mercenaries."[61]

A next major test of the already strained US-Indonesia relationship came during the 1963–1966 period of *konfrontasi* (confrontation) launched by the Sukarno government against the newly formed Federation of Malaysia.[62] This diplomatic and military confrontation produced high tensions across maritime Southeast Asia. Washington openly backed Malaysia over Sukarno's objections. This was a turning point in the US relationship with the Sukarno regime. Washington had its own rationale to recognize the new Malaysian state (not the least of which was its strong tie to the UK and an anti-communist orientation)—but Sukarno saw this as a litmus test of the relationship. His attempt to balance ties with the United States, on the one hand, with Beijing and Moscow on the other, while pursuing his activist "third way" diplomacy with other neutral and developing states—all of this increasingly grated on Washington policymakers. Worse yet was Sukarno's increasing embrace of the PKI, which had grown to about three million members by 1965 (the third largest communist party in the world at the time outside of China and the Soviet Union). In 1963, Sukarno brought leading PKI leaders into his government as ministers.

By the time Sukarno launched his policy of *konfrontasi* in 1963, the United States had been watching him with increasing wariness. But so too were conservative anti-communist officers in the Indonesia military (TNI). Many of these officers had been trained by the United States—and some in the United States—and they shared deep suspicions of communists. As Sukarno lurched increasingly leftward, the US Department of State, National Security Council, and CIA all began to map out a range of actions—many covert—inside of Indonesia to undermine support for Sukarno on the one hand, and the PKI on the other. The conservative TNI officer corps, especially those at the top, were central to this new strategy. It is important to note that there is no available evidence that the United States actually tried to foment a *coup d'état* against Sukarno, but there is considerable evidence of US support for the army's campaign to subvert (and possibly eliminate) the PKI.[63] For his part, Sukarno grew increasingly belligerent on many occasions, including launching repeated verbal attacks against the United States. In March 1965, two months after withdrawing Indonesia from the United Nations in protest over Malaysia's rotational seating on the Security Council, Sukarno told the US ambassador to "go to hell with your aid!"[64] The same month, as relations rapidly deteriorated, an internal US government review of March 1965 assessed that bilateral relations "were on the verge of falling apart"—an assessment seconded by Ambassador Marshall Green in August when he opined that the United States should prepare for a break in relations.[65]

Meanwhile, the cleavage between Sukarno and his PKI-leaning government vis-à-vis the conservative TNI officer corps only widened. Then, suddenly, in the early morning hours of October 1, 1965, a coup attempt erupted. Pro-PKI officers moved first, capturing and killing six of Indonesia's leading generals (half of the Army General Staff). But one escaped: Coordinating Minister of Defense for Security and Armed Forces Chief of Staff General Abdul Nasution. Although the coup plotters had specifically targeted General Nasution, and wound up killing his daughter Irma, the general managed to escape by climbing over a wall at his residence into the adjacent Iraqi embassy and hid there. Awakened at dawn, Major General Suharto, commander of the Army Strategic Reserve, moved quickly to take command and suppress the coup attempt. By day's end General Suharto, now joined by General Nasution, were in control. Washington quickly granted its approval and conveyed its offer of continuing support. Its years of cultivating Indonesia's conservative officer corps had paid off.

Following the abortive coup, and counter-coup, the TNI unleashed a protracted bloodbath against PKI members and sympathizers (many ethnic Chinese) across the country, one of the worst mass murders in history. Conservative estimates claim 250,000 were killed, while other more liberal estimates run as high as two million. The carnage was grotesque in many cases—beheadings, dismemberments, hangings, drownings, summary executions, mass arrests, and massacres. Evidence has now emerged that US embassy staff in Jakarta aided the TNI's bloodbath by supplying lists of suspected PKI members that it had compiled.[66] The mass killings stretched on for months. The PKI was decimated and its leaders executed. The "year of living dangerously" had come to a devastating end.[67]

General Suharto (known in Javanese as Soeharto) quickly consolidated his rule. Sukarno remained president in name, but progressively surrendered his powers to Suharto. In March 1967, Suharto was named acting president, being confirmed in the position by Parliament one year later. He ruled Indonesia for the next 31 years, before being toppled by popular protests in 1998. Domestically, his "New Order" policies were welcomed by Washington. In Indonesia's foreign policy Suharto continued the tradition of non-alignment and neutralism, but in fact tilted distinctly toward the United States throughout the remainder of the Cold War. As long as Suharto opposed communism, he was America's man. As elsewhere around the world, though, this myopic preoccupation led Washington to overlook (and thereby indulge) the regime's repression and corruption.

Post–Vietnam War American Policies and Relations with Southeast Asia

Following the collapse of the South Vietnamese regime in Saigon on April 30, 1975, the United States quite naturally had a tendency to recoil and relatively withdraw from the region. The country was traumatized by more than two decades of costly conflict abroad and divisiveness at home. While a natural consequence, it nonetheless left other American allies in the Asia-Pacific (Australia, Japan, New Zealand, the Philippines, South Korea, and Thailand) wondering about the US commitment to their security. Even before the final dénouement in Vietnam, the Nixon administration had signaled a less directly engaged approach to the region with Nixon's July 1969 Guam speech on "Vietnamization" of the war and shifting more burden for defense on to Asian allies and states (this became known as the "Nixon Doctrine"). Nixon actually presaged his doctrine in his 1967 *Foreign Affairs* article "Asia after Vietnam."[68] This was not a blueprint for regional withdrawal at all—but rather an attempt to transition from a regional policy dictated by the Vietnam War toward the vision of a postwar order in which the American role would be anchored on regional allies and new relationships would be built. It was also in this article that Nixon obliquely signaled a *rapprochement* with China. Eschewing the standard usage of "Red China" or "Communist China," Nixon held out this olive branch:

> Taking the long view, we simply cannot afford to leave China forever outside the family of nations, there to nurture its fantasies, cherish its hates and threaten its neighbors. There is no place on this small planet for a billion of its potentially most able people to live in angry isolation.[69]

Implicit in this vision to bring the People's Republic of China into the "family of nations" was a parallel premise that containing China in Asia was not a permanent policy.

At first, despite the desire to focus more on maritime Southeast Asia, mainland Indochina continued to drive American policy. First, as some predicted, the "dominoes" did fall as the Pathet Lao came to power in Laos and the Khmer Rouge in Cambodia, just prior to the Vietnamese communists' conquest of the south and forced unification of the country on April 30, 1975. All of Indochina had become "red." America's worst nightmare—for which more than 58,000 personnel had lost their lives—had materialized. And it did so, like the rest of the protracted war, on television screens in living rooms across the country. The chaotic images of the fall of Saigon showed US helicopters evacuating American personnel and Vietnamese evacuees from the rooftop of the US embassy on April 29, which was followed the next day by images of some Saigon citizens waving flowers and cheering the "liberating" PAVN forces as their T-55 tanks and soldiers entered the city.

The two-decade American project in Vietnam had come crashing down and was clear for all to see with their own eyes. That day and the entire war had a profound psychological effect on the government and people of the United States. Of course, it had an even more profound effect on the peoples of Vietnam—who lost an estimated two million civilians on both sides, 1.1 million North Vietnamese and Viet Cong fighters, approximately 250,000 South Vietnamese soldiers, and incalculable physical damage to the country.[70] Many Americans were anxious to put the long Vietnam nightmare behind them and to heal the physical and psychological wounds of that traumatic time. Of course, there were some who sought a retrospective answer to the question, "what went wrong?"

Among those dedicated to not only finding explanations, but also coming to terms with the realities, none was more significant than former Secretary of Defense Robert S. McNamara (Fig. 2.9).

Figure 2.9 Robert McNamara
Source: Photo by MPI/Getty Images

In his analytically clinical manner McNamara spent the next two decades of his life meticulously going over the history of the war (aided to no small extent by the "Pentagon Papers" internal study he had ordered). His efforts included visits to Hanoi where he met with General Vo Nguyen Giap, North Vietnam's principal military strategist. The result of McNamara's *gestalt* took twenty years to reach fruition, which emerged in two forms. The first was the publication of his book *In Retrospect: The Tragedy and Lessons of Vietnam* in 1995.[71] The second was the film *The Fog of War* in 2003. The latter grew out of the former. In the film, which earned the Academy Award for Best Documentary Feature in 2003, filmmaker Errol Morris interwove archival film footage with twenty hours of one-on-one interviews with McNamara (plus other principal government officials). The format for the film worked off of eleven "lessons" that McNamara had concluded at the end of his biographical book (although the film's lessons were different from the book). The eleven lessons McNamara himself drew are profound and well worth rereading by all Americans, especially policymakers.[72] McNamara supplemented his eleven lessons with this closing observation:

> Although we sought to do the right thing—and believed we were doing the right thing—in my judgment, hindsight proves us wrong. We both overestimated the effect of South Vietnam's loss on the security of the West and failed to adhere to the fundamental principle that, in the final analysis, if the South Vietnamese were to be saved, they had to win the war themselves. Straying from this central truth, we built a progressively more massive effort on an inherently unstable foundation. External military force cannot substitute for the political order and stability that must be forged *by* a people *for* themselves.

Robert McNamara's reflections sum up the multifaceted impacts of the Vietnam conflict, the broader tenets of the US Southeast Asian regional strategy, and the premises concerning China and the Soviet Union's roles, which had guided a quarter century of American involvement in the region. As a friend of my parents, I personally interacted with McNamara during this period (including visiting China with him) and can attest not only to his personal mission to wrestle honestly with the events and his legacy—but also his deep sense of patriotism to draw the appropriate lessons for the nation and future generations.

Not surprisingly, the Vietnam experience seared the United States so traumatically that the country's (and government's) natural inclination was to withdraw from the region and retreat into isolationism. To some extent, that occurred. But the realities of the region did not permit a total withdrawal. At the time, the United States continued to have seven treaty allies in Asia (Thailand, the Philippines, Australia, New Zealand, South Korea, Japan, and the Republic of China on Taiwan), which all continued to count on the United States for their security. American commerce and cultural linkages continued to be deep across the region. And now, in the aftermath of President Nixon's dramatic opening to the People's Republic of China, a whole new geostrategic shift had occurred. So, as much as Americans' natural inclination was to draw back and nurse its Vietnam wounds, geopolitical realities did not permit it. New challenges lay ahead for the United States in Southeast Asia.

Postwar Indochina: The Ford and Carter Administrations

As the Vietnamese communists swept to victory, their counterparts in neighboring Cambodia and Laos did the same. [73] The Khmer Rouge took Phnom Penh and seized national power on April 17, 1975 (twelve days before Saigon fell), while the Pathet Lao captured Vientiane on December 2, 1975. Although the dominoes fell more or less simultaneously in neighboring Laos and Cambodia, the anticipated monolithic communist bloc in Indochina supposedly directed by Beijing—on which the Americans had justified the war and their entire Southeast Asian policy for two decades—did not materialize. The communist conquests soon gave way to internecine disputes between the Khmer Rouge and Vietnamese communists, and China and Vietnam.

The conquest of Cambodia by the Khmer Rouge unleashed one of the most horrific chapters in world history. Led by Pol Pot, Ieng Sary, Khieu Samphan, Son Sen, and Nuon Chea—all subsequently convicted by a UN tribunal of genocide and crimes against humanity—the Khmer Rouge ruled the country for four years (1975–1979). Their brutal rule took the lives of approximately two million Cambodians, approximately half of the national population.[74]

Less than a month after seizing power, Khmer Rouge forces captured the US container ship SS *Mayaguez*. Although within Cambodia's twelve mile territorial waters, the Ford administration did not recognize the regime and therefore its claims, thus labeling the seizure an act of piracy. This set in motion an assault/rescue operation involving 600 marines and a number of aircraft and helicopters dispatched from Utapao Airbase in Thailand. Unbeknownst to the United States, the Khmer Rouge had moved the crew, so when the assault team descended on Koh Tang beach, where they thought the crew were being held, they were instead met with a blaze of gunfire and needed to call in reinforcements. A fourteen-hour firefight ensued. One Chinook helicopter involved in the operation went down, killing twenty-three airmen, while Khmer Rouge ground fire pierced eight (of the eleven total) helos involved in the rescue attempt. In the aftermath of the firefight, the Khmer Rouge decided to release the crew and the ship.

Following their respective seizures of power in Phnom Penh and Saigon, the Khmer Rouge and Vietnamese communists immediately began to engage in rhetorical barbs and taunts, and military probing of their common border area (which resulted in full-scale battles in 1977). The reports of Khmer Rouge atrocities increasingly filtered out along with refugees into Thailand, and Cambodia (now renamed Democratic Kampuchea) became the object of growing international concern.

I was a young intelligence analyst on the Indochina desk at the Department of State's Bureau of Intelligence and Research (INR) at the time and was on the receiving end of these refugees reports from the Thai border area. Because of a vacancy of the analyst with responsibility for the three Indochina countries, I was transferred from the Northeast Asia division, where I had been part of the China team, to the Southeast Asia Division. There, I dove into the complex subject matter and deluge of daily intelligence, wrote up daily reports for the "Secretary's Daily Brief," and contributed to broader intelligence community assessments. One day I was summoned to the office of Assistant Secretary of State for East Asia and the Pacific Richard Holbrooke, who requested a number of regular briefings from me and other INR analysts on the unfolding situation. On another day, soon thereafter, I was among those summoned to Secretary of State Cyrus Vance's office to brief him.

Then, a few days after that, as the situation in Cambodia was escalating, I was in another interagency meeting at the State Department. During a coffee break I was approached by Michel Oksenberg from the National Security Council staff. Oksenberg was a renowned academic China expert on leave from the University of Michigan to serve as one of Zbigniew Brzezinski's and President Carter's top Asia specialists (Michael Armacost was the other). At the NSC Oksenberg was not only in charge of China but also had the Indochina portfolio, while Armacost had responsibility for Japan, the Korean peninsula, "maritime" Southeast Asia, and the South Pacific islands. Oksenberg began by asking me how I liked working at the State Department? "It's great. I have been given new responsibilities, have worked in the China section and now on Indochina, and am learning a lot," I responded. Oksenberg then suddenly shocked me by asking, "Well, I have heard good things about your work here and I have been reading your reports. How would you like to come over to the NSC and be my assistant?" In astonishment, I splashed the coffee out of my cup (but fortunately didn't drop it), as my hands trembled. As a result, my personal and professional life changed at that moment—becoming entwined with Oksenberg's until his premature death in 2001 (including becoming his PhD student at the University of Michigan). Just talking with Oksenberg in person, whom I had not really met before (having only seen him lecture), was intimidating enough. He possessed a strong and charismatic personality. I was nervous anyway. Now he was asking me to be his assistant at the White House! "Of course," I instantly replied, not really considering the awkwardness of leaving my position at the State Department. "It will take a few weeks to get your clearances transferred over, but I need some assistance on Indochina," Oksenberg told me. As it turned out, beginning in mid-1977 until the end of 1978, I not only followed developments in Indochina full-time, but Mike also had me work on a variety of China-related issues: intelligence assessments of China's internal and external situation, US export controls (the White House was trying to loosen them), commercial "claims and assets" of nationalized American companies in China, and several other practical aspects of necessary policy and legal adjustments should the United States formally diplomatically recognize the People's Republic of China. It was a heady time and I learned an enormous amount. I left the NSC to go to graduate school full-time at the end of 1978, just as the normalization of diplomatic relations between the United States and China was announced. I had been privileged to be a part of the lead-up and had the honor of meeting Deng Xiaoping during his January 1979 state visit. As a result of my positions at State and the NSC, I also had a window into the dynamics of Indochina and Southeast Asia at this transitional time (an abiding interest ever since).

Tensions between the Vietnamese and Khmer Rouge were steadily building. Skirmishes were escalating along the Cambodian-Vietnamese border (particularly in the Parrot's Beak region) and they continued throughout 1977. Finally, on Christmas Day 1978, Hanoi (which had long aspired to a united Indochina under its dominance) took action and invaded Cambodia with 150,000–200,000 forces.

By January 7, 1979 the Vietnamese forces had overwhelmed the Cambodian armed resistance in the eastern part of the country and reached the capital, Phnom Penh. But there was no resistance there, as the Khmer Rouge had already emptied the capital of people following their 1975 seizure of power, eradicating the government and removing the urban population to jungle concentration camps in the interior of the country. As the Vietnamese forces approached, Khmer Rouge forces retreated deep into the jungle interior of the country. As such, upon reaching Phnom Penh, the Vietnamese proclaimed a new People's Republic of Kampuchea, installed Heng Samrin as the puppet prime minister, and began its ten-year occupation of the country.

Deng Xiaoping was newly back in power in Beijing. In May 1978, Beijing terminated all aid to Vietnam and began to publicly criticize Hanoi for its growing ties with Beijing's primary enemy in Moscow. Deng denounced Vietnam as the "Cuba of the East" (a reference to Cuba being a Soviet proxy). In November 1978, Moscow and Hanoi cemented their ties with the signing of a twenty-five-year "friendship" treaty, which included a mutual defense clause. Soon thereafter, Soviet warships entered Cam Ranh Bay (the first time since 1905). China was feeling encircled by the Soviet Union and Sino-Soviet tensions were running high.

In this fluid strategic environment, Deng also accelerated the secret negotiations with the United States for the normalization of diplomatic relations. These were concluded in Beijing and publicly announced on December 15, 1978 (formal ties commenced on January 1, 1979). When Deng visited the United States that month to commemorate normalization of relations, he informed President Carter and his National Security Advisor Zbigniew Brzezinski that he was going to "teach Vietnam a lesson" upon his return to China. Carter disapproved (and told Deng so), but Brzezinski very much supported the punitive Chinese action, as he also viewed Vietnam as the Soviet Union's client state.

Upon Deng's return to Beijing, China attacked Vietnam on February 17, 1979 (which Beijing dubiously labeled a "self-defense counter-attack"). What became known as the Third Indochina War was now in full swing.[75] China had grown increasingly uncomfortable with their former comrades-in-arms (during the Vietnam War, China had dispatched 350,000 of their own military personnel to North Vietnam from 1965 to 1968 and had provided a wide range of material and military aid as well as strategic advice). But with the end of the war, the centuries of Sino-Vietnamese enmity quickly resurfaced. From the Chinese perspective, Hanoi had been insufficiently grateful for China's assistance during the war, and—worst of all—had signed a military alliance with Beijing's erstwhile adversary in Moscow. Moreover, from Beijing's perspective, Vietnam was threatening its longtime client state in Cambodia (both Prince Sihanouk and the Khmer Rouge).

The Chinese attacks, however, did not go so well. Battle-hardened Vietnamese regulars and militia confronted the Chinese invaders in the border region, repelled them, and caused heavy losses (40,000–50,000 casualties) over the month-long conflict. Finally, Chinese forces had great difficulties in even subduing the border towns of Cao Bang, Lao Cai, and Long San. Having attained a minimal objective of reaching these three cities, Beijing proclaimed unilateral "victory" and announced its withdrawal. If anything, the "lesson learned" was not by Vietnam, but by China—the lesson of just how backward and incapable their People's Liberation Army forces were at the time. This was the last time China has fought a war to date.

China's attack on Vietnam actually did nothing to contribute to its two main goals—to evict Vietnamese forces from Cambodia (Kampuchea), and to lessen Moscow's support for Vietnam. Between 1979 and 1981 the Soviet Union supplied Hanoi with $2 billion worth of weapons and military assistance and $1 billion in civilian aid. In addition, 2,000 Soviet military technicians entered Vietnam. Soviet naval deployments to Cam Ranh Bay rapidly escalated—from five to ten ships in port in 1979 to between twenty-five and thirty-five on any given day from 1980 to 1985 (including aircraft carriers, destroyers, frigates, minesweepers, and submarines). Cam Ranh Bay had become Moscow's largest naval facility outside of the Soviet Union—thus doubling Soviet naval deployment capacity in the South China Sea and Indian Ocean theaters. Moscow had finally achieved its long-held strategic dream of a warm-water port. Moreover, Soviet air force deployments at nearby Danang increased from 10–15 to 35–40 aircraft by 1985, including Badger long-range bombers, a squadron of MiG-23s, and numerous long-range reconnaissance and transport aircraft.

Prior to Vietnam's invasion of Cambodia and China's retaliation, back in Washington, the Carter administration was juggling the sensitive questions of whether and how to normalize diplomatic relations with *both* China and

Vietnam. These efforts proceeded on parallel tracks. The Vietnam track was managed primarily by the State Department and Assistant Secretary of State of East Asia and Pacific Affairs Richard Holbrooke—while the China track was concentrated in the White House and National Security Council and overseen by President Carter's chief China advisor Michel Oksenberg. Both tracks were carried out quite independently of the other—until both were nearing fruition in the autumn of 1978. At this juncture, in a meeting in the Oval Office on October 11, Leonard Woodcock, who as President Carter's representative in Beijing had been called back to Washington for consultations as the secret China negotiations were coming to a climax, was asked by the president what he thought would be the likely impact on the secret negotiations which Woodcock was pursuing in Beijing. Woodcock bluntly told Carter and the others present, that his sense was that if normalization with Vietnam proceeded it would "blow normalization with China out of the water."[76] Tensions between China and Vietnam had been mounting and Woodcock had a keen sense of this from his meetings in Beijing. He knew, and told Carter, that the Chinese would feel betrayed and would find such a move by the United States to be duplicitous, at a particularly sensitive juncture in the secret negotiations. Carter heeded Woodcock's advice and normalization of relations with Vietnam was shelved for several years (this is somewhat ironic as a year before being sent as envoy to Beijing, Carter had dispatched Woodcock to Vietnam in March 1977 on an exploratory visit). The negotiations with Vietnam were hung up on the American demands for full accounting of soldiers missing in action (MIAs) and Hanoi's demands for reparations and aid, but the "China factor" killed any further progress. Formal diplomatic relations between the two finally occurred seventeen years later on July 11, 1995.

Despite America's natural instincts to recoil following a quarter century of war in Indochina, with Vietnam's strategic alliance with the Soviet Union and the communist "dominoes" having fallen in Cambodia and Laos, the United States still had serious security concerns in Southeast Asia. These included preventing the Soviet Pacific Fleet from interdicting the Malacca Strait, South China Sea, and the sea lanes up to Japan; preventing Vietnamese military incursions into Thailand or elsewhere in the region; and preventing regional communist insurgencies from threatening the ruling governments in Thailand, Malaysia, Indonesia, Burma, and the Philippines.

To counter these remaining threats, and consistent with the still-existing "Nixon Doctrine" of strengthening the defense capabilities of regional states so that they could better defend themselves and "burden share" in maintaining regional security, the United States thus undertook a new set of cooperative security initiatives with states in the region: Australia, Indonesia, Malaysia, New Zealand, Singapore, and Thailand.[77] However, the loose link in this strategy lay in the Philippines. Despite maintaining 16,000 US military personnel at Clark

Field and Subic Bay Naval Base near Manila, the Philippines government was growing increasingly uncomfortable with the American military presence.

The Reagan Administration

The Reagan administration was quickly confronted with another crisis in Southeast Asia—this time in the Philippines. Ferdinand Marcos, who had been in power since 1965, had turned increasingly authoritarian and dictatorial. He proclaimed martial law in September 1972, after which he cracked down hard on the citizenry, media, opposition, judiciary, and civil society. This had caused frictions with the United States during the prior Carter administration, which championed human rights in its foreign policy. President Reagan initially embraced Marcos, as had all previous American presidents, receiving him at the White House for a state visit in 1982 (Fig. 2.10), and praising him for "sharing the American values of liberty, democracy, justice, and equality."[78]

But Marcos and his hard-fisted rule was becoming increasingly unpopular at home. In 1981, his principal opponent, former Senator Benigno Aquino, who had been imprisoned by the Marcos regime on trumped-up charges of sedition and murder since 1972, was released and allowed to go to the United States for heart bypass surgery. Following his successful surgery, Aquino, now based in

Figure 2.10 President Ronald Reagan with Ferdinand and Imelda Marcos
Source: Ronald Reagan Presidential Foundation

Boston, became a central rallying point for the anti-Marcos opposition world-wide. In August 1983, as Marcos's own health was declining, Aquino was permitted to return to Manila. Thinking he would be safe upon return, Aquino flew back—only to be taken off the plane by Marcos's security forces when it landed and assassinated on the airport tarmac. This was the turning point and beginning of the end for the Marcos regime. Thus began the "people's power" popular movement that would ultimately sweep Marcos and his corrupt family from power in 1986. The United States managed the meltdown of their longtime ally as best possible, pushing him to relinquish power and arranging exile in Hawaii.

Meanwhile, elsewhere in Southeast Asia, the Reagan administration continued the Carter administration's pressure on Vietnam, which continued to occupy Cambodia, dominate Laos, and threaten Thailand. Following the resignation of Alexander Haig as Secretary of State, and his replacement by George P. Shultz in 1982, the Reagan administration's Southeast Asia policy was elevated. Shultz put his personal imprint on Asia policy by relatively distancing the United States from Beijing—which had been the Cold War focus of the United States under Carter and the first two years of the Reagan term—by instead pursuing an "Asia first" (as distinct from "China first") regional policy. Shultz believed that the best China policy was an Asia policy that concentrated America's attention on its allies and partners in the region. This was Shultz's own instinct, but his thinking was also shared and shaped by longtime Asia hands Gaston Sigur, Paul Wolfowitz, and Richard Armitage. Sigur, a professor from George Washington University (and my former professor), was a Japan hand who was also an anti-communist and thus deeply suspicious of cozying up to China. Shultz appointed Wolfowitz as Assistant Secretary of State of East Asia and the Pacific in 1982, before serving as Ambassador to Indonesia from 1986 to 1989. Sigur, who had been serving as Senior Director for Asian Affairs on the NSC staff, had become very close to Reagan and had been instrumental in shaping Asia policy, replaced Wolfowitz as Assistant Secretary of State in 1986 and served until February 1989. It was Sigur who forged Reagan's strong bond with Japanese Prime Minister Yasuhiro Nakasone. Armitage was serving as Deputy Assistant Secretary of Defense of East Asia and the Pacific from 1981 to 1983 and then became Assistant Secretary of Defense for international security policy through 1989. Two other senior officials were also important: James Lilley and Donald Gregg. Lilley had been a CIA operations officer in Laos during the Vietnam War, but also had long-standing expertise in China (where he was born and later served as CIA chief-of-station in the early 1970s and later US ambassador from 1989–1991). Gregg was also a former CIA officer, but with Korea expertise (he served as US ambassador to the Republic of Korea from 1989–1993).

The reason these individuals matter in this story about Southeast Asia is because they all had long experience in the region and were not beholden to the

"China first" approach of many others who had dominated Asia policy from the Nixon through Carter administrations. Thus, one of the legacies of the Reagan administration's Asia policy was to emphasize the "periphery" of maritime Asia, thus putting offshore strategic pressure on China. On the Reagan administration's watch, they managed well the tricky departure of Marcos from the Philippines and engagement with the new democratically empowered Corazón Aquino government (which remained ambivalent about its ties to Washington); they maintained pressure on Vietnam until the Vietnamese withdrew from Cambodia in September 1989 after more than a decade of occupation; they strengthened the alliance with Thailand; they managed prickly relations with Malaysia; and they pushed forward the US-Singapore defense partnership.

The Bush 41 Administration

George H. W. Bush inherited this strong position in Southeast Asia, but his regional perspective was unlike that of George Shultz and the Asia hands of the Reagan administration. For Bush, *China came first*. This was evident early in his presidency. Instead of taking his first trip aboard to the United Kingdom and Europe, as was customary for new presidents, Bush instead chose to travel to Beijing (and Tokyo). Bush had a clear affection for China as a country and Deng Xiaoping as a leader personally, owing to his time as US Liaison Office representative in Beijing during 1974 and 1975. Bush and his wife Barbara cycled around the sleepy Beijing streets, played a lot of tennis, and otherwise socialized with the diplomatic community.[79] This was a period when Deng Xiaoping had just been politically "rehabilitated" from his Cultural Revolution purgatory, and Bush interacted with Deng and came to believe Deng was his "good friend." Bush's faith in his "friendship" with Deng was tested in the aftermath of the June 4, 1989, "massacre" in Beijing, after which he did his resolute best to put the US-China relationship "back on track."[80] For Bush, Japan was important—but it was really China that was the first and foremost priority for the United States in Asia.

As such, Southeast Asia was not terribly consequential in Bush's—or his administration's—worldview or policies. It was on his watch, however, that the lease on the US military bases in the Philippines was running out. Bush dispatched Richard Armitage to renegotiate an extension. Armitage did so successfully—only for the Philippines Senate not to ratify the agreement (reflecting the deep ambivalence in the country about the United States). The Bush administration was also central in forging the UN-brokered Cambodian peace settlement in 1991 (in which State Department official Richard Solomon played a key role). But, otherwise, Southeast Asia did not figure much in Bush 41's foreign policy. Given the dramatic events in China (Tiananmen), the anti-communist uprisings across Eastern Europe, the unification of Germany, the implosion of the Soviet Union, and the first Gulf War, it is understandable that Southeast Asia was not a high priority.

The Clinton Administration

Under President Clinton, Southeast Asia received resuscitated attention from Washington. Clinton came to office, of course, following the 1989 Tiananmen massacre. The human rights situation in China had continued to deteriorate in the three years thereafter. During the presidential campaign Clinton sensed a political vulnerability of Bush's for trying to preserve the relationship with Beijing—criticizing his administration for "coddling dictators from Baghdad to Beijing." Once in office, Clinton continued to distance himself from the post-Tiananmen Chinese leadership, to maintain US and multilateral sanctions on China, and to tie annual renewal of most-favored-nation trading status to identifiable improvements of human rights in China.

This situation naturally led Clinton and his administration to an "Asia first" policy similar to the Reagan approach discussed earlier. There was no value added—either in terms of domestic American politics or in foreign policy—by continuing the Bush 41 approach of trying to reach out to the rulers in Beijing. Quite to the contrary, on the advice of his Secretary of State (Warren Christopher), National Security Advisor (Anthony Lake), and Chief of Staff (Leon Panetta), and Assistant Secretary of State for East Asia and the Pacific (Winston Lord), President Clinton kept a studied distance from China and its leadership during his first term (this would change markedly during his second term).

What this meant for Southeast Asia was a natural re-embrace. Under the counsel and direction of the Assistant Secretary of State for East Asia and the Pacific, the experienced Asia hand Stanley Roth, and his counterpart at the Defense Department, Kurt Campbell, the second Clinton administration definitely was inclined to continue an Asia-first approach and maintain a distance from Beijing. Roth, in particular, had a strong background and interest in Southeast Asia from his previous years working on Capitol Hill. Secretary of Defense William J. Perry and his Assistant Secretary for international security affairs, Harvard professor Joseph Nye, concurred with this overall direction. But the second Clinton administration Asia team had changed and now also included individuals with strong China backgrounds who favored a re-engagement with the Beijing government. This was the impetus of NSC Senior Director for Asia Kenneth Lieberthal and Deputy Assistant Secretary of State Susan Shirk (both leading academic China scholars who had joined government). Despite the 1995–1996 Taiwan Straits crisis—during which China fired ballistic missiles into the waters near Taiwan and the Clinton administration deployed two aircraft carrier battle groups to the area—and the mistaken US bombing of the Chinese embassy in Belgrade, Yugoslavia, in 1997, there was still a desire to put relations with China on a more steady and forward-looking foundation. The NSC and State Department worked out a number of steps to do so, including the exchange of state visits between Clinton and Jiang Zemin in 1997 and 1998, as well as "delinking" annual most-favored-nation trade status from human rights and granting China permanent normal trade relations (PNTR).

In Southeast Asia the Clinton administration also emphasized human rights in the region. Serious human rights abuses were occurring in Burma, Indonesia, and Malaysia at the time. This also came at the time when the "Asian values" debate was taking shape in Southeast Asia, notably in Malaysia and Singapore, both of which pushed back—and hard—against Washington's emphasis on democracy promotion and criticisms of authoritarian regimes. This was the "unipolar moment," the Cold War was over, the Soviet Union had collapsed, and Washington was intoxicated by Francis Fukuyama's liberal "end of history" doctrine. The Cold War policy of "containment" was officially replaced by Clinton's policy of "enlargement" of the world's democracies. While democratic people's power did seem to be playing out in parts of Asia as well—notably South Korea and the Philippines—this was not the case in other Southeast Asian countries. In particular, Malaysia's Prime Minister Mahathir bin Mohamad pushed back against the American human rights evangelism and democracy promotion. So too did some officials in Singapore.

The Clinton administration's relationship with Singapore was further strained by the Michael Fay incident of 1994. Fay, then a nineteen-year-old high school student at the Singapore American School, was arrested for car vandalism and stealing road signs, and sentenced to six strokes by caning (a common punishment in Singapore). Oddly, even though Fay was guilty of petty crimes, his case fueled perceptions in Washington that Singapore abused human rights. President Clinton himself, as well as his administration and several senators, protested the punishment and requested leniency. Fay's sentence was slightly reduced from six to four lashes, but this event added to the strain in bilateral relations over the "Asian values" debate.

The emphasis on human rights, however well intended, definitely undermined Washington's broader agenda in the region and otherwise generally positive relationships. As Singaporean scholar Joseph Liow observes: "On the question of human rights advocacy in US foreign policy, it should be noted that its salience to relations with Southeast Asia was not due to it being a new item on the engagement agenda. At issue, rather, was the zealous vocal, and persistent manner in which the Clinton administration pressed its cause."[81]

Elsewhere in Southeast Asia, US relations with Thailand were on a good footing, as the country was in one of its democratic phases between military coups. A Visiting Forces Agreement (VFA) was concluded in 1998 with the Philippines, allowing again for the American military to establish a continuing presence in the country and to re-engage with its training of the Philippines' armed forces. Notwithstanding the political persecution of opposition leader Anwar Ibrahim by Prime Minister Mahathir, the stirrings of a more robust democracy were also apparent in Malaysia. Things were also looking up in neighboring Burma (Myanmar). Following unprecedented demonstrations against the long-ruling military junta in 1988, nationwide elections were held in 1990. The opposition party—the National League for Democracy—under the leadership of charismatic Aung San Suu Kyi, whom the junta had released from house arrest, won an overwhelming majority in the parliament (392 of 492 seats). However, the ruling junta (the State Law and Order Restoration Council or SLORC) refused to honor the election result, annulled it, and retrenched in their iron-fisted rule. This repressive situation endured until 2012. Indonesia also returned to democracy during the Clinton administration. In 1998, after 31 years in power, General Suharto resigned in the wake of the Asian Financial Crisis and domestic political opposition against decades of violent repression and widespread familial corruption. The Clinton administration played a role in pressuring Suharto to step down and then supported the nation's pathway back to democracy. Thus, in noncommunist Southeast Asia, the Clinton administration witnessed—and supported—the post–Cold War enfranchisement of democracy throughout the region. Even in Vietnam, the administration supported the *Doi Moi* reforms and began the healing process of normalization of relations between the two former wartime adversaries. On July 11, 1995, flanked by war veterans Senators John McCain, John Kerry, and Charles Robb at the White House, Clinton announced that the two countries had established diplomatic relations. Two years later he ended the trade embargo and opened doors to full interaction between the two governments and societies (military exchanges also commenced, although the ban on weapons sales to Vietnam would wait until the Obama administration).

All in all, the Clinton years can be said to have been very positive in US–Southeast Asia relations. The trickiest patch came during the 1997–1998 Asian Financial Crisis—which sent the regional (and global) economy into a tailspin. In Southeast Asia, Thailand and Indonesia were hardest hit, although there was collateral damage in Malaysia, Singapore, and the Philippines. The US approach was to stem the bleeding and currency freefalls—by working both bilaterally and multilaterally with the International Monetary Fund. The IMF, together with supportive bailout packages from the United States, Japan, and other OECD countries, did manage to stabilize a very serious crisis situation. But there was a price. The IMF and United States insisted that various regulatory and legal measures be instituted in affected countries, that addressed the incipient causes of the crisis and would be intended to foreclose the possibility of a repeat. From the region, though, these were bitter pills to swallow. There is a famous indicative photograph of IMF director Michel Camdessus standing with his arms folded over an enfeebled President Suharto, as he signed the terms of the bailout package on January 16, 1998.[82] China, by contrast, quickly offered bailout packages—with no questions asked and no strings attached. Reflecting back on the time and the Clinton administration's response, Singapore scholar Joseph Chinyong Liow observes: "US support for IMF bailouts notwithstanding, at issue for regional states was the perception that American assistance was not only slow in coming, but also that when it arrived, it came with onerous political demands and expectations that invariably contributed to the further destabilization of Southeast Asia."[83] By contrast, China was magnanimous in its "no strings attached" financial support for Indonesia, Malaysia, and Thailand. This was, in a sense, "payback" for Southeast Asia's lack of condemnation of the Beijing authorities following the 1989 Tiananmen massacre. It cast China in a much more beneficial light throughout the region—as the United States was increasingly seen as hectoring and demanding.

The Bush 43 Administration

George W. Bush and his administration succeeded Clinton's in January 2001. As with everything else in US foreign policy during Bush's tenure, the September 11 attacks that year in New York and Washington were defining. Prior to the 9/11 attacks, the Bush administration was already signaling a shift in Asia policy. Criticizing his opponent Al Gore and the Clinton administration's 1998 policy of "[building towards] strategic partnership" with China, Bush countered that China was really a "strategic competitor." While Bush himself seemed to harbor some of his father's perspectives on the need to maintain good ties with Beijing, many of those around the president entered office harboring deep strategic suspicions and dislike for the regime in Beijing and their alleged aspirations to push the United States out of the Asia-Pacific.[84] The May 2000 EP-3 crisis (in which a Chinese fighter intercepted and crashed into a US spy plane and forced it to crash land on Hainan Island in China) only further fueled these perceptions.

It logically seemed, thereafter, that the United States would again practice its "Asia first" regional policy and downgrade China in its approach. Southeast Asia naturally stood to benefit. Then came 9/11. The impact on Washington's view of Southeast Asia only heightened, but for different reasons. Now, post-9/11, China reached out to the United States and became a partner in Bush's "global war on terror" (GWOT). This prompted eight years of the best relations Washington and Beijing have had since the 1980s.

For American relations with Southeast Asia, though, it also served to both elevate, but also narrow, the region in Washington's eyesight. Now, Southeast Asia was designated the "second front" in the GWOT. And for good reasons. Bin Laden's al-Qaeda network had established a presence in Indonesia and the Philippines, and were involved in the Christmas Eve 2000 bomb attacks in Jakarta and eight other Indonesia cities. Al-Qaeda operatives who were trained in its camps in Afghanistan were also detected in Malaysia, the Philippines, Singapore, and Thailand.[85] In December 2001, in the wake of 9/11, during a raid Indonesian police uncovered a document from the al-Qaeda-affiliated Jemaah Islamiyah (JI) extremist group that detailed plans for further attacks in Indonesia, Malaysia, and Singapore. JI were subsequently linked to the Bali nightclub bombings of 2002, an attack on the J. W. Marriott hotel in Jakarta in August 2003, the Australian embassy in Jakarta in September 2004, as well as an earlier plot by the al-Qaeda-affiliated Abu Sayyaf movement in the Philippines to blow up eleven American airliners crossing the Pacific in 1995.[86] A plot to attack US naval ships in Singapore was also foiled in 2002.

Southeast Asia may have been designated the "second front" by the Bush administration, but these plots and other intelligence about the deep links of Saudi and other Middle Eastern backed terrorist groups to counterparts in Southeast • Asia were real and thus made the region a "frontline" in its global anti-terror campaign. Thus, US interactions with Southeast Asian governments were elevated, especially in the military, intelligence, law enforcement, and counterterrorism domains.[87]

These issues really dominated the Bush 43 approach to, and relations with, Southeast Asian governments. They opened the way for the US military to return to the Philippines. In a welcome move, Philippine President Gloria Macapagal-Arroyo invoked the 1951 US-Philippines Mutual Security Treaty and offered the United States use of Subic Naval Base and Clark Air Field for operations, and she publicly said that the Philippines was "prepared to pay any price" to support the US counterterrorism operations.[88] Following the rupture in the American ability to use bases in that country following the Bush 41 administration and the Philippines Senate's rejection of a renewed agreement, this was obviously most welcome news in Washington. As a result, more than a thousand US Special Forces units deployed to the southern Philippines. Similar steps were taken with Thailand, including the establishment of "black site" detention centers where the CIA interrogated and tortured captured al-Qaeda operatives. Malaysia, on the other hand, was much less helpful—indeed it became an impediment from Washington's perspective. Prime Minister Mahathir vocally denounced Bush's "war on terror" and its Islamophobic implications. Because of intelligence that identified al-Qaeda operatives in the country, Washington labeled Malaysia a "Terrorist Risk State" in 2002.

Counterterrorism aside, the Bush 43 years did also produce some forward progress in US–Southeast Asian commercial ties. Negotiations were concluded with Singapore for a bilateral Free Trade Agreement (FTA)—still the only one the United States has in the region. It was also during the Bush years that the Trans-Pacific Partnership (TPP) negotiations were launched, although they are more associated with (and were concluded under) the Obama administration. All in all, the administration of George W. Bush can be quite contented with US relations with Southeast Asia on their watch. None—except perhaps with Malaysia—deteriorated and many improved markedly.

In Retrospect

In this chapter we have witnessed an American legacy in the region that began with traders and missionaries during the first half of the nineteenth century, then progressed to diplomats and official relations during the second half, and then to the arrival of American armed forces at the turn of the twentieth century. Meanwhile, America's commercial interests and footprint continually broadened and deepened. Educational and religious ties also blossomed. America supported self-determination and independence for *all* countries in the region, thus standing apart from its European allies and former colonial powers. Except in the Philippines, America was largely seen as a benevolent partner—but not yet a power. That would change in the wake of World War II and the Cold War.

With advent of communist regimes in China, North Vietnam, North Korea, and the ensuing Korean War, all of a sudden Southeast Asia took on a completely different cast in Washington. Now it became one of two major global theaters of conflict against communism. Thus began America's long and draining involvement in Vietnam and Indochina (1958–1975). This conflict did much to shape US ties with all of the countries in the region, strengthening them in almost all cases. But with the end of the long and exhausting Indochina conflict, which tore the United States itself apart, American attention naturally began to wane and dissipate. Yet, the United States did not have the luxury of really pivoting away— as the nations of Southeast Asia had grown in the interim to be extremely important in their own rights. Events in the region, notably Vietnam's invasion and occupation of Cambodia, would also not permit Washington to let go.

Thus, as we have seen, the United States continued to engage and build its relations with the region from the Carter through the Bush 43 administrations. The engagement may not have always been as strong or consistent as some Southeast Asian countries desired, while for some others it was too strong, but it is clear from the record outlined in this chapter that while the United States may not have always prioritized the region, it has always engaged with it and saw the American role as benign.[89] At least this is how many Americans have viewed their relations with the region. For Southeast Asians, however, the United States has not been so benign. It has often appeared distracted, arrogant, condescending, fickle, and self-preoccupied. This has produced, as Joseph Liow has ably shown,[90] a deep ambivalence toward the United States.

3

America's Contemporary Roles in Southeast Asia

"Early in my presidency, I decided that the United States, as a Pacific nation, would rebalance our foreign policy and play a larger and long-term role in the Asia Pacific. And this has included engagement with Southeast Asia and ASEAN."
——President Barack Obama, February 15, 2016[1]

"ASEAN is central to our vision for the region; it is our indispensable and irreplaceable strategic partner."
——Vice President Mike Pence, November 14, 2018[2]

In the previous chapter we reviewed the history of the American approach to, and roles in, Southeast Asia—from the early nineteenth century through the George W. Bush administration. This chapter picks up from that historical survey and examines the "contemporary" period—the Obama and Trump administrations' policies and actions in the region, before taking stock of three categories of the US footprint at present: commerce, security, and soft power/public diplomacy. Taken together, I argue that the American *presence* and *impact* in Southeast Asia is very large and significant, across multiple categories, even if the *perception* of it is considerably less. The US role is definitely underappreciated by many observers in the region, and it is even taken for granted. As senior Singaporean diplomat Tommy Koh told me: "Your presence hasn't changed. We tend to take it for granted, until it changes. What is new and has changed is China's presence and influence. That is why they get all the attention."[3]

The Obama Administration's Policy Toward Southeast Asia

Southeast Asia never had better relations with the United States, and vice versa, than during the Obama administration (2009–2017). While the previous chapter catalogued the historical ups-and-downs and tradition of "benign neglect" of American attention to the region, throughout the eight years of the

Figure 3.1 President Barack Obama at East Asian Summit
Source: Jim Watson/AFP via Getty Images

Obama administration the region witnessed markedly greater and more consistent attention being paid to Southeast Asia than by *any* previous administration in the post–Vietnam War era. In part this was a byproduct of the Obama administration's "pivot" or "rebalance" policy toward Asia as a whole, in part it was because of the administration's heightened recognition of the importance of Southeast Asia, and in part because of President Obama himself. Obama not only grew up in Hawaii, but he spent the formative years of ages 6–10 in Jakarta, Indonesia—and subsequently had an affection for and understanding of the region. Claiming to be the first "Pacific President," Obama elevated Southeast Asia on his list of foreign policy priorities.

In its first year in office, the Obama administration signed the ASEAN Treaty of Amity and Cooperation (ASEAN's founding treaty) and appointed the first US ambassador to ASEAN (based in Jakarta) in 2011. The Obama administration then elevated its bilateral relations with Singapore to a "strategic partnership" and with Malaysia, Indonesia, and Vietnam to "comprehensive partnerships."[4] Some US officials claim that in practice there is no difference between the two designations, but the latter three governments all balked at the use of the term "strategic"; other former Obama officials note that the "strategic partnership" designation is a term that qualifies that country for more sophisticated weapons purchases as a de facto "major non-NATO ally."

The prioritization of Southeast Asia was highlighted by the convening of annual head-of-state "Leaders Meetings" beginning in 2009. At the conclusion of the first such meeting in November 2009 a wide-ranging Joint Declaration was issued, which mapped out a framework for considerably enhanced US-ASEAN cooperation across a range of areas.[5] In 2016, the United States and ASEAN upgraded their collective relationship to a "strategic partnership" and convened the first stand-alone Leaders' Summit at the Sunnylands estate in Rancho Mirage, California, in February 2016,[6] which resulted in an updated comprehensive joint statement.[7] Beginning in 2014, the US-ASEAN Defense Forum (among defense ministers) was also launched.

The Obama administration's new focus on Southeast Asia was part and parcel of its overall reorientation to the Asia-Pacific region. Believing that the United States had been strategically preoccupied with, and bogged down in, the Middle East and Southwest Asia as a result of the post-9/11 "war on terror," military operations in Afghanistan and Iraq, and hunt for Osama bin Laden, the senior officials of the Obama administration opted to undertake a systematic redirection away from the Middle East and toward Asia in its entirety (south, southeast, northeast, central, Australasia, and the Pacific Islands).

The pivot was largely the brainchild of Kurt Campbell, whom President Obama and Secretary of State Hillary Clinton appointed as Assistant Secretary of State for East Asia and the Pacific (EA/P). Campbell is a cerebral, gregarious, energetic, and dynamic individual who is deeply schooled in the US government. He previously had served as Deputy Assistant Secretary of Defense with responsibility for the Asia-Pacific in the Clinton administration, where he earned high marks. Prior to that Campbell had been selected as a prestigious Presidential Management Fellow and served in the Treasury Department, in the west wing of the White House, and on the National Security Council staff. He also taught at Harvard and held appointments at leading Washington think tanks. Not an Asian regionalist by education (he earned his PhD from Oxford with an emphasis on the former Soviet Union, where he had also studied violin in the former Soviet republic of Armenia), Campbell quickly mastered the Asia portfolio. Campbell's strength on Asia has always been his breadth of knowledge about the region—whereas most Asia hands have deep knowledge of one country (Japan, China, Korea, India, or Southeast Asia), tend to get intellectually "captured" by "their country," know the language of that country, see the region through the prism of their country of expertise, and as a consequence usually do not develop broad regionwide expertise and a balanced perspective. Campbell's regional breadth has been a real asset throughout his career, as he had a good grasp of the many actors in the region. Another notable feature has been Campbell's healthy skepticism of, but not hostility toward, China. He has worked with the Chinese on many issues over the years, in both defense and diplomacy, but he never became beholden to the idea that China was the key nation for the United States in Asia. This earned him the nickname in China of "Dr. Containment"—an unfair moniker actually, as Campbell is a pragmatist who understood that China had to be dealt with and could be useful to the United States on certain issues. Nonetheless, he operated on the principle of "constraining" China through strengthening America's relations with countries throughout the region all around China.

Given this background, Campbell was the perfect choice to be Assistant Secretary of State for East Asia and the Pacific and to conceptualize and engineer the "pivot" to Asia (about which he wrote a book after leaving government).[8] When Secretary of State Clinton was recruiting Campbell to be her principal deputy for the region, she told him: "Asia is the future and our diplomacy must reflect this in a much more fundamental way. . . . China is the big story, no doubt. But for us to be successful, we're going to have to work with others more effectively. We've got to embed our China policy in a larger Asia strategy."[9] To be certain, Campbell was not alone in conceiving and operationalizing the pivot policy. His counterpart as Senior Director for Asia on the National Security Council staff, Jeffrey Bader, was one of the government's most experienced and top diplomats on Asia. Bader was succeeded at the NSC by another seasoned diplomat, Danny Russel, who in turn was succeeded by scholar Evan Medeiros, when Russel became Assistant Secretary of State for East Asia and the Pacific in Obama's second term. Together, and with the collegial participation of many others across government agencies, they put together and implemented the pivot to the Asia-Pacific.

Southeast Asia was a central component. This was a significant shift in American diplomacy, which had always been "Northeast Asia heavy." But Secretary of State Clinton saw it differently, as she noted in her memoir *Hard Choices*: "Stapleton Roy, a former Ambassador to Singapore, Indonesia, and China, urged me not to overlook Southeast Asia, which Jim [Steinberg] and Kurt [Campbell] had also been recommending. Over the years American attention has often focused on Northeast Asia because of our alliances and troop commitments in Japan and South Korea, but countries like Indonesia, Malaysia, and Vietnam were growing in economic and strategic importance. [Ambassador] Roy and other experts backed our plan to sign a treaty with ASEAN, which would then open the door to much greater US engagement there. It seemed like a small step that could yield real benefits down the road."[10] Secretary Clinton made good on her policy by personally visiting all ten Southeast Asian countries, the first US secretary of state ever to do so. Obama's chief Asia advisor on the NSC staff, Jeffrey Bader, echoed this sentiment in his memoirs of the period: "From the time of Secretary of State Clinton's first trip abroad, which included Indonesia, the Obama administration had wanted to signal that our interests in Asia went well beyond the traditional American focus on Northeast Asia. . . . All in all, the Obama administration sought a greater presence in Southeast Asia at the time when the region was finding its place in an emerging world order between a rising China and a rising India. The purpose was not to pursue zero-sum rivalry with China but to be an active player in the region, lest the United States be seen as an increasingly irrelevant power."[11]

During President Obama's tenure, over eight years, he also visited nine of ten Southeast Asian countries (missing Brunei). Many bilateral agreements were signed, including military assistance and Enhanced Defense Agreements with Indonesia, Malaysia, the Philippines, and Singapore. The Obama administration contributed $4 billion in development assistance to the region from 2010 to 2016 and launched the Lower Mekong Initiative to support sustainable development.[12] New bilateral law-enforcement cooperation agreements were concluded with several ASEAN states, and they joined collectively together in the Washington-initiated Southeast Asia Maritime Law Enforcement Initiative—aimed at strengthening the maritime capabilities of Indonesia, Malaysia, the Philippines, and Vietnam. During the Obama administration US-Vietnam relations reached an all-time high, including the lifting of the arms embargo (which had been in existence since the end of the Vietnam War) and establishment of close defense ties between the two former adversaries. The long-troubled US-Myanmar relationship was normalized (except in the defense field), as that country evolved from total military rule to a hybrid system that allowed for some elements of democracy. Relations with tiny Brunei were also improved, with the Sultan paying a rare visit to the White House. However, ties with Thailand, a treaty partner of 184 years and ally of 60 years, became quite strained following the 2014 military coup in Bangkok.[13] Relations with the Philippines took a similar sharp downturn after Rodrigo Duterte became president in 2016.

The intensified US relationship with Southeast Asia was embodied in the ASEAN-US *Plan of Action 2016–2020*.[14] In addition to bolstering wide-ranging exchanges in the cultural and commercial spheres, the Action Plan commits the United States to comprehensive bilateral and multilateral engagement with ASEAN for years to come.

Although many observers in the region became critical of the Obama administration's pivot policy for being more rhetoric than reality,[15] and there is some truth in this, it is still fair to say that US relations with Southeast Asia may never have been better than during the Obama administration. The question in the region when Obama left office was whether the Trump administration would build upon this improved foundation or whether it would revert to the traditional pattern of episodic engagement and relative neglect.

The Trump Administration's Relations with Southeast Asia

Under President Trump the United States returned to its long-standing approach of benign neglect—or what Singaporean scholar Joseph Chinyong Liow aptly terms "ambivalent engagement" in his excellent study of American relations with the region.[16] The Trump administration returned to its traditional pattern of episodic diplomacy, whereby multi-month periods of no or little high-level interaction is followed by bursts of "parachute diplomacy" by US officials who fly into the region, give reassuring speeches of America's continuing commitment and resolve, and then fly out. On some occasions the US government becomes proactive by inviting Southeast Asian heads of state and senior officials to the White House and Washington. But such surges of US diplomacy are normally followed by many consecutive months of relative inattention—before the pattern repeats itself.

Despite the return to episodic engagement by the Trump administration, the regional perception is more different and damning. A 2019 regionwide survey across all ten ASEAN countries of over 1,000 respondents revealed not only a return to benign neglect, but a sharp deterioration in how the Trump administration is viewed.[17] When asked, "The level of US engagement with Southeast Asia under the Trump administration has __?", 51.2 percent said it had "decreased" while 16.8 percent said it had "decreased significantly" (a stunning 68 percent overall). Thus, it must be said that the regional perception is one of *neglect* rather than episodic engagement. There are many measures that contribute to this perception. One may be a lack of ambassadors in key countries (like Singapore and Thailand). Nor did the Trump administration appoint an Assistant Secretary of State for East Asia and the Pacific (David Stilwell) until nearly three years into the president's term. Another key indicator for Southeast Asians is the failure of the president to turn up for key regional meetings—he went only once, instead dispatching Vice President Pence, National Security Advisor Robert O'Brien, and even the Secretary of Commerce Wilbur Ross other times. "Showing up" is judged to be a key indication of interest (or lack thereof) by Southeast Asians.

One can thus understand and forgive Southeast Asian skepticism about the continuity and commitment of the United States to the region. This time around, though, the residual doubts and questions about America's attention span and staying power are greater. In addition to the deeper Southeast Asian sense that America has descended into malaise and protracted national decline (discussed in chapter 1), contemporary doubts are fueled by two further factors: Trump's own unpredictability and capriciousness, and China's rapidly rising role in the region.

Trump has proven himself his administration's own worst enemy. An aggressive early morning tweet or denigrating comments made about a foreign leader, combined with the president's clear disdain for multilateralism, under-appreciation of the importance of alliances, barely disguised racial and religious prejudices, and his simplistic mercantilist view of international commerce *all* have done real damage to US-Southeast Asian relations. As one Malaysian official observed to me: "We Southeast Asians are reserved people, but Trump shoots off his mouth like a gunslinger."[18] Trump's anti-immigration policies and targeting of Muslim immigrants in particular went down very badly in Brunei, Indonesia, and Malaysia. And his abrupt withdrawal from TPP sent irreparable shock waves throughout the region. But, on balance, for Trump personally, it would seem that he harbors no particular animosity toward Southeast Asia, and he has indeed been personally positive during his two visits to the region and in welcoming of the leaders of Malaysia, Singapore, Thailand, and Vietnam to the White House in 2017. Yet, Trump's impulsiveness and capriciousness keeps Southeast Asians on edge. Trump's tariff and trade war with China has also had a direct impact on Southeast Asia, as a number of US companies have begun to rework their supply chains and relocate some of their production facilities from China to the region (mainly Vietnam, Indonesia, and Malaysia).

The second—and major—factor driving the US approach to Southeast Asia under Trump has been China's broadening and deepening footprint across the region. The Trump administration's *Indo-Pacific Strategy Report*, produced by the Department of Defense in June 2019, starkly states: "As China continues its economic and global ascendance, it seeks Indo-Pacific regional hegemony in the near-term, ultimately global preeminence in the long-term."[19] The report criticizes a number of Chinese actions in the region—military, economic, and political—stating: "China is using economic inducements and penalties, influence operations, and implied military threats to persuade other states to comply with its agenda."[20] It particularly takes aim at China's building of islands and expanded military presence in the East and South China Seas. "These actions," the report alleges, "endanger the free flow of trade, threaten the sovereignty of other nations, and undermine regional stability."[21] This critique of China's regional behavior is consistent with the prominent policy statements issued at the outset of the administration, the *National Security Strategy of the United States* and *National Defense Strategy*, both of which labeled China as a "revisionist power."

China's expanded position and influence has indeed been steadily growing, as is described at length in chapter 5, but it has been accentuated (or at least the *perception* of it) by Trump's "America First" foreign policy and episodic engagement with Southeast Asia. Taken together, many analysts see the United States creating a strategic vacuum in Southeast Asia that China is readily and happily filling. This is the pervasive perception and media narrative across the region. No matter where one goes or what one reads, China is seen to be the rising—and inevitable—dominant power in Southeast Asia, while the United States is seen to be increasingly insular, domestically dysfunctional, increasingly unilateral, and in decline. In this context, the parallel narrative has arisen that countries in Southeast Asia are choosing China over the United States and that the latter is "losing" the region to China.[22]

Whether these narratives are empirically accurate is another question. I argue that they are *not accurate*. As will be shown subsequently in this chapter, the United States still possesses substantial strengths—*far greater* strengths than China in the region. But perceptions are not always in line with empirical realities, and they often become a reality of their own (memes). Whatever the perceptions, as discussed in chapters 1, 6, and 7, it is now clearly evident that the United States and China are locked into a protracted comprehensive competition for power and influence.[23]

The Evolution of Trump Policies Toward Southeast Asia

The Trump administration got off to a very slow start in its relations with Southeast Asia. Although Trump invested significant time and attention with Northeast Asian leaders—notably Japan's Shinzō Abe and China's Xi Jinping—Southeast Asia was not initially on his radar screen. The first four months of his term passed without a single meeting or telephone conversation with a Southeast Asian leader, although during the same period he had fifteen phone conversations with heads of state in the Middle East, fourteen from Europe, seven from Latin America, six from Northeast Asia, three from Africa, two from North America, two from Oceania, and one from South Asia.[24]

Trump's action on his third day in office to withdraw from the Trans-Pacific Partnership (TPP), though he had warned he would do so, sent shock waves throughout Asia. I was living in Singapore at the time and experienced the palpable shock and sense of American betrayal. TPP was viewed as the primary economic component of Obama's pivot policy, and Trump's withdrawal deeply damaged the United States' reputation and credibility throughout the region. Several Southeast Asian countries (Brunei, Malaysia, Singapore, and Vietnam) had made wrenching economic adjustments and compromises in order to join TPP. After eight years of Washington cajoling and pressuring them to join, these countries were left in the lurch by Trump's action. But Trump's withdrawal was seen as far more than just an economic action—it signaled to Southeast Asians, once again, that the United States was unpredictable and not to be relied upon. They also found Trump's "America First" rhetoric deeply disturbing,[25] as it led to the widespread perception of an isolationist America—that would unilaterally cede the strategic ground to China.

Beginning during the second quarter of 2017, however, following intensive pleas from US embassies in the region and an internal US government policy review, the Trump team began to focus attention on the region. A carefully calibrated series of steps were taken to send reassuring signals. The vice president, secretaries of state and defense, and the president himself all visited the region. Vice President Pence made a stopover in Jakarta—signing a number of business deals, visiting the US mission to ASEAN, and the ASEAN Secretariat.[26] Secretary of Defense Mattis paid his first visit to the Shangri-la Dialogue in Singapore,[27] and then Secretary of State Tillerson invited all ten ASEAN foreign ministers to meet with him and the administration in Washington.[28] In addition, Trump received the leaders of Malaysia, Singapore, Thailand, and Vietnam at the White House.

With these moves, the Trump administration sought to reassure Southeast Asia of continued US engagement. To some in the region, the signals were encouraging;[29] yet others wondered if they were just the latest examples of Washington's episodic engagement.[30] Other observers noticed a new pattern of "transactional diplomacy" or "gift diplomacy."[31] That is, in line with Trump's "buy American" mantra, visiting foreign leaders now turned the tables on the

Figure 3.2 President Donald Trump greets Philippines President Rodrigo Duterte
Source: Athit Perawongmetha/AFP via Getty Images

superpower by bearing gifts of large-scale commercial purchases from the United States—instead of the traditional pattern of Washington showering visitors with preferential credits, trade deals, and defense arrangements. When Malaysian Prime Minister Najib Razak visited the White House on September 12, 2017, he promptly announced to Trump that he came to purchase twenty-five Boeing jetliners worth $10 billion, offering Malaysian investment of $3–4 billion into US infrastructure, and another $10 billion in technology investments.[32] Thailand's Prime Minister Prayut Chan-ocha had a long and expensive shopping list for F-16 fighter upgrades, Blackhawk helicopters, a Cobra gunship, Harpoon missiles, and other military equipment. He too placed orders for twenty Boeing passenger jets for Thai Airways. Prayut and Trump also signed a series of agriculture and energy deals.[33] Not to be outdone, Singapore's Prime Minister Lee Hsien Loong arrived at the White House offering to buy 39 Boeings. The tables have indeed turned, where now visitors to the White House come bearing gifts of huge commercial deals—rather than being recipients of American-subsidized largesse.

To cap the flurry of US diplomacy in Southeast Asia, President Trump himself visited the region in November 2017 for the annual APEC Summit, the East Asia Summit (which he left early), the US-ASEAN 50th Anniversary Commemorative Summit, and a bilateral state visit to Vietnam. The main policy event of the trip was the president's speech at the APEC CEO Summit in Danang, Vietnam. But Trump used it as an opportunity to give a very toughly worded speech about his "America First" economic agenda. It left many disquieted. While the sheer physical presence of the president of the United States in the region was reassuring to many Southeast Asians, on balance the Trump trip received mixed reactions in the region.[34]

Following the flurry of Washington's re-engagement with Southeast Asia from May–November 2017, the normal pattern of American benign neglect reappeared. No high-level interactions occurred until Trump flew to Singapore for his historic summit with North Korea's Kim Jong-un on June 12, 2018. This, of course, was not a Southeast Asia trip diplomatically—but Trump did have a separate bilateral meeting with Singaporean Prime Minister Lee at The Istana, where he confirmed that he would return in November for the annual ASEAN and East Asia Summits (which he failed to do). The other visit of significance was Secretary of Defense Mattis's second attendance of the Shangri-la Dialogue, where he gave a major speech on June 2, 2018. In it, Secretary Mattis provided a *tour d'horizon* of the administration's regional policies and priorities. It was the fullest exposition to date by a senior US official of the Trump administration's conceptualization of regional order (although it still left much to be desired on a strategic and intellectual level).[35]

As such, Secretary Mattis highlighted the administration's theme of the "Free and Open Indo-Pacific" as the central organizing concept of its Asia strategy and policy. Said Mattis: "Make no mistake, America is in the Indo-Pacific to stay. This is our priority theater. Our interests and regions are inextricably intertwined."[36] The Free and Open Indo-Pacific Order strategy had, in fact, been signaled earlier in the year in the Trump administration's *National Security Strategy of the United States* and the *National Defense Strategy of the United States of America*.[37] Both documents take China to task as the major destabilizing element in the Indo-Pacific region:

> China is leveraging military modernization, influence operations, and predatory economics to coerce its neighboring countries to reorder the Indo-Pacific region to their advantage. As China continues its economic and military ascendance, asserting power through an all-of-nation long-term strategy, it will continue to pursue a military modernization program that seeks Indo-Pacific regional hegemony in the near-term and displacement of the United States to achieve global preeminence in the future.[38]

While they offered hints into the Trump administration's Indo-Pacific strategy, the full elaboration of it came in June 2019 with the *Indo-Pacific Strategy Report*. However, other mid-level Trump officials previewed it in public. Deputy Assistant Secretary of Defense for Asian and Pacific Security Affairs Randall Shriver testified at a Senate hearing that the United States prioritized Southeast Asia.[39] Shriver's counterpart at the State Department, David Stilwell, similarly stated: "Support for a strong united ASEAN remains at the heart of our Indo-Pacific strategy. We see great convergence with ASEAN's outlook on the Indo-Pacific and our vision for the region."[40]

In November 2019, on the eve of the APEC annual meeting and East Asian Summit in Bangkok, the Department of State finally rolled out its own official version of the administration's Indo-Pacific strategy and policy.[41] Entitled *A Free and Open Indo-Pacific: Advancing a Shared Vision*, the document combines together various and sundry US initiatives across the broad sprawling region—from Japan and South Korea in the north; down to Australia, New Zealand, and the Pacific islands in the southeast; to ASEAN in the south; and to India and other South Asian/Indian Ocean countries to the southwest. While the document catalogues a wide range of US programs and initiatives, it states clearly that:

> The US vision for the Indo-Pacific excludes no nation. We do not ask countries to choose between one partner or another. Instead, we ask that they uphold the core principles of the regional order at a time when these principles are under

threat. The United States is strengthening and deepening partnerships with countries that share our values.[42]

By contrast, while not specifically identifying China, when referring to the Mekong River, the report says:

> This region is facing new challenges that put autonomy and economic independence at risk—including debt dependency, a spree of dam-building that concentrates control over downstream flows, plans to blast and dredge riverbeds, extraterritorial river patrols, increasing organized crime and trafficking, and a push by some to mold new rules to govern the river in ways that undermine existing institutions.[43]

If this not-so-oblique reference to China was not clear enough, the official report then goes on to call China out specifically:

> The People's Republic of China (PRC) practices repression at home and abroad. Beijing is intolerant of dissent, aggressively controls media and civil society, and brutally suppresses ethnic and religious minorities. Such practices, which Beijing exports to other countries through its political and economic influence, undermine the conditions that have promoted stability and prosperity in the Indo-Pacific for decades.[44]

Despite such tough language, the report does not anywhere reference an attempt by China to dominate the region (an accusation frequently heard in Washington). Nonetheless, China perceives the Indo-Pacific strategy as thinly disguised containment. One report by the Director of China's National Institute for South China Seas Studies, Wu Shicun, observes "China is the main target . . . the real intention of the Indo-Pacific strategy is to construct an exclusive regional group to counter China."[45]

Following the Trump administration's rollout of its signature Free and Open Indo-Pacific concept, it was initially met with considerable confusion across the region,[46] as well as in Washington policy circles.[47] Some observers saw it simply as a repackaging and updated version of long-standing American preferences for regional order.[48] Some things were seen as new, some things not. For example, the lead sentence of the Pentagon's *Indo-Pacific Strategy Report* explicitly proclaimed for the first time: "The Indo-Pacific is the single most consequential region for America's future."[49] The language concerning China's destabilizing regional role was also new in its explicitness. The Department of Defense document was also not solely focused on the military realm, which is unusual for a Pentagon document. It linked together elements of politics, governance, environment, economics, and other features of regional development.[50] To a certain extent, though, the DoD strategy document was a repackaging of Obama-era policies. For example, the subtitle of the *Indo-Pacific Strategy Report* is "Preparedness, Partnerships, and a Networked Region." *Preparedness* is codeword for upgrading military equipment and readiness, a trend begun under the Obama "pivot" policy. *Partnerships* refers to the strengthening of regional alliances (something all administrations set out to do), solidify non-allied defense and intelligence partnerships with certain countries (such as Singapore), and robust engagement in multilateral forums and institutions. While the latter is also a feature of previous administrations, it is perhaps noteworthy that the Trump administration remains committed to these multilateral mechanisms in Asia—given its wariness, occasionally open disdain, and withdrawal from many (including TPP). *Networks* are also a continuation of Obama-era creation of multinational, multinodal, and multi-service defense networks.

One element that seems to emerge is a revitalization of the "Quad" concept, that is, quadrilateral security cooperation among the United States, Japan, Australia, and India. This is not a new concept (originally a Japanese initiative), but when it was first floated during the George W. Bush administration, it was stillborn because then Australian Prime Minister Kevin Rudd thought it would antagonize China (and hence Australia made clear it would not participate). It seems that Quad 2.0 may fare better—as there does now seem a much greater harmony of interests among the four democracies, Australia is on board, tangible naval cooperation and some intelligence sharing is underway, and all four share a common concern about the rising security role of China across the region.

In sum, with the Trump administration we see elements of both continuity and discontinuity from the Obama administration. The most notable change has been a relative decrease in Washington's prioritization of the region, as compared with the Obama years. But when looked at in the longer term, the Obama administration was the *exception* to the rule. *No* American administration has *ever* prioritized Southeast Asia to the extent Obama did. What we see under Trump is a return to the on-again/off-again episodic pattern of US engagement with ASEAN and its member states. To be sure, and to its credit, the Trump administration did have a very good seven months—from May through November 2017—when it clearly prioritized Southeast Asia. This was a deliberate effort—and it was the result of the apparent vacuum and complete inattention paid during the initial months of the administration. During the initial transition period from Obama to Trump, US embassies in the region seemed to be operating on "autopilot" from the Obama administration—as they had received little policy guidance from Washington (this was the distinct sense I got in visiting several embassies in the region plus India). However, following entreaties from the embassies to Washington and the internal interagency review of April–May

2017, the administration considerably ramped up its engagement with the region and systematically went about initiating official exchanges at various levels throughout the year. Thereafter, US diplomacy in the region fell into remission again—until Vice President Mike Pence's attendance of the 2018 East Asian Summit, APEC Summit, and US-ASEAN Summit, and Secretary of State Mike Pompeo's whirlwind visit through the region in August 2019. Both were classic examples of America's episodic diplomacy—parachute in, deliver reassuring speeches, and depart. Both pushed back against China by giving speeches critical of Beijing's behavior in the region.[51] For his part, Pompeo publicly rejected the idea that China had stolen a march on America in the region—claiming that it was inaccurate to suggest that "some countries in the region were vassal states in the clutches of China."[52] He thus also rejected the accusation that his regional tour was aimed at "winning back" allies and countries, stating: "Our engagement in this region has not been, and will not be, a zero-sum exercise. Our interests simply naturally converge with yours to our mutual benefit."[53]

When it comes to continuities and changes in US-ASEAN relations from Obama to Trump, this is best seen in the continuation of a number of functional dimensions of the relationship. Many of these are apparent when comparing the 2019 State Department report *A Free and Open Indo-Pacific* with similar Obama-era policy documents.

Let us now examine overall US relations with ASEAN and then three key spheres in particular: commerce, security, and public diplomacy.

Overall US Relations with ASEAN

It must be said that ASEAN is as much an idea, or a set of ideals, as it is an institution. It is not an institution in the Western sense, and it certainly is not even the European Union. It is better thought of as an under-resourced and aspiring organization than a centralized and mature institution. This causes no end of problems for foreigners who look for and expect *coherence* and a body that draws together—and *represents*—the different nations of the region. The most fundamental mistakes Americans and the US government make are, first, to think of it as a pan-regional institution that collectively represents its ten member states and is empowered to act on their behalf—and, second, that Southeast Asia equals ASEAN. Neither is the case. ASEAN remains an under-institutionalized and under-resourced body with minimal representative powers and poor capacities for implementation, and it is by no means the same thing as Southeast Asia.

Nonetheless, ASEAN has come a long way since its establishment in 1967, it has recently celebrated its fiftieth anniversary,[54] and it has a record of accomplishments. Suffice it here to note that ASEAN has a relatively new charter

(2008) that tries precisely to deal with the amorphousness of the organization and the valid criticisms of its (in)effectiveness, it is striving hard to find coherence and meaningful consensus (rather than lowest common denominator) on various issues, has prioritized three pillars (the Political-Security Community, Economic Community, and Socio-Cultural Community) around which to organize pan-regional policies, and has redoubled its efforts to engage nations beyond the region in dialogues and exchanges. Originally an exclusive organization, ASEAN now practices inclusiveness (by inviting a wide variety of external "dialogue partners" to interact with it).

For the United States, it officially became a "dialogue partner" of ASEAN in 1977, and by becoming a signatory of ASEAN's bedrock Treaty of Amity and Cooperation in 2009 was able to upgrade and regularize this status. Since 2010 the United States has had a dedicated ambassador to ASEAN and a separate US Mission to ASEAN, both of which are institutionally autonomous but physically embedded within the US embassy in Jakarta, Indonesia. When I visited it in 2018, I found that it is extremely short-staffed and does not even have its own dedicated facilities (by contrast, many other nations have stand-alone offices for their ASEAN missions). Like many diplomatic missions abroad under Trump and following a normal election turnover of political appointee ambassadors, the US Mission to ASEAN had no ambassador in residence at the time. The charge d'affaires and three-member team were courteous enough, but they only gave me a standard boilerplate briefing, measuring their words very carefully and providing little information of substance not available on the mission's website.[55] They did give me a copy of the *Plan of Action to Implement the ASEAN-US Strategic Partnership (2016–2020)*, which is a laundry list of diplomatic language ("support" this, "promote" that, "encourage" this, "strengthen" that) and exchanges built around the three ASEAN pillars noted above.[56] The *Plan of Action* is testimony to the range of engagements the United States has with ASEAN (ranging from political consultations; defense consultations; maritime cooperation; good governance, human rights, and rule of law promotion; trade and investment promotion; support for small and medium enterprises (SMEs); best practices for energy regulation; food and agriculture standards; law enforcement; counterterrorism; disaster management; environment and biodiversity; science and technology cooperation, women's empowerment; etc.).

These are indeed an impressive range of areas in which the United States is engaged on the ground throughout Southeast Asia with both governmental and non-governmental stakeholders. But it seemed clear to me that the job of the US Mission to ASEAN is simply to stimulate liaison between individual US embassies in the ten member states of ASEAN—as they have neither the human nor financial capacity to implement such programs from Jakarta. So, the US Mission to ASEAN is definitely on the *implementation* end of policy and (at best) does not seem to be very engaged in *formulating* US policy toward the region. When I asked them, for example, "What is the US *strategy* what are you doing to monitor and counter China's activities in the region?" my questions were met with an awkward silence and blank stares. Strategy? What strategy? China? Are we in competition with them? Are we supposed to monitor them? This was the unspoken body language I sensed. After an awkward silence, the US chargé d'affaires tersely admitted: "We do not track China regionally."[57]

Perhaps unfair, but my visit to the US Mission to ASEAN left me with the strong impression that US policy toward ASEAN is the sum of the parts of US relations with individual countries in the region and there is little—if any—centralized and coordinated strategy for competing with China in the region. I must say that I got the exact same impression when visiting individual embassies in the region. They all struck me as working on individual pieces of a puzzle (managing bilateral relations with their individual countries) without a sense of the whole puzzle. This said about US embassies in the region, my conversations with senior Trump administration officials in Washington suggest that indeed such a strategy of competing with China *does exist*. So, while there seems to be such strategic thinking in Washington, there nonetheless appears to be a real disconnect with US embassies in the region.

Even if not explicitly aimed at China, the Trump administration has continued to signal, at least rhetorically, ASEAN's importance to US regional strategy. At the Sixth US-ASEAN Summit in Singapore in 2018, Vice President Pence starkly stated: "ASEAN is central to our vision for the region; it is our indispensable and irreplaceable strategic partner. And the members of ASEAN should have no other view."[58] This is a powerful statement by the US vice president, but inquiring minds wonder: are American relations simply the sum of their parts? As the following three sections illustrate, the breadth and depth of US programs and activities in the region—both governmental and non-governmental—is indeed impressive. At the end of the day, it is precisely the *substance* of the American presence and interactions that matter most. Yet, it would be nice if the US Government actually had a coherent, systematic, and well-articulated underlying *strategy* that wove together the many component parts described in the following sections.

US Commercial Relations with ASEAN

Commerce has long been a key anchor of the US engagement with Southeast Asia. From 1873 to 2007, with the exception of the period during World War II, the United States was Southeast Asia's largest trading partner. American companies have deep roots throughout the region. The US trade in goods with ASEAN countries reached $334 billion in 2018 (a quadrupling since the 1990s).[59] Collectively, ASEAN is now America's fourth largest trading partner worldwide. US exports to ASEAN support more than 500,000 jobs in the United States.[60] American exports of goods and services have been growing steadily: $75 billion in goods and $31 billion in services in 2017, a 59 percent increase in a decade.[61] Unfortunately, the United States is running an overall deficit of $83.9 billion (Table 3.1). To date this fact seems to have escaped the attention of President Trump, as he has not (yet) targeted the region with his ire.

More important than trade has been the United States' investment in the region. The cumulative total stock of US direct investment in 2018 reached $329 billion— more than investment by China, Japan, and South Korea combined![62] Annual FDI from US entities reached $24.9 billion in 2017 (almost *twice* that of China's approximately $13.7 billion).[63] ASEAN is the leading destination for US investment in the entire Indo-Pacific region. Meanwhile, ASEAN countries invested $28 billion cumulatively in the United States by 2017.[64] Two-way tourism is also big business— 780,000 people from ASEAN countries visited the United States, while 3.5 million Americans visited ASEAN countries in 2015 (however, this remains a far cry from the 25 million Chinese tourists to ASEAN in 2018).[65]

Although the United States only has one bilateral Free Trade Agreement in the region (with Singapore), various government agreements help facilitate commerce—including the 2006 ASEAN-US Trade and Investment

Table 3.1 US Trade in Goods with Southeast Asia (2016) (Unit = US$ bn.)

Country	Exports	Imports	Balance
Singapore	26,724.9	17,833.4	8,891.5
Malaysia	11,831.9	36,630.0	−24,798.1
Thailand	10,444.9	29,477.0	−19,032.1
Vietnam	10,100.4	42,098.8	−31,998.3
Philippines	8,199.8	10,044.0	−1,844.2
Indonesia	6,023.7	19,194.4	−13,170.7
Brunei	614.7	13.8	600.9
Cambodia	360.7	2,814.3	−2,453.6
Myanmar	192.9	244.7	−51.9
Laos	30.9	55.1	−24.2
Total	74,524.8	158,405.5	−83,880.7

Source: US Census Bureau

Framework Arrangement (TIFA), the 2012 ASEAN-US Expanded Economic Engagement, and US-ASEAN Connect. The last of these initiatives is organized around four program areas to enhance public-private partnerships and cooperation: Business Connect, Energy Connect, Innovation Connect, and Policy Connect.[66]

The Washington-based US-ASEAN Business Council and the American Chambers of Commerce (AMCHAM) in each Southeast Asia country do much to promote two-way trade and investment.[67] Over 4,200 US companies now operate throughout the ASEAN region.[68] This includes 1,782 in Singapore, 784 in Malaysia, 644 in Thailand, 513 in the Philippines, 489 in Indonesia, 309 in Vietnam, 33 in Cambodia, 21 in Brunei, 21 in Myanmar, and 10 in Laos.[69] The 2018 AMCHAM *ASEAN Business Outlook Survey*, based on the annual survey of American companies, was very bullish about opportunities for US businesses in the region: the vast majority of respondents (87 percent) expected their companies' level of trade, investment, and profits in ASEAN to increase over the next five years.[70] Vietnam, Indonesia, Myanmar, Singapore, and Thailand were identified as the fastest-growing markets with greatest growth potential for American business expansion.[71]

The composition of US business in Southeast Asia is quite diverse. General Motors and Ford have had major car and truck production facilities in Thailand for many years (although in early 2020 GM, which had been assembling 50,000 vehicles per year but experiencing weak domestic sales demand, abruptly sold its manufacturing facilities in Rayong province to China's Great Wall Motor).[72] With a five-decade presence in the region (headquartered in Singapore), Caterpillar produces construction and mining equipment, diesel and natural gas engines, industrial gas turbines, and diesel-electric locomotives. General Electric, which first established its business presence in Malaysia in 1975, now employs 1,300 people in the country, from Kuala Lumpur to Sarawak. Intel also has a large plant and is the largest employer in Penang. Also in Malaysia, Coca-Cola, ON Semiconductor, Met Life, and JP Morgan have all established long-term presence in the country.[73] Citibank has been operating in the region since 1902, Procter & Gamble since 1935, and Coca-Cola for over a century. Chevron and other oil majors have been exploring offshore since the 1970s. Boeing does booming business across the region in passenger planes (contracts for at least 75 airliners were signed between 2015 and 2017 alone), fighter jets, transports, helicopters, and other aircraft.[74] Boeing, United Technologies, GE, Lockheed, Booz Allen Hamilton, and others dominate the defense sector across Southeast Asia. Exxon Mobil, Halliburton, Dow Chemical, and other US energy giants have diverse upstream and downstream operations throughout the region. Even Bechtel has returned to the region, following an absence of several years, and is now competing for infrastructure projects.

Under the Trump administration there has also been a marked effort to get back into the infrastructure business and counter China's Belt and Road Initiative. To this end, the Trump administration launched the BUILD Act (Better Utilization of Investments Leading to Development), to which it allocated an initial $60 billion worldwide, and is aimed at offering countries an alternative to China's Belt and Road Initiative. Also, in December 2018 the US Congress passed the Asia Reassurance Initiative Act (ARIA), which has an annual budget of $1.5 billion over five years, much of which is earmarked for Southeast Asia. ARIA stipulates that the administration should negotiate and upgrade "economic and strategic engagement frameworks" within ASEAN and report annually to Congress on its implementation.

Increasingly, though, US business in Southeast Asia has shifted toward diverse services and "soft" industries—including financial services, multimedia, information technologies, consumer retail, e-commerce, pharmaceuticals, insurance, health-care services, consulting services, legal services, accounting services, tourism facilitation, and transportation. This shift is evident in the composition of AMCHAM and the US-ASEAN Business Council member companies, which are increasingly populated by firms such as Adobe, Airbnb, Albright-Stonebridge, Amazon, Apple, The Asia Group, Cigna, eBay, Expedia, Facebook, FedEx, Google, Johnson & Johnson, McLarty Associates, Medtronic, Oracle, PricewaterhouseCoopers, Time Warner, Uber, United Parcel Service, and others. The *ASEAN Business Outlook Survey 2018* noted earlier singles out five sectors as the "most promising" for American businesses: IT/telecommunications, health care, banking and finance, consulting, and education.[75] The standards industry (technical specifications for the manufacturing of products) is also a growth sector for American firms. The US commercial attaché in Singapore, Margaret Hanson-Muse, goes so far as to say, "Standards are *the* No. 1 comparative advantage for US business in ASEAN. Standards equal value."[76] US-ASEAN Business Council executive Michael Michalak agrees: "Services is really the main comparative advantage for the United States in Southeast Asia."[77]

If American business has a weakness in Southeast Asia, it has been slow to get into the e-commerce industry. Southeast Asia's internet economy reached an estimated $72 billion in 2018 and is estimated to grow to $240 billion by 2025, according to the 2018 annual Google-Temasek annual survey of the region's digital economy.[78] US firms are absent in the booming mobile payments industry, which is dominated by China's Ali-Pay, Union Pay, and homegrown Southeast Asian firms.[79] Credit cards denominated by American banks (Visa and Mastercard) are still widely used, but a high percentage of those under fifty in the region increasingly use "e-wallets" (essentially direct debit accounts to their bank or intermediary firms). Online travel accounts for the bulk ($23 billion) of e-commerce revenue in the region, according to the Google-Temasek survey. Online media sales are growing rapidly ($11 billion), owing to the popularity of social media, and ride hailing services are also a huge market ($8 billion) in which the American firm Uber has been usurped by the regional firms Grab (founded in Malaysia and now Singapore-based) and Go-Jek (Indonesia based), and increasingly China's Didi Chuxing.[80]

As a whole, though, the American business and commercial presence in Southeast Asia has never been stronger. It is only due to grow—and grow substantially. One reason is because of the continuing difficulties being experienced by US and Western firms in China. This was true prior to the Trump administration's tariff and trade war with China, when most companies were practicing the "China Plus" strategy, that is, maintaining (but lowering) their production footprint in China by diversifying it to other countries. But, as a consequence of US-China trade tensions and the recalibration of supply chains (so-called "de-coupling"), a considerable number of American firms are now relocating a more substantial part of their business operations to Southeast Asia—notably, Vietnam, Malaysia, Indonesia, and Thailand. ASEAN has thus been a major beneficiary of this diversification and decoupling process.

The US Corrupt Practices Act also gives American businesses a good name and reputation throughout the region. As I traveled and interviewed around the region, this was a point regularly made when I asked businesspeople to contrast American with Chinese business practices. Chinese companies have a deserved reputation for corruption, but American companies are seen to be clean and transparent. The US Secretary of State Mike Pompeo highlighted this in his address to the Indo-Pacific Business Forum on July 30, 2018, when he proclaimed: "American companies have been a force for prosperity and good throughout the Indo-Pacific region. Our good faith as a partner is evident in our support of economic development that honors local autonomy and national sovereignty. The United States does not invest for political influence, but rather practices *partnership economics*."[81] Vice President Pence similarly told the APEC CEO Summit in Papua New Guinea in 2018: "We don't drown our partners in a sea of debt, we don't coerce or compromise your independence. The United States deals openly, fairly. We do not offer a constricting belt or a one-way road."[82] This was an obvious dig at China's Belt and Road Initiative. In addition to passing the aforementioned BUILD Act and working with Japan in particular to compete with China on regional infrastructure projects, the Trump administration is working with other regional states to establish a "Blue Dot Network," a multi-sector platform to evaluate, grade, and approve high-quality infrastructure projects.[83] While agreeing that clean and transparent US corporate practices are valued and respected throughout the region, the US-ASEAN Business Council Senior Vice President and retired Ambassador to Vietnam Michael Michalik told me that: "the biggest US disadvantage is that we just don't have the amounts of cash that China does."[84] Another US initiative is the US-ASEAN Smart Cities Partnership, announced by Vice President Pence in November 2018 at the US-ASEAN Summit, which seeks to connect the American and Southeast Asian public and private sectors in twenty-six member cities to address various problems associated with urbanization and strengthening cybersecurity capacities.

Thus, America's commercial presence in Southeast Asia is extremely broad, deep, and long-standing, and US business practices are respected throughout the region. This is an intrinsic strength that is, at the same time, underappreciated but a real asset.

US Security Relations with ASEAN

Almost all Southeast Asian militaries have extensive ties with the US military. The security/defense relationship is closest with Singapore, growing much stronger with Indonesia, quietly effective with Malaysia, improving significantly with Vietnam, deepening with Brunei, and weathering strains with allies Thailand and the Philippines. In all of these cases, there are extensive training and professional military education exchanges, equipment transfers and sales, joint exercises, high-level leader engagement, and, in most cases, service-to-service exchanges. In some cases (Malaysia, Philippines, Singapore, Thailand), there are US military personnel deployed in-country and American use of host nation military bases and facilities.

US security assistance to Southeast Asia generally includes three main components: the International Military Education and Training (IMET) and Expanded IMET programs, the Foreign Military Sales and Financing (FMS/FMF) program, and the Excess Defense Articles (EDA) program.

IMET is a flagship US military program and is a principal mechanism for training foreign officers in the United States. This occurs at any number of US military bases, staff and service colleges, the National Defense University, and the Asia-Pacific Center for Security Studies (APCSS) in Honolulu (Fig. 3.3). The State Department determines which countries qualify for the IMET program, but the Defense Department implements it. Since US restrictions on Indonesia and Vietnam were lifted, every Southeast Asian country except Myanmar now qualifies to participate in IMET. In Myanmar's case, Congressional staff members adamantly oppose inclusion into IMET and have been successful in blocking it and other forms of normal military-to-military exchanges.

Established in 1995, the Daniel K. Inouye APCSS is a component of IMET and a uniquely important institution and contributor to America's security support for ASEAN (and other Asia-Pacific) countries.[85] APCSS is a poster child for how multinational defense education and security cooperation should operate. Based

Figure 3.3 APCSS National Security Course for Southeast Asia
Source: Official DKI APCSS Photo

in downtown Honolulu, it administers a wide range of conferences and courses for security personnel from across the region. Its mission is "Building capacities and communities of interest by educating, connecting, and empowering security practitioners to advance Asia-Pacific security."[86] APCSS now proudly claims an alumni network of more than 12,000. The distinguished alumni include four presidents and prime ministers, eleven vice presidents and deputy prime ministers, 63 ministerial-level officials, 158 ambassadors, and 852 flag officers.[87] This is *impact!* "We create 'strategic affection' for the USA," I was told when I visited APCSS.[88] It is an extraordinary network of military and civilian alumni spanning the Asia-Pacific. The one country that does *not* participate in APCSS programs is China. When I visited, I was told that this is because the Center accepts personnel from Taiwan.

With an annual operating budget of $21 million, it is supported by the Office of the Secretary of Defense via the Defense Security Cooperation Security Agency. APCSS courses and workshops normally run for five weeks, are of seven different formats, and cover a range of topics: counterterrorism, crisis management, humanitarian assistance and disaster relief, and a range of "nontraditional" security subjects like cyber, water, piracy, and public health. The Advanced Security

Cooperation Course and the Comprehensive Crisis Management Course are flagship programs aimed at "mid-career and senior policy practitioners" (lieutenant colonels, colonels, brigadier generals, and civilian equivalents). The Transnational Security Cooperation Course is targeted at general officers and vice-ministerial-level civilians. The Asia-Pacific Orientation Course and the Senior Asia-Pacific Orientation Course are the bread and butter of APCSS. One unique and important feature is the effort put into role playing in simulation exercises, so as to get visiting military officers and other civilian participants to view bilateral and multilateral security issues from other nations' perspectives.

The Foreign Military Sales and Foreign Military Financing (FMS/FMF) programs now also operate in every ASEAN country except Cambodia, Laos, and Myanmar. In addition to sales of new military equipment and weapons, the Excess Defense Articles (EDA) program transfers used equipment to regional militaries. For example, the Philippines and Vietnam have both received several decommissioned US Coast Guard cutters. The US military also maintains bilateral training programs and undertakes joint exercises with several Southeast Asian militaries every year.[89] In 2015, the US military held three joint exercises with Brunei, four with Cambodia, seven with Indonesia, eight with Malaysia, seven with the Philippines, seven with Singapore, six with Thailand, and three with Vietnam. Another important Department of Defense–led initiative is the Southeast Asia Maritime Law Enforcement Initiative, which was launched in 2012. The US military and civilian intelligence agencies also maintain close ties with their counterparts in many Southeast Asian states.

Through all of these military assistance programs, the United States provides very tangible support for Southeast Asian militaries. These programs are not well known in the region—indeed Southeast Asian governments are quite reticent to allow them to be publicized. Being perceived as close to the United States, particularly in the defense and intelligence domains, is considered a real liability in several countries—most notably in Muslim-majority Indonesia and Malaysia. Even ship visits and routine exercises are rarely reported by the governments concerned or in local media, although US Navy vessels make regular port calls throughout the region.

The Indo-Pacific Command

Operationally, the heart and soul of the U.S. military and security assistance programs lies with the US Pacific Command (USPACOM) in Honolulu, Hawaii. Consistent with the Trump administration's Indo-Pacific strategy, PACOM was renamed the Indo-Pacific Command (INDOPACOM) on May 30, 2018. Actually, despite the change in nomenclature, the command's area of operation (AOR) has

Figure 3.4 Indo-Pacific Command area of operation
Source: US Indo-Pacific Command

always encompassed the Indian Ocean and South Asia (Fig. 3.4). It thus extends all the way from the west coast of the continental United States to Afghanistan and the Middle East (which falls under the Central Command or CENTCOM). It is the largest of America's six regional combatant commands—spanning 100 million square miles, half of the earth's surface, and 36 nations.

When I visited INDOPACOM headquarters at Camp Smith in Honolulu in May 2018, I was given an unclassified briefing that described US military capabilities in the region.[90] Approximately 379,200 military and civilian personnel are assigned to INDOPACOM. This includes the following:

- US Pacific Fleet (140,000 personnel, 1,100 aircraft, 5 aircraft carrier strike groups, and 200 ships).
- US Army Pacific (106,000 personnel, 309 aircraft, 1 corps, 2 divisions).
- US Pacific Air Forces (46,000 personnel, 420 aircraft).
- US Marine Forces Pacific (86,000 personnel, 640 aircraft, 2 expeditionary forces).
- Special Operations Command Pacific (1,200 personnel, 12 aircraft).

Since the Obama administration's pivot initiative, INDOPACOM has become *the favored* regional command in resources, equipment, training, exercises, defense partnerships, and deployments.[91] By 2020, 60 percent of the US Navy's vessels, including 50 percent of the Navy's Littoral Combat Ships (LCS), are deployed in the AOR, as well as 60 percent of US Air Force assets and 50 percent of newest aircraft (F-22 and F-35).[92] Logistics and equipment maintenance were similarly upgraded, with an 80 percent fighter readiness goal.[93] Other force modernization initiatives were identified in the aforementioned *Indo-Pacific Strategy Report*.[94] These include purchase of 110 fourth- and fifth-generation aircraft and 10 more destroyers.

Despite these various initiatives, financial resources from Washington do not appear to be sufficient to support them. On March 22, 2019, the current commander of Indo-Pacific Command, Admiral Phil Davidson, took the unusual step of writing a letter to the Senate Armed Services Committee complaining that the DoD fiscal 2020 budget did not include enough funding to provide "immediate and necessary resources" for INDOPACOM. The letter was not made public, but a copy was leaked to the *Wall Street Journal*, which reported on its contents.[95] Admiral Davidson's letter did not indicate the level of funding he was seeking, but the FY 2018 budget was reported to be $7.5 billion.[96] Davidson laid out a range of immediate needs covering both US forces as well as American allies and partners in the region. Among his requests was for a "permanent and persistent land-based integrated air- and missile defense system to defend the island of Guam"—a vital hub for regional operations.

The admiral's anxiety is fueled by China's ability to rain ballistic missiles down on Guam at present, and to develop the ability to attack the island by air in the not-too-distant future. Indeed, in making his case, Admiral Davidson implored the Armed Services Committee by saying: "I appreciate your continued support and advocacy for those critical capabilities necessary to counter the pernicious actions of our near peer competitor." The not-so-veiled reference to China echoes Davidson's dire warnings that he has given elsewhere. At the 2019 Shangri-la Dialogue, he said that the goal of US military strategy in Asia is to "dissuade China from pursuing their ambitions, which are centered on the first island chain in the near term, but are more broadly and globally ambitious in the long term."[97] These views are not new for Admiral Davidson. Like his predecessor Admiral Harry Harris, who starkly stated that "I believe China seeks hegemony in East Asia,"[98] Davidson has been very candid and direct in describing both the threats he perceives from China as well as the shortcomings in US preparedness to deal with them. In his prepared statement for April 2018 Senate confirmation hearings at the time of his appointment, Admiral Davidson said:

The outcome of war is never certain, and I have increasing concerns about the future. China has undergone a rapid military modernization over the last three decades and is approaching parity in a number of critical areas; there is no guarantee that the United States would win a future conflict with China.[99]

Admiral Davidson's Congressional testimony exemplifies the increasing alarm concerning the perceived dangers that China's dramatically rising military capabilities presents to the United States and its allies. It is important to remember that the United States thinks in terms not only of its *own* defense, but also in terms of defending its *allies and partners* and keeping open the sea lanes and commons throughout the region. Thus, the United States is providing the enormous "public good" of regional security and stability. This has permitted mainly regional militaries—*particularly in Southeast Asia*—to "free ride" on America's provisions for their defense, security, development, and well-being.

To these ends, INDOPACOM and the US Department of Defense undertake a wide range of bilateral and multilateral programs throughout the region. These include joint military exercises, humanitarian assistance and disaster relief (HADR), professional military education (PME), intelligence liaison and training,[100] counter-piracy operations, counterterrorism cooperation, and military training. Activities specifically involving Southeast Asian militaries include military exercises such as Rim of the Pacific (RIMPAC), Cope Thunder, Cobra Gold, Pahlawan Warrior, Balikatan, Pacific Angel, Garuda Shield, Cooperation Afloat Readiness and Training (CARAT), Southeast Asia Cooperation and Training (SEACAT), SEAMLEI (Southeast Asia Maritime Law Enforcement Initiative), and Khan Quest. Bilateral exercises occur with *every* Southeast Asia state except Laos and Myanmar (they are currently in abeyance with Cambodia). For the first time, in 2019 the US Navy undertook a multinational exercise with *all ten* ASEAN members in the Gulf of Thailand and South China Sea.[101] My interviews with INDOPACOM personnel in Honolulu indicated that the annual budget for such exercises is $100 million.[102] Through the Foreign Military Sales (FMS) program the United States also sells, transfers, and maintains various weapons systems for regional militaries. The United States also participates in a number of regional defense diplomacy activities and meetings, such as the ASEAN Defense Ministers Meeting Plus (ADMM+), the ASEAN Regional Forum (ARF), Expanded ASEAN Maritime Forum, the Shangri-la Dialogue, and a variety of bilateral defense and security dialogues with ASEAN member states.

Collectively and multilaterally, through these and other mechanisms the Department of Defense, INDOPACOM, and the individual services of the US military engage and partner with Southeast Asian militaries. Through all of these the United States is deeply engaged in the security and military domains across Southeast Asia. Individual bilateral military-to-military engagements are also extremely deep. The 2019 *Indo-Pacific Security Strategy* specified that "the United States is prioritizing new [defense] relationships with Vietnam, Indonesia, and Malaysia."[103] In addition to these three relatively new priorities, the United States maintains long-standing alliances with the Philippines and Thailand, and a deep defense partnership with Singapore. The following survey highlights many of the main areas of defense cooperation and assistance with Southeast Asian militaries.

The Philippines

The US defense relationship with the Philippines is anchored in their mutual alliance and over a century of close interactions. As discussed in chapter 2, this was not necessarily a pleasant or productive relationship during the colonial period, and there remain residual hard feelings among some of the Filipino public. But for the Armed Forces of the Philippines (AFP), the United States has been an extremely close allied partner and benefactor for more than half a century. American forces liberated the Philippines from Japanese occupation toward the end of Second World War, and this role helped to embed the US military following independence on July 4, 1946.

Soon thereafter, in 1947, the two signed the Military Bases Agreement (MBA) and Military Assistance Agreement (MAA). This relationship was further cemented with the 1951 US-Philippines Mutual Defense Treaty—thus facilitating forty years of a large American military presence in the country, which came to an end with the termination of the MBA in 1991 (see discussion of this period in chapter 2). During this time, and throughout the Vietnam War, the Philippines became a major strategic asset and logistical hub of the US military architecture in East Asia and the western Pacific. Clark Air Base was the headquarters of the US 13th Air Force, which was the command and control hub for all US air operations in the western Pacific and was home to several fighter wings, reconnaissance, and other aircraft.[104] Subic Bay Naval Base similarly was a central link in the forward deployment and projection of American maritime power into Southeast Asia, and between Hawaii, Japan, and the southwest Pacific. At the time, Subic was the largest US naval complex outside the United States and was a "second home" to Hawaii for Pacific Seventh Fleet.

Clark, Subic, and other facilities all fell under the Military Bases Agreement, which was set to expire in 1991. The George W. Bush administration, and particularly Deputy Secretary of State Richard Armitage, made significant efforts to forge a renegotiated and renewed agreement, which took account of Filipino concerns over extraterritoriality, but the final agreement was rejected by the Philippines Senate—thus forcing a complete withdrawal of US forces by 1992.

In the wake of this action, in 1998 the two sides agreed to a Visiting Forces Agreement (VFA). While not granting the United States rights to bases of its own, as under the former MBA, the VFA did provide the legal foundation for a wide range of rotational deployments of US forces, equipment, and personnel in the Philippines (many for lengthy periods), as well as joint exercises, intelligence sharing, and other defense cooperation. It also permitted US use of portions of Philippine bases for logistics. This was further supplemented in 2002 with a Mutual Logistical Support Agreement (MLSA). The events of 9/11 and the Bush administration's "global war on terror" catalyzed closer cooperation. US Special Forces were deployed to the southern Philippines island of Mindanao, where al-Qaeda and ISIS-linked Islamic militant fighters (Abu Sayyaf) were (and still are) engaged in protracted guerrilla warfare and terror operations. This cooperation was enshrined in the Joint Special Operations Task Force–Philippines (JSOTFP).[105] However, in February 2020, President Duterte abruptly gave notice that his government was formally withdrawing from the VFA—throwing into disarray and question the future of bilateral defense cooperation.[106] But being the fickle and unpredictable individual that he is, four months later, in June, the Duterte administration suddenly announced the "suspension" of Duterte's "abrogation." Thus, for the time being, the US-Philippines VFA and deep defense relationship appears to proceed as normal.

The VFA and MLSA were supplemented during the Obama administration with the conclusion of the 2014 Enhanced Defense Cooperation Agreement (EDCA).[107] Under this important agreement, which operates for an initial ten years with automatic renewal, the United States and the Philippines codified a new defense relationship. The agreement gave the United States access to eight Filipino "agreed locations" (bases)—including Clark and Subic again—where the United States can maintain complete operational control of facilities, equipment, prepositioned weapons stockpiles, and personnel. This was all within a new framework and "joint" partnership arrangement that respects Philippines' sovereignty. It also specifies and catalyzes a variety of training and assistance programs provided by the United States to the AFP. This has included the transfer of "excess defense articles," such as retired Hamilton class US Coast Guard cutters, to the Philippines Navy. In particular, the United States is helping to build the Philippines' maritime domain awareness (MDA), coastal security, and incipient naval capabilities. Given the proximity to the South China Sea and China's seven militarized bases there, this is an important initiative. The Philippine Navy is certainly no match for China's navy and armed maritime vessels in the area, but the objective is to build its capacities in order to provide defense of its own claimed territorial waters. The United States has also sold a variety of other weaponry, mainly for police and counterinsurgency purposes. US arms sales in 2018 totaled approximately $100 million.

The US-Philippines defense relationship has also been periodically rocked by the criminal misbehavior of American servicemen, including the conviction for rape and sentencing of a Marine to forty years' imprisonment in 2006. The hiatus caused by the Philippines Senate rejection of the renewed base agreement in 1991 was another blow. The bases—particularly Clark and Subic—provided huge commercial benefits for the local economy, employing thousands of Filipinos and generating considerable revenue. But they also produced simmering resentment, which manifested in repeated demonstrations. Today US embassy officers in Manila told me that US relations with the AFP "proceeds quite well," and that there is a deep reservoir of support for the relationship within the AFP, but not necessarily by President Duterte. US embassy officers also report that there is a "continuing sensitivity and higher level of scrutiny of the American military footprint" by the Philippines Congress.[108]

President Duterte's own anti-Americanism and his administration's embrace of China have been particularly nettlesome obstacles (see discussion in chapters 6 and 7). Duterte has even warned that his government would cease receiving weapons from the United States.[109] His abrupt withdrawal from the VFA is proof positive of his unpredictability. His threats were due to US Congressional criticisms of his violent campaign against alleged drug lords (which has claimed over 7,000 lives) as well as his desire to take delivery of weaponry from China and Russia, which would trigger US sanctions. Duterte made his threats after the United States halted the sale of 26,000 M-4 assault rifles.

Despite these strains, overall, the US military has no deeper, longer, and stronger set of military-to-military ties than with the Philippines (even more so than with Thailand). The stresses in the relationship have been introduced by Duterte himself, whereas the underlying institutional relationships remain quite strong. But this is an example, as we note throughout chapter 6, of how domestic politics in Southeast Asian countries are an independent variable and dynamic in the US-China competition.

Thailand

America's other ally in Southeast Asia is Thailand. Although long-lasting (the alliance dates to 1833), it is a complex, complicated, and sometimes fraught relationship. While it has many trappings of a traditional alliance, it also varies in significant ways. As Southeast Asia scholar Catharin Dalpino has noted, "In contrast to the other US treaty allies in Asia—Japan, South Korea, and the Philippines—the alliance with Thailand is not governed by a written, ongoing treaty that is periodically reviewed and approved by both sides. In lieu of a Status of Forces Agreement (as the United States has with Japan and South

Korea) or a Visiting Forces Agreement (as the US has had with the Philippines), US-Thailand security cooperation is largely based on precedent and ongoing dialogue."[110] The relationship also has no mutual security clause (Article V), the *sine qua non* definition of an alliance, thus making it questionable whether it should, in fact, be termed an "alliance" at all.

The framework for defense ties dates to Thailand's inclusion in the 1954 Manila Pact and the 1962 Thanat-Rusk Communiqué. Following SEATO's demise in 1977, the relationship was restructured and upgraded. As noted in chapter 2, Thailand provided vital basing and other support for US forces during the Vietnam War. In 2003 Thailand received the designation of "major non-NATO ally," which offers non-NATO countries (including non-allies) a range of roughly equivalent level of military and financial assistance. In 2012 the two sides issued the Joint Vision Statement on the Thai-US Defense Alliance, which breathed new life into the military relationship.[111]

As a result of the long-standing military relationship, generations of Thai officers have been trained in the United States or by US personnel in Thailand. By the early twenty-first century, 21,000 Thai officers had been trained in the United States.[112] Thai forces are configured along American lines. Until recently, when Thailand began to buy some weapons from China, the United States had been its sole primary supplier. The military-to-military relationship is very close and tightly integrated. However, it has frequently been challenged by the Thai military's repeated penchant to intervene in domestic politics via *coup d'état* (eighteen since 1947!). Such was the case in 2014, and that coup substantially set back military exchanges. In fact, almost all were suspended by the US side (under congressional mandate). Under Section 508 of the Foreign Assistance Act, the United States is prohibited from continuing to provide military assistance to any country whose elected leader is deposed by a *coup d'état*. As a mandated result, many forms of military assistance and cooperation were suspended. However, the flagship element, the annual Cobra Gold exercises, continued, albeit at a reduced level. After a hiatus of a few very strained years, which one analyst described as "an interval of estrangement," after Trump entered office and invited Thai prime minister Prayut (who had been the senior officer engineering the coup) to the White House, military exchanges began to resume. Consequently, the Pentagon reported "more than 130 [annual] military-to-military 'engagements' took place in 2019".[113] This included full resumption of the annual Cobra Gold joint exercises. In September 2019, Thailand also hosted the first-ever joint naval exercise between the US Navy and all ten ASEAN navies, a five-day maritime drill aimed to "maintain maritime security, focus on prevention, and pre-empt wrongdoing at sea," according to a statement by the US embassy in Bangkok.[114] US forces also continue to have access to Thai bases, notably Utapao Air Base and Sattahip Naval Base. Thailand has again become eligible for the IMET officer training program.

Senior-level military exchanges, up to and including at the defense minister level, have also resumed. Thailand also offers the United States to operate a series of communications facilities of both military and intelligence value (euphemistically described as "cooperative security locations") in country.

Despite the rebound in US-Thai defense cooperation, an unprecedented survey of 1,800 Thai military officers conducted from 2014 to 2017 by two Australian security experts with long-standing connections to the Thai military revealed that a substantial shift in perceptions was occurring among the Thai officer corps in the wake of the 2014 coup.[115] Using the Linkert Scale for measuring influence, their most significant finding was that officers' perceptions of China and its influence were now *more positive* than of the United States, and by a widening margin. By a slight margin, the officers even identified the United States as a greater *threat* to Thai national security than China! The scholars who conducted the survey, Australian National University Strategic and Defense Studies Center's John Blaxland and Greg Raymond, conclude that the findings are not merely a temporary aberration due to anger over the American punitive measures taken after the 2014 coup, but rather reflect a deeper reorientation in thinking among the Thai elite (both military and civilian). Nonetheless, they also conclude that "[English] language and doctrine favor the US alliance rather than China."[116] They point to the continued prevalence of American weapons in the Thai inventory, despite the United States having withheld equipment deliveries post-coup, as well as the low price and ready availability of Chinese weaponry.

The Thai military's budding relationship with China is another real growing problem in US-Thai military relations (from the US perspective). These ties predate the 2014 coup, but they have grown considerably as a result of the US punitive actions following the coup. Described more fully in chapter 5, they include training a large contingent of Thai officers in Chinese military academies (some report as many as half of the Thai officer corps); purchases of Chinese diesel submarines, tanks, light weapons, military vehicles; and the establishment of a joint weapons and munitions manufacturing facility in Thailand. To some extent, Thailand's turn to China for military support was precipitated by the closing off of similar support from the United States—but it also represents a deeper reorientation of Thai foreign policy toward China in recent years. As Thai Vice–Foreign Minister Futrakul told me in an interview in Bangkok, "We will lean as close to China as the West pushes us."[117]

Of all Southeast Asian countries, Thailand is the master of maintaining multiple external relationships, hedging, and balancing them off against one another. As one senior retired Singaporean diplomat put it, "The Thais are the best balancers in the world."[118] But Thailand's recent turn toward Beijing appears deeper and not temporarily tactical. For Americans, therefore, it is important to understand that for the Thais the "alliance" with the United States is not an exclusive (defense) relationship. Americans tend to believe that an alliance means having an *exclusive* military relationship only with the United States—but the Thais do not think this way. In fact, my conversations with a number of Thai officials in Bangkok revealed that the term "alliance" means very little to them. Several of my official interlocutors simply shrugged when asked, and they made no efforts to reassure me of a sense of commonality or commitment to the strategic/military relationship with the United States. The Thais can be thought of as diplomatically and strategically polygamous—owing no particular loyalty to any foreign partner. This may be how they survived as the *only* Southeast Asian country never to be colonized—through constant and adroit maneuvering. But this is not the way Americans think of allies and how Americans expect them to behave.

It is amazing that the Thai-US alliance has endured as long as it has, but there are definite concerns over its durability and longevity on the horizon—especially as the Thai grow ever closer to China. Some longtime observers of the relationship see it at a serious crossroads—and unless Washington takes prompt and sweeping remedial actions, the United States risks losing its most important strategic asset in Southeast Asia.[119] Overall, the Thais do not seem very deeply invested in the relationship and the alliance. It is in real flux at present, with the result that Thailand grows relatively closer to China.

Malaysia

The US-Malaysian defense relationship is considerable, but it operates "below the radar screen." This is intentional. Being an Islam-predominant society, the Malay government has great sensitivities about publicizing its relationship with the United States (particularly in the defense and intelligence realms). In 2014 the United States and Malaysia proclaimed the relationship to be a "Comprehensive Partnership." As part of this, the Pentagon describes Malaysia as a "key player in Southeast Asia" and states, "We conduct more than 100 defense engagements with Malaysia annually, including exercises, subject matter expert exchanges, and partner on common objectives such as maritime security and counterterrorism. We improve our interoperability through combined air, maritime, and amphibious training in multiple locations across the country."[120] While the United States describes the defense relationship in such terms, one would never read such descriptions either in the Malaysian media nor hear about such activities publicly from the Malaysian government. For its part, the Defense Attaché's Office in the US Embassy in Kuala Lumpur described the military cooperation to me as "robust."[121] There are a number of joint exercises every year, while US warships and submarines call at Malaysian ports (mainly in Sarawak, far from urban centers and public attention). Malaysian officers are in residence at the US Army War College in Pennsylvania, Air War College in Alabama, and Naval War College in Rhode Island, while Malaysian NCOs are among the cadets at West Point and the US Air Force Academy in Colorado Springs.[122]

Indonesia

Some of the same religious and political concerns that affect US military cooperation with Malaysia are apparent in Indonesia as well. As with Malaysia, the United States and Indonesia agreed to a "Comprehensive Partnership" in October 2015.[123] The Pentagon's *Indo-Pacific Strategy Report* outlines six areas of joint defense cooperation: "maritime security and domain awareness; defense procurement and joint research and development; peacekeeping operations and training; professionalization; humanitarian assistance and disaster relief; and countering transnational threats such as terrorism and piracy.... Future areas of collaboration include developing defense industry partnerships that will expand coordination on acquisition, technology transfer, cooperative research, industrial collaboration, and logistics support."[124]

From this official description, it is clear that the US-Indonesian defense relationship goes much further and much deeper than that with Malaysia. In particular, as the report's language indicates, it apparently includes a joint weapons development component (not merely weapons transfers), although not much information is available about this. Interviews with the Defense Attaché's Office in the US Embassy in Jakarta in 2018 indicated that the Indonesian military (known as the TNI)[125] had just taken delivery of 24 F-16s C/Ds and 8 Apache helicopters for $1.66 billion.[126] In addition, I was told that the TNI is "closely looking at" at $1.6 billion arms package that would include purchasing new F-16 "Vipers" (a 4.5 generation fighter), C-130s heavy lift transports, Blackhawk, Chinook, and more Apache helicopters.

The decade 1995–2005 badly damaged bilateral defense cooperation, as the United States sanctioned Indonesia and the TNI for human rights abuses in East Timor. Subsequently, though, since 2006 the military relationship has "taken off," in the words of the director of the Office of Defense Cooperation in the US Embassy. During 2018, 222 OAAs (operations, activities, and actions) were planned. These include all the areas noted in the *Indo-Pacific Strategy Report*, as well a bilateral Defense Dialogue, Annual Service Talks (ASTs), and the training of about 900 TNI personnel in all US service war colleges, the Army Ranger School at Fort Benning, and the National Defense University in Washington.

Despite the "robust" nature of US-Indonesian defense ties at present, the legacy of the decade of suspended exchanges lingers in the TNI, which fears it could happen again. Indeed, it could. In 2018 the TNI had contracted with Russia for eleven Su-35 fighters—if the deal goes through, I was told, it would automatically trigger the Countering America's Adversaries Through Sanctions Act (CAATSA). Another area of some friction is the ongoing US refusal to work with the Indonesian Special Forces, the Kopassus, owing to a legacy of human rights abuses. Kopassus are undergoing a process of remediation at present, after which training and cooperation can resume. Those TNI officers who have a vivid memory of the decade of suspended exchanges will begin to retire in 2021, and the United States hopes that the subsequent generation of US-trained officers will help push the relationship forward.

Clearly, Indonesia is seen by the Pentagon (and the US government broadly) to be a very high priority going forward—and for good reason. Indonesia is the largest and most significant country in Southeast Asia—geographically, demographically, strategically, economically, and in other spheres. It is also the de facto leader of ASEAN (although it doesn't act like it). Yet American expectations should be tempered for two reasons. First, like all Southeast Asian states, Indonesia prides itself on its independence and avoiding becoming too close to external powers. Second, Indonesia is a profoundly *domestically oriented* government.[127] This is one reason it abjures a leadership role in ASEAN. Indonesia's insularity is readily apparent in discussions with officials and experts in Jakarta, as well as traveling in the country.

Vietnam

The Socialist Republic of Vietnam has been designated a high priority for building comprehensive overall ties over the past decade. The two governments have overcome ill will from the past and have recognized their many potential commonalities and areas for cooperation. This includes in the defense domain. A 2011 Memorandum of Understanding set out a framework for expanded ties across several areas and armed services.

Nonetheless, from Washington's perspective (and the US Defense Attaché's Office in Hanoi), the military relationship has not developed fast enough—and it is the Vietnamese side that has been slow-walking further development. The United States has proposed a variety of initiatives in recent years, with only about one-third being taken up by the Vietnamese. In March 2018 one persistent "ask" of the Americans was finally realized—to bring an aircraft carrier into Da Nang harbor. The USS *Carl Vinson* (Fig. 0.1) paid a four-day port call, the first since the end of the Vietnam War. This was a symbolic step, on which the United States hopes to build. In March 2020 the USS *Theodore Roosevelt* became the second carrier battle group to pay a port call to Da Nang. But, for Hanoi, like other

Southeast Asian counties, everything is about *balancing* external ties. As one official in the US Embassy in Hanoi put it: "If Vietnam does something with us, they feel they must do the same with China, Japan, India, and Russia. The trajectory of US-Vietnam military ties is positive, but progress is incremental."[128]

While the United States and Vietnam share security and other concerns about China, Hanoi is very careful not to overly provoke Beijing—and, as chapters 5 and 6 illustrate, there are actually comprehensively deep ties between the two communist neighbors. As the director of the Vietnamese Communist Party's (VCP) External Relations Department, Nguyen Vinh Quang, told me: "Vietnam and China have thousands of years of history, including some very friendly periods. There are a lot of complementarities with China, and in politics as well. Our political systems are very similar: socialist. We have tried to learn from each other."[129] After this rather rosy depiction, Mr. Nyugen abruptly pivoted in the conversation and asserted: "In Southeast Asia it is Vietnam that has the most serious problems with China. The problem we have with China now is one of territorial disputes, due to China's attempts to take sole control of the South China Sea. China is getting stronger and stronger, and becoming more and more aggressive, due to its increasing arrogance. Vietnam has not changed anything—it is China that has changed. Its hard power is getting much stronger, and they are consequently getting much more assertive."[130]

As in the US-India relationship, mutual distrust of China is a shared strategic commonality between Washington and Hanoi. This *does* contribute to closer defense ties—yet, at the same time, building US defense ties with Hanoi and New Delhi should be based on a broader conception of the relationship rather than a paradigm of "the enemy of my enemy is my friend."

Singapore

The United States has no more comprehensive and robust defense relationship in Southeast Asia than with Singapore. Although not technically an ally, it is in all but name. It is not clear why the two have never entered into a fully allied relationship (especially when Singapore is a member of the Five Power Defense Arrangement with the Australia, Malaysia, New Zealand, and the United Kingdom), but nonetheless the defense relationship could not be closer (intelligence cooperation is also very close). It is framed by a series of agreements: a 1990 Memorandum of Understanding, the 2005 Strategic Framework Agreement, and the 2015 US-Singapore Enhanced Defense Cooperation Agreement (renewed and upgraded in 2019). The last-named pact designated Singapore a "Major Security Cooperation Partner." At the conclusion of the enhanced DCA, it was reported that "the two sides agreed on a broad framework for defense cooperation covering five areas: military, policy, strategic and technology, along with cooperation against nontraditional security challenges like terrorism and piracy. They also agreed to enhance collaboration in new areas including humanitarian assistance and disaster relief (HADR), cybersecurity, biosecurity and public communications. The enhanced DCA also introduced new high-level dialogues between the two sides."[131]

My discussions with the Defense Attaché's Office (DAO) in the US Embassy in Singapore identified a number of the areas of defense cooperation.[132] The United States has access to both Singaporean air and naval installations. The most significant airbase is Paya Lebar in eastern Singapore, where P-8 reconnaissance regularly land after flying surveillance flights from Okinawa along the China coast and over the South China Sea (which have triggered official Chinese protests to Singapore). It is also a major transit and refueling stop for the US Air Force between Guam and Diego Garcia. A new Changi Air Base East is currently under construction and is expected to take a range of US aircraft on rotation. But, by far, Singapore's major contribution of importance is for the US Navy. Since the "loss" of Subic Bay Naval Base in the Philippines in 1992, Singapore has offered a unique set of naval installations for US ships. This includes most notably Changi Naval Base, which accommodates between 30–40 ship visits per year—including at a specially built pier that accommodates aircraft carriers (it was here that I went aboard the USS *Carl Vinson*, as described in the Preface). Further up the west coast lies Sembawang Naval Base, which offers repair and maintenance facilities for approximately sixty ships per year. Sembawang is also home to the Logistics Group Western Pacific, a key facility for the Seventh Fleet, as well as the USAF 497th Combat Training Squadron. These facilities do not come for free, however. Ships putting into Sembawang for repairs are charged approximately $5,000 per day, while ships at Changyi pay a much higher rate of $23,000 per day (carriers pay more). US submarines also use these bases.

Beyond air and ship visits by American forces, the US and Singaporean militaries are involved in a wide range of exercises and joint training for air, naval, marine, and special operation units. Because Singapore is so small, it maintains several of its fighter and attack helicopter squadrons in the United States—F-15s in Idaho, F-16s and Apache helos in Arizona. Pilot training also takes place in the United States (there are approximately 1,000 Singaporean Air Force personnel in the United States at any given time). Army personnel are also sent to the United States for training (Prime Minister Lee Hsien Loong spent a year at Fort Leavenworth, Kansas, and speaks fondly of his time there). Singapore outspends every military in Southeast Asia, and the United States is its provider of choice—which sells fighters, helicopters, tanks, and a variety of air-to-air missiles.

In sum, the Singaporean defense relationship is vital for the United States' position in Southeast Asia—and the United States is crucial to Singapore's capacity for its own defense. This relationship irritates Beijing no end, but the Singaporean government has—to date—ignored China's protestations, while building its own military-to-military relationship with the PLA (which mainly consists of exchanges of personnel and occasional ship visits). While Singapore is trying to maintain a balanced overall relationship between the United States and China, this is not the case when it comes to defense. It is by no means a one-sided relationship, though, as the facilities that Singapore offers the United States are as important as the military assistance that the United States provides to Singapore. Both sides gain—and gain a lot.

The Others: Brunei, Cambodia, Laos, Myanmar

The other four remaining countries in Southeast Asia all have attenuated defense ties with the US military. None are well developed, but of the four those with Brunei are the best. The Royal Brunei Armed Forces engage in occasional high-level consultations, joint naval and Special Forces exercises, port calls, training programs, and defense liaison. In February 2019 the Deputy Commander of US Army Pacific visited for consultations. In the words of former US Ambassador to Brunei (2014–2018) Craig Allen, "The mil-to-mil relationship is healthy, broad and strong—but not exceptionally deep."[133]

With Laos, defense exchanges are next best. There have been thirteen rounds of the Lao-United States Bilateral Defense Dialogue, but this a fairly pro forma set of contacts. In addition, the two collaborate on military medical training, defense educational exchanges (at APCSS in Hawaii), disaster relief, removal of unexploded ordnance, and regional security workshops.[134]

The Obama administration established military exchanges with Cambodia, but in early 2017 its government abruptly suspended all exchanges (some argue under pressure from Beijing). As described in chapters 5 and 6, Cambodia is a virtual client state of China's.

In the case of Myanmar, defense exchanges are virtually nonexistent. There is a defense attaché in the US Embassy in Yangon—but because of Congressional sanctions and opposition to the Burmese military, no real substantive defense cooperation has been developed. This is not for the lack of desire by the embassy or Pentagon, however. They attribute the block to come entirely from the Congress—and specifically one Congressional staffer on the Senate Appropriations Committee.[135] The only element permitted has been to send some Myanmar military to Asia-Pacific Center for Security Studies workshops and training programs in Honolulu. Thus, in the case of Burma, like Cambodia, politics has impeded military contacts.

US Soft Power and Public Diplomacy Activities in ASEAN

America remains a beacon and magnet of soft power throughout Southeast Asia. Wherever one travels this is evident (even during the Trump era). Even in poorer countries like Myanmar, Cambodia, and Laos, there are multiple examples of American products, American media, American ideas, American educators and English teachers, American sports, American films, and other elements of American popular culture evident.

The US government also maintains a robust series of public diplomacy programs throughout Southeast Asia. Many of these mirror programs administered worldwide, while others are tailored to the region and individual countries. In Washington these are managed principally through the State Department's Bureau of Public Diplomacy and Bureau of Educational and Cultural Affairs. Like all regional bureaus, East Asia and Pacific Affairs (EAP) has public diplomacy officers assigned to it, who coordinate and tailor programs, policies, and messages for Southeast Asian audiences. There is a close working relationship between these departments and embassies in the region. Every three years, embassies and the aforementioned departments put together an "Integrated Country Strategy," which establishes goals, methods, and metrics across a range of areas.

These public diplomacy and education and cultural affairs strategies target different sectors of Southeast Asian societies, institutions, and media; they also employ a wide variety of mechanisms both in-country and in the United States. These include a wide variety of programs, such as the International Visitor Leadership Programs (IVLP) that bring either individuals or small groups (e.g., editors, journalists, think tankers, etc.) to the United States for three-week visits, targeting "current and emerging foreign leaders." IVLP alumni include more than 500 current or former heads of state.[136] The Young Southeast Asian Leaders Initiative (YSEALI), launched by President Obama, has been hugely successful and has involved nearly 150,000 young people aged eighteen to thirty-five with an additional 80,000 engaged in its digital platforms.[137] Students from ASEAN countries also come to US universities in increasing numbers, with approximately 60,000 Southeast Asians studying there in 2019.[138] The ASEAN-US Science and Technology Fellows Program supports ASEAN scientists for bilateral cooperation and policy relevant experience. A wide variety of arts exchange programs exist such as American Music Abroad, Dance Motion USA, and traveling art exhibitions from American museums. Also engaged are touring sports teams; in addition to playing high-profile games, there is a particular effort made to reach marginalized communities. American Spaces, American Corners, and American Centers are all physical spaces for programing, outreach, and various events. The @America Center in Jakarta is a new and particularly noteworthy initiative, and this multimedia interactive facility is serving as a model for emulation in other countries.[139] Radio Free Asia is a US government–sponsored longwave radio service broadcasting 24/7 in a variety of Asian languages. Voice of America also counts millions of listeners throughout the region, broadcasting in local languages to Indonesia, Myanmar, Thailand, Vietnam, Laos, and Cambodia.[140]

Through all of these public diplomacy programs, the United States maintains a robust—but underappreciated—cultural presence throughout Southeast Asia. They contribute to America's vast reservoir of soft power in the region. The Trump administration has, unfortunately, drastically reduced funds for public diplomacy (PD) in the State Department's budget—which is a huge strategic mistake. Prior to the cuts, the PD budget for the *entire* Asia-Pacific region was $52.1 million in fiscal year 2017.[141] This has caused a curtailment of certain programs, although it is unclear what the overall impact has been. The other big change in public diplomacy under the Trump administration has been an explicit shift in priorities from the aforementioned "long-term" programming that was aimed at building personal linkages and promoting American values— to more "short-term" policy-oriented goals. Prior to Trump readjustments, the PD Bureau allocated two-thirds of its funds to "values oriented" programs and one-third to advancing current policy priorities; under Trump this percentage has been reversed.[142] What US public diplomacy in the region does *not* do is counter Chinese propaganda (although it should), nor does it explicitly tout all that the United States offers to Southeast Asia that China does not. The competition between the United States and China in the region will play out in multiple domains—but perhaps none, in my view, is more important that the information domain. The United States must really step up its game in public diplomacy vis-à-vis China in Southeast Asia and worldwide.

In addition, a variety of public and private educational institutions undertake their own cultural and scholarly exchange initiatives with the region. Noteworthy among them is the East-West Center (EWC) in Honolulu and Washington, DC. The EWC offers eight different student scholarship programs for predoctoral students from across the region,[143] as well as several visiting scholar programs.[144] Established by the US Congress in 1960, the EWC administers a wide range of public outreach and cultural exchange programs and has several thousand alumni throughout the Southeast Asian region. These programs have contributed directly and indirectly to "capacity building" in a number of ASEAN countries.

Another very significant institution in the US soft power toolbox is the Asia Foundation. Established by an Act of Congress in 1954, today the foundation operates in eighteen Asia and Pacific nations, including nine in Southeast Asia (Brunei being the exception).[145] Within its broad mandate the foundation has engaged in superb work in education, culture, rule of law, public health, women's empowerment, and other areas.[146] The Asia Foundation has prioritized different countries in its work over time; at present its focus is on Myanmar—which is a ripe operating environment for many of the aforementioned areas of the foundation's legacy and operational experience. Today the Asia Foundation operates on an annual budget of about $100 million and provides approximately 800 grants per year to a wide range of recipients. The Asia Foundation is indeed a significant success story and credit to America's efforts to work with nations, governments, and private entities across the region to promote social development and inclusiveness, good governance, conflict resolution, political participation, strengthened national and local institutions, and intra-regional cooperation.

Thus, while not receiving much media publicity or attention, these governmental and non-governmental public diplomacy and capacity-building programs all contribute a great deal to America's "soft power" appeal throughout Southeast Asia, and directly advance US national interests across the region. This is America at its best.

Net Assessment

The importance of Southeast Asia to the United States has never been greater, and vice versa. For the United States this is true both because of the intrinsic dynamism and diversity of ASEAN countries, as well as its rising strategic importance in the growing US-China regional and global competition. For Southeast Asia, the United States continues to be an important guarantor of regional security and stability—but its commercial contributions and soft power appeal are also strong attractive features.

If America has a pronounced weakness in the region it is in the area of diplomatic engagement. This is not new—as the strategic and economic importance of Northeast Asia and the "tyranny of distance" to Southeast Asia have long conspired to limit Washington's attention span. The Obama administration was the exception to the rule as it prioritized ASEAN as never before. The Trump administration does seem to have relatively downgraded the region when compared with the Obama years. Still, this has been a relative downgrading—and, if anything, a return to the more traditional pattern of episodic US (in)attention.

While there appears to be continuity as well as change in America's approach to ASEAN and its member states, it "takes two to tango." From Washington's perspective, but also very apparent throughout the region, Southeast Asian governments seem unnecessarily reluctant to *openly and publicly* endorse the importance of the United States to the region. During my past three years traveling and researching this book throughout the region, with the notable exception of

Singapore, never *once* did I come across a newspaper article or hear a national-level official publicly praise the role of the United States in the region.

By contrast, ASEAN governments and the regional media narrative are *fixated* on the role and rise of China. Perhaps this is result of the fact that, as Singaporean ambassador-at-large Tommy Koh noted earlier, the United States is *taken for granted*. Perhaps regional governments have been cowed by their increasingly dependent relationships with China and their fear of Beijing's wrath if they were to speak out positively in favor of the US presence and role in the region. Perhaps it is because of religious sensitivities in societies like Indonesia and Malaysia. It is also a fact that anti-American sentiments run strong in several Southeast Asian societies (notably Cambodia, Indonesia, Malaysia, Myanmar, and the Philippines). Whatever the reason(s), it would be nice and appropriate if Southeast Asian governments and media would *openly* acknowledge all that the United States contributes to *their* societies and to regional security and stability. It is this kind of silence that makes some Americans feel unappreciated, taken advantage of, and arguing in favor of drawing down the US presence in the region. It feeds into the isolationist impulse in the United States. If indeed Southeast Asians wish to be dominated by China, this is one way to achieve that end. Southeast Asian silence contributes to American neglect—and that in turn is a recipe for slipping into an unwanted sphere of Chinese influence.

This silence is not only apparent in the region, but in Washington as well. Southeast Asian embassies in Washington really need to step up their presence, become far more publicly involved, and active with the Congress, media, universities, and think tanks.

If Southeast Asians wish to keep the United States engaged, to continue their balancing and hedging behavior, and to limit China's influence in the region—one of the best ways would be to *publicly* acknowledge and thank the United States for all it has done and still does for Southeast Asia. A little credit goes a long way and may result in increased attention and appropriations.

For its part, the best American strategy toward Southeast Asia is simply to remain a steady, present, attentive, engaged, and predictable partner. As David Shear, seasoned former US diplomat, Asia hand, and Ambassador to Vietnam, told me, "Our goal should be to help them hedge."[147] Even Kishore Mahbubani—the former Singaporean diplomat and public intellectual who is known for his sharp criticisms of the United States—argues in his most recent book that America has a reservoir of intrinsic attraction and support in Southeast Asia that, if Washington plays its cards right, could benefit both:[148]

"ASEAN remains a region of great geopolitical opportunity for America. . . . Southeast Asia is one of the most pro-American regions in the world. . . . Happily, this reservoir of pro-American sentiment in Southeast Asia is not

going to disappear soon. If America can work out a sensible, thoughtful, comprehensive, and long-term strategy for ASEAN, it will find a strong partner. . . .
In short, the ASEAN region remains one of the most important regions in the
world if America is interested in trying out a diplomacy-first strategy to match
the growing Chinese influence in the world."

The United States should play to its strengths and work on fixing its
weaknesses. This includes mounting a major public diplomacy campaign to publicize and educate Southeast Asian publics about the value of the United States to
the region, as many are unaware of all that is described in this chapter and that
the United States does in the region. At the end of the day, America's regional
competition with China may be won or lost in the information domain. The
United States needs to do much better in telling its own story—and Southeast
Asian governments and media need to do much better in recognizing the enduring importance of the United States to the region's continuing dynamism,
growth, security, and stability.

PART II
THE CHINESE ENCOUNTER
WITH SOUTHEAST ASIA

4

China's Legacies in Southeast Asia

"At about the same time that the British Isles were first integrated into Roman Europe by Julius Caesar and his successors, the ancestors of the modern Vietnamese people . . . were conquered by Chinese armies and drawn into the ambit of the early Chinese empire."
— Alexander Woodside, historian, 1988[1]

"Partly by governmental design and partly through the play of divergent cultural systems, the Chinese in Southeast Asia achieved a social and economic position always distinctive and usually superior to that of the indigenes. Under these circumstances, Southeast Asian nationalism early developed an anti-Sinitic tradition."
— G. William Skinner, anthropologist, 1959[2]

Historically, China has loomed large—geographically, culturally, militarily, and economically—over Southeast Asia. This was particularly the case before the sixteenth-century arrival of European colonial powers, which encroached upon not only Southeast Asia but China itself, and began to limit earlier Sino-Southeast Asian interactions. Prior to that time, they were a mixture of cross-border migration and economic exchanges; a flourishing maritime trade; outright occupation and subjugation in one case (Vietnam); and ritualistic expressions of the "tribute system" for many others.

The Long Evolution of Sino-Southeast Asian Relations

These four legacies are all extraordinarily complex, for which there are not particularly good historical records. What written records exist largely come from the Chinese side. There are precious few historical records of the early Southeast Asian kingdoms prior to 1600, leaving what the eminent historian of China and Southeast Asia Wang Gungwu (to whom this book is dedicated) describes as a "fragmented and undocumented past."[3] Among other implications, Wang notes that this has served to skew historical interpretations in favor of the Chinese "tribute system" paradigm.[4] As Southeast Asian historian Martin Stuart-Fox further explains, "Climate, the fragility of the treated palm leaf principally used as a writing medium in Southeast Asia, poor storage facilities that allowed the ravages of mildew and insects, and the destruction of war, all have contributed to the dearth of written sources in Southeast Asia compared to China. . . . In few of these can be found any references, however, to political or even economic relations with China. . . . It is not surprising that there is little mention of tributary missions to China. No mention was made of China because to have done so would neither have enhanced a king's glory, nor reinforced the Southeast Asian (Hindu/Buddhist) worldview. By contrast, the records kept by the Chinese of embassies received from even the smallest and most remote Southeast Asian principalities did reinforce the Chinese worldview of magnifying the virtue and might of the emperor as ruling 'all under heaven.'"[5] Wang Gungwu argues that for centuries Southeast Asian traders and tribute-bearers went north with some frequency. They both presented and received gifts. It was thus, he argues, a *reciprocal* relationship of sorts, but only symbolically so.[6] In my interview with historian Nie Dening of Xiamen University, one of China's leading authorities on imperial China's interactions with other regional peoples, Professor Nie also described it as reciprocal: "Our relations (with Southeast Asia) began very early during the Han dynasty. Thereafter, those countries came to China paying tribute (朝贡) and bringing local products that the Emperor had never seen—and we sent them back with some of our products. Before the Ming these missions were not regularized (没有固定的), but after the Ming they became more so. Before the tenth century few Chinese went abroad. Before that, foreigners always came to us, but afterward it changed and Chinese began to go abroad."[7] Nonetheless, in most of his writings Wang Gungwu and most other historians still view the relationships as much more hierarchical than reciprocal, giving Southeast Asian peoples little agency in the long history of interactions with China. Drawing on imperial Chinese archival records, the principal paradigm remains one of China constantly probing and expanding southward—commercially, culturally, ethnically, and militarily.

This perspective, however, also obscures *the major influences* in the region, which was not China—but India and Islam. Hindu traders and Buddhist monks and pilgrims, as well as Arab/Muslim vessels, sailed with some frequency from India and the Islamic world into Southeast Asia for centuries, while Chinese remained continentally contained. There is no evidence of Chinese vessels venturing forth prior to the eighth century, and it was really not until the twelfth and thirteenth centuries that China really embarked on seafaring.[8] So, if there was a dominant external influence in Southeast Asia during premodern times it was not from China, but from India and the Islamic world. The exception to this was the case of Vietnam, but it was indeed an exception to the rule.

Thus, how one interprets these premodern interactions between China and Southeast Asia really does have to do with the available sources, and it seems that the lack of preserved Southeast Asian sources has had the impact of tilting interpretations in favor of the Chinese tributary paradigm. This chapter describes this long sweep of Sino-Southeast Asian premodern and modern interactions in a relatively condensed fashion before turning to the post-1949 period. In so doing, as I am not an historian and had no access to primary sources, I rely on the excellent scholarship of others.

Early Encounters

Although there is some archeological evidence of contact dating as early as the Shang dynasty (1523–1027 BCE),[9] the earliest recorded records of Chinese interactions with peoples to the south date from the Qin dynasty (221–206 BCE) and were with the Yue people. Concentrated south of the Yangzi River in modern day Zhejiang, Fujian, and Guangdong provinces, but also stretching down all along the borderlands of Annam (northern Vietnam) all the way westward to Yunnan (formerly Dai) and northern Siam (Thailand), there were several different types of Yue peoples populating each of these regions, and they became known as the "southern Yue" (南越). There were, in fact, so many different variations of Yue people that they collectively became known as the "Hundred Yue" (百越). Prior to and during the Qin dynasty, Chinese records and archeological finds reveal tribal cultures involved with rice cultivation, fishing, and basic barter. At this time, "Chinese" interactions with the Yue were limited to the borderlands of Guangdong and Guangxi and went no further south than the Red River Valley in northern Vietnam. But after about 1000 CE, evidence emerges of more-sophisticated societies casting bronze for tools, implements, ornaments, and weapons—suggesting interactions and "trickle down" from China's Yangzi and Huai river basins.

China's relations with the southern Yue changed qualitatively following unification under the Qin dynasty. Under Emperor Qin Shi Huang and his powerful armies, all of southern China was brought under more centralized and militarized control. By 214 BCE, after launching five separate invasions and meeting great resistance, his armies had finally subjugated all of the territories occupied by the Yue peoples.[10] This included Annam (Vietnam). From there—the Red River valley in northern Vietnam—for the first time the Han Chinese encountered peoples to the south that were not of Yue stock.[11] They first encountered the Cham people who inhabited central and southern coastal Vietnam (the region known as Champa, which the Chinese called Linyi, 林邑). Then the Chinese moved further south and east, encountering the Khmer people of the Angkor kingdom and modern-day southern Cambodia (which the Chinese called Funan, 扶南).

There is not much historical indication of the nature of these encounters, but they were not (yet) militarized. They seem to be more expeditionary parties that the Han sent south to explore. Nor is there any record of their encountering armed resistance from the fierce Khmers. Indeed, they established a formalized set of interactions—Chinese dynastic histories record that two Chinese envoys visited Funan (southern Vietnam) between 245 and 250 CE, and subsequently the first recorded instance of an "embassy" being sent north to exchange gifts with the Han court, thus probably being the first tributary exchanges in China's relations with peoples to the south.[12]

It is also significant to note that these encounters apparently came over land and not by sea. To the extent that China has any historical validity to its contemporary claims over the South China Sea or Nanyang (南洋), it was not until the eighth through the tenth centuries, under the Sui and Tang dynasties, that there is evidence of Chinese vessels sailing as far south as Brunei, Borneo, southern Sumatra, Malacca, and Java—thus commencing the Nanyang maritime trade. As China's interactions with Southeast Asian territories and peoples expanded to the maritime domain, they did not lose connection on land. For example, Tang dynasty records indicate that during the first decade of the Tang alone no fewer than fifteen embassies were sent from Angkor's (Funan's) successor state Zhenla (真腊) to pay tribute to Emperor Gaozu in the Chinese capital of Chang'an (modern-day Xian).[13]

These early encounters between imperial China and the peoples of pre-modern Vietnam and Cambodia evolved in two significant ways during the Tang dynasty. First, as noted, Chinese became more seafaring, and second, the Vietnamese began to resist Chinese suzerainty and subjugation. We examine these separately in the next two sections, although it is important to bear in mind that they proceeded simultaneously.

The Special Case of Vietnam

While imperial China maintained tributary relations with various peoples and kingdoms of Southeast Asia, its relationship with Vietnam was unique. Over ten centuries (111 BCE–938 CE), Vietnam was dominated and incorporated into the Chinese empire—sometimes directly and as a vassal state—although not continuously. It was not continuous because there were several periods of rebellion against Chinese rule. Other than Korea, no non-Han society on China's periphery was dominated by China for as long or as thoroughly as Vietnam. As in Korea, this produced the cultural "Sinification" of the country, assimilation under Confucian bureaucratic principles, and domination militarily. As Howard French aptly describes it in his masterly study *Everything Under the Heavens*, "Across the centuries, China applied almost every imaginable tactic in order to overcome persistent local resistance to its project [in Vietnam], and none of them enjoyed lasting success. These included scorched earth military campaigns, cultural indoctrination, and stern top-down administration, as well as softer approaches to win hearts and minds of the locals by, among other things, applying light taxation."[14] University of Virginia scholar Brantly Womack similarly argues in his seminal book *China and Vietnam* that the Sino-Vietnamese relationship over centuries embodied a variety of forms of "asymmetry" (no fewer than nine different types)—with China always being the dominant party and Vietnam the subordinate one, but the tactics for both varied over time.[15] For their part, the Vietnamese became very practiced in the art of "feigned compliance."[16] Put another way, for long periods China pretended to rule while Vietnam pretended to be ruled. The Vietnamese feigned deference to the Chinese, but more out of practicality than real respect. The Chinese demanded—and the Vietnamese acquiesced to—all the symbolic trappings of the "tribute system": recognizing the Son of Heaven (天子), sending emissaries to court (朝), who would present gifts (贡) and prostate themselves (口头) in tribute to the emperor. As Womack has aptly observed, "The tribute system was not so much a theory of international relationships as an evolving and ritualistic practice of managing relationships with communities beyond the edge of the empire's control. The basic principle was simple: if the periphery did not challenge the Center—if it showed deference—the Center would not interfere in the periphery's autonomy. The tribute system was a ritualized exchange of deference for autonomy."[17]

As we will also see in the subsequent section concerning maritime trade, Chinese dynasties were under more-or-less constant military pressure from the peoples and kingdoms to the north: Mongols, Xiongnu, Manchus, and Turkics from the northern steppes. There were two consequences of this. First, imperial China's "national security" attention was always focused more to the north than to the south. There were existential reasons for this. Second, territories to the south offered China both a security sanctuary as well as needed economic materiel. China's long dominance produced great resentment among the Vietnamese—contributing much to their own national identity as well as a deeply ingrained sense of independence and resistance. Vietnam's national icons have tended to be those who stood up to, and rebelled against, Chinese rule. None are revered more perhaps than the Trưng sisters (Trưng Trắc and Trưng Nhị), who led a three-year uprising from 40 to 42 CE, before the Han dynasty general Ma Yuan forcibly suppressed it.

No Asian nation has a longer and more scarred history of relations with China than Vietnam. Yet, geography and shared bonds of Confucianism dictated accommodation over time. The long ten centuries of subordination came in four general phases. Armed force was employed in each. Sometimes—as during the Mongol Yuan dynasty and Ming dynasty—it was quite brutal. Hence the Chinese name for Vietnam: Annam or the "pacified south" (安南). The first phase lasted from 111 BCE to 40 CE and the aforementioned rebellion of the Trưng sisters. This period largely coincided with the early Han dynasty (206 BCE–220 CE), in which Vietnamese nobility were allowed a high degree of autonomy. The second phase stretched from 43–544 CE, which overlapped with the later Han dynasty—a period of thorough cultural Sinicization and direct political rule of Vietnam. But, as the Han atrophied and broke up into the Six Dynasties (220–589 CE), Chinese control weakened. As it did, new rebellions broke out in Vietnam—this time in the central Champa region. This led to the third phase of Chinese domination from 602 to 905 CE, which included the late Sui dynasty (581–618 CE) but mostly the Tang dynasty (618–906 CE). The Tang were tough on Vietnam, dispatching their armies numerous times to suppress multiple uprisings, particularly during the period 722–728 CE. One historical source claims that the Tang forces brutally decapitated 80,000 rebels and piled their bodies in a pyramid—as a deterrent symbol for the future.[18]

After the Tang fell in 906, the subsequent Song dynasty was preoccupied with its northern borders and was unable to subdue Vietnam—which thus gained its longest stretch of independence in the country's history to date. This period lasted from 938 to 1407 CE—covering the Ngô, Đinh, and early Lê dynasties. First the Mongol Yuan dynasty tried to invade Vietnam in 1287, but were forcefully rebuffed. Then in 1407 the Ming dynasty again sought to bring Annam (Vietnam) under its control. The Ming emperor Yongle dispatched a military force of a million soldiers to try to bring the Vietnamese to heel. That campaign lasted only a year, but it brought about another experience of forced assimilation and harsh repression to Vietnam, which lasted for twenty years. During this brief time the Ming designated Vietnam as a Chinese province, which they called Jiaozhi (交趾). But this time the Chinese grip was much more tenuous and deeply resented. Vietnamese had tasted their autonomy and independence for the first time over the previous five centuries. A full-scale resistance was mobilized, under the command of a local gentry named Lê Lợi, which was successful in repelling the Ming occupation. Lê Lợi has gone down in Vietnamese history with the Trưng sisters and others for leading anti-China uprisings. For his part, it was a dark stain on the reputation of the Yongle emperor—who was far more successful with the Ming's dramatic maritime expansion (see discussion to follow).

Thus, when considering China's historical relations with Southeast Asia, Vietnam constitutes a special case. On the one hand, no other Southeast Asian people or country were more thoroughly absorbed into the Chinese empire— not merely the Chinese tribute system, but the *empire itself*. No Southeast

Asian country was subjected to as many military invasions and forceful conquests, political subjugation, cultural assimilation, and ideological indoctrination as Vietnam. Yet, on the other hand, none resisted the Chinese as often—unsuccessfully for many centuries, but finally successfully. A national identity born of *resistance* to external control became deeply ingrained in the Vietnamese, which would serve them well in subsequent encounters with the French, Japanese, and Americans. Other Southeast Asian nations also gained their identities and independence through resistance to Western colonizers and the Japanese in the mid-twentieth century—but Vietnam had centuries of prior experience with China. Yet, at the same time, Vietnam's ambivalent experience of "feigning compliance" with China's "tribute system" is another lesson that other Southeast Asian countries have also absorbed.

The Nanyang Trade

The so-called Nanyang (or Nanhai) trade has early roots dating to the second century CE, but did not really fully flourish until the Ming (1368–1644 CE).

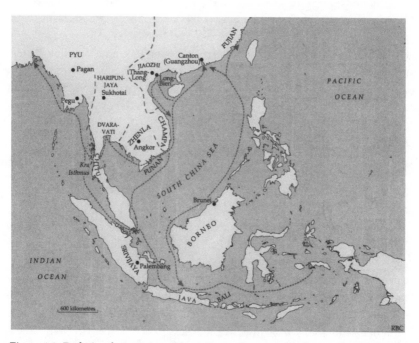

Figure 4.1 Early Southeast Asia and maritime trade routes, third to ninth centuries CE
Source: © Allen & Unwin, created by Robert Cribb

The earliest Nanyang trade can be traced back to southern Yue period (221–111 BCE), according to Wang Gungwu's classic account of it.[19] But this offshore activity was confined to the coastlines of Zhejiang and Fujian, rather than further to the south. It wasn't until the second and third centuries CE that Wang found evidence of maritime coastal voyages south to Funan.[20] By the third century he finds evidence of Chinese voyages through the Malacca Straits and into the Andaman Sea and eastern Indian Ocean (Fig. 4.1)—but no bona fide evidence of maritime contact with the islands of Southeast Asia. One could surmise that these vessels hugged the coastline around mainland Southeast Asia rather than venturing into the far more risky open ocean of the South China Sea. By the fifth and sixth centuries, Buddhist monks and pilgrims began to travel back from India to China on these vessels, thus opening southern China to new religious and cultural influences. The port of Canton (Guangzhou) also became a more active hub for both trading and receiving tribute missions from the south. Chinese dynastic histories record twenty-nine such missions between 420 and 589 CE.[21] But, owing to internal convulsions and rebellions in China, the sea trade thereafter began to contract—which lasted throughout the Tang dynasty.[22] During the Song dynasty (960–1279 CE), sea trade began to pick up again—with a greater range of agricultural products and spices, rubber, and tin, supplementing the earlier Chinese desire for perfumes and jewels.[23] In 1292 and 1293, Kublai Khan, founder of the Mongol Yuan dynasty, sent an expeditionary force of 20,000–30,000 personnel to Borneo and were preparing for an assault on Java—but encountered stiff resistance and were defeated by the forces of the local Javanese kingdom of Singhasari. Kublai Khan's forces were similarly rebuffed in their attempts to conquer Annam and Champa to the south, as well as Japan to the east. Similar losses were suffered in Central Asia. As Chinese historian Nie Dening observed to me: "During the Yuan, the Mongols were very good at conquering others by horseback—but when it came to the sea they had no comparative advantages."[24] This was the apogee of the Mongol empire and thereafter it progressively atrophied until the Yuan dynasty collapsed in China in 1368.

Thus, while there is evidence of some seafaring during the Sui, Tang, Song, and Yuan dynasties, it wasn't really until the Ming that it fully developed. By the Ming a fundamental transformation had occurred, with Chinese building much larger oceangoing ships with far-reaching ambitions to match. This, of course, included the famous voyages of Zheng He (郑和, a.k.a. Ma He). It was during these times that China expanded itself throughout Southeast Asia. By the Ming, huge Chinese oceangoing vessels sailed throughout the South China Sea, up through the Straits of Malacca, throughout the Indian Ocean, to east Africa, as far as the Persian Gulf, Arabian Peninsula, and into the Red Sea! Over these seven centuries China was the premier naval power in the world. Zheng He's fleets, about which much has been written,[25] were dispatched on seven voyages by the Yongle

Figure 4.2 Indonesian postage stamp
commemorating Zheng He voyages
Source: Government of Republic of Indonesia

Emperor from 1405 to 1433. His fleets included gigantic "treasure ships" (宝船)—some more than 400 feet in length, 160 feet in width, with nine masts and a dozen sails, and weighing more than 1,200 tons.[26] His entire fleet during the maiden 1405 voyage had 27,800 men, a fleet of 62 such treasure ships, as well as 200 ships of other sizes.[27] This unfathomable armada became historical lore.

Zheng He himself is venerated throughout the region to this day (Fig 4.2). There is a commemorative museum with a towering statue of him in Malacca City, which was swarming with excited schoolchildren when I visited in 2017. As impressive as Zheng He's voyages were, they mask the fact that Chinese ships and traders had been sailing and traversing the "southern ocean" for some time, putting into ports and leaving behind small communities of ethnic Chinese—thus beginning the intermarriage with Malays, Javanese, and other ethnicities all around what is known today as the South China Sea. Chinese vessels also landed on atolls in what are known today as the Paracel and Spratly islands.

It is on the basis of this historical presence that the People's Republic of China today claims the entirety of the South China Sea as "historical rights"—a claim completely *invalidated* by the 2016 ruling of the international legal tribunal in The Hague (see discussion in chapter 5). China rejected the ruling and even refused to be a contestant party to the case brought by the Philippines. There were many elements to the tribunal's ruling, but it found no valid historical evidence to sustain China's claims.

By the end of the Ming dynasty, China had established an unprecedented presence and network in the region and well beyond. China had become a maritime superpower—dominating not only Nanyang but the Indian Ocean as well. The Ming's maritime thrusts southward and westward were matched with expansion—and aggression—on land as well. The Ming faced hostile pressures from Mongols and Turks to the north, so it became an imperative to stabilize the southern frontier.

Thus, in 1360 the decision was taken to reincorporate Yunnan (then known as Dali) back into the empire.[28] This operation took, according to historian Martin Stuart-Fox, a quarter of a million soldiers and three years just to "pacify" eastern Yunnan and the area around Kunming. The local Mongol forces fiercely resisted the onslaught. Having won the initial victory, Emperor Hongwu's forces thrust further to the southwest up the Li River valley as well as northeastward into Guizhou. Hongwu, who was the Ming dynasty's first emperor, was succeeded from 1402 to 1424 by Emperor Yongle, who spent his entire reign fighting the Mongols. But in 1406 and 1407, Yongle's forces had also invaded Vietnam and again incorporated it under Chinese suzerainty. The Vietnamese chafed under Chinese rule and rebelled in 1418, but the rebellion failed. Having subdued Vietnam (Annam), Yongle set his sights on establishing tributary relations with almost all of maritime Southeast Asia, dispatching 48 seafaring missions in 22 years.[29] These missions successfully established tributary states from the Philippines down through Borneo and Java and west to the Malay peninsula and beyond into the Indian Ocean. Toward the end of his reign, the Vietnamese were again contesting their subordinate status. By the time Yongle died in 1424, the Ming forces had been pushed back over the frontier. Yongle's successor, the Xuande emperor (1399–1435 CE), acknowledged Vietnam's newly independent status, although he insisted on reinstating tributary missions.

The Ming dynasty was succeeded by the Manchu Qing (1644–1911 CE). This is a complicated period in terms of China's interactions with Southeast Asia. After the Ming fleet had been abolished following Yongle's reign, Chinese maritime interchange with southern territories was restricted to a flourishing junk trade. On land, during the 1760s the Qing rulers launched four expansionist military expeditions against Burma, in an effort to expand to the south and reach the Indian Ocean, but each foray was rebuffed by the Burmese.[30] The eighteenth century also witnessed commercial trade and the establishment of physical colonies of Chinese residents throughout the region. Canton, Swatow, and Amoy became the main hubs from where such missions departed. All parts of Southeast Asia— including Siam, Burma, Borneo, Sarawak, Sumatra, the Malay peninsula, and the entire Indonesian archipelago—became populated with Chinese merchants, workers, and adventurers. Intermarriage became increasingly common, and "overseas Chinese" communities—known as the Hokkien—took shape around the region. China was now literally *integrated* into Southeast Asia, and this came about as a result of both "push" and "pull" factors.[31]

However, the subsequent Manchu Qing dynasty sought to stem the tide of emigration to Nanyang, as it feared that the overseas Chinese could become a source of anti-Manchu resistance and subversion.[32] In 1712 the emperor Qianlong issued an edict prohibiting trade and emigration to the Nanyang territories, although it was ignored. This migratory and commercial thrust only continued and was followed during the very late Qing (1885–1886) by more official representations in the forms of Chinese embassies, consulates, and chambers of commerce.

Penang and Singapore were the most flourishing of the "overseas Chinese" (华侨) communities, but ethnic Chinese settled throughout Vietnam, Siam, southern Cambodia, the Philippines and Indonesian (Batavian) archipelagoes, and across the Malayan peninsula and northern Borneo. In Siam alone, the Chinese immigrant population tripled from 440,000 in 1822 to 1.1 million in 1849.[33] Throughout the second half of the nineteenth century a considerable exodus of Chinese left the mainland for points south in "Nanyang." This rapid growth in out-migration forged various bonds—familial, commercial, financial, cultural, political—between the Chinese mainland and Southeast Asian countries. By 1907 there were close to 7 million Chinese in the region, representing the vast majority of the entire overseas Chinese population. This included 2.8 million in the Dutch East Indies, 2.7 million in Siam, 1 million in British Malaya, 200,000 in French Indochina, 134,000 in British Burma, and 83,000 in the Philippines.[34] In order to liaise with this burgeoning diaspora, Qing China established its first overseas consulate in Singapore in 1877.

Meanwhile, in the Qing capital of Beiping (北平), reformers like Zeng Guofan and Li Hongzhang were busy trying to drag China into the modern industrial era via the Self-Strengthening Movement (自强运动), which began in 1872 and lasted until 1894 and included a policy of building "shipyards and arsenals" and a modern navy. The modernization effort was supported by the overseas Chinese throughout Southeast Asia—thus establishing a financial linkage of remittances to mainland China that endures to this day.

Southeast Asia as a Revolutionary Base

Toward the end of the nineteenth century, Southeast Asia assumed an entirely new role for China—as an external base of political movements: the anti-Qing revolutionaries led by Dr. Sun Yat-sen. The overseas Chinese in the region proved crucial for their political and financial support to the ultimate success of the 1911 Revolution (辛亥革命) in China.

Sun and his republican revolutionary comrades were not the only politically active exiled Chinese. Singapore in particular became a haven for various Chinese with different political loyalties. Pro-Qing monarchial loyalists organized a euphemistically titled group known as the "Protect the Emperor Society" (*Baohuanghui*) after the collapse of the Hundred Days Reform in China in 1898. The name is euphemistic because the reforms had been initiated by the Guangxu Emperor before the Empress Dowager Cixi and conservative elites within the imperial court engineered a coup (known as the Wuxu Coup) on October 22, 1898, and put an end to the progressive reforms. While the Guangxu Emperor was

thereafter put under house arrest for the remainder of his life, his supporters—
led by Liang Qichao and Kang Youwei—went into exile in Singapore and Japan.
These were enlightened and liberal intellectuals, but they sought reforms to the
existing order in China and were not yet prepared for revolutionary activity to
overturn it.

There was a second group that had an entirely different and more radical—
revolutionary—orientation. In 1900, Sun Yat-sen (孙中山) first visited
Singapore, but he did not stay long before moving on to Japan, Hawaii, and
San Francisco. He returned to Singapore in 1906 (Fig. 4.3), where, on April
6, he established the Nanyang branch of his exiled revolutionary secret so-
ciety/party the Tongmenghui (同盟会, or United League). There were fifteen
founding members, who signed and swore an oath to "work for the expulsion of the Manchus, the restoration of Chinese sovereignty, the establishment of a republic, and the equalization of land rights."[35] Three years earlier
another group of eighteen Chinese youths gathered in southern Johor, just
over the Malay border from Singapore, and established an underground movement to overthrow the Qing. They called themselves the "Eighteen Saviors."[36]
Eventually their movement was merged into the Tongmenghui. Other groups
of more wealthy overseas Chinese merchants also became politically active in
Singapore—advocating various pseudo-democratic reforms. They too were
kindred spirits for Sun and the Tongmenghui—plus the fact that they had
money. Sun and the League were desperately in need of funds for their cause
in these years, and they spent much time trying to raise financial support in
America, Europe, Japan, and Southeast Asia.

The Singapore branch of the Tongmenghui was to be the headquarters for
the party's activities throughout Southeast Asia. While it was very successful in
raising funds and awareness of the Tongmenghui's program for a future republican China, in 1909 the Nanyang headquarters was moved to Penang (although
the Singaporean branch remained) further up the western coast of Malaya. This
followed the establishment by Sun of ten branches throughout British Malaya
in 1906, during a tour of the region. This included a branch in Kuala Lumpur.
But there was a greater concentration of Chinese in Penang, so the decision was
taken to relocate the regional headquarters of the Tongmenghui there, in hopes
of expanding support throughout the Malay territories and into Siam. There they
were able to tap into a large diasporic community of Chinese that had settled
over the previous century. A year later, on November 13, 1910, it organized the
crucial Penang Conference, which was chaired by Sun Yat-sen and planned an
insurrection in Guangzhou in April 1911 (a.k.a. the Canton Uprising), raised
considerable funds, and plotted the final revolutionary overthrow of the mor-
ibund Qing dynasty.[37] The conference was a crucial turning point in the demise of the dynasty and revolution of 1911. Today the site is preserved as the

Figure 4.3 Sun Yat-sen in Singapore (1906)
Source: Shanghai Museum

Sun Yat-sen Museum (which I visited in 2018). In retrospect, Southeast Asia—notably Singapore and Malaya—was crucial as a base of exiled operations for Sun Yat-sen and the *Tongmenghui*. Of the 102 branches of the United League worldwide, 59 were in Southeast Asia (Nanyang) and more than half of those were in Malaya.[38]

Thus, during the Qing, China's ties with the region qualitatively transformed from barter trade and official tribute to truly integrated connections of lineage and ethnic communities, as well as an exile political base for anti-Qing revolutionaries. China was no longer simply a territorial neighbor—it had now *embedded* itself *in* Southeast Asia.

The Republic of China's Relations with Southeast Asia

The Republic of China's official relations with Southeast Asia during the thirty-eight years of its existence on the mainland (1912–1949) were virtually nonexistent, and thus interactions occurred primarily at the non-state level. China during this period was, of course, consumed by a never-ending series of internal upheavals. The new republican government never really got on its feet—with President Yuan Shi-kai's short-lived presidency and several dissolutions of parliament and constitutional revisions just in the first four years of the infant republic. Thereafter, the nation cleaved into many competing waring fiefdoms during the warlord period (1916–1928). The "Nanjing Decade" (1927–1937) did offer some temporary stabilization and unity, with a semblance of functional central government, but this hiatus was soon overwhelmed by the invasion and occupation of Japan (1937–1945). Following this national calamity, China reverted to internecine strife between ascendant Communists and the declining Nationalists. Throughout, establishing and maintaining foreign relations was an alien luxury. For Chiang Kai-shek's regime, only three partners really mattered: Germany, the Soviet Union, and the United States. Southeast Asia was an afterthought, at best.

Despite the chaos that consumed China, evidently private trade with Southeast Asia continued. According to Xiamen University historian Nie Dening, "Even despite all the disorder in China during the *Mingguo* [republican] period, there was still normal trade by ship with Southeast Asia, although largely with overseas Chinese. This trade came via Xiamen, Guangzhou, Shantou, a little via Shanghai, and trading companies (洋行) played a very key role."[39]

At the state-to-state governmental level, Southeast Asia during this period remained colonized by European powers and therefore there were no regional governments with which to establish diplomatic ties. Only Siam possessed independent sovereignty (Thailand after 1940), but the Bangkok government failed to recognize the new Republic of China (ROC) government. Thus, such as it did, the ROC dealt with the region via the colonial powers. But, even then, it was incomplete. Beiping established formal diplomatic relations with the United Kingdom in 1912 (thus facilitating ties with British Malaya, Borneo, and Burma), with the United States in 1912 (facilitating links with the Philippines), and with France in 1913 (facilitating ties with Indochina), but never did with Portugal or Holland (thus no formal interactions with the Dutch East Indies or Portuguese Timor).

Of course, during World War II Japan not only invaded and occupied mainland China, but also all of Southeast Asia. This included British-ruled Burma, adjacent to southwestern Yunnan province—where the ROC government had withdrawn and from where rearguard resistance was mounted in 1944 and 1945 (the so-called China-India-Burma theater or CBI). The war years and Nationalist China's existential struggle for survival meant that all ties to

Southeast Asia were attenuated. This included most private commerce, as shipping and transport networks were disrupted. Following the war against Japan, some Nationalist forces remained in the border regions of northern Burma, and many more retreated there after the Chinese Communist forces won the civil war (the majority retreated to Taiwan), but the onset of full-scale civil war in China between the CCP and KMT meant continued isolation of China from peripheral states and societies to the south. Moreover, the postwar period witnessed great upheavals and anti-colonial insurgencies across Southeast Asia.

A second dimension of China's interactions with Southeast Asia during the period of Nationalist rule in China, such as it existed, concerned the overseas Chinese throughout the region. These diasporic communities became politically important during the first decade of the twentieth century, as Chinese intellectuals and professionals from mainland China took political refuge and/ or went for professional training (e.g., in medicine). Thereafter, the overseas Chinese were a priority for the ROC government, which established an Overseas Chinese Affairs Commission (侨务委员会) in 1926 to liaise with these communities, build up political support, and gain financial remunerations. The commission also advocated for equal rights and treatment in their countries of residence, as well as having access to a Chinese education. The ROC government continued the Qing practice of granting all overseas Chinese dual citizenship. This was clarified somewhat with the passage of a Nationality Law of 1925, which stated that children born of a Chinese father—no matter where they lived—were of Chinese nationality.[40] Given the large influx of Chinese from the mainland southward during the closing decades of the nineteenth and early twentieth centuries, the dual nationality policy taken together with the increased politicization of these communities by the Kuomintang (Republic of China) party and government, naturally raised suspicions not only among the colonial governments but also among the non-Chinese communities as well. The seeds of suspicion had been sown, and they would continue to grow throughout the twentieth century and into the twenty-first. Even to this day, particularly in Indonesia but also in Malaysia, anti-Chinese tensions remain and occasionally flare up.

The Nationalists were, however, not alone in this endeavor. After the establishment of the Chinese Communist Party (CCP) in 1921, it too established its own Overseas Chinese Liaison Bureau as part of its United Front Work Department, which sought to compete for the loyalties of the Chinese diaspora (especially following the collapse of the first CCP-KMT united front in 1927). This was part of broader, not very successful, efforts by the Soviet Comintern (Communist International) to establish bases of support in Asia and the Middle East.[41] Efforts were made, in particular, to get the Nanyang Communist Party (later Malayan Communist Party) off the ground, and similar underground efforts were underway in Burma, Singapore, and Indonesia. But the most successful ties were forged with the Indochina Communist Party (ICP). Before the first CCP-KMT united front fell apart following the brutal April 12, 1927 "Shanghai massacre," both the Chinese Nationalists and the Communists worked with Comintern representatives in Canton. Some Comintern infiltration occurred surreptitiously in French Indochina, but it was far safer for ICP operatives to be sent to Canton (Guangzhou) for training. One such individual was Nguyen Ai Quoc, a.k.a. Ho Chi Minh. Ho spent two years there, from mid-1925 through mid-1927, receiving training and befriending CCP members.[42]

Thus, owing to the colonization of Southeast Asia by external powers and the domestic complexities in China throughout the Republican era, traditional ties to Southeast Asia were attenuated. This would carry over into the initial years of the new People's Republic after 1949.

The People's Republic of China and Southeast Asia, 1949–2000

The PRC's roles in, and relations with, Southeast Asia prior to 2000 reflected multiple factors and evolved through distinct phases. Generally speaking, like much of China's post-1949 development (internally and externally), the coming to power of Deng Xiaoping in 1978 marks a broad dividing point. Prior to that time, during the Maoist era, China's role in Southeast Asia was quite destabilizing and Beijing's relations were consequently very strained. They were also nonexistent with many countries prior to the 1970s, as China had diplomatic relations with only a handful of countries (Burma, Cambodia, Indonesia, and Laos) prior to that time. After 1978, Deng's recalibration of domestic policies—placing economic development first and downplaying radical Maoist ideology—had real consequences for China's foreign relations.

As a result, China's approach to the region fundamentally changed from a destabilizing one to one of stability and coexistence. To symbolize this shift Deng undertook a personal visit to Thailand, Malaysia, and Singapore from November 5 to 14, 1978. Deng was the first Chinese leader to tour the region since Zhou Enlai in November 1956 and was the *first* Chinese Communist leader to visit these three countries (Zhou had only visited North Vietnam, Burma, and Cambodia).

Prior to 1978 and Deng's reorientation of China's domestic and foreign directions, several factors conditioned the PRC's approach to Southeast Asia, and vice versa:

- The PRC's search for diplomatic recognition as a new state after 1949.
- The Cold War between the United States and its allies and the Soviet Union and its allies (including China before 1960), and China's attempts to undermine the American position in the region.

- China's cultivation of, and support for, communist parties throughout the region—based on Mao's revolutionary ideology and support for fraternal parties.
- China's cultivation of, and association with, newly independent postcolonial countries—and the role Beijing played in the Afro-Asian non-aligned movement.
- China's cultivation and manipulation of overseas Chinese communities as a "fifth column" of the PRC's "united front" to undermine non-communist states and sow revolution throughout the region.
- Following the Sino-Soviet split in 1960, Beijing attempted to blunt and undermine Moscow's role in the region.
- China's comprehensive support for North Vietnam (Democratic Republic of Vietnam) during its civil war with South Vietnam (Republic of Vietnam).

Following 1978, Beijing continued its quest to counter the Soviet Union's role in the region—until the late 1980s and their *rapprochement*. But, otherwise, these hallmark features of China's pre-1978 approach to Southeast Asia were all abandoned. In their place, Beijing terminated support for communist parties (except the Burmese Communist Party), established state-to-state diplomatic relations with all countries in the region, practiced a hands-off policy toward the overseas Chinese, entered into normal trade and cultural exchanges, sought foreign investment from these countries and the overseas Chinese, became more tolerant of the US role in the region, and—following the 1997 Asian Financial Crisis—provided significant financial assistance to many Southeast Asian countries.[43] Taken together, these qualitative changes in Beijing's behavior gradually shifted Southeast Asian perceptions of the PRC from malign to more benign (nonetheless a residue of suspicions remained in many countries).

The Search for Friends

The People's Republic began its existence in international isolation.[44] The emerging Cold War bifurcation of the world into two competing camps definitely impacted "new China's" case for recognition as a sovereign member of the United Nations (UN) and international community. It was denied admission to the UN, and only a dozen countries extended diplomatic recognition in 1949; each was a member of the "Soviet Bloc." In 1950, ten more nations recognized the PRC—four newly independent Asian countries and six Western countries. Even a decade after its founding, Beijing enjoyed diplomatic relations with only thirty-seven states. Mao was fond of counting China's "friends" and "enemies"—the PRC had many more of the latter than the former in the early years of its existence. China was deeply isolated and cut off from ties with the West as well as many in the East. Facing this reality, Mao and the new PRC had little choice but to turn to Moscow for economic assistance and security.

The outbreak of the Korean War in June 1950 only served to solidify China's segregation from the non-communist world and ties to the communist camp, as well as increasing the threats to its national security. It also resulted in frustrating Beijing's attempt to "liberate" Taiwan and close the final chapter of its long-running struggle with the Kuomintang regime—as the United States placed the Seventh Fleet in the Taiwan Strait just as Mao was preparing to cross the strait, attack the island, and forcibly conclude the civil war.

Thus, China's relations with the world during the 1950s were dominated by its international isolation and its allied relationship with the Soviet Union. It is in this context that Beijing sought out support from newly independent post-colonial nations—including India, Pakistan, and those in Southeast Asia. But in Southeast Asia only Burma, Indonesia, North Vietnam, and later Cambodia were interested in establishing diplomatic relations with Beijing. The Democratic Republic of Vietnam (North Vietnam) was the first Southeast Asian state to formally recognize the PRC, establishing relations on January 18, 1950. Indonesia followed suit on April 13 and newly independent Burma on June 8, 1950. Eight years would pass before another Southeast Asian state recognized the PRC, which Cambodia did in 1958. Laos was the next in 1961. In 1965 Indonesia suspended ties with China. Thereafter, another long stretch ensued until Malaysia recognized China in 1974, followed by the Philippines and Thailand in 1975. Another long stretch ensued, until Indonesia renormalized its ties and Singapore officially recognized the PRC in 1990, followed by Brunei in 1991.

Thus, it took more than *forty years* before China had full diplomatic relations with all of the Southeast Asian states. This was not by accident—but reflected the factors noted earlier, as well as the deep levels of distrust of Communist China throughout the non-communist region.

This near-total isolation did not prevent Beijing from trying to forge ties—albeit unofficial ones—in the region. Two international conferences were instrumental in this regard: the 1954 Geneva Conference and the 1955 Bandung Conference. Each international meeting allowed the PRC, and its Premier and then Foreign Minister Zhou Enlai, to take their first steps on to the world stage.

After three years of horrendous war in Korea the battle lines stalemated near the 38th Parallel and an armistice was signed in 1953. Thereafter, the major powers convened for the Geneva Conference from April through July 1954 (see discussion in chapter 2).

Zhou Enlai earned high marks for his calm demeanor, personal sophistication, and diplomatic acumen at Geneva. Zhou's performance stood in stark contrast to the more belligerent image the PRC had cast during its initial years.

The US delegation, led by Secretary of State John Foster Dulles, did its best to ignore and marginalize China's participation in the Geneva Conference[45]—but symbolically, China had taken its initial steps into the international diplomatic arena. Substantively, Zhou and the Chinese delegation were instrumental in forging the conference's Final Declaration, which included a temporary ceasefire for Indochinese states, the creation of an International Commission to monitor the ceasefire, the partition of Vietnam (pending nationwide elections), and other provisions. Zhou's support for these initiatives put it at direct odds with its erstwhile communist partner in Hanoi, but it reflected Zhou's pragmatism.[46]

The following year, in April 1955, the Bandung Conference in Indonesia offered the PRC another international platform, but with a different audience. Again, as at Geneva, Zhou Enlai played a prominent role and performed admirably (Fig. 4.4).

Also known as the Asian-African Conference, representatives of twenty-nine nations from these two regions gathered to offer a "third way" between the two competing Cold War camps (the socialist camp and the imperialist camp).[47] Mao himself declared this to be the "intermediate zone" in world affairs.[48] The Bandung Conference paved the path to the creation of the Non-Aligned Movement (in which China became an observer but not a member). It also offered the PRC the opportunity to advertise its "second identity" as a developing postcolonial nation (its first identity was as a socialist-communist state) and

Figure 4.4 Zhou Enlai addresses the Bandung Conference (1955)
Source: Keystone-France/Gamma-Keystone via Getty Images

to begin to broaden its diplomatic ties with these countries.[49] The declaration adopted by the conferees also reaffirmed many of the elements that China and India had incorporated the previous year into their Five Principles of Peaceful Coexistence.[50]

Beijing tried to capitalize on the modest openings that Geneva and Bandung provided. During November 1956, Zhou Enlai embarked on a tour of the handful of Asian countries with which it had diplomatic ties: Afghanistan, Burma, Ceylon, India, Nepal, North Vietnam, and Pakistan. Cambodia was added to the itinerary despite not yet having established official relations. Zhou had also visited Rangoon, Burma, in 1954, where he and U Nu signed a bilateral trade agreement and communiqué recognizing the Five Principles of Peaceful Coexistence (the Sino-Burmese Border Treaty was signed in 1961). China and Indonesia forged particularly close ties as both sides sought to embolden the "united front from above" strategy embedded in the Afro-Asian movement. The potential problem was that Beijing was simultaneously supporting the Indonesian Communist Party (PKI) in a "united front from below."[51] But as Sukarno increasingly moved politically to the left he began to forge closer links with the PKI, even bringing several senior members into his cabinet. For Beijing this became an increasingly tenuous situation, as Mao and the CCP increasingly urged and supported the PKI to undertake "armed struggle." As discussed in chapter 2, the situation came to a head with an attempted coup on October 1, 1965, led by leftist PKI-associated officers. The coup failed, the PKI was decimated, and a bloodbath against ethnic Chinese ensued. So much for the vaunted "Beijing-Jakarta axis." Indonesia suspended diplomatic relations.

While the Geneva and Bandung conferences, and Zhou's 1956 tour, did offer the new PRC government useful opportunities to engage with international actors other than the Soviet Union and its satellite allies, China still remained relatively isolated in the world. By the end of the 1950s, it only had formal diplomatic ties with twenty-seven nations. Moreover, as domestic Chinese politics became more radical beginning with the Anti-Rightist Campaign (1957), commune movement (1958), and Great Leap Forward (1958–1960), Sino-Soviet frictions also began to metastasize. What seemed like an opening for Beijing following Geneva and Bandung was overwhelmed by a combination of Mao's lurch leftward domestically, his growing desire to confront the United States worldwide, and then the open split with the Moscow in 1960.

Support for Communist Parties

While the PRC was not able to establish normal state-to-state diplomatic relations with most of its Southeast Asian neighbors—other than Burma, Cambodia,

Indonesia, and North Vietnam—what Beijing did do was to cultivate ties with, and extend material support for, a variety of nascent communist movements in the region. Even *within* three of these four countries with which it had official relations, the CCP continued to cultivate party-to-party relations with indigenous communist parties and insurgents that were attempting to overthrow the established governments. China thus pursued a two-level dual political approach to the region: state-to-state and party-to-party.[52] In some countries it adopted a third approach—the united front—trying to push communist parties into coalitions with other parties.[53] These efforts began in the 1950s and continued until the late 1970s. They accelerated following the Sino-Soviet split in 1960 as the two communist powers began to compete worldwide for the allegiance of leftist parties, and it reached its apogee during the Cultural Revolution decade 1966–1976, before being largely terminated after 1978.[54]

During this lengthy period, the CCP supported the Vietnamese Communist Party, Burmese Communist Party, Khmer People's Revolutionary Party (later Khmer Rouge), Lao People's Revolutionary Party (Pathet Lao), Communist Party of Thailand, Malayan Communist Party, North Kalimantan Communist Party (operating in Borneo), Communist Party of Indonesia (Partai Komunis Indonesia, PKI), and Communist Party of the Philippines (New People's Army). These are hugely complicated relationships in each case, about which much has been written. Suffice to say that types of support varied in each case.

In the case of North Vietnam, at one extreme, it involved full and sustained military assistance, and provision of materiel, throughout the war with the United States.[55] In 1973, for example, China provided the North Vietnamese with 233,600 guns, 9,912 artillery pieces, 40 million rounds of bullets, 2.2 million artillery shells, 4,335 radio transmitters, 120 tanks, 36 aircraft, and 1,210 vehicles.[56] Supplies in other years fluctuated, but were not dissimilar. Throughout the war China also advised the Vietnamese on military strategy. China's support also included the stationing and rotation of 320,000 active-duty Chinese PLA personnel in North Vietnam—largely for the purposes of engineering and construction, logistics, and manning of anti-aircraft batteries.[57]

China's support for communist parties elsewhere in Southeast Asia was on a much lesser scale than Vietnam, as they were not involved in hot wars, but nevertheless Beijing consistently supported a variety of communist insurgent movements. In the case of the Malayan Communist Party (MCP), Chinese support included propaganda in the form of radio transmissions known as the Voice of the Malayan Revolution (which broadcast from November 1969 to June 1981), secret communications channels, clandestine funding, as well as on-and-off supply of light arms and ammunition. MCP leaders were mainly ethnic Chinese, and several went to China for training and medical treatment.[58] China also beamed broadcasts for the Voice of People's Thailand, and Voice of the People of Burma from long-range transmitters based in Yunnan Province.[59] In all of the cases of Burma, Cambodia, Indonesia, Laos, Malaysia, Thailand, and the Philippines, China's support included provision of weapons (mainly light arms) for these communist parties to undertake "armed struggle" (武器斗争).In the Cambodian case, China was the sole benefactor of the murderous Khmer Rouge, leaving a very dark stain on the PRC's image and legacy.[60] In the Burmese case, beginning in 1962, China stepped up its military supplies for the Burmese Communist Party (BCP) and by 1968 had formed a joint force with People's Liberation Army (PLA) regulars. This BCP-PLA joint force was well armed with artillery, anti-aircraft guns, and other conventional equipment. In early 1968 they mounted an offensive with the objective of seizing Mandalay, but were beaten back by Burmese military forces and contained in the China-Burma border region, where the BCP had de facto control until the early 1980s.[61] In Thailand, the Thai Communist Party had an estimated 5,000 armed soldiers by 1973, but their operations were confined to jungle regions in the northern and southern parts of the country.[62]

China's support for armed insurgencies did not go down well with the established governments they were attempting to overthrow. In the cases of Cambodia, Laos, and Vietnam they succeeded. In the cases of Burma, the Philippines, and Thailand, the communist insurgent movements never mounted a credible and direct threat to central governments, although in each case they did control large rural and jungle areas of these countries. In the case of Burma, Chinese political agitation did reach the streets of Rangoon during the summer of 1967 as members of China's diplomatic mission and state news service (Xinhua) went into the streets to demonstrate and distributed Mao buttons and other Cultural Revolution propaganda.[63] Similar subversive actions occurred in Phnom Penh, Cambodia. In each case it caused a diplomatic kerfuffle with Beijing (Burma even temporarily suspended relations). As discussed in chapter 2, Indonesia came the closest of any Southeast Asian country to an armed seizure of power by a local communist party—with the attempted coup of October 1965. For several years prior, the CCP had been smuggling money and weapons to the PKI and hosted its leader D. N. Aidit in Beijing on multiple occasions. On August 5, 1965, Aidit met with Mao in Beijing, who strongly encouraged him to "eliminate all the reactionary generals and officers in one blow."[64]

MAO: You should act quickly.

AIDIT: I am afraid the army is going to be the obstacle.

MAO: Well, do as I advise you and eliminate all the reactionary generals and officers in one blow. The army will be a headless dragon and follow you.

AIDIT: That would mean killing some hundreds of officers.

MAO: In northern Shaanxi I killed 20,000 cadres in one stroke.[65]

In the same discussion, Mao promised to ship 30,000 light weapons to the PKI. These arms were delivered during September. As such, China was strongly suspected of helping to foment the (failed) September 30, 1965 coup attempt in Jakarta, and indeed was so accused by the surviving junta led by General Suharto. But subsequent information reveals no direct linkage—no proverbial "smoking gun"—between the CCP, PKI, and coup plotters.[66] Nonetheless, Jakarta blamed Beijing for helping to instigate the coup, and the junta's horrific post-coup massacre against ethnic Chinese, which claimed the lives of more than a million, fueled tensions. Relations subsequently became very strained before Indonesia officially suspended diplomatic ties with the PRC in 1967. China's ties to the PKI were also decimated along with the PKI. More broadly, China's careful cultivation of Indonesia (and vice versa) over the previous fifteen years had fully collapsed in failure. [67]

In the other cases across Southeast Asia, though, China continued its support and material aid to communist parties through the end of the 1970s. But then in 1978, as has been noted, Deng Xiaoping indicated China's intention to cease such active support during his tour of Malaysia, Singapore, and Thailand. By 1981, when Premier Zhao Ziyang toured the region, he repeatedly made the point that the CCP's relations with regional parties was only "moral and political" and that China would not interfere in the internal affairs of either these parties or countries in the region.[68] While this was welcome news to the established governments that China had previously been trying to undermine—the residual distrust festered from three decades of subversive and destabilizing behavior by Beijing.

The Sensitive Issue of Overseas Chinese

Prior to the 1980s, the legacy of distrust of China in Southeast Asia also had much to do with Beijing's relations with the ethnic overseas Chinese diaspora throughout the region. During the 1950s, 1960s, and 1970s, overseas Chinese (华侨) were viewed suspiciously as subversive "fifth columns" by many Southeast Asian governments (the term "fifth column" grows out of the Spanish civil war in 1936 when the nationalist General Emilio Mola and his supporters besieged Madrid with four columns of troops, but he claimed that a "fifth column" of clandestine supporters were waiting in the city to aid them). But after 1978 and China's turn to economic development as the overriding national goal, ethnic Chinese in Southeast Asia (and worldwide) were viewed as potential contributors to modernization rather than exporting revolution. At that time, in 1978, there were 14.5 million ethnic Chinese in Southeast Asia.[69]

As noted earlier in this chapter, ethnic Chinese migration from mainland China to Southeast Asia has a history dating back centuries. They have been the purveyors of commerce, culture, and familial ties. During the early twentieth century the ethnic Chinese population in Singapore and Malaya became involved in mainland Chinese politics, as Sun Yat-sen organized *Tongmenhui* (United League) revolutionary activities there. The overseas Chinese, especially in Southeast Asia, provided crucial financing to Dr. Sun's movement.

Following the 1949 seizure of power by the CCP on the mainland, and the retreat to Taiwan by the Nationalists, the two rivals competed fiercely for the political allegiance of the overseas Chinese in Southeast Asia. Each government had its own Overseas Chinese Affairs Commission (华侨事务委员会), which undertook to liaise with Chinese communities worldwide, including in Southeast Asia. But, owing to the fierce anti-communist orientation and sedition laws of most Southeast Asian governments, Taiwan had the upper hand from the 1950s through the 1980s. Taiwan-affiliated groups during these decades dominated the local Chinese diaspora newspapers, which mainly publicized anti-communist articles. Those with sympathies for the new People's Republic were viewed with deep suspicion among the diasporic communities. Nonetheless, some ethnic Chinese either possessed leftist political leanings and/or took pride in the newly established PRC, and these individuals "returned to the motherland" during the 1950s (how many is unknown). Others remitted personal funds to the PRC but did not physically move to the mainland. Hong Kong played a central role in funneling these remittances from Southeast Asia to the mainland. One study calculated that such remittances via Hong Kong amounted to $28–$35 million *per annum* between 1950 and 1964.[70] These were not insignificant amounts (especially in today's currency equivalent) and the remittances evinced a significant degree of sympathy and support for the communist-led PRC.

The principal question of concern during these years was what the official policy of the Beijing government was toward the citizenship of overseas Chinese. At first, the new PRC regime continued the Qing dynasty and Republic of China policy that children born of a Chinese father—no matter where they lived—were of Chinese nationality, and on this basis extended the offer of dual citizenship if sought by the individual. Then, in 1957, Beijing made a fundamental change by abandoning dual citizenship (applying equally to foreigners living in China who sought Chinese citizenship)—and, moreover, Beijing encouraged overseas Chinese to integrate themselves into the societies in which they lived and to adopt local citizenship. This was an important shift in PRC policy and it was welcomed in the region. It was presaged by the April 1955 China-Indonesia Treaty on Dual Nationality, which encouraged Chinese in Indonesia to adopt Indonesian citizenship.[71] The policy change introduced a linguistic distinction used by the PRC authorities: *huaqiao* (华侨) vs. *huaren* (华人). The former referred to Chinese living overseas who were citizens of China, while the latter referred to people of Chinese descent who were citizens of foreign countries.[72] The shift can be at least partially explained by Zhou Enlai's attempts to cultivate support for China among Southeast Asian countries in the post-Bandung period. Nonetheless, the staunchly anti-communist Southeast Asian governments continued to view ethnic Chinese as a potential source of potential subversion. As Beijing began to actively back communist parties and insurgent movements throughout the region, as discussed earlier, this fear heightened.

Nowhere was this more the case than in Indonesia. Despite the Dual Nationality Treaty of 1955 and the 1957 decree on assuming local citizenship, Beijing continued to step up its close contacts with the Indonesian Chinese community, as well as the Indonesian Communist Party (PKI). In December 1959, Beijing shifted course and launched a campaign to call all overseas Chinese back to the "warm bosom of the motherland." Fang Fang, vice chairman of the PRC Overseas Chinese Affairs Commission, declared that "we want none of our dear ones to suffer in foreign lands, and it is our hope that they will all come back to the arms of the motherland. The Chinese government has decided to receive all returned overseas Chinese whether they are half a million, a million, or several million."[73] This new policy inflamed Sino-Indonesian relations, and continued to fester until the failed coup of 1965—after which extreme retribution was taken against the ethnic Chinese community, killing more than a million in a two-month bloodbath.

The Indonesian case was an extreme one, as such violence was not generally perpetrated on ethnic Chinese in other Southeast Asian societies. But then, in the wake of the North Vietnamese victory in its civil war in 1975, the new communist regime undertook a systematic repression of ethnic Chinese in Vietnam (known as the Hoa)—interning many in jungle concentration camps, while tens of thousands of others escaped Vietnam in daring small boat voyages (known as the "boat people"). A quarter of a million more Hoa escaped to China, where they were resettled. This Vietnamese persecution was one of the rationales for China's punitive attack on Vietnam in 1979.

Becoming a More Normal Neighbor

While the main pivot point in China's approach to Southeast Asia came with Deng Xiaoping's return to power in 1977, following the arrest and overthrow of the Gang of Four in October 1976, some nascent steps toward normalization were taken near the tail end of the Maoist era. Malaysia and China formally recognized each other in 1974, as did the Philippines and Thailand in 1975. These moves were facilitated by several factors: China was now a member of the United Nations, President Nixon's 1972 visit had opened the door for US allies to develop their own relations with China, the American war in Vietnam had ended, and Premier Zhou Enlai was fashioning a foreign policy that would contribute to China's post-1974 mission of the "four modernizations." In each of these cases, establishment of diplomatic relations with Beijing necessitated breaking them with Taipei—a difficult, but necessary, price to pay in each case.

While Beijing's ties with these three key ASEAN states were opening, with Vietnam they were deteriorating. As Robert Ross's careful and classic account of the period 1975–1979 delineates, this is a period of rapidly shifting alignments among multiple actors.[74] Despite China's steadfast support for North Vietnam during the wars against the French and Americans, Beijing had also long feared Vietnamese dominance over Indochina. It was also very uneasy about Hanoi's ties with its erstwhile adversary the Soviet Union. Not long after North Vietnam's military conquest of the south and unification of the country in 1975, these twin fears were realized in 1978. In November, Hanoi signed a Treaty of Friendship and Cooperation with a mutual defense clause with Moscow and the Soviet navy began docking at Vietnamese ports. The following month Vietnamese forces invaded Cambodia, overthrowing the genocidal Khmer Rouge regime (and China's client state), while Vietnamese party cadres and army units infiltrated the Laotian regime. Vietnamese dominance over all of Indochina was a reality, as Vietnam effectively controlled the region (except pockets of jungle where remnant Khmer Rouge guerrillas had sanctuaries). Moreover, by the summer of 1979 Vietnamese forces had pushed to the Thai border and were engaging Thai forces in the border region. I traveled to the region northeast of Chiang Mai that summer, climbed a hill, and witnessed (from 2 miles away) the battle for Poipet, a Cambodian border town. Vietnamese forces never successfully penetrated into Thailand, but there was plenty of nervousness that they would.

As a deterrent and contingency plan, China urgently rushed weapons to the Thai military and offered to intervene if Thailand requested it. In February 1979, an estimated 200,000 Chinese PLA forces crossed the border and attacked Vietnam from the north, proclaiming that China sought to "teach Vietnam a lesson." Beijing deemed the "lesson" necessary for several reasons: Vietnam's incursion into Cambodia and Laos, Hanoi's apparent lack of gratitude for all of China's support during the war with America, Vietnam's treaty with Moscow and the deployment of Soviet naval forces to China's south, the persecution of ethnic Chinese in Vietnam, a disputed Sino-Vietnamese border, and armed border clashes that Beijing claimed were incursions into Chinese territory. For all of these supposed reasons, China unleashed its ire by attacking Vietnam (hypocritically dubbed a "self-defense counterattack" by China). After three weeks of fighting, in which Chinese forces bogged down and were beaten back by 70,000 battle-hardened Vietnamese troops before finally seizing the border village of Long San, after which they proclaimed "victory" and withdrew. The brief border war was a military humiliation for China. If anyone was "taught a lesson," it was the PLA—which demonstrated general incompetence, lack of coordination, no air cover, disrupted logistics supply lines, and no interoperability, and thus endured heavy losses (perhaps as many as 25,000 killed in action and 40,000 casualties).[75]

While the campaign was a military failure, China maintained a large contingent of troops on the Vietnamese border for the next decade, attempting to "bleed" Vietnam's occupation of Cambodia by forcing the Vietnamese to maintain a large contingent of their troops there. Finally, following a UN-brokered arrangement, Vietnam withdrew its forces from Cambodia (and Laos) by the end of 1989—although the client leader (Heng Samrin) and regime Hanoi installed remained in place through 1992 and nationwide elections. The Cambodia settlement opened a new era in China's relations with Southeast Asia, as well as the gradual process of re-normalizing party-to-party and state-to-state relations between China and Vietnam.

The 1990s: Progressive Warming

Just as China was emerging more fully on the regional and global stage, with significant economic and political reforms being implemented at home by CCP leader Zhao Ziyang, its momentum was arrested as a result of the Tiananmen Incident of June 4, 1989. Following six weeks of massive pro-democracy demonstrations in Beijing and across the country, Deng Xiaoping personally took the decision to remove Zhao from power and to use lethal force to clear the city of demonstrators. Between 1,500 and 2,000 died. China, which had made impressive progress in "reform and opening," now found itself the object of international condemnation and isolation . . . almost. While the G-7 and Western nations enacted sanctions against the Chinese regime, the rest of the world remained relatively silent over the tragic events in Beijing. Japan joined in the G-7 sanctions, but within a year wriggled out of them. The South Korean government only noted that it was a "regrettable incident." Southeast Asian states were also circumspect. On the one hand, Singapore's senior statesman Lee Kuan Yew issued a public statement saying, "My cabinet colleagues and I are shocked, horrified, and saddened by this disastrous turn of events." This was, in Lee's view, a simple statement of fact, but not a condemnation. In his memoirs, Prime Minister Lee observed: "I did not condemn them. I did not regard them as a repressive communist regime like the Soviet Union."[76] Subsequently, Prime Minister Lee led the way among Asian states in maintaining contact with Beijing, arguing that it would be counterproductive in the long term to isolate China. Lee's view at this troubled time was consistent with his overall strategy of integrating and binding China positively into the East Asian region.[77] The Malaysian and Thai governments simply stated that it was China's "internal affair."

Thus, as traumatic as the events of June 1989 were for China's reputation internationally, Beijing was not at all isolated in the Asian region. Thereafter, the ASEAN states led a diplomatic campaign to "engage"—rather than isolate—China.[78] This did not go unnoticed in Beijing. As the leaders struggled with their own post-Tiananmen domestic politics, with Western sanctions, with the overthrows of communist party-states in Eastern Europe, and then the disintegration of the Soviet Union in a brief two-year span, Southeast Asia offered a rare bright spot for Beijing. In August 1990, China and Indonesia renormalized their relations following a twenty-three-year hiatus. Singapore, which had never established formal diplomatic ties since its independence in 1965, followed suit in October 1990. Brunei came next in September 1991, followed by the renormalization of Sino-Vietnamese ties in November 1991. For the *first* time, China now had formal diplomatic relations with *all* Southeast Asian states. During 1990 and 1991, China and ASEAN also explored establishing formal diplomatic links. China became a "dialogue and consultation partner" in 1991, becoming the first non-regional state to accede to ASEAN's Treaty of Amity and Cooperation. This opened the door to participating in all ASEAN facilitated sub-organizations and meetings.

Thereafter, a seven-year period of gradual and mutual integration of China into ASEAN multilateral mechanisms ensued. Between 1992 and 1999, China overcame its suspicions that Asian multilateral organizations were instruments of American efforts to contain China; it did so by progressively attending, and then joining, a number of regional groupings. ASEAN was central in this process of reassurance and learning for Beijing. "It was a gradual learning process for us, as we needed to become more familiar with how these organizations worked and to learn how to play the game," reflected Cui Tiankai (then Director General of Asian affairs in China's Ministry of Foreign Affairs and currently Ambassador to the United States).[79] By the end of the decade, China and ASEAN had forged quite close relations, which were solidified by a variety of bureaucratic consultation mechanisms. Lee Kuan Yew's vision for integrating China into the region was being realized.[80]

This process occurred almost by stealth, as the rest of the world was consumed with the meltdown of the Soviet Union, end of the Cold War, dissolution of the Warsaw Pact, reunification of Germany, establishment of new democratic governments in Eastern Europe, and a self-congratulatory "end of history" hubris. The United States, it told itself, had "won the Cold War." In this context, China was viewed as being on the "wrong side of history," and it was only a matter of time before "history" caught up with it and the CCP joined other former communist parties in the Marx's proverbial "dustbin of history."

Such was the prevalent *zeitgeist* in the West. But not in Asia, and certainly not in Beijing. For China's leaders, there was absolutely no doubt that they had done the right thing on June 4, 1989; had they not used force to suppress the "counterrevolutionary rebellion" (反革命暴乱) that posed a severe political threat, the CCP and PRC may not have survived. Having thus done what was necessary to face down the politically existential challenge, the questions now were threefold: first, how to overcome China's international isolation and continue the process of becoming a global power; second, what lessons to learn from the collapse of the Soviet Union and communist party-states elsewhere; and, third, how to implement these lessons domestically so that there would never be a repeat of 1989.[81] In all three cases, China's leadership determined that maintaining China's opening to the world was key to overcoming these challenges. The broader and deeper China's external linkages, the more difficult it would be for others to isolate or manipulate it.

Asia was key in this process and beginning in 1999 Beijing prioritized the region in its global diplomacy.[82] With its new peripheral diplomacy (周边外交) initiative, Beijing set out to build on its foundation with Southeast Asia to strengthen ties all around China.[83] This emphasis was part of a deeper set of debates and rethinking among Chinese foreign policy practitioners and experts during the 1996–1999 period.[84] China's positive response to Southeast Asian nations affected by the Asian Financial Crisis of 1997 had a large impact in shifting regional perceptions of China in a more positive direction. How this all became operationalized in the twenty-first century is explored in the next chapter.

5

China's Contemporary Roles
in Southeast Asia

"China is committed to pursuing partnership with its neighbors and a neighborhood diplomacy of amity, sincerity, mutual benefit and inclusiveness, and fostering a harmonious, secure, and prosperous neighborhood."

—China's President Xi Jinping, Singapore, 2015.[1]

"China is a big country and other countries are small countries, and that's just a fact."

—China's Foreign Minister Yang Jiechi, Hanoi, 2010.[2]

"The Chinese government has not decided to break up ASEAN. . . . Yet its actions have weakened ASEAN, a dangerous thing to do to an organization that is inherently fragile—perhaps as fragile as a Ming vase."

—Kishore Mahbubani, National University of Singapore, 2016.[3]

China's relations with Southeast Asian countries and ASEAN have grown dramatically since the turn of the twenty-first century and have now achieved a high degree of interactions. Some statistics are illustrative. By 2018 ASEAN's total trade in goods with China had expanded to $587 billion, China's total foreign direct investment (FDI) into ASEAN increased to approximately $84 billion with annual $13.4 billion inflows, Chinese tourist arrivals in ASEAN totaled 20.3 million people and over 38 million trips were taken in both directions, over 200,000 students are studying in each other's universities (80,000 Southeast Asian students are enrolled in Chinese universities with 124,000 Chinese students in ASEAN universities), more than 3,000 flights shuttle back and forth every week, and a variety of other indicators reveal a considerable density of interactions.[4] There has been a particularly notable uptick in all spheres since around 2015 (pre-COVID-19).

China's contemporary approach toward Southeast Asia is shaped by multiple factors. Among them, perhaps geography is the most important. China's close geographical proximity facilitates easy access and regular presence. This has led to growing economic interconnectedness, buttressed by transportation links. This relative proximity also facilitates tourism, academic exchanges, and a regular presence of Chinese officials visiting the region.

China's Assessments of Southeast Asia

How does China perceive Southeast Asia and the dynamics in the region, and what does it reveal about Beijing's strategy toward the region? A sampling of recent publications by China's Southeast Asia specialists, combined with official documents, is revealing on a number of levels.

First, it must be said that there is surprisingly sparse expertise on Southeast Asia in China. This is a curious anomaly given the relative importance of the region to China. Compared with other academic disciplines focused on regions of the world (such as American Studies, European Studies, African Studies, Latin American Studies), Southeast Asian Studies in China today is relatively underdeveloped.[5] This is not to say that the field is in any way absent, but I find it underdeveloped when compared with these other area studies. This is particularly the case in Beijing. There is, for example, no separate institute for Southeast Asian Studies in the Chinese Academy of Social Sciences (CASS). Other Beijing think tanks—such as the China Institutes of Contemporary International Relations (Ministry of State Security) and China Institute of International Studies (Ministry of Foreign Affairs)—generally only have a couple of researchers each devoted to the entire region (who tend not to speak regional languages), and they tend to concentrate on security issues rather than domestic affairs, foreign relations, or ASEAN itself.[6] Occasionally, faculty at China Foreign Affairs University (CFAU) publish on Southeast Asia, although the university has no dedicated institute (the same applies to Peking University, Renmin University, and Tsinghua University—all of which have established international relations and a variety of other regional studies programs).[7] Thus, there is a real dearth of expertise on Southeast Asia in the capital city.[8]

Conversely, the strengths of Southeast Asian regional studies lie outside of Beijing. There are several universities in the southern part of the country that have institutes or programs of Southeast Asian Studies: at Jinan University (Guangzhou), Xiamen University, Yunnan University, Guangxi University, Guangxi Normal University, and Zhongshan University. Research in these institutions tends to be heavily oriented toward ethnographic, historical, and cultural studies (including overseas Chinese), with some social science or international relations work being undertaken. The exceptions to this rule are Xiamen University and Jinan University (Guangzhou), which are more comprehensive in scope and publish the two leading contemporary studies journals in China,

Southeast Asian Affairs (南洋问题研究)[9] and *Southeast Asia Research* (东南亚研究) respectively. The Yunnan and Guangxi Academies of Social Sciences also each have research institutes on Southeast Asia, the first of which has published a number of volumes on contemporary Southeast Asian affairs.[10] Despite these pockets of expertise, I am still struck by the dearth of expertise in universities and think tanks given the size, proximity, and importance of Southeast Asia to China.

Of these institutions, the Research School for Southeast Asian Studies in the College of International Relations at Xiamen University in Fujian is the oldest and best in China. The beautiful Xiamen University campus is nestled seaside, where the island of Jinmen (Quemoy) is visible just 2 miles offshore. Jinmen was the site of high tensions in the period 1954–1960, when it was aptly described as the "frontline of the Cold War" (along with Berlin), as it was the forwardmost military outpost of the Chinese Nationalists (with 58,000 soldiers deployed on the tiny island) after they retreated to Taiwan. Jinmen was the epicenter of two Taiwan Straits crises of 1954–1955 and 1958–1960 when Chinese Communist forces began artillery shelling of the island (along with neighboring Matzu), thus triggering US military responses (and fierce debates between Kennedy and Nixon during the 1960 presidential election). In the midst of these crises the central government ordered the establishment of the Nanyang Research Institute (南洋研究所) at Xiamen University in 1956, to concentrate on the study of overseas Chinese and Southeast Asia. In 1974, following clashes with South Vietnam over some disputed islands in the Paracel chain (which China seized following brief firefights), the institute took on the added research responsibility for South China Sea studies. In 2000 the Ministry of Education elevated it to the status of "key point" (中点) national research center (研究院). Thereafter, the institute broadened its focus to international relations of the region and established eight specialized research centers including an ASEAN Studies Center. When I visited the school in October 2019, as part of researching this book, I was impressed by the quality of the faculty and earnestness of the student body (over 400). Its 25 faculty offer a range of regional courses for BA, MA, and PhD concentrations, the library has an extensive collection of over 100,000 volumes, and the school engages in multiple exchanges with institutions in Southeast Asia.

In terms of analytical tendencies, Chinese analysts of Southeast Asia evince several. First, they tend to adopt a big power approach and thus are preoccupied with the role of the United States—and China's competition with it—in the region. Part of this perspective is related to China's desire to create its own sphere of influence in the region, while part of it is related to China's defense posture of trying to push the US military as far away from its shores as possible.

This tendency in Chinese publications is also a by-product of Chinese scholars' readings of American analyses, as they show considerable familiarity with US scholarship (ironically, however, they do not often reference Southeast Asian scholarship). There is thus not a great deal of originality in Chinese writings, as many tend to repackage or cite Western scholarship. Second, however, Chinese scholars do carefully monitor the cohesion and orientation of ASEAN—for any signs that the grouping is developing in an anti-China direction. Conversely, Chinese observers are keenly aware of ASEAN's frequent and systemic disunity—and prefer to keep the organization that way. A unified ASEAN has the potential to be oriented against Chinese interests, while a disunited ASEAN is more malleable and easily manipulated by Beijing.

Yet some Chinese analysts are particularly critical, even scathing, in their assessments of ASEAN. Some see it as a weak organization and dismiss "ASEAN Centrality" as a mere slogan. On the occasion of ASEAN's 50th anniversary in 2017, one analyst in the Ministry of Foreign Affairs–affiliated China Institute of International Studies noted four systemic weaknesses of ASEAN: (1) "Building of the ASEAN Community is still flawed"; (2) "ASEAN has not solved the problem of internal leadership"; (3) "ASEAN's ability to coordinate with its dialogue partners is limited"; and (4) "ASEAN's performance in promoting regional cooperation remains to be improved."[11] Despite these criticisms, this analyst and other Chinese observers always maintain that "China always attaches great importance to its cooperative relations with ASEAN . . . and accepts ASEAN's central role in regional cooperation."[12]

Overall, though, Chinese analysts see an increasingly competitive strategic dynamic between the United States and China across the Indo-Pacific region, but particularly in Southeast Asia.[13] This is not a new dynamic, as Chinese strategic analysts have been arguing that regional strategic competition (地区战略竞争) and structural contradictions (机构性矛盾) began to rise during the Obama administration.[14] Many articles accused the Obama "pivot" or "rebalance" policy as thinly veiled "containment" (遏制). While many Chinese analysts see the renewed American attention to Southeast Asia as beginning with the Obama pivot, many think the competition has continued under Trump.[15] One analyst from Xiamen University acknowledged that the increased attention paid to Southeast Asia by the Obama administration did have a negative impact on "political mutual trust" (政治互信) between China and ASEAN states, and he argued (in 2014) that China needed to step up its game to win back the region's mutual trust.[16] This required a comprehensive approach involving cultural, economic, diplomatic, and institutional efforts. He also noted the sensitivities of disputed claims in the South China Sea and that "China should take care of the interests of the disputed parties while safeguarding its sovereignty but avoid establishing a unilateralist image in its diplomacy."[17]

In dealing with the United States in Southeast Asia, some analysts acknowledge that some ASEAN countries support the United States in balancing against China

(借美制华), though not specifying which ones, but they do argue that China still has greater "strategic capital" (战略资本) in the region than does the United States, and therefore it should exercise "strategic patience" (战略定力).[18] Other authors view Southeast Asian states' position vis-à-vis China and the United States as dependent on the country's "capacity" and "will":[19]

> Considering regional characteristics, we might be able to classify the strategies of neighboring countries towards China into four distinct categories: balancing, accommodating, opportunism, and hedging. Specifically, if a neighboring state has both strong capacity and will ... such a state will have a preference towards balancing. ... If, on the other hand, a state only has strong capacity to balance, but is lacking in will, it will prefer accommodation. If on the other hand, a state's capacity to balance is weak, but has strong will, it can lean towards opportunism, such as Vietnam. If a state's will and capacity to balance are both weak, such a state is likely to follow a hedging strategy.

Some authors, though, see Southeast Asian states as trying to avoid "bandwagoning" (with Beijing) by "hedging" and trying to maintain an equidistant position between the United States and China. "An equilibrium strategy has gradually become the preferred strategy that Southeast Asian countries employ to maximize their strategic interests," argues one author from Shanghai Foreign Trade University.[20] Another argues that hedging is the "default strategy" for ASEAN states.[21]

Another assessment by a scholar at the China Foreign Affairs University divides ASEAN countries into three types in terms of their approaches toward China: friends and collaborators; enemies and opponents; and uncertain hedgers.[22] The first group are those countries that have largely been "absorbed into China's economic system" (Myanmar, Cambodia, Laos). The second group seek to "counterbalance China," mainly by aligning with the United States (Singapore, Vietnam, Philippines). These countries seek to "befriend distant states" (远交), but not "attack those nearby" (近功). However, the author sees this tendency declining as the "China threat theory voices are slowly disappearing in the mainstream Southeast Asian countries." The third group are those practicing the two-dimensional "hedging strategy" (两面注战略)—Thailand, Malaysia, and Indonesia. This last group seeks a relationship between ASEAN and China that is "not close but not distant" (不远不近) and "neither friend nor enemy" (非敌非友).[23] This author concludes that in the fluid environment of Southeast Asia, China should prepare for surprises in its relations with Cambodia and Myanmar as "problems may arise," but that there is no need for undue pessimism about relations with Vietnam and the Philippines, and that China's wisest approach is to actively engage in ASEAN's multilateralism.[24]

Many other authors think that China holds natural appeal in the region. Some hark back to the October 2013 Peripheral Diplomacy Work Conference and argue that continued attention to China's neighborly policy of "amity, sincerity, mutual benefit, and inclusiveness" should be sufficient to assuage the region,[25] while others hold that Xi Jinping's "China-ASEAN Community of Common Destiny" is of intrinsic attraction.[26] Yet others question this optimism, arguing that while China enjoys extensive economic complementarities with Southeast Asia, there simultaneously exists considerable political mistrust and friction, which have compromised Chinese diplomatic initiatives.[27] Moreover, this author, who is identified as working at the Chinese Academy of Social Sciences Asia-Pacific and Global Strategic Research Institute, argues that China's soft power (软实力) has not been very effective in changing the "strategic mentality" (战略性思潮) of ASEAN.[28]

Others, sensing more urgency, argue China has to be particularly "vigilant" against US inroads—especially in Indochina and the lower Mekong region.[29] Chinese military analysts point to strengthened military ties between the United States and India, Vietnam, Singapore, Indonesia, Brunei, and the Philippines.[30] One PLA researcher at the National Defense University Institute of Strategic Studies meticulously catalogued the range of joint military exercises the United States carries out in the region: Cobra Gold (multinational based in Thailand), CARAT (multinational conducted in South China Sea), Balikatan (Philippines), Angkor Sentinel (Cambodia), Cope Tiger (Singapore, Thailand), and Strikeback (Malaysia). He also surveyed Foreign Military Sales (FMS) arms transfers and the International Military Education Training (IMET) officer training program.[31] One article by professors at the Public Security University in Beijing carefully traced the history of IMET with the Indonesian military (one wonders if IMET is a model for what the PLA aspires to in its foreign military assistance in the future?).[32] Also of particular interest to Chinese military analysts was the April 2014 Enhanced Defense Cooperation Agreement (ECDA), concluding that it permitted the US military to be "almost permanently stationed in the Philippines."[33] Others argued that the best way to blunt US encirclement was not militarily—but to deepen the region's economic dependency on China,[34] and to leverage China's comparative advantages by stepping up its "economic diplomacy" in the region.[35]

While Chinese publications on Southeast Asia do exhibit a preoccupation with the roles of the United States in the region, and the positioning of ASEAN member states in this great power competition,[36] there are also analyses of more discrete topics. Quite a number focus on trade and investment patterns in the region.[37] The annual "Blue Book" on Southeast Asia, published under the auspices of the Chinese Academy of Social Sciences, concentrates entirely on economic trends in the region.[38] A few analysts write about domestic politics in some Southeast Asian states,[39] and some analyze the South China Sea disputes. But very little, if any, is written about cultural issues, social trends, demographics, religion, ethnicity (other than overseas Chinese), terrorism or successionist movements, or other internal affairs of Southeast Asian societies. As a result, admitted Dean Li Yiping of Xiamen University, "We know a lot about economics, overseas Chinese, and current events—but we do not have a very good understanding about how and why things occur."[40] Thus, China's Southeast Asianists exhibit pockets of specializations, but do not demonstrate through their publications either very broad or very deep understanding of the region.

Beyond perceptions, how does China actually interact with Southeast Asia? China has been steadily extending and deepening its presence throughout the region in recent years. In doing so, it has used diplomatic, cultural, economic, and security instruments in its "toolbox."

China's Diplomacy in Southeast Asia

Bilaterally, China maintains a consistent and thick set of high-level exchanges with ASEAN member states. Beijing prioritizes its relations with Indonesia, Malaysia, and Thailand. Singapore and Vietnam are secondary priorities. Brunei, Cambodia, Laos, and Myanmar are of lower priority (although Cambodia can be characterized as a client state).

As Table 5.1 indicates, China's bilateral diplomatic relations have been established at different times over the past seventy years, and thus have developed at different intensities.

Table 5.1 China's Bilateral Diplomatic Relations in Southeast Asia

Country	Establishment of Diplomatic Relations
Democratic Republic of Vietnam	1950
Republic of Indonesia	1950
Union of Burma (Myanmar)	1950
Kingdom of Cambodia	1958
Kingdom of Laos	1961
Malaysia	1974
Republic of the Philippines	1975
Kingdom of Thailand	1975
Republic of Singapore	1990
Brunei Darussalam	1991
Democratic Republic of Timor-Leste	2002

Today there is a very high degree of interactions. In his study of China's regional bilateral diplomacy from 2013 to 2017, American scholar Eric Heginbotham found there are an average of 4.4 high-level (president, vice president, premier, state councilors, foreign minister) visits *per country per year*, with Indonesia, Cambodia, and Vietnam topping the list.[41] From 2003 to 2014 there were ninety-four Chinese leadership visits to ASEAN countries, sixty-two of which occurred between 2009 and 2014.[42] Every year, a number of Southeast Asian leaders are also invited to Beijing for lavish state visits. In 2017 every single Southeast Asian leader visited Beijing.[43] Before his fall from power in 2018, Malaysia's Najib Rizak was a frequent visitor (and recipient of Beijing's financial largesse). Singapore's Lee Hsien Loong also visits annually, and Cambodia's Hun Sen as well. Xi Jinping has also made concerted efforts to court Aung San Suu Kyi and Joko Widodo since they became Myanmar's and Indonesia's heads of state, respectively, and they too have realized the imperative of dealing with China. In Myanmar's case, one Yangon-based expert observed to me: "Aung San Suu Kyi has made her peace with China. She knows she cannot afford to alienate China. But she doesn't have any kind of China strategy or policy, and there are zero China experts in the government."[44]

The greatest diplomatic triumph for China, however, came with the much-ballyhooed visit by Philippines President Rodrigo Duterte to Beijing in November 2016, where he announced his country's "separation" from the United States and the beginning of a "special relationship" with China. Since then Duterte has made four more official visits to Beijing in the course of just three years—in search of Chinese investment, infrastructure, and commercial trade.

Bilateral meetings between President Xi Jinping or Premier Li Keqiang are also often piggybacked on to multilateral ASEAN gatherings. Seven ASEAN heads of state were among the 29 leaders and 1,500 delegates to participate in the Belt and Road Forum in Beijing in May 2017. The Chinese Communist Party's International Department also engages in exchanges with some ASEAN countries (notably, Laos, Malaysia, Myanmar, and Vietnam). China's Foreign Minister Wang Yi and State Councilor Yang Jiechi also regularly interact with their counterparts, usually in multilateral settings. In sum, there is a high tempo of bilateral diplomatic interactions between China and Southeast Asian states.

In more recent years, China has established a range of different types of partnerships with each country (Table 5.2). Half of these were upgraded and harmonized (in terms of language) during 2018.

Multilaterally, in 1996 China became a full and official "dialogue partner" of ASEAN, beginning a process of annual China-ASEAN summits. ASEAN's other official "dialogue partners" are Australia, Canada, the European Union, India, Japan, South Korea, New Zealand, Russia, and the United States—but in August 2019 at their annual ASEAN-China ministerial meeting in Bangkok, the

Table 5.2 China's Diplomatic Partnerships in Southeast Asia

Country	Type of Partnership	Year Established/Upgraded
Brunei Darussalam	Strategic Cooperative Partnership	2018
Cambodia	Comprehensive Strategic Cooperative Partnership	2018
Indonesia	Comprehensive Strategic Partnership	2013
Laos	Comprehensive Strategic Partnership of Cooperation	2018
Malaysia	Comprehensive Strategic Partnership	2013
Myanmar	Comprehensive Strategic Cooperative Partnership	2012
Philippines	Relationship of Comprehensive Strategic Cooperation	2018
Singapore	Comprehensive Cooperative Partnership Progressing with the Times	2015
Thailand	Comprehensive Strategic Cooperative Partnership	2012
Vietnam	Comprehensive Strategic Cooperative Partnership in the New Era	2018
ASEAN	Strategic Partnership for Peace and Prosperity	2003

ASEAN foreign ministers proclaimed China to be *the* "most important" of all of the association's dialogue partners.[45] Back at the seventh summit in October 2003, the two sides first established a "strategic partnership for peace and prosperity," which endures by this title to this day. In the same year China signed the ASEAN Treaty of Amity and Cooperation (TAC), becoming the first foreign country and ASEAN dialogue partner to do so. In 2008, China established a separate diplomatic mission to ASEAN and appointed its first ambassador to the organization. When I visited the mission in Jakarta in 2018 (Figure 5.1) Minister-Counselor Jiang Qin kindly provided a thorough briefing on China-ASEAN ties (Ambassador Huang Xilian was away), and she said that the mission is now staffed with twenty persons representing various Chinese ministries,

Figure 5.1 Author with Minister-Counselor Jiang Qin at China's Mission to ASEAN, Jakarta
Source: Author's photo

including the PLA.[46] This contrasts with the handful of officers in the US Mission to ASEAN, although when needed it can additionally call on staff in the US embassy to Indonesia, where it is physically located (the Chinese Mission to ASEAN has its own stand-alone offices separate from the Chinese Embassy in Jakarta). The disparity in staffing levels is indicative of the importance each government attaches to ASEAN.

Multilaterally, the China-ASEAN relationship is deeply institutionalized—on paper at least—including more than ten joint ministerial mechanisms and more than twenty senior official mechanisms, according to Minister Counselor Jiang. Dozens of Memoranda of Understanding (MoUs) and agreements have been signed over the years in a wide-ranging variety of fields—including public health, defense, transnational crime, nontraditional security, maritime emergencies, agriculture, information and communications technology, transport and civil aviation, tourism, sanitary and phytosanitary standards, science and technology, education, youth exchanges, cultural cooperation, environmental protection, disaster management, food safety and security, intellectual property protection, small and medium enterprise (SME) development, production capacity, media exchanges, and other fields.[47] Some of these areas of cooperation are bureaucratically backstopped by joint ministerial or director-general level committees, such as those noted in Table 5.3.

These areas of cooperation and interaction have been set out in two successive Plans of Action (PoA), running from 2011–2015 and 2016–2020. These are extremely detailed documents that evince the breadth, depth, and degree of institutionalization of China-ASEAN relations.[48] The 2016–2020 Plan contains no

Table 5.3 China-ASEAN Institutions and Mechanisms

ASEAN-China Summit

ASEAN Post-Ministerial Conference with China (PMC+1)

ASEAN-China Senior Officials Consultations

ASEAN-China Joint Cooperation Committee

ASEAN-China Free Trade Area Joint Committee

ASEAN-China Ministerial Dialogue on Law Enforcement and Security Cooperation

ASEAN-China Defense Ministers Informal Meeting

ASEAN-China Ministerial and Senior Officials Meeting on Transnational Crimes

ASEAN-China Joint Science & Technology Committee

ASEAN-China Science and Technology Partnership Program

ASEAN-China Environmental Cooperation Forum

ASEAN-China Business and Investment Summit

ASEAN-China Expo

ASEAN-China Cultural Forum

ASEAN-China Justice Forum

ASEAN-China Cyberspace Forum

ASEAN-China Business Council

ASEAN-China Youth Camp

ASEAN-China Ministerial Meeting on Youth

ASEAN-China Forum on Social Development and Poverty Reduction

ASEAN-China Transport Ministers Meeting

ASEAN-China IT and Telecommunications Ministers Meeting

ASEAN-China Health Ministers Meeting

ASEAN-China Senior Officials Meeting on Health Development

ASEAN-China Ministerial Meeting on Quality Supervision, Inspection, and Quarantine

ASEAN-China Connectivity Cooperation Committee

Table 5.3 *Continued*

ASEAN-China Police Academic Forum

ASEAN-China Agriculture Cooperation Forum

ASEAN-China Customs Coordinating Committee

ASEAN-China Prosecutors General Meeting

ASEAN-China Heads of Intellectual Property Offices Meeting

ASEAN-China Education Ministers Meeting

ASEAN-China Economic Ministers Meeting

ASEAN-China Ministers Responsible for Culture and Arts Meeting

ASEAN-China Cooperation Fund

ASEAN-China Public Health Cooperation Fund

ASEAN-China Fund on Investment Cooperation

Lancang-Mekong Cooperation Mechanism

Network of ASEAN-China Think Tanks

ASEAN-China Center

China-ASEAN Environmental Cooperation Center

ASEAN-China Friendship Organizations Meeting

Sources: Plan of Action to Implement the Joint Declaration on ASEAN-China Strategic Partnership for Peace and Prosperity (2016–2020); Ministry of Foreign Affairs of the People's Republic of China and the ASEAN-China Center, *1991–2016—25 Years of ASEAN China Dialogue and Cooperation: Facts and Figures* (Beijing: ASEAN-China Center, 2016); Ministry of Foreign Affairs of the People's Republic of China, *China's Foreign Affairs* (2015); Xu Bu and Yang Fan, "A New Journey for China-ASEAN Relations," *China International Studies* (January/February 2016): 64–78.

fewer than 210 initiatives.[49] The nineteenth ASEAN-China Summit in 2016 in Vientiane, Laos, commemorated the twenty-fifth anniversary of ASEAN-China dialogue relations and also offered an opportunity to produce a joint statement that took stock of the relationship and produced a long list of achievements and joint programs.[50] There has been a clear and apparent effort on China's part since 2016 to energize and upgrade its ties with ASEAN. Some of this new thrust may have been stimulated by the Obama pivot and renewed American attention to the region, but it more generally has grown out of the PRC's increased emphasis on "peripheral diplomacy" (周边外交) and availability of enormous funds to spend. Whatever the stimuli, there is now considerable momentum in China's diplomatic attention and diplomacy toward the region.

Recognizing this new momentum and the plethora of programs and mechanisms established, since ASEAN itself is much more of an association than an institution, it does not have very effective enforcement powers and thus its ability to implement these accords is actually limited by lack of resources (institutional, human, financial). Unlike the European Commission, the ASEAN Secretariat does not have a true mandate or large bureaucracy dedicated to implementing pan-regional policies and agreements—rather, implementation is often passed on to the member states for follow-through. When this occurs, it comes only with some ASEAN funding to help facilitate implementation—usually far from enough, and individual governments normally do not earmark funding for these ASEAN-wide programs themselves, and there are no real costs imposed for non-implementation. As a result, this is why ASEAN has earned a reputation as a "talk shop"—it is very good at convening (lengthy) meetings, adopting resolutions (if they can get to consensus—a big "if"), and concluding agreements with external states that are impressive on the surface but normally achieve only partial implementation.

Thus, when evaluating the broad-gauge and impressive list of mechanisms between ASEAN and China, observers should be sober about the reality of actual cooperation. Moreover, remember that ASEAN has struck these types of agreements with many countries around the world. It is simply impossible for the ASEAN Secretariat to maintain all of these exchanges in actual practice. When I visited ASEAN Secretariat headquarters in Jakarta in 2018 (Figure 5.2), the relative lack of capacity of the organization was readily apparent. As of August 2019, the ASEAN Secretariat had only 131 recruited staff representing each of ten ASEAN member countries, with an additional 237 locally recruited staff (Indonesian nationals).[51] The Secretariat's organizational structure is represented in Figure 5.3. The

Figure 5.2 The ASEAN Secretariat
Source: Author's photo

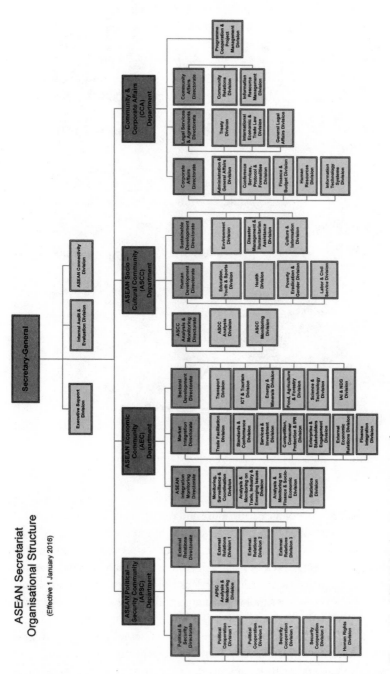

Figure 5.3 ASEAN Secretariat organizational structure

Source: https://asean.org/asean/asean-structure/organisational-structure-2/

Figure 5.4 Author with ASEAN Secretary-General Dato Lim Jock Hoi
Source: Author's photo

Secretariat itself is more of a clearinghouse and repository of information, and a convener of meetings among regional governments and external dialogue partners, but is not a supranational institution that coordinates and enforces policies and actions across its ten member states or in concert with non-ASEAN states. As the ASEAN Secretary-General Dato Lim Jock Hoi from Brunei (Figure 5.4) told me: "ASEAN will never be a supranational organization like the EU. It was never intended as such."[52]

Nonetheless, ASEAN is very good at generating a large number of meetings—something the Chinese also excel at—and these generate a large number of agreements and aspirational documents. I am by no means dismissing these as unimportant—but am simply trying to caution analysts and observers from overestimating this thicket of bureaucratic modalities and agreements. Similarly, the Chinese are very good at generating catchy phrases to depict relationships. An example is the "2 + 7 Initiative" that Premier Li Keqiang unveiled at the 2013 ASEAN-China summit in Bandar Seri Begawan, Brunei.[53] The first element had to do with "two fundamental principles": to "deepen strategic trust and good neighborly relations, and to focus on economic development and expand win-win results." Given these foundational principles, Li then recommended seven specific action items to implement in the coming years. These included signing a new China-ASEAN Treaty of Good Neighborliness and Cooperation; beginning an annual China-ASEAN defense ministers' meeting; upgrading the ASEAN-China Free Trade Agreement of 2010 and reaching $1 trillion in two-way trade by 2020; expediting development of infrastructure building; expanding financial cooperation including *renminbi* (RMB) currency swaps, trade invoicing, and banking services; building maritime cooperation in the South China Sea; and promoting cultural, scientific, and environmental cooperation.

The 2 + 7 initiative is a clear example of China being the proactive party in pushing forward relations with ASEAN. And, it must be recognized that seven years later all but the first action item (a new treaty) and the $1 trillion two-way trade target have been achieved. Not to be content with these rapid achievements, at the ASEAN+3 foreign ministers' meeting in 2015, China's Foreign Minister Wang Yi put forth a further ten-point proposal for taking the China-ASEAN relationship to the "next level."[54] Many of these suggestions were repackaged in the 2016–2020 Action Plan already noted.

From these examples, it is clear that Beijing is trying to drive the relationship with ASEAN. This produces a certain sense of being overwhelmed and "dialogue fatigue" among member states and certainly with the ASEAN Secretariat in Jakarta.[55] This is a refrain I often heard in discussions with individual governments throughout the region. One of the key challenges facing Beijing in the future, therefore, will be to more carefully calibrate these exchanges with ASEAN—as there is already a pervasive and growing sense of China's "over-whelming" nature. China's geographic proximity to Southeast Asia, the enormity of its governmental apparatus, its multitude of semi-governmental actors, and its unrelenting persistence can all turn out to be negatives that produce asymmetric dependencies and alienate Southeast Asians. China's attempts to "pull" the region within its grasp actually can have the exact opposite effect of "pushing" it away.

Chinese regional diplomacy also sometimes exhibits a distinct pushiness and demanding posture. A senior Thai official described it to me this way:

Thirty-five years ago when Chinese ministers came here, they were quite humble—nowadays it's no longer so. China now has power, and they are acting like it—they come here and tell us to do this and do that. The Chinese have a saying: "The sky is high and the emperor is far away." But the emperor is not so far away now. The emperor now has both the will and capability to enforce its desires.[56]

Bilahari Kaukisan, the former high-ranking Singaporean diplomat, further observes:

> Chinese diplomats also whine about ASEAN "bullying" China or "ganging up" against China. All ten members of ASEAN combined are smaller than China. This absurd complaint is, in effect, a threat. It sets up a false dilemma as if ASEAN'S only choice is to agree with China or be against China, with the obvious insinuation that this would be unwise.[57]

Perhaps the single most troubling diplomatic (and security) issue for Southeast Asians is the South China Sea (SCS) and China's land reclamation of submerged "features" into full-blown islands—and islands that are increasingly militarized. There are two main clusters of islands—the Paracels (西沙)in the north and the Spratlys (南沙) in the south. Through its expansive "Nine Dash Line" (which appears like a giant tongue; see Figure 5.5) China claims the *entirety* of the SCS based on what it asserts are "historical rights" and previous precedent of the Republic of China's assertion of these claims in 1947 (when it was an eleven-dash line).

China's assertions are contested by six other claimants: Brunei, Indonesia, Malaysia, the Philippines, Vietnam, and the Republic of China (Taiwan). In July 2016 an Arbitration Tribunal of the United Nations Law of the Sea in The Hague, Netherlands, ruled on the case brought by the Philippines that contested China's asserted claims. The Tribunal ruled unanimously that there was *no* legal basis for China's "historic rights" claims and nine-dash line. Faced with this unambiguous rebuff, the government of China refused to participate in the arbitration case and rejected outright its findings. Instead, Beijing issued its own White Paper reiterating its "unyielding position."[58] In addition to not recognizing other nations' competing claims, China's long-standing position has also been, contradictorily, that it is only willing to negotiate *directly* and *bilaterally* with the other contestants—and never in a multilateral setting or subjecting itself to any international mediation or imposed settlement. What China has been willing to do is to sign on to a Declaration of Conduct (DOC) in 2002, and more recently to enter into negotiations (near conclusion) on a revised and full Code of Conduct to govern states' behavior under conditions of contested claims. The operative clauses of the 2012 DOC were:

> Clause 4: The Parties concerned undertake to resolve their territorial and jurisdictional disputes by peaceful means, without resorting to the threat or use of force, through friendly consultations and negotiations by sovereign states directly concerned, in accordance with universally recognized principles of international law, including the 1982 Convention on the Law of the Sea.

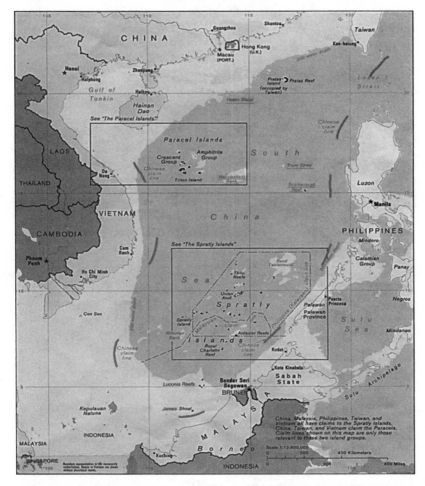

Figure 5.5   China's nine-dash-line claims in the South China Sea

Source: US Central Intelligence Agency, Asia Maps (1988), Courtesy of The University of Texas Perry-Castañeda Library

Clause 5: The Parties undertake to exercise self-restraint in the conduct of activities that would complicate or escalate disputes and affect peace and stability, including, among others, refraining from action of inhabiting on the presently uninhabited islands, reefs, shoals, cays, and other features and to handle their differences in a constructive manner.[59]

Of course, one major problem with this sensible declaration is that China has demonstrably violated Clause 5 by reclaiming seven submerged shoals ("land features") into full-blown islands, building structures and infrastructure on them, inhabiting them, and preparing them for an array of military equipment—from

Figure 5.6 A Chinese Island (Subi Reef) in the South China Sea
Source: Digital Globe via Getty Images

long-range radars to deep-water ports and submarine pens to 10,000-foot runways for bombers and fighters to land-based missile emplacements to housing for troops (see Figure 5.6). Beijing is also apparently making unreasonable demands of the other Southeast Asian states, which would, in effect, give China a veto over resource exploration or joint naval exercises with other countries (such as the United States). Thus there is still a fair amount of skepticism as to whether the revised Code of Conduct will be completed by its 2021 target date.[60]

To be sure, China is not the only claimant country to have inhabited or built military encampments on islands (Vietnam has, as well as Taiwan and the Philippines to a much lesser extent), but the PRC is the only one to have built artificial islands and militarized them to such an extent.[61] As a whole, China's claims and physical presence in the South China Sea are cancers on its overall image and relations with the region.[62]

People-to-People Exchanges

People-to-people exchanges between China and Southeast Asian societies have expanded rather dramatically in recent years. They are embodied in the Action Plan of China-ASEAN Cultural Cooperation (2014–2018) and include a variety of activities.[63] As part of its effort to get 250,000 Southeast Asian students studying Chinese, since 2009 China has sent more than 2,000 Chinese-language teachers and 15,319 volunteers to ASEAN countries, while the PRC's China International Educational Foundation (formerly the Hanban) has also established 33 Confucius Institutes and 35 Confucius Classrooms, and provided 6,210 scholarships.[64] The China Scholarship Council has also committed to providing more than 20,000 government scholarships for ASEAN students between 2018 and 2021.[65] In an attempt to project its soft power, China has also established a number of Chinese Cultural Centers across the region (Figure 5.7), as well as a dedicated ASEAN-China Center in Beijing (Figure 5.8).

Figure 5.7 China Cultural Center in Singapore
Source: Author's photo

Figure 5.8 ASEAN-China Center in Beijing
Source: Photo courtesy of John Holden

Tourism

Chinese tourism in Southeast Asia is booming and is an increasingly important source of revenue for regional economies,[66] growing fivefold over the past decade and now accounting for roughly one-fifth of all visitors to ASEAN.[67] No doubt that the coronavirus pandemic will impact the flow of tourists in the short-term, but long-term growth trends remain robust. Tourists from outside ASEAN totaled 62.91 million in 2015, of whom 18.59 million came from China.[68] By 2018, the number topped 20 million, according to China's Ambassador to ASEAN, thus becoming the largest source of tourism to ASEAN countries.[69] Ten million alone visited Thailand, four million visited Vietnam, three million visited Singapore, and two million each visited Indonesia and Malaysia in 2017, according to the McKinsey Global Institute.[70] This is not insignificant given the dependency of these countries on tourism as a source of income (for example, tourism accounts for 28 percent of Cambodia's GDP and more than 20 percent of Thailand's, according to *The Economist*).[71] McKinsey estimates that Chinese tourists spent on average per visit $3,000 in Singapore, $2,000 in Thailand, and $1,000 in Indonesia, Malaysia, and Vietnam.[72] In 2015, 630,300 Chinese tourists visited the Philippines and spent $19 million in total.[73] The number of

Figure 5.9 Young Chinese tourists at Marina Bay Sands in Singapore
Source: Image Professionals GmbH/Alamy Stock Photo

flights each week from China to Southeast Asia, especially on budget airlines, is skyrocketing—and some regional airports are struggling to keep up with the volume. The number of Chinese tourists from interior so-called tier-two cities is also rapidly growing.[74] Altogether there are 5,000 flights per week connecting Chinese and ASEAN cities.[75] Most come on group package tours, but wealthy and mobile "Chuppies" (Chinese yuppies) are traveling in small groups or individually (Fig. 5.9).

Chinese tourists are drawn to the region by a variety of attractions. Shopping opportunities may be at the top of the list, but Southeast Asia's relatively clean and less-populated beaches are also appealing. Direct flights connect multiple Chinese cities to Boracay and Cebu in the Philippines, Bali and Kuta in Indonesia, Langkawi in Malaysia, Phuket in Thailand, and other tropical destinations. Gambling is also a huge driver—especially to Cambodia, the Philippines, and Singapore. Chinese also have been buying property all across the region. Given the relatively inexpensive real estate, Thailand and the Philippines have become increasingly popular for Chinese who can afford it; Singapore, however, is too expensive for many Chinese to afford. Cheap currencies in several countries help to fuel the boom. And, of course, many Chinese like to visit relatives among the diaspora communities in Southeast Asia.

Educational Exchanges

China-ASEAN educational exchanges are also booming. As of 2016, they totaled approximately 205,338 (81,210 ASEAN students in Chinese universities and 124,178 Chinese in ASEAN higher education institutions), according to official Chinese figures.[76] An unknown number additionally study in high schools, notably in Singapore. The number of Southeast Asian students has now overtaken that of South Koreans as the largest on Chinese campuses. Table 5.4 provides the national breakdown of Southeast Asian students in China, with students from Thailand leading by a significant margin, followed by Indonesia, Vietnam, and Laos.

The two sides marked 2016 as the China-ASEAN Year of Educational Exchange. For Southeast Asian students, Chinese universities and vocational schools offer a higher quality of education than can often be found at home (except in Singapore), and the cost of education is very inexpensive as compared with Western universities. Moreover, the Chinese government provides scholarships for many. In 2016, the government allocated $3.6 billion in 50,400 full scholarships covering tuition, accommodation, and living expenses, according to Zhou Dong, chairman of the China University and College Admission System (CUCAS).[77] Southeast Asian graduate students can also often matriculate for their PhD degrees by only spending one year in residence in China and

Table 5.4 Southeast Asian Students in Chinese Universities (2016)

Country	Number
Brunei Darussalam	70
Cambodia	2,250
Indonesia	14,714
Laos	9,907
Malaysia	6,880
Myanmar	5,662
Philippines	3,061
Singapore	4,983
Thailand	23,044
Vietnam	10,639
Total	**81,210**

Source: Ministry of Foreign Affairs of the People's Republic of China, *China's Foreign Affairs 2017*.

then are permitted to return to their home country, including the submission of the dissertation.[78] Additionally, southern Chinese provinces—notably Fujian, Guangxi, and Yunnan—are providing their own separate sources of funding to Southeast Asian students.[79] ASEAN students studying in Guangxi alone totaled nearly 10,000 in 2017.[80] Another novel experiment is the branch campus of Xiamen University outside Kuala Lumpur, Malaysia—the first Chinese university to open a campus in the region.[81] Chinese educational administrators are hoping to produce Southeast Asian students who "know China and are friendly to China" (知华友华).[82]

In the other direction, there has been a particular surge of Chinese students into Thai universities of late.[83] In the 2017–2018 academic year, 8,455 Chinese students were enrolled in Thai universities—a doubling from the previous year.[84] Thai universities are cost-effective for Chinese students (tuition averages just $3,700), a range of degrees and majors are offered, and Chinese language is easily used.

Influence Activities

China also is involved in a multifaceted effort to shape perceptions throughout Southeast Asia. As it is doing across the world, China has embarked on a major effort to create a positive image of China, influence elites and publics in a pro-China direction, and undertake "external propaganda/publicity" (外宣) work.[85]

These efforts take a variety of forms. Some are legitimate, transparent, and normal public diplomacy. But others are covert, manipulative, and subversive. Much of the latter involves "united front work" (统战工作) that primarily targets the overseas ethnic Chinese communities. Some are in the gray zone between overt and covert—such as when PRC media reports are republished in Southeast Asian newspapers or social media (sometimes with attribution to Xinhua or other Chinese media, sometimes not). This is definitely the case in most Chinese-language media in Southeast Asia (Singapore's *Lianhe Zaobao* is an independent exception), as is the case in many other countries. In Australia, New Zealand, the United States, and Europe, the Chinese diaspora media are now almost entirely owned and controlled by PRC entities.[86] Chinese films and television series are gaining increased viewership across the region—particularly in Myanmar, the Philippines, Singapore, Thailand, Vietnam, and increasingly in Malaysia.[87] But the PRC's media penetration also reaches into English-language publications and social media, such as the *Vientiane Times* in Laos, *Khmer Times* and *Cambodia Daily* in Cambodia, *The Star* in Malaysia, *Khaosod English* in Thailand, and the *Manila Bulletin* in the Philippines, which all regularly run Xinhua articles and commentaries.[88] Actually, this is not that unusual in developing countries. Across Africa and increasingly in Latin America, Xinhua provides low-cost or free content to local media—which is an important financial consideration for cash-strapped multimedia in less developed countries.[89] In addition to Xinhua, the state news agency, other major Chinese media platforms also beam their transmissions directly to Southeast Asian (and other) audiences. The most notable of these at CGTN (China Global Television News) and China Radio International. In 2018 these two entities were amalgamated, along with CCTV-I (China Central Television International) and China National Radio into one mega state-run national media network called the Voice of China (since then Beijing has dropped the name, although the conglomerate continues).[90] CCTV, CGTN, and Xinhua also all provide free content (video, digital, and print) to Cambodian National Television and the Cambodian New Agency. This is also the case with Malaysian and Thai TV.[91]

While a considerable amount is now known about China's influence activities around the world and a significant number of studies have been published over the past few years,[92] surprisingly little is known about China's activities in Southeast Asia and virtually nothing has been published on the subject.[93] This is something of a mystery. It is certainly not because Chinese influence activities do not exist, yet not much is known about their covert or disguised activities (outside of regional intelligence agencies). What is occurring are activities run by the Chinese Communist Party's International Department (中共联络部 or CCP-ID),[94] the CCP United Front Work Department (中共统战部 or UFWD),[95] the Overseas Chinese Affairs Office of the State Council,[96] the Chinese People's Institute for Friendship with Foreign Countries (中国人民对外友好协会 or CPIFFC),[97] and the Chinese People's Institute of Foreign Affairs (中国外交学会 or CPIFA).[98] While there is information available in China about these organs, they are not well known in Southeast Asia.

The CCP-ID is the most active of these organizations and is a Central Committee–level department.[99] It carries out exchanges with a wide variety of political parties, parliamentarians, and retired politicians in all Southeast Asian countries. The vast majority are with Vietnam (as a fraternal communist party), but a review of their exchanges in 2018 and 2019 reveals a considerable number of exchanges with Thailand and Malaysia, followed by Indonesia.[100] A survey of the UFWD's website concerning overseas Chinese exchanges with Southeast Asia reveals a number of activities and delegations with Malaysia (the most), followed by Thailand, Indonesia, and the Philippines in 2018 and 2019.[101] CPIFFC exchanges with Southeast Asia are few—only receiving visitors from Laos, Myanmar, and Thailand in 2018 and 2019.[102] While CPIFA maintains exchanges with all parts of the globe, Southeast Asia does not seem to be a very high priority. During the period 2018–2019, for example, it received two former heads of state (Myanmar's U Thein Sein and the Philippines' Gloria Macapagal

Arroyo), met with the Singaporean ambassador in Beijing, and carried out three annual bilateral forums (the China-Singapore Forum, China-Philippines Roundtable, and Seminar on China-Malaysia Relations).

Since 2009, when the Ministry of Foreign Affairs established its Office of Public Diplomacy, the Chinese government has also begun to invest much more heavily in traditional public diplomacy (公共外交) programs. Taking a leaf out of the United States' public diplomacy playbook, the Chinese government brings significant numbers of influential "opinion shapers" and local officials to China on all-expenses-paid "soft power tours." When I visited Yangon, Myanmar, I was told that the PRC has made a significant effort in this regard, after the government there abruptly terminated the Myitsone dam project in 2011—which totally surprised the Chinese concerning the extent of local opposition to the project (although the dam was symptomatic of broader and deeper Burmese concerns about Chinese penetration of their country). Thereafter, the PRC began bringing "hundreds" of Burmese to China on these tours in an attempt to co-opt them.[103] Another source places the number between 1,000 and 2,000 since 2013.[104] The PRC also runs a series of training courses in China for regional journalists and other professions. China's 2014 Foreign Aid White Paper stated that from 2010 to 2012, China had trained over 5,000 officials and technicians.[105]

By far, the most systematic assessment of Chinese public diplomacy programs in Southeast Asia was a 2018 joint project of AidData (based at the College William and Mary in the United States), the China Power Project of the Center for Strategic and International Studies in Washington, and the Asia Society Policy Institute.[106] The report describes the "targets" of public diplomacy to include "public officials, civil society or private sector leaders, journalists, academics, students, and other relevant socio-economic or political sub-groups."[107] The study thus cast its net widely—to include China—sponsored cultural events, Confucius Institutes, Chinese Cultural Centers, training programs, media dissemination, political parties exchanges, military exchanges, sister city programs, professional and scholarly exchange programs, friendship associations, student educational exchanges, and economic assistance (including humanitarian aid, infrastructure, debt relief, and budget support)—and it found that the Chinese government is active in all of these domains. In terms of results, it found that Beijing's most effective tools are media penetration (especially among the Chinese diaspora), sister city and friendship association ties, Confucius Institutes, infrastructure building, development assistance and poverty alleviation projects, elite-to-elite exchanges, and professional training programs. In the case of Confucius Institutes, for example, as of 2018 there are sixteen in Thailand, seven in Indonesia, four in Malaysia, four in the Philippines, two in Cambodia, two in Laos, one in Singapore, and one in Vietnam.[108] China's national government agencies can be expected to continue to carry out, refine, and ramp up its public diplomacy efforts in all of these areas in Southeast Asia in the future. Chinese provincial organs—particularly in Fujian, Guangxi, and Yunnan—are also extremely active in their own exchanges with Southeast Asian countries.[109]

A more recent survey of China's reputation and influence in the region is the "State of Southeast Asia 2019" annual survey undertaken by the ISEAS–Yusof Ishak Institute in Singapore. When asked, "What country/regional organization has the most influence politically and strategically in Southeast Asia?," 45.2 percent replied that China did (United States came second at 30.5 percent).[110] Since ASEAN itself was included in the potential answer (20.8 percent), this is a little distorting. Nonetheless, China clearly is viewed as the most influential country in the region. When the same question was asked about economic influence, China scored even higher (73.3 percent). Yet China came dead *last* in "trust" rankings among Southeast Asians: Japan (65.9 percent), European Union (41.3 percent), United States (27.3 percent), India (21.7 percent), and China (19.6 percent). Conversely, in the "distrust" rankings, China came out on top (51.5 percent). So, clearly, influence and trust have an inverse correlation when it comes to China in Southeast Asia. The more China's presence and influence grows, the less it seemingly is trusted.

The reason that the ISEAS survey is so useful and important is because it covers all ten ASEAN societies. Other global polling normally only includes two or three ASEAN countries. Take, for example, the Pew Global Attitudes Survey. In 2018, in its global poll evaluating views of China, it only included Indonesia and the Philippines. In Pew's rather crude and oversimplified "favorability" ratings, an identical 53 percent viewed China favorably in each country.[111] Another Pew survey in 2017 polled Indonesia, Philippines, and Vietnam. When asked if they viewed China's rise as threatening, fully 80 percent of Vietnamese did, while 47 percent of Filipinos and 43 percent of Indonesians did.[112]

The Overseas Chinese Diaspora

A primary target of China's influence activities in Southeast Asia are the Chinese diaspora communities. For many years the PRC has done battle with Taiwan for the political loyalties of overseas Chinese, and since the 1980s Beijing has courted these communities for investments in China's modernization drive. In more recent years, Beijing has based its appeals on global Chinese patriotism, admiration of China's "great rejuvenation" (中国的大复兴), and Xi Jinping's "Chinese Dream" (中国梦). Xi Jinping also announced a new "Grand Overseas Compatriots" (大侨务) policy intended to integrate a variety of overseas Chinese initiatives.[113] He has also launched a new "three benefits" initiative: "to benefit China, to benefit host countries, and to benefit Chinese overseas."[114] The Chinese diaspora are, in particular, supposed to "act as a bridge to advance and implement China's signature Belt and Road initiative," according to the director of Peking University's Center for the Study of Chinese Overseas.[115]

Despite Beijing's outreach, ethnic Chinese have continued to live under suspicion in some Southeast Asia societies. By 2010 the number of overseas Chinese totaled 28.5 million.[116] Of this figure, the composition by country is reflected in Table 5.5. Chinese in Southeast Asia represent approximately 70 percent of the total in the world. And many are extremely wealthy. According to *Forbes*, in 2019 overseas Chinese in the region accounted for three-quarters of the $369 billion in billionaire wealth.[117] Overseas Chinese control a "bamboo network" of firms throughout the region.

Occasionally anti-Chinese violence flares up—as it did in Indonesia in 1998, 2015, and 2019; in Vietnam in 2014; and in Myanmar in 2015. While there have not been any public incidents of large-scale anti-Chinese riots in Malaysia since 1969, in 2015 there were two minor incidents that inflamed passions. Following these incidents, then Chinese Ambassador to Malaysia Huang Huikang gave a public speech, on the occasion of the annual September Moon Festival, in which he stated: "We will not stand idly by as others violate the national interests of China, or infringe upon the legal rights of Chinese citizens and companies."[118]

Table 5.5 Number of Overseas Chinese in Southeast Asia, 2010

Country	Overseas Chinese Population
Indonesia	8,011,000
Thailand	7,513,000
Malaysia	6,541,000
Singapore	2,808,000
Philippines	1,243,000
Myanmar	1,054,000
Vietnam	990,000
Laos	176,000
Cambodia	147,000
Brunei Darussalam	50,000
Total	**28,536,000**

Source: 2011 Statistical Yearbook of the Overseas Chinese Affairs Council, Republic of China (Taiwan), 11.

This speech attracted much attention in Malaysia, Singapore, and throughout Southeast Asia. But then, a week later, Ambassador Huang made an even more provocative statement in a speech to a Maritime Silk Road forum, in which he asserted: "I would like to stress once more, overseas *huaqiao* (华侨) and *huaren* (华人), no matter where you go, no matter how many generations you are, China is *forever* [emphasis added] your warm maternal home (娘家)."[119] This statement was widely interpreted in regional media as a significant qualification of China's Nationality Law and raised concerns that China was again asserting some kind of legal provenance over Chinese diaspora abroad. The Nationality Law of 1980 reaffirmed that China does not extend or recognize dual nationality (Article IV), while Article V categorically clarifies that "any person born abroad whose parents are Chinese nationals, or one of whose parents is a Chinese national, has Chinese nationality. But a person whose parents are Chinese nationals and have settled abroad, or one of the parents who is a Chinese national and settled abroad and has acquired foreign nationality on birth, does not have Chinese nationality."[120]

For those Chinese who have emigrated from the PRC to Southeast Asian societies, there can be significant problems of social adjustment and conflicted identities. One study focusing on recent arrivals in Singapore conducted by Liu Hong, a well-known professor and former Dean of the College of Humanities and Social Sciences at Nanyang Technological University in Singapore, found that the new immigrants still identify their patriotism much more with the PRC than with their new native countries, they tend to socialize together and not integrate into local diaspora communities, are not very cosmopolitan, and have a hard time adjusting to local customs, rules, and laws. Many also have difficulties adjusting to multicultural societies. On the other hand, Professor Liu's study found the opposite problem with long-resident overseas Chinese. Many had been "de-Sinified" (去中国化), having been away from mainland China for so long, and thus were in need of "re-Sinification" (再华化) in order to re-establish their "Chineseness" (华人性) and cultural connections to China.[121]

Thus, the overseas Chinese issue has remained a complex and sensitive one in many Southeast Asian countries since the establishment of the PRC. As one of the world's leading experts on overseas Chinese, Leo Suryadinata of the Institute of Southeast Asian Studies in Singapore, observed in his recent definitive study of the subject: "Beijing has attempted to blur the distinction between Chinese citizens and foreign citizens of Chinese descent, as reflected in various recent external and internal events involving the Chinese overseas. China has also begun to show its intention to protect not only Chinese nationals overseas, but also those Chinese overseas who have become foreign nationals. It seems that Beijing has forgotten its earlier policy of encouraging the Chinese overseas to integrate into local society and respect the rules and regulations of their adopted countries."[122]

The United Front Work Department (统战部) is clearly the most important institutional actor vis-à-vis overseas Chinese in Southeast Asia. Following a reorganization and bureaucratic upgrading of the department in 2018, the State Council's Overseas Chinese Affairs Commission (侨务委员会) was moved under the CCP UFWD, and a separate Overseas Chinese Affairs Bureau (the UFWD's ninth bureau) was established to coordinate work worldwide.[123] The China Council for the Promotion of Peaceful National Reunification, a united front organization that is under State Council auspices (rather than the UFWD),[124] is also an important player and has long had branches and affiliated organizations in several Southeast Asian countries (Cambodia, Indonesia, Laos, Malaysia, Philippines, Thailand).[125] In addition to carrying out activities in the region, the council also convenes a global conference that brings delegates from all over the world to Beijing (during which presumably they receive instructions for their annual work).[126] This meeting usually coincides with the annual united front Chinese People's Political Consultative Congress (CPPCC) every March.

In business circles, China also has established and operates Chinese Chambers of Commerce (CCOC or中国商会) in all ASEAN countries.[127] These are not merely targeted at overseas Chinese business circles, but toward the commercial sector in those countries more generally. The CCOC in Myanmar was established in 1996; Vietnam in 2001; Brunei, Indonesia, and Laos in 2005; Thailand in 2006; the Philippines in 2007; and Cambodia in 2009. The CCOC in Malaysia dates its origins to 1904 and the one in Singapore to 1970. These organizations undertake a wide range of national and community activities: trade and investment promotion, local philanthropy and charity work, government liaison, commemorative cultural events (e.g., Moon Festival, Lunar New Year), contributing to disaster relief, and staging exhibitions.[128]

Although generally dormant following the persecution of the Hoa population in Vietnam in the years 1975–1978, the sensitivities surrounding overseas Chinese have occasionally flared up in Indonesia, Malaysia, Myanmar, and Vietnam. Since China introduced its Patriotic Education Campaign in the early 1990s, this has been extended to overseas diaspora communities through the UFWD and Overseas Chinese Affairs Commission. The majority of Chinese-language newspapers and media abroad are now owned and controlled by united front affiliates. The increased penetration of overseas Chinese communities by the CCP united front organs (including appointing prominent members of overseas Chinese communities as deputies of the Chinese People's Political Consultative Congress) has raised concerns,[129] and is an increasing concern and priority for a number of intelligence agencies in the region.

Chinese citizens overseas have also become much more active in public demonstrations that promote the PRC and denounce groups that criticize China. Such demonstrations are often orchestrated and coordinated with local Chinese embassies or consulates. Chinese officials abroad have also become more assertive in speaking out. Thus, after many years of relative quiescence, it is apparent that China has again begun to be more proactive concerning overseas Chinese.

Commerce

Although traditional diplomacy and people-to-people exchanges are important elements in China's regional toolbox, trade and investment are far and away the most important. They dominate China's regional footprint in Southeast Asia and both dimensions are growing rapidly. Chinese companies are all over the region, with more than 6,500 registered in Singapore alone.[130] However, getting fully accurate and consistent statistics on China's regional trade, and particularly investment, is not easy.

China-ASEAN Trade

China has been ASEAN's largest trading partner since 2009, accounting for $587.87 billion in 2018 (excluding trade via Hong Kong), according to data from the China's Ministry of Commerce.[131] This represents a nearly 900 percent increase since 2001 (see Figure 5.10). China's trade with Cambodia, Laos,

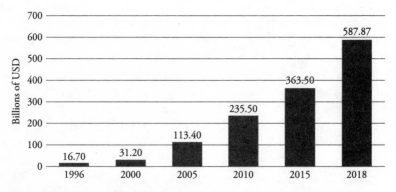

Figure 5.10 China-ASEAN trade, 1996–2018
Source: ASEAN Focus; ASEAN Secretariat

Myanmar, and Vietnam have grown the fastest: 24 percent, 37 percent, 33 percent, and 30 percent on average, from 2001 to 2014.[132] By mid-2019 ASEAN had, in fact, overtaken the United States as China's second largest trading partner.[133]

The trade relationship received a big boost in 2010, when the China–ASEAN Free Trade Area (CAFTA) came into effect. CAFTA includes a combined population of 1.9 billion and $4.5 trillion in trade volume. Under CAFTA, China and ASEAN agreed to zero tariffs on 90 percent of each other's goods. China and ASEAN "upgraded" CAFTA in 2018 and both sides set the goal of $1 trillion in total trade by 2020 (while having grown rapidly this was an overly ambitious target). By 2018, according to the CEIC database,[134] China's trade with countries in the region was: Vietnam ($106 bn.), Singapore ($100.2 bn.), Thailand ($80.2 bn.), Malaysia ($77.7 bn.), Indonesia ($72.6 bn.), the Philippines ($30 bn.), Myanmar ($11.7 bn.), Cambodia ($7.7 bn.), Laos ($3.47 bn.), and Brunei ($1.8 bn.).[135] However, among its ASEAN trading partners, in 2018 all countries except Laos and Singapore ran a trade deficit with China.[136] Collectively, ASEAN ran a $90.5 billion deficit in that year, with Vietnam, Thailand, and Indonesia being by far the largest.[137] The rate of growth of imports from China in Indonesia, Malaysia, the Philippines, and Thailand from 2013 to 2018 has been particularly dramatic (and their trade deficits have consequently ballooned).

Southeast Asian countries are also increasingly settling commercial transactions in Chinese *renminbi*. Currency exchange swaps are already in practice for the Indonesian rupiah, Malaysian ringgit, Philippines peso, Singaporean dollar, Thai baht, and Vietnamese dong—while China and ASEAN have agreed to moving further toward "de-dollarization" by expanding local currency settlement. Also, with the United States' withdrawal from TPP, ASEAN and China are pushing ahead with the Regional Comprehensive Economic Partnership (RCEP) initiative, essentially an Asian regionwide free trade area between the ten members of ASEAN and six other regional countries.

While the joint aspiration of achieving $1 trillion in China-ASEAN trade by 2020 fell short, there is no disputing the rapid and dramatic upward trajectory in two-way trade. And with trade comes interconnectivity (human and digital). The interconnectivity is further fueled by investment. China and ASEAN are quickly and increasingly becoming deeply integrated economically. This trend is only likely to grow and accelerate.

Chinese Investment in ASEAN

Chinese investment into ASEAN has also been spiking upward, reaching $13.7 billion in 2017 before sliding back to $10.1 billion in 2018 (see Figure 5.11).

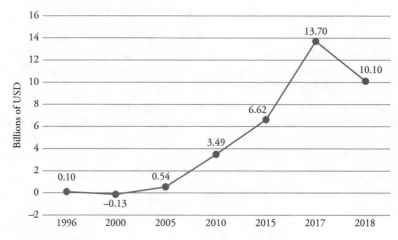

Figure 5.11 Chinese investment in ASEAN, 1996–2018
Source: ASEAN Focus; Financial Times

Establishing an accurate estimate for the total FDI stock of China in ASEAN is not easy, but by combining official Chinese and ASEAN statistical sources a reasonable estimate is $84.7 billion by the end of 2018.[138] While this overall cumulative total is not that much (especially when compared with that of the United States or EU), China's annualized FDI inflows to Southeast Asia have been trending upward in recent years. It more than quadrupled between 2010 and 2018. China is already the largest total foreign investor in Cambodia, Laos, and Myanmar.[139] In 2017, China accounted for 40 percent of Singapore's inbound FDI, 16 percent of Indonesia's, 14 percent of Malaysia's, and 30 percent of the other seven ASEAN members.[140] Over time from 2003 to 2014, according to one study, Singapore was the largest recipient of Chinese FDI (37 percent), followed by Indonesia (15 percent), Laos (10 percent), Thailand and Myanmar (9 percent), Cambodia (8 percent), Vietnam (5 percent), Malaysia (4 percent), Philippines (3 percent), and Brunei negligible.[141]

Despite the sharp increase of Chinese investment flowing into the region since 2010, this must be kept in comparative perspective. In 2017 a total of $154.7 billion was invested in the region from abroad according to ASEAN statistics.[142] The United States came first ($24.9 bn.), followed by Japan ($16.2 bn.), the European Union ($15 bn.), and China ($13.7 bn.).[143]

Chinese investment is expected to grow severalfold in coming years (DBS Bank in Singapore estimates it will reach $30 billion by 2030),[144] stimulated in particular by China's 21st Century Maritime Silk Road initiative (half of One Belt, One Road, a.k.a. the Belt and Road Initiative).[145]

The Belt and Road Initiative in Southeast Asia

The Maritime Silk Road is a sprawling set of projects spanning Southeast Asia to Southeastern Europe. In Southeast Asia, it includes a number of separate country "corridors" and economic cooperation zones—such as the Bangladesh-China-India-Myanmar Corridor, China-Indochina Peninsula Economic Corridor, Nanning-Singapore Economic Corridor, Guangxi Beibu-Brunei Economic Corridor, Pan-Beibu Gulf Economic Cooperation Zone, Lancang-Mekong Cooperation Zone, and China-Vietnam Two Corridor and One Circle Cooperation Zone. Some of the more important projects include:[146]

- an 1,800-kilometer highway from Kunming, the capital of Yunnan Province, to Bangkok;
- three separate high-speed rail lines from Kunming down into Myanmar, Vietnam, and Laos—the latter connecting to Thailand, Malaysia, and ultimately Singapore;
- a 150-kilometer high-speed rail line between Jakarta and Bandung in Indonesia;
- an East Coast Rail Link (ECRL) in Malaysia, with a cross-peninsula line connecting the Klang and Kuantan ports with points north along the east coast of the country up to the Thai border;
- major port building and upgrading at Klang, Kuantan, Kuala Linggi, Malacca, and Penang in Malaysia; Kyaukphyu and Maday Island in Myanmar; Tanjung Sauh, Jambi, and Kendal in Indonesia; Kompot and Sihanoukville in Cambodia; and Maura in Brunei;
- a 479-mile oil and gas pipeline from Yunnan through Myanmar to the Bay of Bengal;
- major bridge projects in Penang, Malaysia; southern Leyte to Surigao City, Luzon-Samar, and Panay-Guimaras-Negros in the Philippines; and across the Mekong River between Laos and Thailand;
- a new airport in Phnom Penh, Cambodia, and expansion of the airport in Luang Prabang, Laos;
- an expressway from Phnom Penh to Sihanoukville, Cambodia;
- metro expansion in Hanoi, Vietnam;
- four hydropower dams in Laos, two dams and two hydropower plants in Cambodia, one plant in Myanmar, two in Indonesia, and one in Vietnam.

These and many other projects are already underway, with more on the drawing board or in negotiation stage. In 2019, BRI projects and investments showed a sharp rise to $11 billion just in the first half of the year.[147] As of 2019, one report indicates that among BRI projects either "at the stage of planning, feasibility study, tender, or currently under construction," Indonesia currently leads the way ($93 bn.), followed by Vietnam ($70 bn.) and Malaysia ($34 bn.).[148] Let us examine one national case that illustrates both the extent and the problems with China's BRI initiative in Southeast Asia: Malaysia.

The Special Case of Malaysia

Overall, Malaysia has been a particular beneficiary of OBOR/BRI, with many major projects launched during the rule of Prime Minister Najib Razak (2009–2018). This included projects such as Melaka Gateway ($10 billion), Bandar Malaysia ($8 billion), Kuala Linggi International Port ($2.92 billion), Robotic Future City in Johor ($3.46 billion), Kuantan industrial park and port expansion ($900 million), Samalaju Industrial Park and Steel Complex ($3 billion), Penang waterfront land reclamation project ($540 million), Pahang Green Technology Park ($740 million), Forest City mixed-development project ($100 billion), and the East Coast Rail Link ($16 billion).[149] I discussed the Forest City and Melaka Gateway projects in the Preface.

Taken together the investment footprint in Malaysia is the largest of all BRI recipient countries in Southeast Asia. So sweeping is the footprint of BRI projects in the country, that one Malaysian academic I met with described his country as "ground zero for OBOR."[150] Another Malaysian Foreign Ministry official echoed this: "We are the indispensable country for BRI, and the Chinese know this."[151] Malaysia and China clearly had big plans for commercial cooperation. Between 2010 and 2016, China invested $35.6 billion in construction projects in Malaysia, according to the Malaysian Department of Statistics.[152]

Despite this optimistic overall atmosphere, several of the ambitious projects began to hit hurdles in 2017—both financial and political. In May of that year, Chinese funders withdrew their financing that was to cover 60 percent of the Bandar Malaysia project.[153] More significantly, a major perceptual shift was taking place across the country. Malaysians feared the country was being overrun by Chinese investment and that the terms of indebtedness and ceding of sovereign access to China would be far too great a burden for the country to bear.[154]

One notable Malaysian who shared and tapped into these sentiments was then ninety-two-year-old former Prime Minister Mahathir Mohamad—who decided to come out of retirement and challenge Najib in the 2018 elections. Najib's political party, the United Malays National Organization (UMNO), used to be Mahathir's too and it had *never* lost a national election. But Mahathir achieved the unthinkable and defeated Najib at the polls. His skepticism of China's financial footprint in the country was a key plank of his election platform. Chinese had been on a buying spree beyond BRI infrastructure, including huge rubber and palm oil

plantations, beachfront properties and hotels, and industrial parks—and it reso-
nated with the electorate.[155] In January 2017, in a public speech, Mahathir railed
against "foreigners being given large tracts of land to build property that will be
occupied by them.... Singapore was our territory, but not now. If we think a little
bit, this is happening again. Our heritage is being sold, our grandchildren won't
have anything in the future."[156] In 2019, Mahathir further reflected in an interview on American public television: "Everything was imported, mostly from
China—workers were from China, materials were from China, and payments
for the contracts were made in China. That means that Malaysia doesn't get any
benefit at all. The whole thing was done in a hurry by the previous government
without due regard for the interests of Malaysia."[157]

Najib was politically vulnerable not only over the Chinese investments in his
country, but also because of accusations of deep corruption involved with the
1MDB banking scandal—both factors contributed directly to his electoral defeat in 2018. Najib's dramatic downfall and Mahathir's unlikely return to power
opened the door to re-evaluate the broad swath of Chinese BRI projects in
Malaysia. Right after his surprise election victory, Mahathir moved swiftly to
freeze a number of China's BRI projects in the country. These included the $20
billion East Coast Rail Link,[158] the $16 billion high-speed rail link between Kuala
Lumpur and Singapore,[159] and two natural gas pipelines in Sabah state.[160] "We
don't think we need those two projects. We don't think they are viable. So if we
can, we would just like to drop the projects," Mahathir said at the time.[161] He also
estimated that Malaysia could cut almost one-fifth of its $250 billion national
debt by scrapping the projects.[162] Mahathir's new finance minister, Lim Guan
Eng, explained it in less pragmatic terms: "We don't want a situation like Sri Lanka
where they couldn't pay and the Chinese ended up taking over the project."[163]
Mahathir, in an interview with the *New York Times*, framed it in an even broader
and comparative historical context: "China knows very well that it had to deal
with unequal treaties in the past imposed upon China by Western powers. So,
China should be sympathetic towards us. They know we cannot afford this."[164]
Mahathir then went up to Beijing to explain his position about freezing the project pending renegotiation of the terms. By April 2019, after widely fluctuating
reports that the 648-kilometer East Coast Rail Link was on-again and off-again,
it was announced that China had agreed to reduce the cost of construction and
completion—from $15.81 billion down to $10.7 billion.[165] The project restarted
in July 2019. Some analysts see Beijing's willingness to renegotiate terms as an
indication of its flexibility and responsiveness to criticisms of its BRI "debt diplomacy."[166] Xi Jinping did indicate such flexibility in his comments to the Second
Belt and Road Forum in 2019.

Generally speaking, there has been much enthusiasm about China's BRI
throughout Southeast Asian governments and societies. This is reflected in the

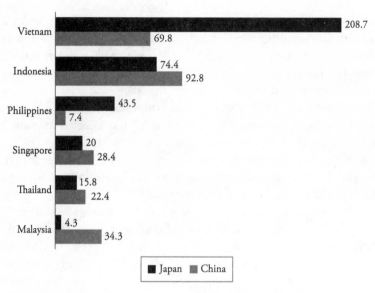

Figure 5.12 Japan vs. China infrastructure investments in Southeast Asia
Source: Fitch Solutions

fact that a quarter of the heads of state who attended the Second BRI Forum in Beijing in April 2019 hailed from Southeast Asia. There is certainly enormous need and appetite for infrastructure across the region. The Asian Development Bank in Manila has estimated that the region will require $1.7 trillion *per year* in infrastructure investment to 2030.[167] And China is by no means the only nation involved in building infrastructure in the region—in fact, Japan still outspends China ($367 bn. vs. $255 bn.).[168] The two nations' comparative spending is captured in Figure 5.12. As Thai scholar Pichamon Yeophantong notes, "Compared with Japanese-financed projects in the region that are popularly perceived as building—with superior skills and technology—vital connectivity infrastructure, Chinese projects are often viewed negatively as being of lower quality and geared towards exploiting the region's natural wealth to serve Chinese interests."[169]

While there has been a general welcoming of China's infrastructure investments, beginning in 2017 concerns have also arisen over the terms of financing and potential for excessive debt, the quality of the infrastructure, and the geopolitical implications of China's expanded reach into the region. Thus the region can be said to be not of one mind concerning BRI. One study divides ASEAN countries into three camps: "highly enthusiastic," "cautiously enthusiastic," and "cautiously supportive."[170] The first camp is composed of Brunei, Cambodia, Laos, and Thailand—they have been the greatest beneficiaries of BRI to date and have been the most publicly supportive. The second includes Malaysia, the Philippines, and

Singapore—each of which has its own domestic constraints that make them more ambivalent and guarded, although still supportive. The third is Myanmar and Vietnam—both of which have BRI projects but view the entire initiative primarily from a geostrategic perspective and are troubled by the implications on that basis. While this is an interesting division by two knowledgeable regional scholars, one should not consider the countries in each camp as fixed. Indeed, several are very fluid. It will be interesting to see if Malaysia's and Mahathir's standing up to—and renegotiating with—China on the terms of BRI projects will be something that other Southeast Asian (and other) countries do as well. Of course, China has a variety of economic projects in all other ASEAN countries. I have only used the example of Malaysia here—but offer a fuller accounting of each ASEAN country's economic engagement with China (and the United States) in the next chapter.

Security

The fourth and final dimension of China's policy toolbox vis-à-vis Southeast Asia is in the defense and security realm.[171] China is increasingly active in its military-to-military exchanges—but these come nowhere near the United States in terms of weapons sales, "after-sales service," officer training, joint exercises, intelligence collection and sharing, and military education programs.

China's weapons transfers/sales have been edging up in recent years, now accounting for 6.8 percent of global totals,[172] and ranking China the third largest weapons exporter in the world, following the United States and Russia. The quality of Chinese arms has improved considerably, and they are no longer mere Soviet/Russian knock-offs. Also, their prices are about 20 percent lower than those of Western nations (owing in part to state subsidies). Most Chinese transfers go to Pakistan (two-thirds of its arms exports), Bangladesh, and several African states. Recipients in Southeast Asia remain few—Cambodia, Myanmar, and Thailand primarily, with Malaysia and the Philippines becoming more recent markets. Transfers amounted to $2.1 billion in 2016, according to the authoritative Stockholm International Peace Research Institute.

Myanmar receives the lion's share, importing a range of equipment (frigates, armored personnel carriers, tanks, helicopters, jet trainers, trucks, and light arms). In 2017, Thailand ordered three 039A Yuan-class diesel-electric submarines, purchased forty-nine MBT-3000 tanks, and took delivery of twenty-eight VT4 tanks and thirty-four armored infantry fighting vehicles, and concluded an agreement for a joint weapons manufacturing facility to build and repair a range of conventional weapons for the Thai military.[173] Meanwhile, Malaysia has entered into a co-production agreement for four Littoral Mission Ships for the Royal Malaysian Navy, and discussions about a range of other equipment are ongoing.[174] Cambodia is virtually dependent on China's largesse for its nascent armed forces.[175] Indonesia has begun to buy some of its weapons from China—anti-ship missiles, precision-guided munitions (PGMs), portable surface-to-air missiles, radars, and Type 730 close-in weapon system for ships.[176] The Philippines has received light weapons from China, and in 2017 China provided the Philippines with a $14 million line of credit to purchase military equipment.[177]

In addition, China trains officers from these four countries at installations both in China and in-country. The Malaysian and Thai armed forces engage in annual military exercises. Malaysia and China are also said to have entered into a defense intelligence-sharing arrangement including secure communication links; Thailand is reported to have done the same.[178]

Most Southeast Asian militaries have regularized bilateral defense exchanges—what the Chinese refer to as "defense diplomacy" (军事外交)—with their counterparts from the PLA. These started at different times: with Thailand in 2001, the Philippines in 2005, Indonesia in 2006, Singapore in 2008, and Vietnam in 2010. It is unclear if Brunei, Cambodia, Laos, and Myanmar have such bilateral defense dialogues. Since 2002, China also interacts with Southeast Asian defense ministers at the annual Shangri-la Dialogue in Singapore, although the PLA has been distinctly wary of this meeting since its inauguration (only twice sending its defense minister). Beijing is much more comfortable with the ASEAN Defense Ministers Plus (ADMM+) multilateral mechanism, as well as its own annual Xiangshan Forum.[179] Beginning in 2015 they inaugurated an annual China-ASEAN Defense Ministers Special Meeting.[180] At the 2017 meeting, the two sides also agreed to the first-ever joint maritime exercise, to be held in 2018.[181] This took place off the southern Chinese coast in October 2018 with vessels from Brunei, the Philippines, Singapore, Thailand, and Vietnam participating (Cambodia, Indonesia, Malaysia, and Myanmar sent observers).[182] The second annual joint exercise occurred off of Qingdao in April 2019.[183] China, Laos, Myanmar, and Thailand have also engaged in joint patrols of the Mekong River since 2012.[184]

Other confidence-building measures—notably ship visits—and exchanges among different military services also occur with some frequency. Institutionalized bilateral exercises (primarily naval) occur every year with Cambodia, Laos, Indonesia, Malaysia, Singapore, and Thailand. Chinese writers say that the overall goal of these bilateral and multilateral defense diplomacy mechanisms is to build a "China-ASEAN Security Community" (中国-东盟安全共同体).[185] In 2017, China produced its first White Paper on Asia-Pacific Security Cooperation, in which Beijing laid out its vision for regional security. This included four main principles.[186] First, the future regional security framework should be "multi-layered, comprehensive, and diversified." Second, it should be adopted as a "common cause" by all countries in the region. Third, it should be based on consensus.

Fourth, it should be advanced in parallel with the development of a regional economic framework. Premier Li Keqiang echoed these themes, albeit with slightly different language in a 2016 speech at the ASEAN Secretariat in Jakarta, when he said: "We are ready to work with countries in the region to build an ASEAN-centered, open and inclusive security architecture in the Asia-Pacific on the basis of international laws and rules."[187]

Despite all of these activities, China's military relationships in Southeast Asia remain quite limited and rather shallow. With the exceptions of Cambodia and Myanmar, they come nowhere near the breadth and depth of the US military presence or assistance programs in the region.

Broadening and Deepening China's Footprint in Southeast Asia

Through these four dimensions of China's "toolbox"—diplomacy, people-to-people exchanges, commerce, and security—the PRC has established a broad and increasingly deep footprint across all of Southeast Asia. Yet the extent of Beijing's influence along these different dimensions is uneven—both by category and by countries. Clearly, China's economic/commercial impact is largest and growing rapidly. Societal-level people-to-people ties are the second largest element. Beijing's diplomacy is impressive on paper (as evident in the plethora of multilateral mechanisms identified in Table 5.3), yet discussions with Southeast Asian diplomats suggest that these are more pro forma than substantive. Bilaterally, China's diplomatic ties are generally good—but there are also frictions with many countries. In terms of military/security ties, China's position is not very deep at all (especially when contrasted with the United States).

But how is China actually viewed in the region? How are regional states adapting to its rapidly growing presence? And how are they navigating between, and managing, their relations with the United States and China respectively? We turn to these questions in the next chapter.

PART III
SOUTHEAST ASIAN ENCOUNTERS WITH AMERICA AND CHINA

6

Navigating between the Giants

ASEAN's Agency

"The US is a very important partner for ASEAN. We have good relations with the US."

—Dato' Lim Jock Hoi, Secretary General of
the ASEAN Secretariat[1]

"We have always attached high importance to ASEAN and ASEAN-China relations."

—Jiang Lin, Minister Counselor, Chinese Mission to ASEAN[2]

"ASEAN can no longer sit and watch extra-regional powers actively shape the future of the region."

—Rizal Sukma, senior Indonesian diplomat[3]

Having examined how China and the United States have approached Southeast Asia in the previous chapters, this chapter reverses the picture by examining how the ten Southeast Asian countries each try their best to navigate between the two big powers. In other words, the previous chapters viewed Southeast Asia from the "outside in" (from the perspectives of the two powers), while this chapter views America and China from the "inside out" (from the perspectives of regional states).

Not a single country in the region is entirely under either Chinese or American influence. Cambodia comes the closest, but it too maintains some modest defense and commercial ties with the United States and is beginning to chafe under Chinese dominance. Nonetheless, Cambodia should be considered a Chinese client state. Most Southeast Asian states "hedge" to some extent; they seek to maintain their independence and freedom of choices and action; most seek benefits from each while avoiding dependency; and all have to simultaneously navigate bilaterally with each power, trilaterally with both powers, and multilaterally with other significant regional powers (Australia, India, Japan, and South Korea) and within the framework of "ASEAN centrality."

Surprisingly, given the importance of China to Southeast Asia, there appears to be a parallel dearth of expertise on China in Southeast Asia. By far, the largest concentration of China expertise in the region is at the Vietnam Academy of Sciences Institute for China Studies.[4] The second largest and best concentration is the East Asia Institute at the National University of Singapore—which, despite its name, is devoted entirely to the study of contemporary China. EAI is of very high quality—yet the staff are almost entirely from mainland China. It was established originally in 1983 to study political economy, then philosophy, but in 1997 (under the new directorship of Wang Gungwu) it reoriented itself again—this time to be a China-related think tank for the Singaporean government. After that, there is a small Center for Chinese Studies in Jakarta, but it is not really an institution per se, as it mainly serves as a convening forum for local professionals interested in China. Surprisingly, Malaysia, Thailand, and the Philippines each have only a handful of contemporary China scholars, but no centers for Chinese studies. Also surprising is that the leading institute on the region, the ISEAS–Yusof Ishak Institute in Singapore, has no section or researchers specifically dedicated to studying China's roles in the region.

Given this context, among the ten states I find one notable overarching characteristic: *pervasive ambivalence*. That is, all ten countries exhibit ambivalence about *both* powers—not fully trusting either.

China's Growing Presence and Southeast Asian Ambivalence

While China's expanding footprint in the region seemingly has an inexorable momentum that binds China and Southeast Asian societies increasingly together, and there has been an evident regionwide trend toward "bandwagoning" and aligning with China, it simultaneously has a downside for many Southeast Asians: China is *too close* and *too omnipresent*. Whereas the United States has the opposite problem—the so-called tyranny of distance and the perception of episodic engagement—China's sheer size and proximity are overwhelming to many Southeast Asians.

China's contemporary relationships in Southeast Asia are also deeply framed by history (as discussed in the previous chapters). The legacy of China's "tribute system" lurks in the minds of many Southeast Asians,[5] as well as mainland Chinese, and this is reinforced by China's close geographic proximity. Recall from chapter 4 that the tribute system was hierarchical, essentially peaceful and noncoercive, highly ritualistic, deferential, involved trade in goods, had both continental and maritime linkages, and was filled with symbols of China's supposed cultural superiority. Some observers in the region see signs that Beijing is trying to re-create at least the practices of the ancient tribute system—a kind of Asian "Finlandization." But this is the twenty-first century—not the Ming dynasty. The problem for China is that, today, most countries in the region do not wish to slide back into such a dependent and subservient relationship. As retired senior Singaporean diplomat Bilahari Kausikan poignantly observes, "In East Asia, the assumption of Chinese centrality and superiority is particularly difficult to accept because it seems to encompass a strong element of revanchism."[6] Southeast Asia's reluctance to acquiesce to Beijing's revived tributary approach takes a variety of forms, but deference is one key element. As Kausikan describes it:[7]

> China does not merely want consideration of its interests—it expects deference to its interests to be internalized by ASEAN members as a mode of thought. It wants the relationship to be defined not just by a calculation of ASEAN interests vis-à-vis China, but "correct thinking" which leads to "correct behavior." ... The very triviality of the behavior China sometimes tries to impose underscores the cast of mind it seeks to embed in ASEAN through its almost Pavlovian process of conditioning. It does not always work. It can be counterproductive. But it works often enough and well enough with enough ASEAN members for China to persist.

Although they may not know or like it, ASEAN states are already conditioned not to criticize China publicly or directly. Thus, a deafening silence can be heard throughout the region when China says or does something that Southeast Asians do not like; much hand-wringing and complaining takes place privately, but Beijing has so successfully co-opted and intimidated the ASEAN states that they quickly and quietly yield. It is a form of "veto power." This reluctance is particularly evident in the realm of diplomacy, where statements and communiqués issued at ASEAN meetings are regularly devoid of any mention of China, particularly its island-building and militarization in the South China Sea. In 2012, China succeeded in blocking a joint ASEAN statement for the first time ever when the grouping met for its annual summit in Phnom Penh. China almost succeeded again during the 2017 summit in Manila, before a bland pro forma statement was issued several days after the meeting adjourned.

Despite this diplomatic kowtowing to Beijing, and the realities of increasingly thick economic and cultural ties, under the surface many Southeast Asians remain deeply ambivalent about their countries' increasing coziness with—and deference to—China. The 2020 coronavirus pandemic crisis has also contributed to the region's ambivalence about Beijing, with mainland Southeast Asian countries generally being more positive than maritime countries about Beijing's role during and after the initial outbreak.[8] Southeast Asian governments have also shown a distinct coolness toward Xi Jinping's concept of an "ASEAN-China Community of Common Destiny."[9] Moreover, many still clearly recall Beijing's "year of assertiveness" from 2009 to 2010 when Beijing bullied a number of China's neighbors, and the older generation remember China's decades of support for regional communist insurgencies and support for ethnic Chinese as a subversive "fifth column" when the PRC attempted to subvert many regional governments (as discussed in chapter 4). But, as leading Thai scholar Thitinan Pongsudhirak of Chulalongkorn University points out, "On its own, no Southeast Asian state can afford to stand up to China."[10]

There is also growing concern throughout Southeast Asia about China's real estate acquisitions, the financial terms of Belt and Road infrastructure projects, and the growing indebtedness that some countries face. China's stepped-up united front operations are also a growing concern. So are the influx of organized crime triads, smuggling operations (drugs and human trafficking), and money laundering. For downstream Mekong countries, China's upstream damming has become a major problem. China's island-building and militarized fortifications in the South China Sea, as well as China's dramatically increased naval presence in the region, also generate deep anxieties throughout the region.

In China, though, there is little official recognition or nervousness about Southeast Asians' concerns. Chinese officials, think tanks, and media all remain on message about "good neighborliness" and "win-win cooperation." As President Xi Jinping put it in a speech in Singapore during his 2015 tour of the region: "Together we can achieve open, inclusive, and win-win cooperation among neighbors that is based on mutual respect and mutual trust, expanding common ground and narrowing differences."[11] Xu Bu, China's former ambassador to ASEAN, similarly asserted: "Through the past 25 years of continued dialogue and deepening reform, China and ASEAN have built solid foundations for political mutual trust. China, as always, upholds the neighborhood diplomacy principles of amity, security and prosperity. The ASEAN countries follow the one-China policy, support China's peaceful reunification, and accommodate China's concerns on major issues of principle involving China's sovereignty."[12] These kinds of diplomatic statements are regular and ritualistic. One rarely, although occasionally, finds awareness of Southeast Asian suspicions of China and their hedging strategies in Chinese analyses.[13]

Thus, despite the intensity and density of China's diplomatic outreach in Southeast Asia, Beijing's behavior displays distinct vulnerabilities that may compromise its relationships in the region over time.[14] As Australian National University scholar and Southeast Asia expert Evelyn Goh notes: "Chinese policymakers and analysts seem to have two blind spots in their relations with small developing neighbors. The first is a tendency to downplay the autonomous agency of these weaker states, preferring to attribute their lack of acquiescence to the machinations of other great powers. The second is to overlook the connection between China's more benign modes of influence and the undermining effect of its, at times, inconsistent or coercive behavior on the very same issues."[15] The telling indicator will be whether Beijing senses these behavioral vulnerabilities and recalibrates its diplomacy to be less pushy and more respectful of Southeast Asian sensitivities. Real listening, taking criticism constructively, and recalibrating its diplomatic practices accordingly are not necessarily characteristics that China is known for. Big powers get criticized—it is part and parcel of being a power. But mature powers listen to, reflect on, accept criticisms, and adjust their policies and behavior accordingly. China's party-state still has a long way to go in this regard—unless and until Beijing begins to demonstrate such a capacity, it will find that others will treat its pronouncements and behavior with skepticism.

Sources of Southeast Asian Ambivalence about the United States

Similarly, pervasive ambivalence exists about the United States. There are a number of reasons and causes why Southeast Asians have mixed feelings about, or distrust of, the United States.

Many see the United States as just another Caucasian imperialist power, reminding them of their colonial pasts. As Southeast Asians have profoundly defined their contemporary identities in terms of rejecting their colonial pasts, and the legacies of the European powers, it does not matter much to them that the United States played a relatively minor role in the region during the colonial era (the Philippines being the major exception, of course). Nor does it matter that Washington touted an "open door" egalitarian trade policy under Presidents William McKinley and Theodore Roosevelt—or that President Franklin Delano Roosevelt sought decolonization and tried (before his death) to keep the European colonial powers from repossessing their colonies following the defeat of Japan in the Second World War. While Americans are credited by some Western historians with practicing progressive policies in East and Southeast Asia, the United States is generally not viewed this way in the region—where it is frequently lumped together with the European imperialist powers.

A second related reason is that the United States was not supportive of—indeed was very suspicious of—Southeast Asian attempts at neutralism and nonalignment during the 1950s and 1960s. My university colleague and historian Gregg Brazinsky's excellent study *Winning the Third World* is replete with countless examples of American policymakers in Washington and diplomats in the region who sought to undermine national and regional efforts to gain autonomy during the early Cold War years.[16]

The third, and again related, reason was America's lengthy war in Vietnam. This bitter and costly conflagration brought catastrophe to the peoples of Vietnam, Cambodia, and Laos, and it polarized the region. For a region with common colonial histories that were trying to find some unity and forge a "third way" between the contending powers of the Cold War, the American war in Vietnam was profoundly destabilizing. The United States may have thought itself to be a progressive force for good and bulwark against communist aggression, but that is not the way many in the region viewed Washington's war.

Then, with the end of the war, another new form of American intervention appeared during the Carter (and later Clinton) administration: promotion of democracy and human rights. There was not a single democracy in the region in the 1970s; indeed, many countries were ruled by a combination of highly corrupt despots and praetorian militaries. President Carter was more of a promoter of basic human rights, while President Clinton was more an advocate of democratic expansion (and implicitly the toppling of autocratic regimes)—but in both cases the region found Washington's proselytizing to be offensive, arrogant, and unwelcome.

With the end of the Cold War, a fifth American tendency became apparent: blunting China's rising influence in the region—at a time when most Southeast Asians saw opportunity and generally welcomed expanded ties with China (particularly following the 1997 Asian Financial Crisis).[17] While Washington sought to work with China in some Southeast Asian contexts, it was increasingly the case after 1989 that Beijing's growing roles in the region were not necessarily in America's best interests—indeed were counterproductive. As the twenty-first century dawned, this viewpoint became even more pronounced in Washington. As a result, Southeast Asian regional states became increasingly caught in the growing competition for regional influence between the two powers. As this book argues, that trend has sharply accelerated and intensified in recent years. For Southeast Asians, the efforts to counter China smack of their earlier experiences of manipulation at the hands of external powers.

Throughout all five of these phases, except during the Vietnam War, one overarching characteristic always defined Washington's approach to—and hence reception in—the region: its distracted and episodic attention. With the exception of the Obama administration, this tendency has been consistent over time. Joseph Chinyong Liow captures and elucidates this perfectly in his careful study *Ambivalent Engagement*.[18] For all of these reasons, Southeast Asians rightfully hold ambivalent views of the United States. This is one thing that the United States and China share in common in the region.

With this backdrop, let us now proceed in the remainder of this chapter to "look from the inside out" and survey each of ASEAN's ten member states' attempts to navigate between the two major powers. As noted, no nation in Southeast Asia has found a "sweet spot" of establishing an equidistant position between Beijing and Washington, as all manage to "tilt" more toward one or the other. This said, as noted in chapter 1, there *has been* a noticeable qualitative shift *toward China* on the part of the majority of Southeast Asian states in recent years. Let us now explore how Southeast Asians navigate the divide, trying to maximize the benefits of relations with both powers, while doing their best to maintain their independence and autonomy.

Thailand

No country may be more important in the US-China contest in Southeast Asia as Thailand. Given its size and strategic location, its large population (70 million), its GDP ($529 billion), and its founding role and active position within ASEAN, Thailand is one of the most significant countries and actors in Southeast Asia. Its location—straddling the Gulf of Thailand and South China Sea to the south, the Andaman Sea and Indian Ocean to the west, and just north of the Malacca Straits—makes Thailand strategically important. Successive Thai governments have also demonstrated long-standing diplomatic independence, befitting of the only Southeast Asian nation never to be colonized, and Bangkok has pursued an activist foreign policy in the region and beyond.[19] Bangkok is the master of hedging and omnidirectional foreign policy, flexibly maneuvering constantly. It has been observed that, "Like Schrödinger's cat in quantum mechanics, both dead and alive, Thailand views great powers as simultaneously threats and allies."[20] Its monarchy has provided political continuity and national pride, even if Thailand's fractious political parties and interventionist military have proven to be very disruptive.

Thailand has had official ties with the United States dating to 1818, forged its first bilateral treaty in 1833, and has had a mutual security treaty since 1954 (reaffirmed by the 2012 Joint Vision Statement on the Thai-US Defense Alliance). Thailand's ties to China are even more long-standing, as we saw in chapter 4, although not nearly as close as with other Southeast Asian countries that border the South China Sea. While it is true that Thailand is not as large or important overall in Southeast Asia as Indonesia or Vietnam, it is *the* most important "swing state" in the US-China strategic contest in the region. While Thailand has long been an American ally and has leaned toward the United States (given Thailand's strong independent streak), Bangkok has been noticeably swinging toward Beijing in recent years. This tendency was apparent prior to 2014, but since the military *coup d'état* of that year and Washington's punishment of the praetorian junta that seized power, Bangkok's gravitation toward China has been more and more apparent. Should the United States "lose" Thailand in this contest, it would be a devastating blow to America's strategic position in the region— even more so, I would argue, than if its other ally, the Philippines were to fully swing into China's orbit.

Thailand's Approach to the United States

It may already be too late for the United States. Many close observers already perceive that Thailand now leans much more closely toward Beijing than Washington.[21] If there is debate on this question it is *when* rather than *whether* this shift occurred. Some date it to the end of the Vietnam War, when the US military bases in Thailand were no longer in as high demand. Yet, Vietnam's 1978 invasion of Cambodia and de facto annexation of Laos was a genuine threat to Thai national security and sovereignty, which held the strategic bond between Washington and Bangkok together through the 1990s. However, the attempted Vietnamese takeover of Indochina also brought Beijing and Bangkok together for the first time (and began tangible military material support). The tepid US support for Thailand's economy during the traumatic 1997 Asian financial crisis was a turning point, though—especially as Beijing came to the financial rescue of Thailand (and Indonesia) with "no strings attached." The post-2001 US "war on terror" revealed Thai ambivalence about helping the Bush 43 administration. On the one hand, Bangkok acquiesced to allowing the CIA to set up secret "black site" prisons for the detention and interrogation (and torture of) captured al-Qaeda terrorists captured in Afghanistan, Pakistan, and elsewhere. On the other hand, Bangkok did not accept US requests for the use of several military bases (including Utapao) for its military operations in Afghanistan and Iraq.[22] This ambivalence was reflected in a telling interview that I had with a former staff member of Thailand's National Security Council. In the immediate aftermath of 9/11, the Thai prime minister wondered whether the "alliance" with the United States contained an "Article V" clause such as with NATO and some other US bilateral alliances (whereby the alliance partner is obligated to come to the reciprocal defense of the United States). The NSC staff carefully read all related documentation and found no such obligation or mandate—to the apparent great relief of Prime Minister Thaksin Shinawatra.[23]

The US-Thailand "alliance" may not really be an alliance per se. It is the by-product of the 1954 Manila Pact and the 1962 Thanat-Rusk communiqué. The former was the underpinning of the Southeast Asia Treaty Organization (SEATO, which became defunct in 1977), but its Article IV *did* include a mutual security clause: "This treaty provides that, in the event of armed attack in the treaty area" each member would "act to meet the common danger in accordance with its constitutional processes."[24] But since the dissolution of SEATO, the Thai have taken a very "elastic" view of the defunct treaty and its obligations. The aforementioned former Thai national security official describes Bangkok's approach this way: "The Thais see the US alliance as symbolic of friendship—there is no sense of formal obligation. They see the alliance as a form of prestige and don't think of it as a military pact."[25] Thai scholar Pongphisoot Busbarat similarly writes, "Alliances, such as the one Thailand has with the United States, are simply a formalized form of alignment."[26] Even some American observers admit, "The alliance has struggled to find a clear direction for over forty years."[27] Moreover, there is no joint command or integration of armed forces—such as exists in America's alliances with Australia, Japan, and South Korea—although there is joint training and arms transfers (consistent with Thailand's designation as a "major non-NATO ally").

Despite these characteristics, the US-Thai alliance has endured over many decades and has been relatively durable. It has had to be—because it has been frequently rocked by Thai military coups, which have resulted in reciprocal retaliation from Washington. The most common—and indeed first—form of retaliation is to suspend or cut off military assistance. The most recent case was the 2014 coup, Thailand's twelfth since 1932, after which Washington immediately suspended $3.5 million in Foreign Military Sales (FMS) plus $85,000 in IMET training funds.[28] This was mandated by US law. The annual Cobra Gold joint exercises were also substantially scaled down, although not terminated. When I visited the US Embassy in Bangkok in 2017, I was flatly told by the Deputy Chief of Mission: "The last two years have been the lowest point *ever* in the Thai-US relationship."[29] Although the military dimension of the relationship was scaled down substantially and bilateral diplomatic ties were strained, the massive US embassy complex and personnel in Bangkok remain the largest in the region, as it serves as regional headquarters for a variety of US government agencies.

But with a change in government in Washington in 2017, the Trump administration moved to repair ties. Prime Minister Prayut (the general who seized power in the coup) was invited to and fêted at the White House on October 2, 2017. President Trump indulged his authoritarian impulses by congratulating Prayut for "restoring political stability" in the wake of the 2014 coup.[30] This visit went a long way toward repairing and restoring ties. The two sides signed an MoU on cross-investment, while Prime Minister Prayut agreed to purchase 20 Boeing aircraft, 150,000 tons of coal, and an arms package that included helicopters, missiles, and F-16 upgrades.[31] Subsequently, Cobra Gold also ramped up again (6,800 US military personnel participated in 2018, a doubling over the previous year). In 2018, Thai Deputy Army Chief-of-Staff Apirat visited Washington and signed a weapons deal worth $261 million.[32] The Trump administration also "removed the human rights factor" from strained ties as well, according to a close observer in Bangkok.[33] Longtime and astute Thai journalist Kavi Chongkittavorn succinctly observed: "After hitting an all-time low in the 200 year history of Thai-U.S. relations. . . . After Prayut's visit, Thailand-US cooperation intensified at full-throttle."[34] Defense Secretary Mark Esper met his Thai counterpart and signed a "US-Thailand Joint Vision Statement" in November 2019. Two-way trade is now over $40 billion. Leading Thai imports from the United States include machinery, aircraft, gold, optical and medical goods, and agricultural products.[35] The United States is also one of the largest investors in Thailand, with a cumulative $11 billion invested as of 2015. According to the State Department, "the United States' partnership with Thailand spans the areas of public health, trade, science and technology, wildlife trafficking, education, cultural exchanges, law enforcement, and security cooperation."[36] The positive role played by American commandos, working together with their Thai counterparts (who had been trained by the United States), in rescuing the twelve stranded boys of a Thai soccer team from an underground cave in July 2018 also went far to repairing the image of the United States with the Thai public. American "soft power" and popular culture also remains very prevalent in Thailand. At the same time, one author notes the Thai saying "Amerika Maha Mit" or "America the Great Friend," and the fact that "many Thai public servants, both civilian and military, received their training and education in American educational institutions, creating a large cadre of American-oriented Thais that [have] provided support for the re-lationship."[37] With these steps forward, very strained bilateral ties have begun to be repaired to some extent.

Nonetheless, while welcome, this restoration of Thai-US ties should not be overstated. There remains a brittleness and fragility to the relationship among the Thai elite. As a Thai scholar puts it: "Thai elites interpreted America's un-willingness to tolerate the military coups as a sign that Washington does not value the friendship, minimizing Thailand's trust in the United States."[38] Another Thai academic echoed this sentiment and criticized the Trump administration for indulging the Prayut regime with a White House visit.[39] When Washington punishes Bangkok following military coups, it grates on the Thai military and strains their allegiances toward the United States. As one Thai army officer put it, "We bled with you on the battlefields of Korea, in Laos, in Vietnam, and in the war on terror. But when we needed your understanding during a deteriorating security situation, you didn't treat us as your friend and ally: you constantly scolded and humiliated us!"[40] As a result, one close analyst of the relationship observed: "Despite the contradictions in the relationship, it still serves the po-litical interests of both Washington and Bangkok to avoid a public and messy divorce . . . but Thailand is clearly hedging by doing the barest minimum to keep the alliance alive."[41]

Thailand's Cozy Relationship with China

This kind of sentiment plays directly into the other side of Thailand's conflicted external relationships—with China. Thailand's relations with China have steadily grown since the 1980s and, as such, Beijing has become more and more central to

Bangkok's calculations. As Southeast Asian expert Ian Storey of the ISEAS–Yusof Ishak Institute in Singapore put it: "China has clearly emerged as Thailand's preferred major power partner since the May 2014 coup."[42] Benjamin Zawacki, a resident of Bangkok and author of a significant study of Thailand's relations with the United States and China,[43] goes so far as to say, "Since 2014 Thailand has engaged China to a greater extent than *any* other nation."[44]

However, Thailand's increasing orientation toward China is not simply recent, tactical, or expedient—as the relationship has grown deep roots over several decades and there is genuine closeness in the way that most Thais feel about China. Thailand is home to one of the largest overseas Chinese communities in the world (8 million), which account for 14 percent of the entire Thai population.[45] Ethnic Chinese have extensively intermarried and intermingled in Thai society and now occupy the upper echelons of Thai society, business, government, and increasingly the military. Even Thailand's royal family has some Chinese ancestry. Thai royal Princess Sirindhorn speaks fairly fluent Chinese, practices calligraphy, and was awarded China's honorary Friendship Medal (the highest honor given to foreigners) by President Xi Jinping at a ceremony in Beijing's Great Hall of the People in October 2019. This fraternal closeness is sometimes referred to as *Zhong-Tai yijiaqin* (one big Chinese-Thai family). Thailand's ethnic Chinese community is Southeast Asia's best example of successful assimilation—a not insignificant accomplishment given the difficulties that ethnic Chinese have encountered in many other societies. In addition, an estimated 400,000 mainland Chinese have moved to Thailand, while 8.8 million Chinese tourists visited in 2016.[46]

China is also increasingly important to the Thai economy—becoming Thailand's leading trading partner in 2013 with two-way trade totaling $75.7 billion in 2018. China accounts for about 20 percent of Thailand's foreign trade. Chinese companies, such as Haier and SAIC Motor, have established large factories in Thailand. Many of Thailand's largest companies are owned by overseas Chinese Thai citizens who maintain close business links with the PRC. One prominent example is Charoen Pokphand (CP) Group, the country's preeminent conglomerate with annual revenues of $68 billion (according to *The Economist*).[47] People-to-people exchanges are also extensive: Thailand sends more than twice as many students to study in China than any other Southeast Asian country (23,000), while 10 million Chinese tourists visited Thailand in 2018 for the first time.[48] Chinese are also buying up a lot of property in Thailand, mainly in the country's famous beach resorts. China has also established thirty-five Confucius Institutes and Confucius Classrooms in Thailand (more than in any other Southeast Asian country). Thailand is home to Huawei's 5G regional data center, and the Chinese company dominates the telecom industry in Thailand (and throughout Southeast Asia). The intensity of Chinese-Thai diplomatic interactions are also "frequent" in the words of China's Foreign Ministry,[49] while military-to-military relations have been steadily building. Geographic proximity is also an important magnetic factor drawing the two societies together. But, from Bangkok's perspective, China's real appeal has been a combination of complementarities and Beijing's consistent support over time. As Thai scholar Pongphisoot Busbarat has noted: "Beijing is viewed as increasingly appealing for two reasons. First, its economic and military resources can meet Thailand's needs. Second, China shares a closer cultural affinity and shows greater understanding and acceptance of changes in Thailand."[50]

Bangkok has been responsive to Beijing diplomatically. For example, when China requested that ethnic Uighurs who had fled Xinjiang in western China and taken refuge in Thailand be rounded up and deported back to China, Bangkok complied. Over 350 were detained, placed in detention facilities, and many were repatriated in 2015.[51] The United Nations High Commissioner for Refugees and human rights advocacy groups denounced Thailand's actions as "a flagrant violation of international law."[52] Chinese security personnel also brazenly kidnapped a Hong Kong bookseller while on vacation in Thailand in 2015 and took him back to China. The Thai government offered no public protest. Gui Minhai was one of several Hong Kong booksellers that sold racy books about Chinese politics who were abducted by Chinese security agents (the others were seized in Hong Kong and taken across the border). However, while born in China, Gui is a Swedish citizen. He remains in detention in China, despite persistent diplomatic efforts to free him, and this has become a major tension in China-Sweden relations. But *not* in China-Thai relations. Apparently the Thai don't mind such extraterritorial and extrajudicial renditions from their soil. These kinds of actions reflect the kind of subservient political-diplomatic relationship Bangkok has developed with Beijing.

In terms of security relations, the Thai armed forces began their relationship with the Chinese PLA following the Vietnamese invasion of Cambodia in 1978. During the decade of Vietnamese occupation, China supplied a range of light and heavy arms (tanks, armored personnel carriers, and rocket launchers). Beijing viewed Thailand as a "frontline" state against Vietnamese expansion— and indeed there was some danger of Vietnamese incursions from Cambodia into Thai territory (as discussed in chapter 5). Following the Vietnamese withdrawal from Cambodia at the end of the 1990s, the Thai continued their military interactions with China, but on a much lesser scale. Nonetheless, from the Thai perspective, China had been there in time of need—a pattern that would repeat itself during the Asian Financial Crisis of 1997–1998. These were very important confidence builders. As Southeast Asia expert Ian Storey has observed:[53]

> Thailand has always been able to rely on China's support during crisis periods: e.g. during the 1973 energy crisis when China sold oil to Thailand at "friendship prices"; China was Thailand's primary strategic ally during the

decade-long Cambodian crisis; Beijing provided financial support when the Thai economy buckled during the 1997–98 Asian Financial Crisis; and after the 2006 coup, China recognized the new government immediately and bilateral relations continued as normal. In Thailand, these events, among others, have created a very positive image of China as a country that always has the Kingdom's national interests at heart, irrespective of who holds power in Bangkok. In contrast, the United States is often perceived as self-interested, uninterested in Thailand's problems and, when political power shifts, punitive.

In this context, China-Thai military exchanges have grown steadily since the 1990s. Thailand was the first ASEAN member to establish annual defense and security talks with China, and the two conducted their first joint exercises in 2005.[54] The Royal Thai Armed Forces have conducted more bilateral exercises with the PLA than any other Southeast Asian country. They have occurred on a more or less annual basis since 2005.[55] These have included several air exercises (Falcon Strike) and in 2019 the first naval exercise (Blue Strike). While notable, the sophistication of these exercises come nowhere near those carried out with the United States— either bilateral or multilateral ones like Cobra Gold. The Thai military have been sending increasing numbers of their officer corps to China in recent years (particularly post-2014); although the exact numbers are uncertain, one Thai scholar in Bangkok told me that as many as half of the officer corps could have received some sort of training in China.[56] Other informed sources, though, place the numbers at only thirty to fifty Thai officers per year.[57] By contrast, some 21,000 Thai officers have trained in the United States by the early twenty-first century, averaging about 350 per year.[58] Even in the wake of the 2014 coup, from that year through 2016, 1,084 Thai military personnel came to the United States for training.[59]

In addition to human military exchanges, the Sino-Thai relationship includes arms sales and joint production of weapons. In addition to the tanks, APCs, and rocket launchers sold in the 1980s, Thailand took delivery of six Jianghu class frigates during the 1990s, and other shore patrol vessels, radars, and anti-ship missiles during the 2000s. In September 2019, Thailand contracted for a Chinese built Type 71E amphibious assault ship (25,000 tons). Other recent purchases include CX-1 anti-ship cruise missiles and CM-708 submarine launched anti-ship missiles.[60] Chinese arms sales grew from $20 million in 2012 to $77 million in 2016 (exceeding US sales by $30 million in that year).[61] But in 2015–2016 a new threshold was crossed with the delivery of forty-eight VT-4 main battle tanks (MBT), and agreement for three *Yuan* class diesel electric submarines valued at $1.03 billion (each costing $390 million).[62] This is the largest single arms deal in Thailand's history, and includes crew training and ten-year payment plan, according to one analyst.[63] In 2017 the two sides announced the purchase of an additional ten VT-4 tanks,[64] which were delivered along with thirty-four VN-1 armored personnel carriers (a $76 million total package) in December 2019.[65] In addition, there have been repeated reports of the establishment of a joint Sino-Thai munitions factory in Thailand—which the former PRC defense attaché in Bangkok (now in Washington) claims is really an assembly facility for weapons parts manufactured in China (mainly armored personnel carriers).[66] All considered, it has to be said that while China-Thailand military exchanges have grown, they still are dwarfed by those Bangkok has with the United States and they are not very multifaceted or sophisticated. The Chinese side likes to play it up,[67] and it attracts regional media attention, but substantively it is not that significant.

Economic ties have also had their limitations. A long-negotiated 542-mile high-speed rail (HSR) project, which will link northeastern Thailand with Laos and China, finally broke ground on 2017.[68] There are four other Chinese-built HSR lines planned to run south from Yunnan province into Thailand (collectively dubbed the "five fingers"),[69] but the cost of these projects has raised strong concerns in Thai society.[70] These concerns paralleled those next door in Malaysia. This also reflects a view among many Thais that their country should not become too dependent on China and, by moving much closer to Beijing since 2014, Thailand's famous omnidirectional foreign policy and independence is being compromised. As Vice Foreign Minister Futrakul told me, "We want a balance in our relations with the USA and China . . . but it is a fluid balance. It depends on the American attitude and policies. We will lean as close to China as the West pushes us."[71] In contrast, one of the vice minister's other Foreign Ministry colleagues was more resigned to the Thai tilt to Beijing: "It's too late to get out of China's embrace, it's too late. China's increased self-confidence means that now they come and just tell us to do X or Y. Thailand's reality is to learn how to be embraced but not crushed. I am not sure that Thais have enough strength to stand up to China. We can't get out of China's embrace—we just have to make the best of the situation."[72] He continued: "The Chinese are tough. There is no friendship in the way China has negotiated the railway issue, for example. Thirty-five years ago when Chinese ministers came here, they were quite humble—nowadays no longer so. The relationship is changing. China now has power and they are acting like it." Such sentiments reveal that while Sino-Thai relations may appear quite close on the surface, all is not necessarily well underneath.

Myanmar

The Republic of the Union of Myanmar, as it is officially known (having changed its name from the Union of Burma in 1989), is a large and strategically located country straddling South and Southeast Asia (it also abuts China's southwestern Yunnan Province). Sandwiched between India, China, and Thailand, Myanmar also has a long seacoast on the Andaman Sea and Bay of Bengal. Despite this fortuitous location for external trade and foreign interactions, Myanmar has traditionally been quite insular and isolated internationally. With a population of 54 million, it is the most multi-ethnic country in Asia (the Myanmar government claims 135 distinct ethnic groups in the country). Stitching together such a diverse socio-ethno-religious fabric has been the central government's principal challenge since independence from colonial Britain in 1948. The ethnic diversity is spread among fourteen separate states and regions across the country, with several (notably in Arakan/Rakhine, Kachin, Karen, and Shan states) experiencing long struggles for autonomy within the Burmese union. The Burmese Communist Party (BCP) insurgency was also long active until its demise in 1989.[73]

Politically, following the 1962 coup led by General Ne Win (then commander of the Burmese Army) that overthrew the U Nu government, Myanmar endured a lengthy period of military rule and a succession of juntas from 1962 through 2011. Ne Win's rule was marked by a heavy security hand combined with nationalization of the economy and control of all strategic natural resources by the military. Ne Win ruled until 1988, when he and his Burmese Socialist Program Party were ousted by dramatic nationwide demonstrations led by students and Buddhist monks but ultimately embracing a wide swath of society. After a month of mass unrest, the military moved and forcefully suppressed the movement, resulting in thousands of deaths and arrests.

Thereafter, another cabal of generals established SLORC (the State Law and Order Restoration Council). Under intense international pressure, SLORC acquiesced to holding national elections in 1990. Aung San Suu Kyi, the daughter of the modern father of the nation Aung San and who had risen to prominence during the August 1988 demonstrations, led the National League for Democracy (NLD) in the elections and swept 81 percent of the vote. But the SLORC generals (led by Saw Maung) would not tolerate the electoral outcome, nullified the results, seized complete control of power, and put Suu Kyi under house arrest. Her strong persona, beauty, charisma, and articulateness, and the iconic image of such a slight female figure challenging the military state earned her further international attention and acclaim (for which she was awarded the Nobel Peace Prize in 1991). She remained under house arrest from 1989 to 1995 and was released for five years until being detained again in 2000 for nearly two years. She was released again in May 2002 but re-arrested in May 2003 and held until November 2010. Altogether she had been detained for fifteen of the previous twenty-one years.

It was an untenable situation, yet the junta continued their iron grip on power throughout. Aung San Suu Kyi's incarceration attracted international attention and condemnation. Finally, she and SLORC—which changed its name to the State Peace and Development Council (SPDC) in 1997—made peace with each other and she was released, allowing her to stand for election with the reinstated and permitted NLD. In any event, the truce did not hold. As part of its "pathway to democracy," in November 2010 the SPDC junta called new national elections, but the NLD boycotted them. Consequently, the Union Solidarity and Development Party (USDP) won nearly 80 percent of parliamentary seats. The NLD and foreign states and NGOs denounced the elections as rigged and fraudulent. With such a domineering majority the SPDC was dissolved. After much protest, the USDP acquiesced to another round of by-elections to fill 48 vacant parliamentary seats. In April 2012 the NLD swept 43 of these seats.

This set the stage for fully contested national elections in 2015. This time the NLD did not boycott, and Aung San Suu Kyi and her popular party swept seats nationwide—winning majorities in both the upper and lower houses of parliament. While this landmark election constituted the first real civilian government after more than five decades of military rule, under the constitution the military retained significant authority. Because she had been married to a foreigner (deceased Oxford scholar Michael Aris), as stipulated under the constitution Aung San Suu Kyi was not allowed to serve as head of state. Since then she has been de facto leader of Myanmar, often representing her country internationally, although others (Htin Kyaw and Win Myint) have served as president. Since 2017, Aung San Suu Kyi's rosy international image has been badly tarnished by the military's ethnic cleansing campaign in Rakhine state, which has resulted in approximately 700,000 refugees fleeing into neighboring Bangladesh, and for which she represented the country against charges of genocide in the International Court of Justice in The Hague.

Myanmar's Approach to America

Throughout this saga, the United States (together with many other nations and NGOs) had pushed hard for her release, an end to martial law, an end to civil war, release of political prisoners, and restoration of democracy.[74] The State Department describes the American approach as follows: "The United States has employed a calibrated engagement strategy to recognize the positive steps undertaken to date and to incentivize further reform. The guiding principles of this approach have been to support Burma's political and economic reforms; promote national reconciliation; build government transparency, and accountability and institutions; empower local communities and civil society; promote responsible international engagement; and strengthen respect for and protection of human rights and religious freedom."[75]

In November and December 2011 Hillary Clinton became the first American secretary of state to visit Yangon (formerly Rangoon), where she held an emotional and highly publicized meeting with Aung San Suu Kyi. Clinton returned eleven months later with President Barack Obama for an equally emotional encounter (Figure 6.1).[76]

This state visit symbolized a dramatic rapprochement between the United States and Myanmar (although the US government still officially refers to the country as Burma). The two countries have held diplomatic relations since 1948 but had been estranged for decades. I remember visiting Burma in the summer of 1979 and attending the US Embassy's Fourth of July reception (to be appropriately attired for the occasion I had to borrow a jacket and tie from a waiter at the famous Strand Hotel!). Even at that time the embassy had a skeletal staff and very few Americans visited the country (foreigners were only given seven-day visas). Throughout the ensuing three decades the United States had no real relationship with Burma/Myanmar, having closed its AID mission and other in-country activities in 1989 and placing the country under sanctions following the coup and

Figure 6.1 Aung San Suu Kyi with Hillary Clinton and Barack Obama
Source: AP Photo/Pablo Martinez Monsivais

massacre. But with Myanmar's restoration of democracy after 2011, Myanmar more generally opened to the West.[77]

Washington welcomed this trend and was quick to re-establish ties. Even before the national elections the new Obama administration, which entered office in 2009, began to signal a new policy flexibility of "pragmatic engagement." Sanctions were eased. Assistant Secretary of State for East Asia and Pacific Kurt Campbell visited Yangon and Naypyidaw (the new capital post-2005), and Washington appointed the experienced Asia hand and Burma specialist Derek Mitchell as the first US ambassador to be posted to the country in twenty-two years. USAID reopened its office and began providing $80–$100 million in development assistance per year.[78] A variety of semi-governmental and private democracy promotion organizations are also active in Myanmar (the National Endowment for Democracy, International Republican Institute, National Democratic Institute, and Open Society). The Peace Corps, Fulbright Program, Drug Enforcement Agency, and Centers for Disease Control and Prevention are also active in-country. It has been difficult, however, to initiate US military links with the Myanmar military—mainly because of staunch opposition by a small handful of Congressional staffers who adamantly oppose it.

Overall, though, the restoration of full diplomatic relations and "opening" of Myanmar were true accomplishments of the Obama administration's foreign policy. Since then, however, bilateral relations have been strained by the Rohingya human rights abuses—and there is a palpable perception in Yangon and the capital Naypyidaw that the relationship has drifted since around 2015.[79] There is a sense among many I spoke with that the United States has dropped the ball and failed to sustain the momentum of the 2012–2015 period. Even US Embassy officers lamented the downturn and drift in relations.[80] Several of my interlocutors in Myanmar attributed this atrophy to limitations placed on the relationship by Congress, notably in the military and security assistance domain. This downturn stimulated the Myanmar government to engage in an alien undertaking—lobbying on Capitol Hill—with the hiring of the lobbying firm the Podesta Group to help influence opinion in Washington, DC.[81]

Myanmar's Relationship with China

While America's ties to Myanmar are recent, by contrast, China's are much deeper and more long-standing. Beijing has been one of the few external actors that a succession of Burmese military juntas could rely on. Burma was the first Asian nation to officially recognize the People's Republic of China. Their relationship is frequently referred to as *pauk phaw* (kinship or fraternity). Despite China's unique role in post-independence Burma/Myanmar, the Burmese have long had ambivalent views of their giant neighbor to the north. Part of the ambivalence was due to the Burmese own deeply ingrained sense of independence, neutralism, and non-alignment (I recall one of my undergraduate professors, Harold C. Hinton, observing that "Burma is so non-aligned that it doesn't even attend non-aligned conferences"). Burma actually withdrew from the Non-Aligned Movement in September 1979. Burma's isolation was particularly the case during the U Nu's rule (1948–1961), but it also characterized Ne Win's reign (1962–1987). The Chinese were suspicious of Ne Win's "Burmese road to socialism," but continued to aid his regime. They also had disagreements over their common border, until an agreement was reached in 1960. There was a falling-out between Rangoon and Beijing in the summer of 1967 at the height of the Cultural Revolution, when Chinese embassy personnel sought to spread Maoist propaganda and foment unrest (see discussion on chapter 5). Anti-Chinese riots ensued. This caused a rupture in relations, with both sides withdrawing ambassadors (until 1970). Beijing also terminated its aid program and launched a fusillade of propaganda invective against the Ne Win regime.

Another result of the rift was that the CCP stepped up its support for the insurgent Burmese Communist Party (BCP), and its splinter group the "White Flags," in the northern regions of Burma. The BCP received substantial military aid and financial support from Beijing and built up a significant force of approximately 15,000–20,000 members and fighters,[82] but it never truly threatened to seize national power in its four-decade-long struggle (1948–1988). During the decades of China's support for the BCP, Beijing supplied more military assistance than to any other communist insurgency in Asia outside of Indochina.[83] However, following Deng Xiaoping's return to power in 1978 he cut off China's support for all communist insurgencies in Southeast Asia, although an exception was made for the BCP. Over the following decade, though, Beijing gradually tied off its aid and support. Deng symbolized his new departure in China's approach to Burma with a visit in January 1978, the first by a Chinese leader since Zhou Enlai's secret visit in 1964. As a result of Deng's visit and policy shift, official relations resumed, and China began to resume its aid to the Burmese military and restarted some aid projects.

The ultimate disintegration of the BCP in 1988–1989, combined with the draconian military crackdown following large-scale pro-democracy unrest and a national general strike in 1988, opened another new chapter in Burma's relations with China. On China's part, it too was dealing with the aftermath of its own brutal military suppression in Beijing on June 4, 1989. Both bloodstained and isolated regimes found common cause with each other. As a Burmese government press release bluntly stated: "We sympathize with the People's Republic of China as disturbances similar to those in Burma last year broke out in the PRC."[84] As one former member of the SLORC regime described it in an interview with me, "Our relationship with China was one of dependence by necessity."[85]

Beijing's subsequent support for Burma flowed over the next two decades. In October 1989 a twenty-four-member Burmese military delegation visited China and signed a massive arms deal worth $1.4 billion (no small amount for the poor country)—including fighter jets, naval patrol craft, tanks and armored personnel carriers, anti-aircraft batteries, artillery, communications equipment, and small arms and ammunition.[86] Thereafter, a variety of projects for mineral extraction, hydroelectric power, road and rail construction, and port development ensued. One significant project was a pair of oil and natural gas pipelines that that would traverse Myanmar, connecting Yunnan province with the port of Kyaukphyu (which China also reconstructed) in Rakhine State on the Bay of Bengal (Figure 6.2). Kyaukphyu

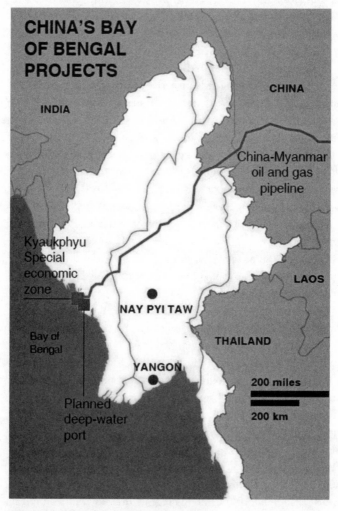

Figure 6.2 China's Bay of Bengal projects
Source: Frontier Myanmar

is one of a number of Chinese Belt and Road projects in Myanmar.[87] When Xi Jinping visited Myanmar in January 2020, China committed an additional $1.3 billion to the project as part of thirty-three agreements.[88] With the completion of this project, which began to carry 12 million tons of oil to China in 2017,[89] China now has achieved its centuries-long ambition of a direct link to the Indian Ocean.[90] More immediately, it also permits China to circumvent the strategically vulnerable Straits of Malacca, through which much of its imported oil and gas pass.

Chinese investments are substantial. By 2011, China had become Myanmar's top foreign investor with cumulative investments of $13 billion.[91] The investment was supplemented by an array of loans and other commercial support, as well as military assistance. Myanmar bought $1.4 billion in weapons from China from 2000 to 2016, accounting for the lion's share of the country's arms imports.[92] For a nation still experiencing international isolation and sanctions for its human rights abuses, China's economic and military assistance was critical. Chinese investment flooded into Myanmar.[93] China's commercial thrust into Myanmar had come quickly—*too fast* for the Burmese, according to David Steinberg, a leading scholar of Burma, who notes: "Military equipment, training, and aid poured in, with close relations developing to a degree that the Burmese themselves felt the equilibrium needed to be restored to maintain balance. The Chinese tide was running too high."[94] The deep Burmese sense of independence was being compromised. Not only was Chinese money flooding into the country, but so too were Chinese traders and migrants. Chinese merchants had always operated in the porous cross-border regions, but now Chinese goods and people had begun to penetrate into Myanmar's cities such as Mandalay.[95] The Chinese population in Mandalay swelled from 1 percent of the population in 1983 to between 30–50 percent today—where 80 percent of the hotels and 70 percent of restaurants are owned and operated by Chinese today.[96]

Domestic resentment was growing. In 2011 it snapped. On September 30 of that year the Thein Sein military junta suspended work on the huge $3.6 billion hydroelectric Myitsone dam project, which was being built largely by China and would be the fifteenth largest in the world. It was the largest of three large hydro projects China was constructing in the northern part of the country. The dam is located at the confluence of several tributaries that flow into the Irrawaddy River, Myanmar's principal source of inland water, and was due to pump out 6,000 megawatts of power generation—with one problem: the power was to primarily be exported into China's Yunnan Province. There were also other local environmental concerns. The dam project had become a symbolic lightening rod among many Burmese—symbolizing China's increasingly exploitative position in the country. "It was a classic case of familiarization breeding contempt," according to one observer in Yangon.[97] Finally—much to the surprise of Beijing—the military government acted.

The Myitsone decision was part and parcel of Myanmar's leaders seeking a more balanced approach in its external relations—including the opening to the United States, and developing multifaceted ties with other ASEAN states, Japan, and India. China viewed Myanmar's opening to the United States with particular concern.[98]

China also recalibrated its approach as a result of the surprising decision on the Myitsone dam. Beijing had not seen it coming. This is often the case with Chinese projects in many countries—they just plough ahead with little awareness of (or care for) local interests. Such behavior triggers bitter memories of colonial times—resulting in accusations against China of "neocolonial behavior." In the case of Myanmar, after digesting the shock, the authorities in Beijing came back with a multifaceted public relations offensive to influence several sectors of Burmese state and society. This has involved four levels of intensified engagement: government-to-government, military-to-military, party-to-party, and people-to-people.[99] At the first level, Beijing (and Xi Jinping in particular) have sought to cultivate Aung San Suu Kyi (Fig. 6.3)— who, in the words of one seasoned observer in Yangon, has "made her peace with China."[100]

The military component involves intelligence sharing, officer training, and arms transfers. Party-to-party exchanges are managed by the CCP's International

Figure 6.3 Aung San Suu Kyi meets Xi Jinping
Source: Damir Sagolj/AFP via Getty Images

Department (中共中联部). These exchanges not only involve the NLD and the Union Solidarity Development Party—which have reportedly "sent hundreds of members to China from 2015–2018," as well as "around one hundred" members of the United Nationalities Alliance (an umbrella organization of fifteen minor parties).[101] The people-to-people component has involved bringing several thousand Burmese journalists, educators, NGO members, professionals, religious and community leaders, and other local stakeholders to China on so-called study tours (some locals refer to this as China's "soft power offensive").[102] Xinhua News Agency has even started a Facebook page in Burmese (which has received over 30 million "likes"), and Xinhua supplies news feeds directly to Myanmar newspapers and media outlets.[103] These are mainly organized by the China-Myanmar Friendship Association or the China NGO Network for International Exchange, but other Chinese institutions are also involved. These exchanges are all classic forms of "influence operations" and united front work.[104] The question is whether these influence/propaganda activities—and that is what they are—are having their intended effect? A report based on interviews with participants in these tours concludes with a mixed result: "Many of the people interviewed for this report remain critical of China's intentions. Yet, this multilayered engagement strategy has created a more positive perception of China among the participants."[105]

Taken together with the decline of attention paid by Washington since about 2015,[106] and particularly since Trump entered office, Beijing has recovered much of its lost ground and damaged image in Myanmar by 2020.[107] This was symbolized by Xi Jinping's state visit in January 2020, the first by a PRC head of state in nearly twenty years.[108] To be sure, there remain contentious issues from the Burmese perspective—notably China's military support for the United Wa State Army (with an estimated 20,000 fighters) in the Kokang region of Shan State bordering on China's southwestern Yunnan Province, and continuing sensitivities over Chinese exploitation of Burmese natural resources. But, on balance, Myanmar's ties to China are strong and have been strengthened since the Myitsone episode (particularly post-2017). The Chinese government has also been playing a role as broker and convener of a negotiated peace process among the multiple armed groups operating in the Kachin and Shan states. This role has generally been welcomed by—but de facto forced upon—the Myanmar government in Naypyidaw. Although it has yet to produce a resolution of the complex ethnic conflicts, Beijing's role has helped to stabilize the situation to some extent.[109] China's role concerning the Rohingya crisis has been less than constructive, however. The PRC has opposed or weakened United Nations resolutions condemning the Myanmar military (known as the Tatmadaw) for its ethnic cleansing offensive in Rakhine state (which has resulted in hundreds of thousands of refugees).

Thus, after attempting to decrease its dependence on China and escape Beijing's tightening grip in 2011, the Myanmar government has allowed itself to slide back into a semi-dependent relationship with its patron to the north. Meanwhile, its furtive opening to the United States has stalled and relations with Washington lack intrinsic strength. The Burmese have tried to multilateralize their external relations to some extent—with India, Japan, and ASEAN—but none of these ties has really reduced Myanmar's close and dependent relationship with China.

Laos

Laos[110] is a small landlocked kingdom sandwiched between Vietnam and Thailand, while sharing relatively short borders with Myanmar, Cambodia, and China. Half of the population of 7 million are ethnic Lao, while the other half are a composite of other ethnic groups and hill tribes. Politically, since the Pathet Lao took power in December 1975, Laos has been one of the five remaining communist party-states in the world (along with Vietnam, China, North Korea, and Cuba).

If Laos is caught in a rivalry between external states, it is between China and Vietnam—not the United States and China. The Vietnamese and Lao communist parties share long and deep relations, as do the two militaries. After Vietnam's invasion and occupation of Cambodia in 1979, the Vietnamese also stationed 50,000 soldiers in Laos.[111] While Vietnam has held the greatest influence over Laotian affairs, the Lao have been quite adroit at balancing Hanoi's influence by maintaining ties with China, Thailand, Russia, and ASEAN (which it joined in 1997). As one regional observer noted, "Lao PDR's approach is a textbook case in the practice of small state diplomacy. Lao PDR finds itself in a position where it must swim with the sharks or be eaten."[112]

Laos' Relations with the United States

The United States has been a relative non-factor in the country's calculations— until the Obama administration. Secretaries of State Hillary Clinton and John Kerry both visited the kingdom and in September 2016 President Obama became the first American president to ever visit Laos. Some regional media interpreted the visit as an attempt by Vientiane to counterbalance Chinese influence.[113] As a result of these visits, a Joint Declaration,[114] and declaration of a "comprehensive strategic partnership," the United States began to develop a series of ties and in-country programs. A USAID mission opened and is involved in sanitation, public health and medicine, HIV/AIDS prevention and care, forestry, hydropower, protection of endangered species, and environmental programs. Preventing human and wildlife trafficking is also a priority. Laos (along with Cambodia, Myanmar, Thailand, and Vietnam) also participates in, and benefits from, the US Lower Mekong Initiative (LMI)—a multifaceted series of programs in six principal areas: agriculture and food security, connectivity, education, energy security, environment and water, and public health.[115] The United States and Laos also cooperate in law enforcement and counter-narcotics trafficking, child nutrition, legal reform, gender equality, youth education, and English-language training.[116] Other priorities of the United States in Laos are to recover the remains of 301 missing Americans from the Vietnam War (273 have been recovered), as well as clearing unexploded ordnance. During the war, American bombers pummeled the country with 2.5 million tons of ordnance. There is some military-to-military interaction: a Bilateral Defense Dialogue and collaboration on military medical training and defense educational exchanges (at APCSS in Honolulu).

Laos's Relations with China

By comparison, China's role and influence in Laos is far more considerable. It is predominantly economic—but also includes political and military ties. While today China's presence is palpable, this was not always the case. Following the Pathet Lao's seizure of power in December 1975 it aligned closely with the North Vietnamese communists. This included persecuting ethnic Chinese (as was the case in Vietnam post-1975). Many ethnic Chinese were forced to repatriate across the border back into China—dropping the population of the Lao Chinese community from 100,000 to approximately 10,000 by the early 1990s.[117] But in 1990 Chinese Premier Li Peng paid a visit to Laos, which kick-started a range of interactions. The first manifestation was an influx of petty traders from Yunnan Province, which "transformed the socio-economic landscape of northern Laos, in both urban and rural areas," according to a French specialist on the country.[118] This was followed by four subsequent phases.

First, beginning in the late 1990s and early 2000s, the Lao government decided to "turn land into capital" and launched a policy by that moniker. This new policy was tailor-made for China. Immediately Chinese companies (many state-owned) moved into four areas of Laos' natural resources: mining, forests, agriculture, and water. Chinese companies began logging timber, extracting minerals and jewels from mines, building dams on rivers (China is planning or has already built no fewer than eight dams along the Mekong on Laotian territory),[119] and taking control of banana groves and fruit orchards. In the last case they began applying pesticides (mainly to bananas), which caused polluted run-off into the water table and downstream rivers and lakes. This caused 63 percent of banana plantation workers to fall ill, according to the Laos Agricultural and Forestry Institute.[120] Many villagers also had to curtail their traditional fishing practices as a result.[121]

The next phase of China's economic foray (some locals label it an "invasion") into Laos came in the early 2000s with the creation of several Special Economic Zones (SEZs). These are simply districts that operate under relaxed (or unenforced) regulatory procedures or control by the Lao government. The Chinese sold the idea on the basis that it would stimulate indigenous industries and cross-border tourism. They certainly did the latter, but for one purpose: gambling. Several giant casinos were constructed. While one (Golden Boten City) was shut down by Chinese authorities following lurid news reports of extortion, kidnappings, and killings, others have proceeded. The Kings Roman Casino in the Golden Triangle SEZ—euphemistically dubbed "Laos Vegas"—attracts over 1,000 gamblers per day[122] and has its own international border checkpoint, river port, banks, multiple hotels, a Chinatown, and restaurants and shops.[123]

The third phase of the Chinese influx has come in the cities and outskirts of Luang Prabang and Vientiane, where Chinese companies have built roads, office buildings, shopping complexes and malls, restaurants, and other commercial establishments.[124] A joint commercial cooperation agreement signed by the two governments in May 2019 opened the door for even greater Chinese investment into the country.[125] China is now the largest investor in Laos and second leading trade partner.[126]

The fourth phase concerns China's Belt and Road infrastructure projects in Laos, the most noteworthy of which is the construction of the high-speed rail link that runs from Kunming right down through the center of the country and into Thailand (where it is planned to connect to another segment to Bangkok and then down the Malay peninsula to Singapore).[127] The $6 billion project is predominately being funded by China (70 percent), while Laos's 30 percent is being paid via loans from China. It will require 100,000 workers, who are already blasting through mountains and laying track across 4,000 hectares of requisitioned land.[128] By the end of 2017 one-fifth of the 414-kilometer project had been completed—and when finished (target date December 2021) the path through the mountainous country will traverse 75 tunnels and 167 bridges.[129] Not unsurprisingly, the mammoth project is stirring discontent in the country. The question is, will the high-speed rail project produce a "Myanmar moment" for the Laotian government, similar to the Myitsone dam episode that reflected the Burmese reaction to the similar influx of Chinese presence in that country? Time will tell, but the conditions are very similar.

Cambodia

Cambodia cannot even be described as "bandwagoning" with China—it has become a full-blown Chinese client state. No nation in the world may be as dependent on China as is Cambodia. Together, Cambodia and Laos are the closest to China of all Southeast Asian nations.[130] While there are some signs of simmering discontent with its subservient status, the country is fully in the grip of China.

Cambodia-American Relations

For its part, the United States has a minimal presence in Cambodia. From 1998 to 2007, Congress prohibited any assistance to Cambodia, largely because of human rights concerns. Since then, however, various development assistance programs have been authorized by Congress ($79.3 million in 2018).[131] Bilateral trade remains a paltry $3.6 billion. Ironically, though, the currency of preference in the country is the US dollar (in far wider circulation that the Cambodian *riel*). The Obama administration also started low-level military exchanges, which the Hun Sen government suspended in 2017 but restarted in early 2019. Diplomatic relations remain frosty—owing to the repression, corruption, and election rigging of the Hun Sen regime.[132] As a result, the US Congress has taken a number of measures recently to punish and sanction the Cambodian regime, including passing the Cambodia Democracy Act and Cambodia Trade Act in 2019 (both of which include various punitive measures but also hold out incentives for improved relations). Since his arrival in Phnom Penh in late 2019, the new US ambassador Patrick Murphy has tried to re-engage the Hun Sen regime, including restarting military cooperation (halted since 2017).[133] Murphy also arrived bearing two letters from President Trump. This is another example of Trump's engagement of authoritarian leaders. But it is unclear, as of this writing, where the new outreach will lead.

　　While not at all in good shape, US-Cambodian relations could improve if Phnom Penh sours on its over dependence on China or if the Hun Sen regime—which has been in power since 1985—ends. This could occur if Cambodia also experienced a "Myanmar moment." Let us now examine the various ties that bind Cambodia tightly to China.

China's Grip

China has a long history of backing successive Cambodian regimes. First it was Prince Norodom Sihanouk's government, which forged close ties from the mid-1950s through the mid-1960s. As elsewhere in the region, the Chinese embassy in Phnom Penh tried to propagate Maoism during the Cultural Revolution during 1966 and 1967. As a consequence, Sihanouk temporarily soured on Beijing—but when he was ousted from power and the throne in a coup by General Lon Nol in March 1970, Sihanouk was given sanctuary in Beijing. Lon Nol reoriented Cambodia toward the United States. Thereafter, China intensified its backing of the communist insurgent Khmer Rouge—which seized power in 1975 and unleashed a horrific genocide that took the lives of an estimated 2 million Cambodians. Throughout this gruesome period, China was the sole patron of the Khmer Rouge movement and regime. Consequently, China also bears responsibility.

The brutal and ruthless regime was overthrown by a Vietnamese invasion in December 1978 and driven deep into the country's jungles where they continued to wage armed insurgency and massacres in the "killing fields." Vietnam ruled the country and installed Heng Samrin as puppet prime minister when it invaded the country in 1978—who ruled until his power and position were usurped by Hun Sen in 1985 (although Heng Samrin remains an honorific figure in Cambodian politics to this day). In 1988, under intense international pressure, Vietnam announced it would withdraw its forces and international peace talks commenced in Paris under the auspices of the United Nations. After two years of negotiations the external powers came to agreement that UN peacekeeping forces would be deployed to disarm the warring factions and supervise security while UN-supervised elections would be held in 1993. The elections produced an unstable, and ultimately untenable, coalition government led by Prince Sihanouk's son and Hun Sen. At first Hun Sen, who had also been originally installed during the period of Vietnamese occupation, was not well disposed toward China—but as personal and political relations between Prince Ranariddh (one of Sihanouk's sons) and Hun Sen deteriorated in the mid-1990s, Hun Sen began to warm to the Chinese, and vice versa. In July 1996 he visited Beijing and signed several agreements with Beijing. A year later, in July 1997, he ousted the prince in a coup and took sole control of power. From then until the present day, Hun Sen has been in Beijing's pocket.[134]

China has far and away been Cambodia's leading economic benefactor. "China has achieved nearly pervasive economic influence in Cambodia," finds one study.[135] Another concludes that China has altogether provided about $13 billion in aid, grants, and concessionary loans.[136] By contrast, all other aid from OECD member states totaled only $2.36 billion over the same period.[137] Nearly half of Cambodia's external debt is owed to China. In addition, China is the largest foreign investor with a cumulative stock of approximately $15 billion,[138] while China-Cambodia trade was $5.8 billion in 2017.[139]

China's investment involves a wide range of projects in a wide range of sectors: infrastructure, agriculture, industries, energy, telecommunications, services, tourism, education, and media.[140] Some of the more noteworthy ones are a new international airport, national long-distance highways (National Roads 6, 57, 58, 59, 76), the Vaico irrigation network, a national electrical grid, numerous bridges, and seven dams across the Mekong River. Phnom Penh is one big construction site—with high-rise buildings, office blocks, private apartments, parks, streets, flyovers and bridges—most being built by Chinese firms. There is so much construction ongoing that what normally is a half-hour drive from the city center to the airport can now take up to three hours. Outside of the capital, the southern seaside port city of Sihanoukville (Kampong Som) has been transformed into a Chinese casino and tourism mecca. Says one local: "Everything has changed in Sihanoukville in just two years. Before it was really quiet here, but not anymore with all the Chinese construction. There will be no Cambodia left in Sihanoukville."[141] A Chinese-built $2 billion four-lane highway connects Sihanoukville with Phnom Penh. Human trafficking, ivory and wildlife trafficking, pimps and prostitution, money laundering, drugs, and organized crime have all accompanied the gambling invasion of Sihanoukville. One study found that 150 of the 156 hotels, 414 of the 436 restaurants, 48 of the 62 casinos, 41 karaoke clubs, and 46 massage parlors in Sihanoukville were Chinese-owned.[142] Fifty Chinese nationals were arrested there in August 2019 in a crackdown on prostitution rings, while 68 percent of *all* those arrested in Cambodia in the first six months of 2018 were Chinese citizens, far outnumbering other foreign nationals.[143] All over the country there has been an enormous influx of Chinese migrants, businesspeople, tourists, gamblers, and pleasure seekers. In 2018, Chinese accounted for one-third of the country's 6.2 million visitors. When I visited Angkor Wat in 2017 perhaps half of the visitors were Chinese. Battambang and Siem Reap are also quickly being visibly "Sinicized."

In 2018, to commemorate the sixtieth anniversary of diplomatic relations between the PRC and Cambodia, Premier Li Keqiang visited the country in February and signed nineteen new agreements.[144] President Xi Jinping also visited in October and signed more deals. For his part, Prime Minister Hun Sen visited Beijing in January 2019 and received Chinese commitments of $588 million in aid over the next two years.[145] One example of Cambodia's client state status, that is frequently cited, was when Cambodia served as the rotating chair in July 2012 of the ASEAN Ministers Meeting (AMM). For the first time in ASEAN history, the meeting failed to adopt a communiqué. This was because there was no unanimous consent concerning verbiage concerning the South China Sea—all members were in agreement on lowest common denominator language, but Beijing still took umbrage at it and got the Cambodia government to block the adoption of the communiqué.[146]

China is also Cambodia's main military supplier. To be sure, the Cambodian military is not a formidable force—but it too is dependent on China. This includes transfers of weapons, training, and joint exercises.[147] A new package of military aid was agreed during Minister of Defense Tea Banh's visit to Beijing in October 2019.[148] One aspect of the military relationship that has garnered a lot of attention is an apparent secret agreement signed between the Cambodian and Chinese militaries in the spring of 2019, but revealed by the *Wall Street Journal*.[149] The deal, if accurately reported, would give China a thirty-year lease to use part of Cambodia's largest naval base at Ream as well as an adjacent airfield facility 50 miles away across the isthmus at Dara Sakor, for which a murky Chinese company has secured a ninety-nine-year lease. The developer and the Cambodian government claim that the runway will become an international airport and will serve a large resort complex. The runway at the airfield is currently being extended to 2 miles, long enough to handle long-range bombers and military transports, while the Ream deep-sea port facility will cover 190 acres and includes two new piers large enough to handle China's large destroyers, frigates, and possibly two aircraft carriers.[150] The physical proximity of the facilities, which lie on the Gulf of Thailand, would hook up with China's reclaimed island bases in the Spratlys in the South China Sea. Despite much media attention to the projected deal for bases, as well as inquiries by the US embassy in Phnom Penh,[151] and complaints from the Pentagon in Washington,[152] both the Cambodian and Chinese governments have adamantly denied it.[153] Hun Sen did not disavow it, however, calling reports "distorted."[154]

Yet, China's largesse is not appreciated by all Cambodians. Anti-Chinese sentiment and resentment has been brewing under the surface of Cambodian society.[155] The sheer volume of the influx of Chinese people is one catalyst. Chinese tourists and visitors are also not always the best behaved. As in so many other countries, Chinese shops have sprouted like bamboo shoots in a spring rain—often overtaking local petty entrepreneurs. Chinese-made products fill the shelves of stores, even those managed by Cambodians. Not all Chinese in Cambodia are traders or builders—many organized crime triads have also infiltrated the country. The amount of Chinese construction is also overwhelming to many Cambodians—and the Chinese-character signs that hang on construction sites are visible reminders of their presence.

Given this growing subterranean sentiment, which should not be overstated, there are two views of Hun Sen's position. One is that he is doubling down, is unapologetic about Cambodia's close dependency on China, and rejects any suggestion he is selling out his country. In March 2018 he said: "The Chinese leaders respect me highly and treat me as an equal. Let me ask those of you who have accused me of being too close to China, what have you offered me besides cursing and disciplining me, and threatening to put sanctions on me?"[156]

There are others, though, who see him as trying to hedge, gain some distance from China, and gain investment from other outside countries too.[157] "He sees himself as a modern-day Sihanouk, playing big powers off against each other," observes Jim Laurie, a longtime journalist and visitor to Cambodia who has met and interviewed Hun Sen.[158] Several Cambodia watchers believe that Hun Sen has a severe case of "Sihanouk envy," seeing himself as a contemporary inheritor of both the prince's political stature and diplomatic acumen, as well as his royal honorifics. In May 2016 he gave himself the semi-royal title of "Samdech," which roughly translates as "Glorious Lord."

Thus, despite its dependency on China, there are clear signs of simmering unease with the relationship among some Cambodians—and much of China's ties to the country depend on Hun Sen himself. If he were overthrown, or when he dies, much could change. Whether this will produce a "Myanmar moment" for that country remains to be seen.

Vietnam

If Cambodia is the nation most aligned with China in Southeast Asia, next door the Socialist Republic of Vietnam is the nation most distant from and antagonistic toward China. Of course, this does not pertain to geography, as they share a 796-mile land border and overlapping sea claims. Their physical proximity is simultaneously a source of exchanges and friction. Quite a lot of cross-border trade takes place, and there are a variety of political and cultural exchanges between the two. But the two communist countries have viscerally disputed overlapping maritime claims in the South China Sea and Paracel Islands. Of course, as described in chapters 4 and 5, the antagonism between China and Vietnam runs deep and is centuries old. Vietnam also has its historical issues with the United States owing to their fifteen-year war—but, remarkably, both sides have been able to put that traumatic period (described in chapter 4) behind them and have been able to build comprehensive well-rounded relations. This would likely have occurred on its own merits and at its own pace, but Vietnam's ambiguous yet essentially antagonistic relationship with China has certainly been a driver in forging ties between the United States and Vietnam.

While the United States and China figure prominently in Hanoi's strategic thinking and foreign policy, Vietnam's external relationships are quite diversified. Ever since the SRV's troop withdrawal from Cambodia in 1989 and the 1991 Paris settlement, Hanoi has taken a variety of steps to diversify its external relations. Joining ASEAN in July 1995 was a major step toward integration into Southeast Asia. Under the rubric of Đổi Mới (the policy of economic "renovation" begun in 1986), Vietnam has actively sought foreign commercial partners and is now the 21st largest export economy in the world. Today, Vietnam has diplomatic ties with 188 nations and most multilateral institutions. It officially practices a foreign policy of "diversifying and multilateralizing" (*Đa dạng hóa, đa phương hóa*). Since adopting this approach in the early 1990s, Hanoi has been able to pursue a diversified and flexible external strategy that has behooved the country.[159] Such diversification helps Vietnam (as others in Southeast Asia) from falling into a relationship of excessive dependency on, and pressure from, China.[160]

Vietnam's Asymmetry, Hedging, and Schizophrenia vis-à-vis China

While Vietnam deserves, and has received, high marks for its foreign policy, clearly its most difficult relationship is with China. As I was told by Nguyen Vinh Quang, Director-General of the External Relations Department of the Vietnamese Communist Party (VCP), when I met him at VCP headquarters in Hanoi in 2017:[161]

> There are a lot of economic complementarities with China, and in politics as well. Our political systems are very similar: socialist. We have tried to learn from each other. But, within Southeast Asia, it is Vietnam that has the most serious problems with China. China is getting stronger and stronger, and becoming more and more aggressive, due to its increased arrogance. Vietnam has not changed anything—it is China that has changed. Its hard power gets much stronger and they are increasingly getting much more aggressive.

Echoing this sentiment, another senior Vietnam Foreign Ministry official, told me: "After 5,000 years China still does not accept us or others as equals."[162]

As University of Virginia scholar Brantly Womack elucidates in his seminal book on China-Vietnam relations, Hanoi finds itself in a relationship of complex "asymmetry" vis-à-vis China.[163] Asymmetry, Womack argues, is a *structural* factor in the relationship, not a policy preference. Asymmetry brings with it vulnerability on the smaller country's part—thus the need for flexible strategies to navigate and survive. Dealing with asymmetry requires much more, he argues, than simply traditional "balancing" or bandwagoning" strategies and tactics often deployed by weaker states vis-à-vis stronger powers—it is a far more complicated phenomenon that requires a combination of the two plus a good deal of interdependence and pragmatic interactions. Womack also argues that asymmetry affects mutual perceptions—which, in turn, calibrates behavior: "Characteristic patterns of misperception can develop in which the stronger side makes errors of inattention while the weaker makes errors of over-attention, and these misperceptions can amplify one another into a crisis."[164] Le Hong Hiep, a leading scholar of Vietnam's relations with China, goes further by describing Hanoi's China strategy as a "multitiered omnidirectional hedging strategy, made up of four components: economic pragmatism, direct engagement, hard balancing, and soft balancing."[165]

These perspectives help to explain why there is an odd kind of schizophrenia in Vietnam's relationship with its northern neighbor. On the one hand, there is clear antagonism owing to the historical record of subjugation by China, to the 1979 border war, to contemporary maritime disputes, and to periodic race riots against ethnic Chinese or Chinese commercial entities. In Vietnamese society fully 80 percent view China as "threatening," according to a 2017 Pew poll.[166] On the other hand, the two were kindred allies during the anti-colonial era and anti-US war periods, the two ruling communist parties enjoy fraternal and extensive ties, the two governments interact across a range of functional areas, the two societies enjoy exchanges, and significant trade and investment anchor the economic relationship. Thus the apparent schizophrenia is manifest in these two dimensions: extensive bilateral exchanges combined with "hard" and "soft" multilateral balancing behavior.

At the party-to-party level, from 1991 to 2017 Vietnamese Communist Party (VCP) general secretaries visited China eleven times while CCP general secretaries visited Vietnam five times, and the respective prime ministers paid official visits eleven times.[167] Beneath the most senior leaders, a wide variety of party departments (Propaganda, Organization, International Liaison, party training schools and research institutes) and government ministries undertake regular exchanges. During these visits numerous party-to-party and governmental communiqués and agreements have been signed, which are filled with effusive rhetoric and tangible cooperation. A Joint Steering Committee for Bilateral Cooperation also meets annually (Politburo member and foreign policy czar Yang Jiechi usually represents China). The two militaries also engage in exchanges "in such fields as border defense, peacekeeping, national defense industry, academic research, medical science, media, and personnel training,"[168] as well as joint sea exercises.[169] The respective coast guards and internal security ministries also cooperate. A variety of other joint working groups and ministry-to-ministry and cultural exchanges are institutionalized, as well.[170]

A notable indication of the two countries' extensive cooperation was Xi Jinping's official visit to Hanoi and Da Nang in 2017. Xi was warmly received, signed fifteen agreements, and ironically proclaimed that the two nations' ties were "forged in blood." In an article published in the Vietnamese state media (*Nhan Dan*) on the eve of his visit, Xi effused about the history of fraternal ties between the two communist parties and militaries, noting that Ho Chi Minh had "spent twelve

long years in China for revolutionary activities."[171] Xi called for expanding bilateral exchange mechanisms in many fields. Xi further noted that China had been
Vietnam's largest trading partner for thirteen consecutive years, claiming that bilateral trade had reached "nearly $100 billion" in 2016 (although other sources in-
dicate trade that year was only around $70 billion).

The amount of two-way trade is actually not that great, given the two countries' proximity. By contrast, China's trade with neighboring South Korea in
2017 was $280 billion. China is also only the eighth largest foreign investor
in Vietnam, with 1,616 projects worth $11.19 billion in 2017.[172] According to
Vietnam's Foreign Investment Department, Chinese investments exist in 54
of Vietnam's 63 provinces and cities.[173] There is certainly scope for increased
Chinese investment, particularly in the context of the Belt and Road Initiative
(of which Vietnam is part). Vietnam has significant need for infrastructure that
China could help with, yet Hanoi has been reluctant to enter into joint projects
with China.[174] The degree of Vietnam's economic engagement with China will
also be dictated by the future nature and scope of its domestic reforms.[175] More
than most, Vietnam remains wary of any type of dependency on China, and their
conflicting maritime claims cast a long shadow over potential cooperation.

One other economic aspect worth noting is that Vietnam has been a beneficiary of the US-China trade frictions. To the extent that American firms are
"decoupling" from China and moving their supply chains elsewhere, many
have relocated some of these linkages to Vietnam (and elsewhere in Southeast
Asia).[176]

These elements of Vietnam's bilateral interactions with China are all important and not to be dismissed as ephemeral. I say this because many American
observers do not appreciate the breadth and depth of Sino-Vietnamese ties and,
second, they overemphasize what they perceive to be a pro-American tilt by
Hanoi. These ties are part and parcel of Vietnam's hedging strategy, but are also
important to the country in their own right.

To be certain, Vietnam has no illusions about China and it has concrete areas
of dispute. No issue is more contentious that their maritime disputes in the
South China Sea (which Hanoi refers to as the East Sea). These primarily lie in the
Paracel island chain (called Hoang Sa in Vietnamese and Xisha in Chinese)—
just south of Hainan Island, where China's South Sea Fleet is based—but also
further south in the Spratly chain. Of all the five Southeast Asian states with
which China has conflicting claims, those with Vietnam seem most acute. There
have been military clashes dating back to 1974. More recently, during May and
July 2014, tensions flared when a major Chinese oil company (CNOOC) pro-
vocatively deployed a mega-size deep-sea oil drilling platform, the *Haiyang
Shiyou 981*, just 120 miles off of Vietnam's coastline (within Vietnam's 200-mile
Exclusive Economic Zone). A major stand-off ensued, with both sides deploying

coast guard vessels and issuing bellicose statements against the other. The incident also triggered large-scale anti-China demonstrations in Vietnam. Although China ended up abruptly withdrawing the oil rig in July, it was a watershed event and rude reminder for Vietnam of China's capacity for brazen actions. It also caused Hanoi to step up its own military modernization program and arms imports from abroad, particularly for its coast guard. From 2014 to 2017, Hanoi imported coast guard vessels from the United States, the Netherlands, Japan, and South Korea.[177] The Vietnamese coast guard and navy began to increasingly interdict Chinese survey vessels within its EEZ.[178] On the other hand, the 2019 *Vietnam Defense White Paper* was remarkably conciliatory, calling for mutual restraint, establishment of a series of confidence-building measures (CBMs), and concluding further bilateral agreements with China (beyond the existing Agreement on the Basic Principles Guiding the Settlement of Sea-Related Issues, the Agreement on Maritime Boundary Delimitation in the Gulf of Tonkin, and Agreement on Fishery Cooperation).[179]

Growing Closer to America

The other manifestation of the 2014 oil rig crisis was to increase Vietnam's ties with the United States. Of course, this was already well in train before the incident—but it focused policy minds in Hanoi. Viewed from Hanoi, and reflected in my conversations with Vietnamese officials there, a closer relationship with the United States is primarily motivated by national security considerations.[180] While the United States can offer Vietnam considerable trade, investment, development assistance, and opportunities to train students—all contributing to Vietnam's development—it is the allure of the United States as a strategic counterweight to China that primarily motivates Vietnam's America policy. "China is *the* priority for Vietnam—they calibrate everything around it," a US embassy officer in Hanoi told me.[181] Such an approach dovetails to some extent with Washington's calculus, although my sense is that the United States is more interested in building a comprehensive and long-lasting relationship with Vietnam—whereas Vietnam sees greater national security expediency in its approach to ties with the United States.

If this is the case, it is something of a mystery (and a frustration for the US Defense Department) that Hanoi has been slow-walking the defense relationship with the United States. While military-to-military relations have developed since the signing of a Memorandum of Understanding on Advancing Bilateral Defense Cooperation in 2011, the US-Vietnam Joint Vision Statement on Defense Relations in 2015, and the lifting of the arms sales embargo in 2016, and the symbolic high-profile visit of the aircraft carrier USS *Carl Vinson* to Da

Nang in 2018 and the USS *Theodore Roosevelt* in 2020—from Washington's perspective there nevertheless is too slow momentum in developing defense ties. As a US defense attaché in Hanoi put it: "The US-Vietnam military trajectory is positive, but progress is incremental."[182] The Vietnamese limit the United States to only one ship visit per year, refuse to engage in joint training, send officers to the US National Defense University and Army War College only for academic exchanges, do not permit US military personnel or equipment to be stationed in-country (unlike Thailand and the Philippines), do not permit US logistics facilities in-country (unlike Thailand, Singapore, or the Philippines), do not engage in complex bilateral or multilateral air or naval exercises (unlike with Thailand, the Philippines, Singapore, Indonesia, or Malaysia), and purchase only a minimum of American weapons. "Vietnam does not want to be beholden to the US, instead aiming to maintain a broad, diversified base of arms partners from South Korea to India, but primarily from its traditional source Russia," notes Collin Koh, a specialist at the S. Rajaratnam School of International Studies in Singapore.[183] The US Defense Attaché in Hanoi echoed this perspective concerning Vietnam's military preferences: "If Vietnam does X with us, they feel the need to do the same with Japan, China, India, and Russia."[184]

Thus, Hanoi's relative reluctance to engage in extensive military exchanges with the United States is at seeming variance with its desire to have the United States counterbalance China, particularly in the South China Sea. But it may also indicate that Vietnam's interests are really all about the South China Sea, and that their real preferences are to maintain diversified relations with many countries and not get too close to the United States (thus it may be a strategic misperception in Washington that Vietnam seeks a strategic relationship with the United States). Another indication of Vietnam's reluctance is that it has only agreed to a "comprehensive partnership" with the United States, whereas it has "strategic partnerships" with sixteen other countries (including China).[185]

Nonetheless, since the formal normalization of diplomatic relations in 1995, there has developed a closeness between the two sides in recent years. President Obama visited Vietnam in 2016 and President Trump in 2017, while Vietnamese Communist Party leader Nguyen Phu Trong and Prime Minister Nguyen Xuan Phuc also visited the White House in 2015 and 2017 respectively. Trade is also steadily growing—reaching $62.6 billion in 2018, but with a $39.5 billion surplus in Vietnam's favor.[186] This deficit caught the attention and ire of President Trump, who lashed out against Vietnam in a FOX News interview on June 26, 2019, labeling Vietnam as "almost the single worst abuser of everybody. . . . Vietnam takes advantage of us almost even worse than China!"[187] Despite Trump's tantrum, overall ties between the two countries remain quite positive and show much scope for further development.

Malaysia

Malaysia is a critically important and strategically located country in the US-China competition in Southeast Asia. With a population of 33 million and GNP of $358.5 billion Malaysia is the thirty-fifth largest economy in the world and attractive for trade and investment. China ranks as Malaysia's largest trading partner, while the United States is third largest. Although Malaysia is covered with palm (oil) and rubber tree plantations and is the world's largest producer of each, the national economy depends less and less on agriculture as it has become a full-fledged newly industrialized economy (NIE).

While Kuala Lumpur has forged comprehensive ties with the United States, and on many levels they are deep, there has nonetheless been an underlying ambivalence about them. By contrast, successive Malaysian administrations have tilted toward Beijing. This represents Malaysian hedging, allowing it to maintain its official adherence to a foreign policy of neutrality, but in fact is a "tilted" form that aligns with and favors relations with China.

Malaysian Relations with America

The United States has had a long-standing diplomatic (consular) and commercial presence in Malaya, North Borneo, and Sarawak since the 1800s. In more modern times formal diplomatic relations were immediately established upon the Malaysia's independence from Britain in 1957. Today the United States and Malaysia do a robust $52.2 billion in trade (2018) while the United States is the largest foreign investor in the country with a total stock of approximately $15.1 billion.[188] A considerable number of American companies have manufacturing plants in Malaysia, as well as in financial services and the energy (oil and gas) sectors. The United States also exports machinery, aircraft, agricultural products, optical and medical instruments, and plastics to Malaysia.[189] Educational, public diplomacy, and cultural exchanges are also extensive. The Fulbright Program in Malaysia is one of the largest in the world, while the US Department of State public diplomacy exchanges count 6,000 Malaysians among its alumni.[190] Moreover, hundreds of young Malaysians have participated in the US-sponsored Young Southeast Asian Leaders Initiative (YSEALI), and several of those participants have assumed high-level government positions in recent years. Defense cooperation is also extensive, although the Malaysian government does not like to publicize it (see discussion in chapter 3). My discussions with defense attachés in the US Embassy in Kuala Lumpur detailed a variety of programs in joint training, ground force and naval exercises, arms sales and service, counterterrorism, non-proliferation, and intelligence sharing.[191] A special area of recent cooperation has been US assistance to improve the Malaysian air force and navy's "maritime domain awareness"—important given the country's crucial location straddling the South China Sea, Andaman Sea, Gulf of Thailand, and the critical Straits of Malacca. Yet none of this defense cooperation is publicized in Malaysia.

Diplomatically, ties between the United States and Malaysia have generally been sound, but have also endured some difficult times. Such was the case during Prime Minister Mahathir Mohamad's long rule from 1981 to 2003, as Mahathir was a frequent outspoken critic of the United States. Following the September 11, 2001, terror attacks in the United States and the Bush administration's "war on global terror," the tensions intensified as Malaysia (a predominantly Islamic country) objected to the invasions of Afghanistan and Iraq. After Najib Rizak's assumption of power as prime minister in 2003, relations began to stabilize (although Najib tilted even further toward Beijing). President Obama even visited the country in 2014, the first by an American president in forty-eight years. But as Najib became embroiled in the 1MDB (One Malaysia Development Berhad) investment scandal,[192] the Obama administration distanced itself from Najib.

1MDB was a state-owned investment firm set up by Najib and of which he was the chairman. The problem was that large sums began to disappear from the fund's coffers—with $700 million reappearing in Najib's personal accounts in 2015, as exposed in investigative reporting by the *Wall Street Journal* and other publications.[193] Najib's efforts to move the embezzled funds offshore resulted in investigations by the US Justice Department, which froze his assets and filed a civil suit against him (not so named but dubbed "Malaysian Official No. 1") in 2016. As rumors of his corruption began to fly, Najib became an ever more regular presence in Beijing. His November 2016 visit resulted in a $33.6 billion package of investments and loans; no wonder that during the visit Najib pronounced China-Malaysian relations as the "best ever."[194] By 2017 his reputation and position came under increased scrutiny and criticism at home and abroad. Mahathir decided to challenge him directly in the 2018 election—and won.

Defeated, Najib was arrested at home on July 3, 2018, by the Malaysian Anti-Corruption Commission and was subsequently prosecuted on thirty-two charges, including corruption, illegal gains, wire fraud and money laundering, misappropriation of public funds, criminal breach of public trust, and abuse of power. Najib's wife Rosmah Mansor was also arrested and charged with money laundering. Frequently compared to Imelda Marcos, Mansor had expensive tastes. When they raided Najib's home, police seized 1,400 necklaces, 567 handbags, 423 watches, 2,200 rings, 1,600 broaches, and 14 tiaras worth $273 million.[195] At the time of this writing, Najib's and his wife's trials had not yet concluded.

Before Najib's downfall and arrest, a new American president had entered office: Donald Trump. In September 2017, Trump hosted Najib on a state visit at the White House. Less than a year later he was under arrest. Subsequently, US ties with Mahathir's new administration remained stable but were not particularly close. Mahathir was consumed with cleaning up domestic corruption in the wake of the 1MDB scandal, as well as recalibrating Malaysia's relations with China. Then, in a surprise political shock, Mahathir was suddenly removed from power by the king on March 1, 2020. The abrupt action was precipitated by parliamentary maneuvering and the apparent loss of a majority for Mahathir's Pakatan Harapan (Alliance for Hope) majority bloc.[196] Mahathir was replaced by veteran politician Muhyiddin Yassin, leader of the Malaysian United Indigenous Party. His leadership was confirmed in an abruptly called session of Parliament in May. At the time of this writing much still remains fluid and unsettled, but two things seem apparent.[197] First, Najib has been permitted to retain his seat in parliament and is a member of the new ruling coalition—but, at the same time, his (and his wife's) trial is proceeding. Second, Belt and Road projects with China will continue on the terms renegotiated by Mahathir.

Malaysia's Relations with China

As described in chapters 4 and 5, Malaysia and China have long-standing cultural, ethnic, and commercial linkages. Since formal diplomatic relations were established in 1974 under Najib's father Abdul Razak Hussein, relations have consistently developed. The only persistent glitch (a not insignificant one) are the two countries' contested claims in the South China Sea. In April 2020 China's coast guard escorted a Chinese seismic survey ship into waters falling within Malaysia's 200-mile exclusive economic zone. But with the renegotiation and recalibration in BRI projects under Mahathir, and the tumult in domestic Malaysian politics, the overall Malaysia-China relationship is returning to more solid footing, despite their ongoing maritime territorial disputes in the South China Sea.[198] Even with the hiccups of Chinese ambassador Bai Tian's (my former student) interference in the 2018 Malaysian election (when he only campaigned for Najib), and his predecessor Huang Huikang's 2015 provocative comments about overseas Chinese (see chapter 5), these incidents do not seem to have had any lasting fallout.

According to Malaysia's former ambassador to China Dato' Abdul Majid Ahmad Khan (1998–2005), "China is pursuing a sophisticated strategy on many levels: state, party, people-to-people, soft power, investment, bilateral, multilateral—they integrate all these elements very well."[199] Commercial links are very thick. Bilateral trade totaled $108 billion in 2018. In 2018 the People's

Bank of China and Bank Negara Malaysia signed a three-year $26.26 billion currency swap agreement to facilitate trade and investment.[200] Beyond BRI infrastructure projects, Chinese investments in Malaysian real estate, agriculture, energy, and manufacturing are extensive—amounting to tens of billions. Chinese tourism in Malaysia is booming with over 2 million visitors a year. Thus, the economic relationship is paramount.

Beyond this dimension, the Chinese Communist Party has maintained close party-to-party links with the long-ruling United Malays National Organization (UMNO) and the Malaysian Chinese Association.[201] These party linkages go well beyond exchanges of delegations and include training of Malaysian officials and politicians at the CCP Central Party School in Beijing and China Executive Leadership Academy in Shanghai. There they are taught how to manage state and private media, control civil society, and stifle political opposition.[202] On the diplomatic level, the two countries are "comprehensive strategic partners" and hold annual "Strategic Consultation" meetings annually.

Defense cooperation is also considerable, dating to the 1990s. Mutual annual visits by defense ministers began in 1992, and the two sides have signed three successive defense cooperation agreements (1999, 2005, and 2014) that specify the particular elements of cooperation. These include an annual a Defense and Security Consultation (DSC) mechanism, joint exercises (ground, air, and naval), exchange of military students and officer training (in China), ship visits, exchange of information and intelligence, military-industrial co-production, and arms transfers.[203] In 2017 the two sides agreed to co-production of four Littoral Mission Ships (LMS), the first two of which to be built in China and the second two in Malaysia. The first was delivered to the Malaysian navy in January 2020. When compared with Malaysia's defense cooperation with the United States as well as with the UK, Singapore, and Australia (via the Five Power Defense Arrangements), its cooperation with China is considerably less (but growing).

Looked at over a long period, Malaysia has always prioritized its relations with China since diplomatic ties were established in 1974 (Malaysia was the first ASEAN country to established diplomatic relations with China). Dr. Mahathir was a regular visitor to Beijing during his long first term in office (1981–2003), and comprehensive and deep ties were forged during this era. He continued to visit (nine times) in his retirement (2003–2018).[204] Despite his campaign criticism of the terms of China's Belt and Road projects and suspension of $22 billion in ongoing projects following his election, after he forced the renegotiation of terms of many of these projects, Mahathir returned to his more traditional pro-China policies. As Chinese Foreign Minister Wang Yi noted in 2018: "Dr. Mahathir is an old and good friend of the Chinese people. He knows China well and he is friendly toward China."[205]

Tilted Hedging

Thus, in the future US-China regional competition, Malaysia can be expected to continue tilting toward Beijing—while keeping its diplomatic distance from Washington. Commercially and culturally, however, Kuala Lumpur seeks strong ties with the United States, and it also values its discrete defense ties even though it does not like to discuss them publicly. This is a form of what I would describe as "tilted hedging." Others view Malaysian diplomacy as more fluid and equidistant between the United States and China. Professor Cheng-Chwee Kuik of the National University of Malaysia has written extensively about his country's and ASEAN's hedging behavior, offering nuanced examinations of different hedging strategies. He correctly notes the deep ties that Malaysia has to the United States—which the Malaysian government and media do not like to publicize—which he characterizes as "light hedging" vis-à-vis China, as distinguished from how he characterizes Vietnam's "heavy hedging" policy that is more openly confrontational toward China and embracing of America.[206] Malaysia, Kuik argues, has considerable "ambivalence" about China—but it avoids "direct balancing" or "heavy hedging" approaches. At the same time that Malaysia extensively engages with the PRC, he argues that it avoids "binding engagement" or "pure bandwagoning." This kind of carefully calibrated and fluid approaches to juggling relations with the United States and China is, he maintains, the distinguishing characteristic of Malaysian diplomacy. Looking back, Malaysia has been quite successful in managing this juggling act—but going forward, like all other ASEAN states, it may become increasingly difficult to navigate.

Brunei

The monarchy of Brunei Darussalam is a tiny Muslim state strategically located on the northern coast of Borneo at the geographic center of Southeast Asia. Only 2,226 square miles in circumference with a population of only 442,000, it nonetheless has the fifth highest per capita income in the world ($84,000). This is due to its extensive deposits (onshore and offshore) of oil and natural gas. It also possesses other raw materials. The country only has a small industrial base, but with a GDP of $36.8 billion it is officially classified as a developed country. The kingdom gained its independence from the UK in 1984, but it maintains close relations with London (including a defense agreement that allows for a small garrison of British troops as well as a battalion of 600 Nepalese Gurkhas). It also joined ASEAN following independence and is a regular participant in ASEAN activities. Given its location, Brunei maintains particularly close ties with Malaysia, the Philippines, and Singapore.

In terms of navigating the US-China competition in the region, like other Southeast Asian states, it has tried to maintain a balance between the two—but finds itself increasingly the object of Chinese attention and influence. The former US ambassador to Brunei Craig Allen (2014–2018) describes Brunei's orientation this way: "Today, Brunei and the United States maintain a strong partnership, especially in the military and security area. While Brunei is cautious about Chinese activity in the South China Sea, they welcome increased Chinese investment into the Sultanate. Culturally, Brunei remains rooted in ASEAN and maintains especially close ties with Singapore, Malaysia and Indonesia."[207]

While not a high priority for Washington, especially compared with other maritime Southeast Asian countries, Brunei and the United States do maintain a range of exchanges and official dialogues. A Senior Officials Dialogue commenced in 2011 and meets periodically (often on the sidelines of the annual US-ASEAN Summit). A defense cooperation agreement came into effect in 1994 and involves a range of exchanges (described in chapter 3) including joint exercises, US Navy port calls, training of Bruneian military personnel in US military academies, and participation in the Cooperation Afloat Readiness and Training (CARAT) annual multinational exercises. Although the UK remains Brunei's main external supplier of military equipment, the United States has also sold Sikorsky Blackhawk helicopters, avionics and other electronic monitoring equipment, as well as some training aircraft to the Royal Brunei Armed Forces.[208] Altogether, bilateral trade totaled $365 million in 2018.

Since establishing diplomatic relations with China in 1991 (Brunei was the last ASEAN state to do so), bilateral ties have grown steadily—although their disputed claims in the South China Sea are divisive issue (Brunei claims a 200-mile box-like economic zone jutting out into the South China Sea), Brunei has been studiously quiet about it and has not openly challenged Beijing's claims. In April 2016 Chinese Foreign Minister Wang Yi publicly claimed that Brunei supported China's position, which the Brunei government did not contradict. Brunei's ties with China are predominantly economic. In 2014 Bandar Seri Begawan (the Bruneian capital) and Beijing agreed to open the Brunei-Guangxi Economic Corridor (odd, given that Guangxi is a landlocked Chinese province), which qualifies Brunei as an official Belt and Road partner country. China is also investing in a number of infrastructure projects—perhaps the most noteworthy of which is a $3.4 billion major petrochemical complex near the capital. This is Brunei's single largest foreign investment project.[209] Chinese firms are also involved in upgrading ports and building roads and bridges. Altogether, China's investments in the tiny kingdom now total $4.1 billion.[210] Beijing also lavishes Brunei with diplomatic attention. Xi Jinping has met Sultan Haji Hassanal Bolkiah several times, most recently receiving him in the Great Hall of the People on April 26, 2019. Foreign Minister Wang Yi has also visited the Bruneian capital several times. As elsewhere in Southeast Asia, showing up counts for a lot. Brunei's gravitation to China was well captured in a discussion I had with officials at the Bruneian Foreign Ministry in Bandar Seri Begawan, where one senior official simply stated: "We have interacted with China for 2000 years. One of our previous Sultans is buried there (in Nanjing)."[211] Concerning and contrasting Brunei's relations with the United States, the official continued: "We see China as a neighboring power that is here to stay, which is not so clear with the USA. America is a new power in Asia, China is not. For us, US power is waning and China's is rising. The last 200 years have been an aberration in China–Southeast Asian relations—it is now returning to a more traditional state."[212]

Singapore

If there is one country in the world that punches above its weight—well above— it is the Republic of Singapore. A small city-state of 5.6 million that became fully sovereign in 1965 (following its expulsion from the Malaysian Federation), Singapore has earned the respect of its neighbors and the world. Singapore boasts the fourth highest GDP per capita in the world ($104,000) and ranks in the top ten globally on many human development indicators. Its educational system, health-care system, legal system, civil service, and corporate environment are all world class. It is also a successful multi-ethnic and secular society. Its political system, while dominated by the People's Action Party (PAP), is a functioning democracy with an active civil society and a considerably (but not totally) open media. All of Singapore's accomplishments owe to its industrious and disciplined population, a first-class civil service, the value of meritocracy and hard work, its strategic geographic location, market economy, lack of corruption, and the visionary leadership of founding father Lee Kuan Yew (1923–2015).

Lee ruled Singapore throughout his lifetime, serving as prime minister from 1965 to 1990, after which he was given the titles of "senior minister" and then "minister mentor," but continued to exercise a guiding hand over the republic.[213] Lee was widely revered at home and around the world. I had the personal honor and professional pleasure of meeting and talking privately with him in his office at the Istana on a number of occasions. As with many others,[214] I was enormously impressed by his intellect, charisma, grasp of issues large and small, sophisticated views of international affairs, his probing mind, his ability to listen, and his understanding of China (about which most of our conversations revolved). While Lee had an outsized imprint on Singapore, he certainly did not do it alone. I have already referred to the world-class Singaporean civil service, but there were also a number of other notable leaders who succeeded him as prime minister (Goh Chok Tong and Lee's son Lee Hsien Loong), eight presidents (including Yusof

Ishak, Ong Teng Cheong, S. R. Nathan, and Tony Tan), as well as a number of very capable senior ministers. Singapore has been blessed with highly competent public servants and leaders. It has also had a number of significant intellectuals, many of whom served in government and others in academia. This group notably includes Wang Gungwu, Bilahari Kausikan, Kishore Mahbubani, Peter Ho, Chan Heng Chee, Tommy Koh, Joseph Chinyong Liow, and others—all of whom are globally recognized public intellectuals who have helped to promote Singapore's views on world affairs.

Given Singapore's size and location, it has behooved the government to practice a multidirectional foreign policy that balances its relations with many powers (including the United States and China), as well as all of its neighbors and being an active participant in ASEAN. This said, Singapore has long had tensions with neighboring Malaysia (owing to its incorporation in, and expulsion from, the federation), as well as being acutely sensitive to the complexities of its larger neighbor to the east: Indonesia. But, on balance, Singaporean foreign policy has been remarkably successful in maintaining good and positive ties with many nations.[215] This is no small accomplishment. As current Foreign Minister Vivian Balakrishnan said on the floor of the Singapore Parliament: "We are still a tiny island in an uncertain neighborhood. We still have to try our best to build a wide network of friends. We have to be a relevant, valuable, reliable partner and, at the same time, be realistic about our place in the world."[216]

Singapore Navigates between Beijing and Washington

Vis-à-vis the United States and China, Singapore has tried hard to *balance* its relations with the two giant powers. While it is much closer to the United States in the security-military sphere (a de facto US ally), in all other spheres Singapore maintains deep and extensive ties with China (as it does with the United States). For example, Singapore is the *world's* leading investor in China, and China is Singapore's largest trading partner ($50.4 bn. in 2018). Yet, for Singapore, it is a delicate balancing act—which requires constant engagement with both Beijing and Washington. Until 2015 it was managing pretty well, but between 2016 and 2017 Singapore's relations with China became strained—as Beijing showed displeasure and sought to "punish" Singapore for several actions it deemed "unfriendly."[217]

First, Singapore's military relationship with the United States was of increasing concern. Singapore has long hosted the US Navy at Changi and Sembewang naval bases, while Singaporean fighter pilots train in the United States, and there is an extensive range of other military and intelligence cooperation as well. This also includes the US use of Singaporean Paya Lebar air base for refueling its reconnaissance flights that regularly run from Okinawa along the China coast-line across the South China Sea, down to Singapore and back up to Okinawa. Beijing seemed to become increasingly intolerant of this US military presence.

Beijing's pressure campaign concerning the US military presence began to seep into the local press. The very day I arrived for my sabbatical stay in Singapore I was greeted by a prominent article in the *Straits Times* entitled, "Time for Singapore to Move Away from Uncle Sam's Embrace?" The article argued that "the Singapore-China relationship was at a crossroads," and that "Singapore is perceived by some as being too close to the US and as being unfriendly to China"—thus arguing that the only way forward was to distance itself from the United States.[218] The authors argued that "Singapore's journey away from the embrace of Uncle Sam should be gradual and graceful. It will not be easy, but it must be done—for the sake of Singaporeans who must live in a new world."[219]

Second, Singapore seemed to openly side with the Philippines after the international tribunal in The Hague issued a ruling in 2016 that invalidated China's expansive claims and "nine-dashed line" in the South China Sea. This coincided with Singapore's chairing of ASEAN in 2017, when it did not do Beijing's bidding on the South China Sea and other issues.

Third, although Beijing had long tolerated it, China began to express displeasure to the Singaporean government and military over its training of ground forces on the island of Taiwan. To be sure, this was a unique arrangement that had been worked out between Lee Kuan Yew and Deng Xiaoping at the time of normalization of relations in 1990. But with the passing of Lee, Beijing apparently felt that it was no longer bound by the agreement and began to rachet up complaints and pressure on Singapore. One way it did so was in November 2016 when Hong Kong authorities impounded nine Singaporean (Terrex) armored infantry vehicles as they were being transshipped from Taiwan through Hong Kong en route back to Singapore. The holding of the Terrexes went on for several months before a behind-the-scenes negotiation facilitated their release. I was living in Singapore at the time and can attest to the widespread public, media, and government discontent with China over the incident.[220] But Beijing was "putting down a marker" about its discontent with the Taiwan training. Despite its pressure, the training continues.

For these reasons, Beijing mounted a concerted campaign to intimidate Singapore during 2016 and 2017. One way it showed its displeasure was by not inviting Prime Minister Lee Hsien Loong to the inaugural Belt and Road Summit in Beijing in May 2017. Lee was the only Southeast Asian head of state of a BRI partner country not invited. Another way was to slow down one of Singapore's three major commercial government-to-government development projects, the China-Singapore (Chongqing) Connectivity Initiative (CCI). The CCI was launched in 2015 as part of an effort to channel investment, trade, digital connectivity, and professional interactions between western China and Southeast Asia, via the mega metropolis of Chongqing.[221] Singapore's previous such projects were the Suzhou Industrial Park (1994) and the Tianjin Eco-City (2008). Another way Beijing expressed its pique with Singapore was to delay scheduling their annual Joint Council for Bilateral Cooperation for 2017. Other pressure tactics were not very subtle. Madame Fu Ying, a former senior Chinese diplomat and at that time chairwoman of the National People's Congress Foreign Affairs Committee, visited Singapore and met with a number of officials—and, according to one present, she said: "China is geography, the US is policy. Figure out which is more important."[222]

By the summer of 2017, however, this multi-pronged pressure campaign eased and relations began to return to an even keel. It is still unclear exactly how the tensions were finessed, and what (if anything) Singapore had to do to accommodate Beijing—but they seemed to begin easing following the visit to Beijing in February 2017 by Deputy Prime Minister and Coordinating Minister for National Security Teo Chee Hean. A Singaporean Foreign Ministry diplomat deeply involved with China relations at the time asserts that no secret compromises, no private exchange of letters, or quid pro quos were reached in order defuse tensions.[223] Subsequent to Teo's visit, though, the Singaporean

Figure 6.4 The author with Singaporean Prime Minister Lee Hsien Loong
Source: Author's photo

media began reporting of improved bilateral ties.[224] Despite the recalibration, from my many discussions while living in Singapore and researching this book at the time, I can attest to the angst that was felt by Singaporean government officials and ex-officials during this period. Even a discussion with Prime Minister Lee and several ministers over dinner at the height of the crisis (Fig. 6.4) concentrated on how far China was prepared to go in "punishing" Singapore— although, truth be told, the prime minister himself evinced the calm view that it was "just a rough patch" that would pass. In retrospect, I had this conversation with Prime minister Lee just three weeks before Deputy Prime Minister Teo made his February 26–28 visit to Beijing, so he was well aware of his government's behind-the-scenes efforts to defuse the intensifying crisis.

While the "rough patch" was weathered and bilateral relations returned to a normal keel, Beijing had definitely put Singapore through an extended period in the "penalty box," as it has done with so many other countries. Unlike other cases, though, the Chinese government never publicly described Singapore's "transgressions" and never publicly criticized Singapore for specific "unfriendly" acts. Thus, Singaporeans were left wondering exactly *what* it had done and exactly *how* to assuage Beijing to repair ties.

This type of oblique reprimand is one form of how China punishes others when they offend Chinese sensibilities or "core interests." The tactic keeps the other side guessing, groveling, and searching for ways to please Beijing—without ever having publicly displayed its displeasure. It's the "silent punishment" treatment. Sometimes it is paired with oblique statements by the Chinese side to the effect that "he who ties the knot has to untie the knot," or the other party "knows what it has done and should reflect on its errant ways." Eventually, though, the other party (in this case Singapore) capitulates, moderates its behavior, apologizes or makes assurances behind the scenes, or takes other steps to accommodate Beijing. As a retired senior Singaporean diplomat said at the time, "If you do what China asks you will never be rewarded. The Chinese will tell you to stand, then they will tell you to sit, but if you do both they will next tell you to kneel. It will never stop."[225] I know these Chinese tactics personally. After I published an article in the *Wall Street Journal* in 2015 I have endured five years of the oblique "deep freeze," as I was "punished" for the article, which offended the sensibilities of the Chinese Communist Party and government.[226]

It remains unclear exactly what Singapore did or said to defuse tensions either before or during Deputy Prime Minister Teo's visit to Beijing—but that visit seemed to be a turning point, after which China backed off, the strains were eased, and relations returned to normal. What is clear is that Singapore did not have to terminate its infantry training on Taiwan (which continues to this day), although I know from discussions with those close to the Ministry of Defense that MINDEF had begun an aggressive search for alternative training sites in

Australia, India, Indonesia, and the Philippines, in case it lost the use of Taiwan. Ironically, China apparently offered its own Hainan Island as an alternative, which was politely declined by Singapore.

Relations between Singapore and China have not always been strained as they were in 2016 and 2017—quite to the contrary, Singapore has enjoyed wide-ranging cooperation since diplomatic relations were established in 1990 (even pre-normalization). This has not only included the substantial trade and investment relationship noted earlier, but also political, diplomatic, and cultural ties. These comprehensive ties were catalogued in a Joint Statement by the two governments in 2018.[227] For many years, China saw Singapore as a political model to be studied.[228] Thousands of Chinese Communist Party, government, and provincial delegations have visited the city-state. As of 2015, Singapore had provided training for 50,000 Chinese officials and cadres, according to then President Tony Tan.[229] On balance, despite the "rough patch," Singapore-China relations are quite comprehensive, sound, and mutually beneficial.

The same can also certainly be said of the US-Singapore relationship. It too is comprehensive in scope, as described in chapter 3. More than 1,700 American companies have offices in Singapore, and trade and investment relations are thick. The United States is Singapore's largest investor ($288 billion), with bilateral trade totaling $45 billion in 2016.[230] Extensive academic and cultural exchanges exist. I taught in one Singaporean university (Nanyang Technological University) and was a visiting scholar at another (National University of Singapore) and can personally attest to the excellent quality of higher education (the best in Southeast Asia by some measure). Diplomatic relations and consultations are very close. Defense ties could hardly be thicker, as also described at length in chapter 3. Although not a formal treaty ally of the Singapore, the United States has no closer partner nation in ASEAN (including with its formal allies Thailand and the Philippines).

Going forward, like all Southeast Asian countries, Singapore will continue to try and navigate the great power competition by maintaining substantive relations with both America and China. This will not be easy, especially for a small city-state like Singapore, and there will be continuing debates within Singapore about just how to manage this situation. At the 2019 Shangri-la Dialogue, held annually in Singapore, Prime Minister Lee Hsien Loong devoted his entire address to the US-China relationship and growing competition, but he was sanguine that Singapore and other ASEAN states could continue to effectively navigate the growing great power rivalry without having to "choose" one over the other.[231] On another occasion, in a high-profile article in the American flagship journal *Foreign Affairs* in June 2020, Lee again directly addressed the impact that the US-China rivalry is having on the region:[232]

The two powers must work out a *modus vivendi* that will be competitive in some areas without allowing rivalry to poison cooperation in others. Asian countries see the United States as a resident power that has vital interests in the region. At the same time, China is a reality on the doorstep. Asian countries do not want to be forced to choose between the two. And if either attempts to force such a choice—if Washington tries to contain China's rise or Beijing seeks to build an exclusive sphere of influence in Asia—they will begin a course of confrontation that will last decades and put the long-heralded Asian century in jeopardy.

This is what Singaporeans and other Southeast Asian certainly desire, but as this book argues, it may be increasingly difficult. Other Singaporeans are sober-minded about the pressures they face. Bilahari Kausikan, the retired senior diplomat, has observed: "What Singaporeans need to understand better is that, under present circumstances, there may be no sweet spot we can occupy that will keep the Chinese and the Americans simultaneously happy. There is no silver bullet, and it's a fool's errand to look for one."[233] In looking forward, Singaporeans would be well advised to look backward to the wise perspectives of their founding father Lee Kuan Yew. Among Lee's many keen observations and prescient predictions, he said the following about the Sino-American competition in the region:

> The Chinese know that they are the biggest boy in the neighborhood and that as they grow in power, they can expect respect for their rights from their neighbors. It is therefore in the interest of other Asian countries, including those in ASEAN, that the Americans maintain a significant presence in the Asia-Pacific region to balance China.... For years, America's presence has been an important stabilizing factor for the region.... In the end, I do not see the Chinese being able to squeeze the Americans out of the western Pacific.[234]

With reference to China's role in the region, Lee observed in 2012:

> China's strategy for Southeast Asia is fairly simple: China tells the region, "come grow with me." At the same time, China's leaders want to convey the impression that China's rise is inevitable and that countries will need to decide if they want to be China's friend or foe when it "arrives." China is also willing to calibrate its engagement to get what it wants or express its displeasure. China is sucking the Southeast Asian countries into its economic system.... Economics sets underlying trends. China's growing economic sway will be very difficult to fight.[235]

Such foresight and geostrategic perspectives—although contradictory—were a distinguishing feature of Lee Kuan Yew. His countrymen—and the entire region—would be well served by keeping them in mind.

Indonesia

Indonesia is the largest Southeast Asian nation in many respects: by population (267.6 million) and largest Muslim population in the world (227 million), geography (735.4 square miles and 17,000 islands), GDP ($1.1 trillion), second largest defense spending ($7.6 bn.), largest multiparty democracy, and other measures. While by these and other indicators Indonesia can be said to be the "most important" nation in Southeast Asia, in its foreign relations—both inside and outside of ASEAN—it does not act like it. Indonesia "punches way below its weight." It is an extremely insular country and government, preoccupied with domestic affairs. In terms of its foreign policy, we have already discussed at some length in chapters 2–5 how Indonesia has clung to a neutralist foreign policy and postcolonial identity—championing non-alignment, South-South relations, and Islamic transnationalism. Indonesia takes ASEAN seriously, but "leads from behind" at best. ASEAN is an organization crying out for leadership and Indonesia is the "natural" leader—but it refuses to act like one. This contributes a great deal to the failure of ASEAN to take tough decisions and act with coherence on the regional and global stage. Under Sukarno and Suharto, Indonesia acted with greater purpose and a stronger international identity, but since 1999 five successive presidents (Habibie, Wahid, Sukarnoputri, Yudhoyono, and Widodo) have pursued very insular policy agendas and have eschewed assuming a leadership role in the region or acting like a middle power internationally.

In chapters 2–5 we also examined at some length how Jakarta managed its relations with the United States and People's Republic of China. Sukarno aligned Indonesia closely to China during the Cold War—until the 1965 failed *coup d'état*. Thereafter, Suharto tilted more toward the United States. In the post-Suharto era, successive Indonesian governments have tried to maintain good ties with both. If anything there has been a slight tilt toward Beijing. The US "war on terror" under the Bush 43 administration and the targeting of Islamic immigrants by the Trump administration have strained bilateral ties in recent years. Despite these temporal strains, ties with the United States are multifaceted and quite strong.

Indonesia's Current Relations with the United States

The two countries enjoy what they describe as a "strategic partnership" (while a commonly used term in Chinese diplomacy, it is unusual in American diplomacy) since 2015. In 2018 bilateral trade was $33.8 billion. US investment in Indonesia is $11.1 billion (total stock). Although technically a middle-income country ($11,600 per capita income), Indonesia remains a very large developing country. As such, the US government undertakes a number of aid and development programs in-country. USAID administers numerous poverty alleviation, institutional capacity building, public health, education, civil society, rule of law, and environmental programs. The Peace Corps is also active, particularly on Java. Law enforcement cooperation is also deep. A lot of effort is devoted to fostering entrepreneurship and SMEs (small-medium enterprises). As US Ambassador Joseph Donovan put it to me: "A democratic, secure, prosperous and active civil society and protection of human rights is in the national interests of the United States. Our relationship with Indonesia is not a sub-set of our relationship with China. It is vitally important in its own right."[236] The United States also invests a great deal in public diplomacy, cultural exchanges, and outreach programs. The Young Southeast Asian Leaders Initiative (YSEALI) has 28,000 members in Indonesia.[237] The Fulbright Program is also fairly active.[238] But the most noteworthy component of US public diplomacy in Indonesia is the wildly successful @America Center. A multimedia "edutainment" and "digital hub" venue located in an accessible downtown shopping mall, @America was launched in 2010, is open 365 days a year, hosts multiple events, and attracts 3,500–4,000 Indonesians (mainly between 18–35) per week.[239] When I visited in 2018 I was very impressed and found it to be a very vibrant, very interactive, and very well conceived venue. So successful is @America that it is being copied and replicated by the State Department in other countries around the world. @America is a great example of successful public diplomacy and American soft power.

Turning to "hard power" and the US-Indonesia defense relationship, it too has become a notable positive dimension of the bilateral relationship. Although there was a "bad decade" from 1995 to 2005 when the US Congress sanctioned the Indonesian military (TNI) for human rights abuses in East Timor, since 2006 the defense relationship has resumed—and indeed has taken off! Similar to the case of Malaysia, however, owing to its sensitivities as an Islamic nation, the Indonesian government does not like to publicize the relationship—but a lot is going on. I was fortunate to receive a detailed briefing from the US Office of Defense Cooperation in the US Embassy on one of my visits to Jakarta. I was told that India, Indonesia, and Vietnam are the Department of Defense's new "priorities" in the Indo-Pacific region. DoD administered 222 OAA's (Operations, Activities, and Actions) with the TNI in 2018.[240]

When US Secretary of Defense James Mattis visited Jakarta in January 2018, he noted the large number of US and Indonesian militaries' joint activities. When Acting Defense Secretary Patrick Shanahan visited Jakarta in May 2019, the two sides signed a joint cooperation agreement to deepen and expand these exchanges.[241]

In sum, the trajectory of Indonesia-US relations is positive, and there is much scope for further development.[242] The United States is fully prepared to advance the relationship—the question is, however, is Jakarta as well?

Indonesia's Approach to China

As described in chapters 4 and 5, Indonesia's relationship with the PRC dates to 1950 when it was one of the earliest countries to establish diplomatic relations with the new regime, but it has had its ups and downs subsequently. We also noted in chapters 4 and 5 the particular problems that Indonesia's Chinese diaspora have played in the relationship. Today, there is an odd kind of duality in Indonesia's approach to China. On one level, there are the normal types of governmental and commercial interactions—but, on another level, there is not much knowledge in Indonesia about China and, to the extent there is, a deep *ambivalence* is apparent. As Jusuf Wanandi (Chairman of the Board of Trustees of the Center for Strategic and International Studies in Jakarta and seasoned observer of Indonesian foreign policy) said at a 2017 conference in Singapore:

> Ambivalence is the key characteristic [in Indonesian views of China]. Anti-Chinese feelings still exist. The Chinese diaspora have become kind of compradors between PRC and Indonesian business. We Indonesians don't really understand China, we don't have connections there, and vice versa. There is a huge gap in understanding and mistrust. The issue is not too much Chinese influence—but not enough! We need to build basic understanding of China—we have none. Nobody speaks Chinese in Indonesia. There are only seven Confucius Institutes in Indonesia—we need 4,000! Indonesians are totally mixed up about China—their baseline knowledge is very poor.[243]

When I met with Wanandi a couple of months later he further lamented: "There is an abysmal level of knowledge in Indonesia about China. It is a product of the past 65 years, but also the insularity of Indonesia. On the surface there are all kinds of government-to-government agreements—but no implementation. The two countries really don't know each other."[244]

Based on my interactions with the Indonesian China studies community in 2017 and 2018, I have to agree with Wanandi's observations (although he was referring to Indonesian society broadly). For such a large country it is rather shocking how small a community of academic China specialists there is. A leading scholar of Chinese politics, Wibowo Wibosono (my PhD student at SOAS), unfortunately prematurely passed away in 2009, and since then (according to a University of Indonesia academic): "Nobody does internal politics."[245] There is only one young lecturer at the University of Indonesia studying China's foreign relations, and I did not meet China scholars at other local universities I visited. One scholar further observed: "It is ironic because we study Chinese, but not China. Japanese studies is very well developed, but not Chinese studies. Last year the University of Indonesia organized a national conference on

China, but only five papers were submitted."[246] There is a "Center" for Chinese Studies in Jakarta, but it functions more as an association than as an institution and has no physical premises or teaching functions. When I gave a lecture there (in a downtown office building) in 2018 I was struck by the pro-China sentiments expressed. Director Natalia Soebagyo said, "Many of us in Indonesia and the region have a sympathetic view of China—because we only really care about economics. Moreover, we don't know what is going on inside China. As long as we can ride the wave of Belt & Road, we Indonesians will be happy."[247] One of her colleagues echoed this sentiment: "We see China has economic strengths that we admire and need."[248]

All of this is indicative of Indonesia's overwhelming insularity as a nation. It is a country totally preoccupied with itself. Major powers like the United States and China are abstractions at best. That also explains why it is difficult for Indonesia to be very active in—much less lead—ASEAN. These sentiments also reflect a certain—indeed considerable—naïveté about China. My discussions with officials in Indonesian ministries reinforced this impression.

Recognizing this ambivalence and lack of Indonesian understanding of China, nonetheless the government has built a number of institutional mechanisms and interactions to reflect the "China-Indonesia Comprehensive Strategic Partnership."[249] China is Indonesia's largest trading partner ($60.1 bn. in 2017),[250] while China is the third largest investor in the country ($2.67 bn.).[251] Chinese tourist visits are significant (2.14 million in 2018), as they visit Bali and other beach resorts in large numbers.[252] But this figure is way below the number of Chinese tourists visiting Thailand (8.87 million in 2016),[253] and as a result the Jokowi government set a target of increasing Chinese tourist numbers to 5 million by 2020. A considerable number of Indonesian students also study in Chinese universities (14,000 as of 2017), and almost all attend with full Chinese scholarship packages.[254] This compares to 9,000 Indonesians now studying in the United States. It is now not uncommon to meet young Indonesian academics who did their PhD degrees in China. When I asked one why he did so—he replied that only six to eight months in residence was required, all expenses were paid, he could then return to Indonesia to work full-time while completing his dissertation, and once it was submitted (to Xiamen University) it was summarily approved. As noted, there are also seven Confucius Institutes in Indonesia— although they are not all known as such. When I visited the one at Al-Azhar University I was told that, owing to sensitivities over promoting Chinese culture in Indonesia and at an Islamic university, they had named their CI as the "Mandarin Language Center" (Pusat Bahasa Mandarin) instead.[255] There have been a number of frictions over the naming and operations of CIs in Indonesia. As one careful study concluded: "The long prevalent racial and political narratives on China and Chinese-Indonesians in Indonesia have been the source of frictions."[256]

In terms of Indonesian military ties with China, they are similar to Thailand's defense ties with the PLA in one respect: when the United States sanctioned the Indonesian military (TNI) from 1995 to 2005 for human rights abuses, the TNI turned to the PLA just as the Thai military did following the US sanctions following the 2014 coup. China smelled an opportunity. Beginning in 2000 and continuing to present, a number of military delegations are exchanged every year, annual joint exercises occur (Sharp Knife), TNI officer and pilot training takes place in China, and joint defense industry cooperation began in 2012. Indonesia has also permitted Chinese naval vessels and submarines to pass through Indonesian territorial waters.[257]

The most sensitive issues in Indonesia's relations with China are the South China Sea around the Natuna islands, and China's Belt and Road Initiative (BRI) projects in the country. Interestingly, given that Indonesia has the world's largest Muslim population, one issue that has not been particularly sensitive has been the incarceration of Uighurs in "re-education" camps and prisons in Xinjiang province in China. Indonesia's relative silence on the issue has been the result of intensive lobbying efforts by China among the Indonesian government, religious authorities, and journalists—according to an article in the *Wall Street Journal*.[258] This issue notwithstanding, let us examine the Natunas issue first and BRI second.

Despite China's expansive claims to the South China Sea, Beijing has long recognized the Natuna Islands as Indonesian territory. The islands themselves lie outside of China's "nine-dash line" claims, but Indonesia's EEZ extends across the southwestern most part of China's line and claims. Beginning in 2016 there have been an increasing number of Chinese fishing boats that have entered Indonesian waters, and some of these incidents have involved large Chinese Coast Guard ships confronting Indonesian attempts to enforce Indonesian sovereignty. There have been a number of close encounters between Chinese Coast Guard and Indonesian naval vessels.[259] In July 2017 the Indonesian Ministry of Maritime Affairs issued a new map that officially renamed that part of the South China Sea as the "North Natuna Sea"—which enraged Beijing and drew official protests. Since this time and to the present the issue remains contested, unresolved, and sensitive between the two countries.

The other sensitive issue concerns the terms of China's BRI projects in the country. There have been several Indonesian concerns: the environmental impact of many projects (particularly mining projects in Kalimantan); the large number of Chinese workers imported into the country (an estimated 31,000 in 2016);[260] the cost and local impact of the Jakarta-Bandung High Speed Rail (HSR) project;[261] the extraction of minerals and raw materials; the dominance of Chinese companies in the projects; and loan financing and debt problems.[262] The Indonesian government has announced that BRI projects in the country will be concentrated in four locales—North Kalimantan (Borneo), North Sulawesi, North Sumatra, and Bali—with a whopping $45.98 billion in total investment.[263] The Sulawesi projects are mainly mining (nickel) and tourism, while Kalimantan involves energy and hydropower. On Java the most notable project is the Jakarta-Bandung high-speed rail connection— which after much back-and-forth is finally in final construction. There will likely be more to come. At the Second Belt and Road Forum in Beijing in March 2019 (where nine of the thirty-six heads of state in attendance came from ASEAN), Indonesia signed twenty-three cooperation agreements for a proposed twenty-eight projects worth $91 billion to the Chinese side.[264]

The BRI in Indonesia has become a very sensitive issue and it played a role in the 2019 national elections.[265] President Jokowi was put on the defensive about it but did his best to avoid it in public commentary. The sub-issue of the large number of Chinese workers in the country was particularly criticized, especially when there are millions of unemployed Indonesian workers. A national survey found that 26.6 percent of Indonesians felt that Chinese workers should be banned altogether, while 50.2 percent said that their numbers should be strictly limited.[266] Indonesian elite perceptions of China have long been more positive than those of the population at large.[267]

For these reasons, the Indonesian government seems to have taken heed from the experiences of other countries and have set down several conditions for BRI projects in the country. Some Chinese experts have taken note of this. Professor Lin Mei of Xiamen University, China's leading specialist on the Indonesian economy, told me: "On the one hand, Indonesians are very eager to embrace BRI—but, on the other hand, they are very sensitive to labor, financing, environmental issues, even political sensitivities. Many Indonesians—politicians, scholars, journalists, and average citizens—talk about 'neo-colonialism' and they are quite worried about a negative impact of BRI."[268] Discussions with senior Indonesian officials also evinced these sentiments. When I interviewed the Indonesian minister overseeing BRI, Minister of Maritime Affairs Luhut Pandjaitan, he set down a number of conditions: transparency; the transfer of first-class technology; creating value added from upstream to downstream industries; respecting the environment; maximizing the use of local labor in projects; and a debt-to-GDP ratio of less than 30 percent.[269] The minister completed our discussion by forcefully proclaiming: "No way we will become dependent on China—no way! But they need us and we need them."[270]

Thus, overall, Indonesia's relations with China are not without their frictions— but Jakarta has been able to maintain generally sound relations while managing the many domestic constituencies that are involved (not the least of which are the Chinese diaspora). In many ways, China seems to be a more combustible issue in Indonesia than in other Southeast Asian societies. As one senior Indonesian think tanker put it, "Anti-Chinese sentiment in Indonesia is still strong. One nudge and it will ignite."[271]

The Philippines

If there is one country in Southeast Asia where a change in leadership has brought with it a dramatic change in orientation vis-à-vis America and China, it is the Philippines under Rodrigo Duterte since he assumed the presidency in June 2016 and embraced China. Prior to that time, the Philippines was strongly rooted in and oriented toward the United States. In fact, so much so that it was the *least* involved Southeast Asian nation with China. Thus—in a real way—the Philippines' broadening and deepening of its relations with China, and recalibration away from the United States under Duterte, places the Philippines in a more equidistant hedging position *similar to* all other ASEAN states. This observation is not to excuse the abrupt, and perhaps unwise, nature of Duterte's shift toward and embrace of China; it is simply to note that this places the Philippines in a similar position with all other ASEAN states—trying to get as much economically out of relations with China as possible while still simultaneously benefiting from ties to the United States. As the Philippines foreign secretary noted in 2017: "Our relationship with Washington is not a marriage that forbids us from pursuing relations with other countries such as China."[272]

What makes the Philippines somewhat different is that it is a long-standing treaty ally of the United States dating back to the 1951 Mutual Defense Treaty. There is also more than a century of close Philippine-American ties, dating to the colonial period, with an estimated 4 million American citizens of Filipino ancestry and more than 220,000 American citizens currently living in the Philippines. A thick and dense web of ties have been built up over the past century (trade, investment, tourism, and people-to-people exchanges). Chapters 2 and 3 detailed these long-standing ties (which have been a mixture of negative and positive). The decision by the Philippines Senate in 1992 not to extend US use of the military bases (notably Clark and Subic Bay) was indicative of the sensitivities that Filipinos feel about their national sovereignty and autonomy.

Despite the ambivalence among some Filipinos about ties to the United States, and some who oppose it forthrightly, public opinion polls nonetheless regularly show that the United States is the most widely liked foreign country among Filipinos. The defense relationship with the Armed Forces of the Philippines (AFP) is particularly close, with generations of officers who have been trained by and in the United States. AFP military doctrine is shaped by the United States and military equipment all comes from there as well.[273] As described in chapter 3, under the Enhanced Defense Cooperation Agreement

(EDCA) of 2014, US military forces have regained periodic access to Filipino bases and continue to deploy troops in the country. The operative clause of the Mutual Defense Treaty (Article 4) has been reaffirmed by both sides in recent years, and both the Obama and Trump administrations have made it explicit that it applies to the Philippines' claims and deployments in the South China Sea. When he visited Manila on March 1, 2019, Secretary of State Pompeo explicitly stated: "As the South China Sea is part of the Pacific, any armed attack on Philippine forces, aircraft or public vessels in the South China Sea will trigger mutual defense obligations under Article 4 of our Mutual Defense Treaty."[274] Such explicit statements are warranted because of lingering Filipino uncertainty about whether the United States will actually "have their back" in a military confrontation with China over their conflicting claims in the South China Sea. Even President Duterte has publicly questioned American commitments in this regard. Commenting on the 2012 Scarborough Shoal stand-off, Duterte was quoted as saying: "Why did you not send the armada of the Seventh Fleet, which is stationed in the Pacific, to just make a u-turn and go there and tell them right to their face, stop it!"[275]

But on February 11, 2020, Duterte threw the US-Philippines defense cooperation into further confusion when he abruptly announced that the Philippines would withdraw from the 1998 Visiting Forces Agreement (VFA).[276] His unilateral withdrawal is valid under the terms of the original agreement, which either party can withdraw from (with 180 days' notice). In doing so, Duterte justified his decision by saying it was in retaliation for a US Senate resolution condemning his government for thousands of extra-judicial killings as part of its alleged anti-drug war. As noted in chapter 3, in June 2020 the impulsive Duterte walked his decision back by "suspending" it for the time being. Although the 1951 Mutual Security Treaty would remain in force, the withdrawal from the VFA would fundamentally affect the full range of US-Philippines defense cooperation.

Duterte's China Pivot

Since coming to power in 2016, Duterte has undertaken a quite critical and confrontational posture toward the United States—while undertaking a radical reorientation of Philippines foreign policy toward China. In October 2016, Duterte made a heralded visit to Beijing, where in a speech in the Great Hall of the People he stunningly announced: "In this venue I announce my separation from the United States—both in military, but in economics too. America has lost. The only hope of the Philippines economically, I will be frank with you, is China."[277] Duterte went further by claiming that he is of Chinese ancestry. For his gushing pivot to Beijing, Duterte was rewarded with a $24 billion economic package ($16 billion in FDI and $9 billion in aid). In total, 13 bilateral cooperation agreements were concluded during Duterte's visit. When I asked Duterte's hand-picked ambassador to China, Chito Romana (whom I have known for forty years), why this abrupt embrace of China had occurred, he replied: "Duterte views China almost entirely through an economic lens—what China can do for the Philippines."[278] This dimension is likely uppermost in President Duterte's mind, but other observers in Manila also note his personal antipathy for the United States and ideological affinity for socialist China.[279] "Duterte is more anti-American than he is pro-Chinese," one scholar noted.[280]

This was just the first of seven meetings Duterte and Xi Jinping had between 2016 and 2019. In November 2018, when Xi Jinping paid a state visit to the Philippines, a thirty-one-point Joint Statement was issued[281] and 29 further cooperation agreements were inked, including a framework agreement for joint exploration of oil and gas in the South China Sea, the establishment of a number of bilateral consultation mechanisms, further collaboration in trade and investment, and defense cooperation. Unlike Duterte's amateurish and emotional display in Beijing two years earlier, Xi Jinping conducted himself with characteristic calm and statesmanlike stature.[282] Subsequently, in September 2019, Duterte returned for his fifth visit to China in three years. This time around he was more restrained and less provocative, but he came away empty-handed.[283]

Yet, three years later after his initial visit to Beijing, Duterte actually has little to tangibly show for his pivot. Very little of the originally promised $24 billion economic investment and aid package has materialized.[284] In fact, Duterte's China pivot has been widely criticized in the Philippines media, among parliamentarians, from some academics, and among the armed forces.[285] Meanwhile, Chinese intrusions into Philippines territorial waters have continued unabated, causing a firestorm of controversy in Manila. Another controversy involves massive Chinese involvement in online gambling in the Philippines. An influx of Chinese workers and human trafficking has become a further irritant.

While President Duterte has managed to reorient his country's foreign policy away from the United States and more toward Beijing, it remains very much a work-in-progress that is afflicted by domestic controversy and opposition. It is very much of a leader-driven policy, and as soon as he leaves office in 2022, Philippine policy could well tilt back toward the United States.

ASEAN's Range of Relationships

In this chapter we have examined all ten ASEAN states' relationships with both the United States and China, largely from their *own perspectives*. Whereas chapters 2–5 examined the two powers' approaches toward Southeast Asia, this chapter turned the analysis around by examining how each of the ASEAN ten have sought to juggle their relations with each power. What we have discovered is that, while all seek to juggle and "hedge" between the United States and China (with the exceptions of Cambodia and Laos), no two are alike. They all fall along a spectrum, but one that is fixed and not static. We explore this, as well as the likely future of the region's ties with the major powers, in the last chapter.

PART IV

THE FUTURE OF GREAT POWER
RELATIONS IN SOUTHEAST ASIA

7

Sino-American Competition in Southeast Asia

Polarization or Competitive Coexistence?

"I think it is very desirable for us not to have to take sides, but the circumstances may come when ASEAN may have to choose one or the other. I am hoping that it's not coming soon."
—Singapore Prime Minister Lee Hsien Loong[1]

"We don't ever ask any Indo-Pacific nations to choose between countries. Our engagement in this region has not been, and will not be, a zero-sum exercise."
—US Secretary of State Mike Pompeo[2]

"The US has proved that it always uses a big stick, and very little carrot. This has not happened with the Chinese. It's not the Chinese way."
—Malaysian Prime Minister Mahathir Mohamad[3]

This book accepts that the *primary dynamic* in international affairs today—and into the indefinite future—is *comprehensive rivalry* between the United States and China. The Sino-American competition is multifaceted in scope—including diplomacy, economy (trade, investment, aid, and standards), technology, security (military and nontraditional), the information domain (media, propaganda, and public diplomacy), political influence activities, ideology, competing models of development and governance, culture, and soft power. The also spans the entire globe. It is the "new normal" in bilateral Sino-American relations as well as international relations more generally. Recognizing this reality, the relationship is not entirely devoid of cooperation or interdependence—but both have shrunk in recent years, as the competitive dynamics have grown greater and some "decoupling" occurs.

While the Sino-American rivalry is increasingly global in nature—spanning every continent—it is most apparent and acute across the vast Indo-Pacific region.[4] The Trump administration's *National Security Strategy* reflects this and flatly asserts: "China seeks to displace the United States in the Indo-Pacific region, expand the reaches of its state-driven economic model, and reorder the region in its favor."[5] The Chinese government, of course, disputes and denies this characterization and continues to claim that it does not seek to expel the United States from the region. Experts are divided on this question—with many believing that expelling the United States from the region and dominating Asia is indeed the *eventual* goal for China. This cohort of analysts sees China constantly probing and eating away at America's position—practicing incremental "salami-slicing tactics" rather than immediately or frontally confronting the United States directly. Other analysts believe that it is not China's goal to force the United States out of the Asia-Pacific and that Beijing can live and coexist with the United States in the region.[6]

While spanning the world as well as the vast Indo-Pacific, this book argues that the strategic competition is increasingly centered in Southeast Asia. In my view, Southeast Asia is *the epicenter* of this global competition and the region will be considerably impacted by the US-China rivalry—much more than most ASEAN states recognize or care to admit. Unfortunately, there exists a considerable amount of denial and excessive preoccupation with internal affairs among Southeast Asian states. This will cloud their perspectives about the larger dynamics swirling around them. There is an ancient Asian adage that when the elephants fight, the grass is trampled. Such is the danger for Southeast Asia as the geo-competition between the United States and China heats up and becomes more and more acute. While neither Beijing nor Washington are at present asking nations to "choose" one over the other—as this would be a counterproductive strategy for each—there nonetheless *are* considerable implicit inducements and pressures being pursued by both powers vis-à-vis third states.

The Sino-American rivalry in Southeast Asia is thus going to be an epic challenge for regional governments (and ASEAN itself) to maneuver effectively between the two major powers, maintain their independence of action, and protect their national sovereignty. Southeast Asia is certainly no stranger to great power competition—indeed it has been the *norm* throughout the modern era. Over time, ASEAN states have become masters of "hedging" behavior and shifting alignments,[7] but navigating it this time around will not be so easy for regional states. While Southeast Asia had to maneuver between the United States' and China's interventions during the Cold War, which was quite intense and indeed the major catalyst for the Vietnam War, this new era of Sino-American competition is quite different—because today Chinese capabilities and influence are considerably greater. Conversely, the power and influence of the United States in the region has *relatively* declined—particularly after the Obama administration.

Thus, the dynamics of Southeast Asia's relations with the two great powers has shifted and remains fluid.

ASEAN's Spectrum of Relations

As described in chapter 6, this has resulted in recalibration by several ASEAN states of their relations vis-à-vis the United States and China. In particular, the Philippines and Thailand have drawn demonstrably away from the United States and toward China.

We see in Figure 7.1 that, as of 2020, seven of the ASEAN ten are closer in their comprehensive relations and strategic orientation to China than to the United States (Brunei, Cambodia, Indonesia, Laos, Malaysia, Myanmar, and Thailand). These seven are not even neutral (although Indonesia may think that it is). They all align with and tilt toward China. On the other hand, three countries (the Philippines, Singapore, and Vietnam) are closer to the United States. Given what we have just seen in chapter 6 about Duterte's pro-China policy, readers may wonder why I place the Philippines to the left of the neutral line. The short answer is the bedrock US-Philippines Mutual Defense Treaty and the totality of deep economic and social bonds with the United States—although Duterte's February 2020 withdrawal from the Visiting Forces Agreement throws into serious question the future of defense ties. Nonetheless, unless and until his government reorients its defense ties from the United States to China, I would still place the Philippines on the American side of the neutral line. But Duterte is a real wild card and has done considerable damage to US-Philippine relations.

I hasten to add that these are my own subjective and considered judgments, but they are based on the empirical evidence described for each nation in previous chapters of this book. Moreover, these are judgments made in mid-2020.

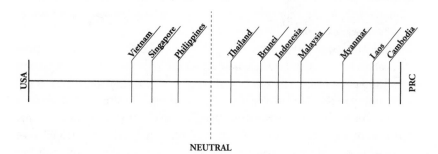

Figure 7.1 Spectrum of ASEAN states' relations with the United States and PRC
Source: Diagram courtesy of Alexander Shambaugh

These relationships are *fluid* and subject to change. Four or five years ago I would not necessarily have placed Indonesia, Myanmar, the Philippines, and Thailand where I do today. Two or three years from now there may be further "movement" along the spectrum. If countries like Cambodia and Laos have what I described in chapter 6 as "Myanmar moments," they could easily pull away from China. Similarly, post-Duterte, the Philippines may well shift back more toward the United States. Thailand could possibly do so too. So, readers should bear in mind that this is something of a "fluid" spectrum in 2020. Things can easily change.

Comparative Advantages and Disadvantages

Both major powers bring certain comparative advantages and disadvantages to their interactions with different Southeast Asian countries. Each has strengths and weaknesses.

Although all Southeast Asian nations engage with the United States and China, this book has demonstrated that there has been a noticeable gravitational shift on their collective part toward China since 2017. While recognizing that China's position and influence in the region has increased considerably, neither should it be overstated. Although China primarily remains an economic power, other dimensions of its power and influence are developing as well. China's diplomatic and political influence in the region must now be said to be greater than America's, while it military prowess and footprint are growing steadily. Once China forward-deploys air and naval assets on its seven reclaimed islands in the South China Sea, and possibly in Cambodia as well, it will be a game-changer for Southeast Asian security. Nonetheless, China's primary strengths are its geographic proximity and deep financial pockets. Beijing showers its ASEAN neighbors with money and projects. Its BRI and building of much-needed infrastructure throughout the region is a distinct comparative advantage. China's commercial footprint is huge—exchanging $587 billion in traded goods in 2018. Beijing's lack of criticism concerning human rights and governance is also appreciated by regional states.

On the other side of the ledger, China's weaknesses are, ironically, its geographical proximity (perceived as too near and too overbearing), its expansive South China Sea claims, its occasional diplomatic manipulation of ASEAN, no real ability to provide security/defense for the region, a "tin ear" of inability to listen and take criticism constructively, and the historical suspicions that Beijing uses ethnic Chinese communities as "fifth columns" in several Southeast Asian societies. China also does not seem to possess much soft power in the region. As Singaporean scholar and one of the most astute regional experts Joseph Chinyong Liow has observed, "Ideational aims do not figure very prominently in China's relations with Southeast Asia."[8] Liow further notes that Beijing fails to articulate a coherent policy vision for the region: "China does not appear to be making any attempt to clearly articulate its military, economic, and ideational interests in the region and to knit together the efforts across the Chinese state to pursue these interests."[9] Despite all of the money and effort expended by Beijing into united front, media, and propaganda work in Southeast Asia (which we discussed at length in chapter 5), it does not seem to be getting much return on its investment (this is true elsewhere in the world as well). China's negatives are perceptually reflected in the ISEAS-Yusof Ishak Institute *State of Southeast Asia 2020 Survey Report*, which asked 1,308 respondents about the "perception of China's political and strategic influence" in the region. Fully 85.4 percent of those surveyed surprisingly responded "worried," while only 14.6 percent answered "welcome."[10] China thus has a major reputational problem, despite its increased presence and influence. In fact, its reputation seems to correlate inversely to its rising regional role. The stronger China becomes, the more it is feared and the more anxiety it produces. These are all distinct shortcomings of China's role in the region.

For its part, the United States also brings multiple assets to bear in its relations with Southeast Asian states and societies. The United States is truly a multidimensional actor. The United States' greatest strength and asset remains its hard military power. The United States is far and away the leading provider of security assistance to Southeast Asian militaries—training, doctrine, provision of weapons, and other areas of support. The forward presence of the US Navy is also unparalleled. Although China's navy now encompasses more ships in the region than the United States, many are not yet "blue water" capable (open ocean). It is the US Navy that keeps the sea lanes of communications (SLOCS) open. America's investments and commercial presence is also substantial. US-ASEAN trade was $334 billion in 2018. Most impressively, the cumulative stock of American direct investment ($329 billion) is four times *larger* than China's and, as previously noted, is greater than that of China, Japan, and South Korea *combined*. America's soft power appeal through media, movies, sports, higher education, technology, and investment are second to none and remain considerably greater than China's regional cultural impact. Even the annual expenditure of US aid programs in the region outstrip China's by a factor of about 4 to 1.

Nevertheless, the United States' weaknesses in its competition with China are many: its geographic distance from the region (the "tyranny of distance"); its emphasis on democracy, human rights, and good governance (which are not intrinsically bad and are consistent with American democratic values, but they do not generally go down well with Southeast Asian governments); Washington's impatience with the slow "ASEAN Way" of diplomatic consensus building; and a lack of government funds to match China in investment and infrastructure projects (the BUILD Act is commendable but a drop in the bucket compared with China's BRI). Another major problem is Washington's episodic diplomacy and failure to regularly send high-level officials to the region. The United States is simply seen as diplomatically disengaged and undependable.

Another weakness is America's reputation in the region and the failure of Southeast Asians to appreciate the breadth and depth of US engagement. As senior Singaporean diplomat and Ambassador-at-Large Tommy Koh described it to me: "In the contest for influence in ASEAN between China and the US, the Chinese are winning the competition. The US has to work harder to strengthen its economic, cultural, political, and security ties with ASEAN."[11] Reporting on China *dominates* regional media in Southeast Asia, while articles and reports about the United States are few and far between. Recognizing this, the United States needs to develop a comprehensive plan to effectively compete with the predominant "China narrative" in the region and undertake a *major public diplomacy effort* to educate Southeast Asians about what the United States contributes and has to offer the region. This has to be well-resourced and consistent, and US public diplomacy officers in the region need to become much more proactively engaged in shaping public opinion about the United States, while countering China's propaganda. Indicative of this dilemma is the aforementioned *State of Southeast Asia 2020 Survey Report*, which asked respondents across the entirety of ASEAN to identify the "most influential political and strategic powers in Southeast Asia": 52 percent of respondents said "China," only 26.7 percent replied "United States," while 18.1 percent identified ASEAN itself.[12] Clearly, the United States has its public diplomacy work cut out for it.

Overall, Washington should substantially raise Southeast Asia as a strategic priority in its Asian and global foreign policy—it is too important of a region to cede to China. Perhaps most important, the United States needs to remain steady, supportive, and engaged with the region. If and when China becomes overly assertive or aggressive in the region—and, as we have seen in previous chapters, there are already signs of this occurring—the United States needs to be present and supportive, offering ASEAN states a viable alternative.

Future Directions

While the Sino-American competition and rivalry in Southeast Asia is increasingly and comprehensively competitive, it remains fluid and can develop differently in the future. Competition for position and influence is not going to stop—indeed it is likely to intensify. But what will be the outcome of it? To my mind, there are four distinct possibilities.

Scenario 1: Further Bandwagoning

We have seen evidence in chapters 5 and 6 (and earlier in this chapter) of a demonstrable shift by many Southeast Asian states *toward China* in recent years. Countries that were "hedging" and trying to maintain a more neutral position (Indonesia) or were more pro-American (the Philippines and Thailand) have distinctly swung toward China. Those that were trying to escape from China's tight grip and establish closer ties with the United States (Myanmar) have slipped back into China's fold. Malaysia was already tilting heavily toward China under Najib—and after a brief recalibration (mainly over renegotiating terms of BRI projects in the country), Mahathir and his successor seem to have continued Malaysia's long-standing pro-China tilt. Cambodia and Laos have become completely dependent on China and can only be described as Beijing's client states. Tiny Brunei also leans much more toward China than the United States. Even Singapore, which maintains close commercial and security ties to the United States, is *deeply* engaged with and in China. Vietnam is also deeply involved in multiple spheres with China, and as we described in chapter 6 the perception in Washington that Hanoi is a de facto ally is deeply misplaced.

So, pro-China bandwagoning and alignment is the current megatrend and it is a strong one.[13] It could well continue to develop even more deeply—and the United States could find itself ostracized across the region.

Scenario 2: Continued "Soft Rivalry" and Competitive Coexistence

I would define the Sino-American competition at present as *soft* rather than *hard*, and *indirect* rather than *direct*. What does this mean? It means that during the Cold War the global rivalry between the United States and the Soviet Union was one of direct action-reaction, tit-for-tat, zero-sum competition. If Moscow made a move, Washington attempted to directly counter it, and vice versa.

The Sino-American competition in Southeast Asia today is not like this (at least not yet). Both Beijing and Washington pursue policies and activities in the region to advance their interests rather than to directly counter the other. They certainly keep a close eye on each other's actions, but there is relatively little evidence that either is calibrating its actions, policies, and presence to directly counter the other. Both powers are on a kind of "autopilot" whereby they work to advance their own position without directly trying to undermine the other's.

This is a situation that behooves Southeast Asian states, as they can try to maximize benefits from both powers.

Because the Sino-American competition in Southeast Asia is not (yet) a direct tit-for-tat, zero-sum, Cold War–type of struggle, I argue that a kind of "competitive coexistence" between the two powers is the current situation, and could be sustained into the future. This is a "good news" scenario. Thus, the US-China strategic competition can be successfully kept from becoming fully adversarial or kinetic. Southeast Asian states have a vital role to play in this regard, through exercising their own agency and by pursuing their traditional, neutralist hedging strategies. Their recent gravitation toward China is thus not helping them, and it puts pressure on Washington to fashion counter-China strategies.

Scenario 3: "Hard Rivalry" and Polarization

In this scenario, the United States *and* China would either individually—or in tandem—both increase and intensify their competition for Southeast Asian loyalties. As during the Cold War, each would directly calibrate its actions to counter the other. For this to occur, China would need to substantially step up its game in the security and defense realm and begin to provide regional states with real alternatives to American weapons and training. China has a *very* long way to go before it will be able to compete with the United States in security assistance. China also has a long way to go to compete with the United States in commercial *services*. As we saw in chapters 3 and 5, China *builds* things, while US companies *facilitate* commercial activity. China also has a very long way to go to compete with the United States in soft power. Thus, for a "hard rivalry" of tit-for-tat direct competition to develop, China's ability to compete in these spheres would need to increase substantially.

Scenario 4: More Neutral Hedging

If Southeast Asian states were to move away from their current bandwagoning toward China and back toward a more neutral "hedging" position, it would likely be triggered by the *overreach* of China. They would experience what I have referred to in this book as "Myanmar moments." That is, regional states (and societies) would need to come to *resent* China's overwhelming and overbearing presence and grip—and would thus seek to maneuver relatively *away from* China into a more neutral position or even slightly tilt toward the United States. Full bandwagoning with the United States does not seem a realistic possibility to me. Those days are over, including for American allies in the Philippines and Thailand. The *best* the United States can hope for is a more neutral hedging type of behavior and partial strategic alignment with Washington.

The possibility of this scenario is not unrealistic. As we saw in chapter 6, several Southeast Asia states (Cambodia, Indonesia, Laos, Malaysia, and Myanmar) are all currently feeling overly dependent on China and there is substantial simmering discontent with China among these societies. Moreover, at least in the Cambodian case, the overdependence is directly related to the ruler (Hun Sen). This was certainly the case in Malaysia under Najib as well, although Mahathir's actions and words concerning BRI alleviated the domestic discontent to some extent. This is also very much the case with Duterte in the Philippines. Jokowi in Indonesia is also politically vulnerable with regard to China. Laos and Myanmar are not dissimilar, but in these cases it is more the regime than the leader.

Thus, in each of these societies the potential for an anti-China backlash is not insignificant. But, if and when it occurs, the result would not be a flip-flop toward a similar dependency on the United States—but much more likely a shift back toward the traditional Southeast Asian "sweet spot" of neutralist hedging.

Implications for the Two Major Powers

How should Beijing and Washington thus proceed in Southeast Asia? Far be it for me to give advice to either (particularly China), but this book does lead me to a few concluding observations.

For China, above all Beijing needs to become *more sensitive* to, and genuinely understanding of, Southeast Asian fears and anxieties about its ambitions and actions. Southeast Asians possess acute memories of the imperial "tribute system" and they do not wish to become tributes again. For *both* powers, understanding the deep and abiding twin sentiments of independence and neutralism embedded in the DNA of Southeast Asian societies is the *starting point* of fashioning a successful regional strategy and policies. Without a genuine and deep appreciation of this factor, any external power will fail in Southeast Asia. For Beijing, this requires an appreciation of the *resentment* felt by many Southeast Asians over China's imperial approaches to the region—and this very much includes the continuing ethnic sensitivities concerning overseas Chinese (*huaqiao*) in several societies. China's expansive and illegal territorial claims to the entirety of the South China Sea, and the building of military facilities there, is also a major *vulnerability* and weakness of China's in the region. As long as this territorial expansionism continues, there will be deep suspicions, fears, and resentment. It could well trigger what I call the "iron law of international relations"—the law of "counter-balancing." If Beijing wishes to provoke Southeast Asian states to align more closely with the United States, its South China Sea claims and militarization are a sure way to achieve it. If Beijing were strategically smart it would adhere to the international legal ruling, abandon its absurd nine-dashed line, and follow international precedent of dividing overlapping claims at the midway points with other states. Such moves would instantly—and lastingly—win China greater trust and support in the region. The terms of China's commercial presence—including BRI—are also a potential vulnerability. China is simply overwhelming many Southeast Asian societies economically—and its hard-nosed, often mercantilist, commercial practices raise resentment as well.[14] The environmental impact of many Chinese projects—particularly, but not exclusively, including the construction of eleven dams that directly impact down-river Mekong countries—is also of concern. These are all distinct vulnerabilities for China and are time bombs waiting to detonate. Thus, if Beijing is wise, it would activate its cultural antennae and pay much closer attention to these anxieties and growing resentment—listen carefully and recalibrate many of its offensive activities.

For its part, Washington should be adroit in how it plays its hand in Southeast Asia. Above all, its needs to *pay attention and show up* in the region.[15] The return to neglecting the region during the presidency of Donald Trump is deeply concerning to many Southeast Asians.[16] Washington should also avoid any temptation to mount a coordinated containment strategy against China in the region, as no single Southeast Asian state would go along with such an effort. Similarly, the *worst* thing that the United States could do would be to try to force a (false) choice on regional states that they must "choose" the United States over China.[17] Such efforts to contain or choose would be very counterproductive—as several states would actively resist Washington and thus most likely align more closely with Beijing. As one official in the Malaysian government told me: "Don't ask us to choose, as you may not like the answer."[18] If anything, one of America's greatest advantages in the region may be China's own unique proclivity to overreach, overstep, bully, intimidate, penetrate, smoother, and overwhelm Southeast Asian states and societies (indeed this applies to other parts of the world as well). Beijing's leaders and their officials abroad all live in a kind of propaganda echo chamber and have not demonstrated that they are capable of listening constructively. In various countries (although not yet so much in Southeast Asia), Beijing has used economic instruments to "punish" others for offending China's many sensitivities. Also, with "wolf warrior" public diplomacy, Chinese diplomats are alienating multiple constituencies around the world. Thus, one of America's greatest assets in its regional and global rivalry with China, may well be Beijing's own increasingly coercive and hegemonic behavior.

At the same time, many Southeast Asian states also look to the United States as an "offshore balancer," a role that the United States can and should play. This role should not be confined only to the security realm but should be comprehensive in scope—including the diplomatic, cultural, public diplomacy, and economic instruments discussed earlier. The United States also needs to *be confident about itself.* The United States has many intrinsic strengths and advantages to draw on in the region.[19] As noted, when China overreaches and becomes too assertive, which I think is quite likely, then the United States needs to be physically present and be perceived to be a reliable partner for Southeast Asians. It is high time for Washington to overcome its history of episodic engagement with Southeast Asia, to realize the strategic significance of the region, and to make it a priority among US global commitments.

Acknowledgments

Researching and writing a book requires the assistance of many. During this three-year endeavor I have been the beneficiary of institutional, financial, and personal support from a variety of sources.

During 2017 I had a sabbatical from George Washington University, which permitted half a year in Southeast Asia. During this time, I was based in Singapore as Distinguished Visiting Professor at the S. Rajaratnam School of International Studies of Nanyang Technological University. I cannot say enough good things about RSIS and all of those affiliated with the school. RSIS has established itself as the premier professional school of international relations in Asia and it is filled with a very diverse range of faculty and scholars working on an extremely broad range of topics. The MA students, with whom I had the pleasure of teaching, are also of high caliber. Particular thanks go to Deputy Chairman of the Board of Governors Ong Keng Yong, current Dean Ralf Emmers, and former Deans Barry Desker and Joseph Liow for inviting me to RSIS. The genuine hospitality I felt from staff and fellow faculty was very much appreciated.

While I got an enormous amount of research accomplished during my stay at RSIS, as well as extensive travel in the region (visiting nine of the ten ASEAN countries), during the summer of 2018 I returned to Singapore again to finish up research for the book. This time I experienced a different institution and was fortunate to be a Visiting Senior Fellow at the Institute of Southeast Asian Studies (ISEAS)–Yusof Ishak Institute. Established in 1968, ISEAS is well known to all in the field as the premier center for the study of Southeast Asia in the region, if not in the world. The library is extraordinary, and the architecturally inviting building is brimming with expertise on different dimensions of Southeast Asia. Again, I was made to feel most welcome and am deeply grateful for the hospitality extended. Particular thanks go to Director Choi Shing Kwok and Daljit Singh, coordinator of the Regional & Strategic Studies Program, as well as Ian Storey, Malcolm Cook, Lye Liang Fook, and Leo Suryadinata for making me feel welcome.

During both stays in Singapore I had the good fortune to live at the Treetops apartment complex, a wonderful respite from the busy world. I wish to thank the staff at Treetops for all of their warmth and hospitality, which made living there a real pleasure.

In addition to the institutions that hosted me in Singapore and around the region, I owe a deep personal debt to the following individuals, each of whom took time to discuss various aspects of the book with me (many more than once). When I began this project I was a true novice on Southeast Asia. It was largely terra incognita. The following individuals in Southeast Asia did a great deal to open my mind and deepen my understanding of this extraordinarily diverse, complex, and fascinating region. Their perspectives are all those with long-time and deep experience in Southeast Asia. They were most gracious with their time, patient and thoughtful in responding to my queries, and most helpful in suggesting others whom I should meet. I list them alphabetically here: Craig Allen, Ang Cheng Guan, Richard Bitzinger, Ralph "Skip" Boyce, Brian Bridges, Andrew Browne, Chan Heng Chee, Peter Chang, Kavi Chongkittavorn, Malcolm Cook, Camille Dawson, Barry Desker, Joseph Donovan, Ralf Emmers, Don Emmerson, Paul Evans, Jon Fasman, Chris Fussner, Virasakdi Futrakul, Nisid Hajari, Pete Haymond, Peter Ho, Abdul Majid Ahmad Khan, Bilahari Kaukisan, Khong Yuen Foong, Tommy Koh, Cheng Chwee Kuik, Nadav Lahavy, Lye Liang Fook, Yerimiah Lalisang, Frank and Anne Lavin, Li Mingjiang, Shahriman Lockman, Kishore Mahbubani, Michael Michalak, Raja Mohan, Chow Bing Ngeow, Nguyen Xuan Cuong, Ong Keng Yong, Desra Percaya, Thitinan Pongsudhirak, Kitti Prasirtsuk, Chito Romana, Daljit Singh, Natalia Soebagjo, Ian Storey, Leo Suryadinata, Stephanie Syptak-Ramnath, Tan Chin Tiong, Tang Siew Mun, Michael Vatikiotis, Yusuf Wanandi, Wang Gungwu, Greg Wiegand, Raymond Wong, and Friedrich Wu.

Back in the United States, I similarly benefited from conversations with Amitav Acharya, Kurt Campbell, Satu Limaye, Amy Searight, Jonathan Stromseth, Michael Yahuda, Brantly Womack, and participants in the monthly Southeast Asian Roundtable in Washington, DC, who have all provided important input. Steve Jackson also helped track down some arcane references. In addition, I particularly benefited from the following colleagues who read portions of the draft manuscript and offered crucial corrections and useful suggestions for improvement. Their eagle eyes and deep knowledge were truly helpful contributions: Richard Bush, Nayan Chanda, Paul Heer, Jim Laurie, Joseph Chinyong Liow, Derek Mitchell, Sheldon Simon, Robert Sutter, and Wang Gungwu.

A multinational project of this nature requires significant financial assistance, and I am most fortunate to have been selected for competitive grants and programs that facilitated the research, travel and living abroad, salary, and benefits.

First, I must thank my home institution, the Elliott School of International Affairs and Department of Political Science at George Washington University, for the sabbatical that started this entire project. Sabbaticals are truly one of the great things about being a professor—if used wisely they permit one to really broaden their horizons and build new intellectual capital. Sabbaticals are partially paid leaves, so GWU is the first source of financial support for which I am very grateful. The Sigur Center for Asian Studies has long offered a collegial work environment for me in Washington. Miriam Grinberg, manager of research programs in the Sigur Center, deserves special thanks as she has managed the grants and all of the complicated financial aspects of this project. Dean Rueben E. Brigety II was particularly supportive of this project. I have also benefited from many discussions with my faculty colleague Robert Sutter, himself a leading scholar and specialist on the region. I also thank Jo Spear, who runs the Elliott School's National Security Manager's Course for Department of Defense Foreign Area Officers (FAOs) and senior officials, which has afforded me informative interactions with senior military officers deeply involved in US military programs in the Indo-Pacific region. This book also benefited from the research assistance from three of my former students, Nico Han, Doris Xu, and Summer Tan—for which I am most grateful.

Secondly, I was the beneficiary of the US Department of State's Speakers Program, administered by the Bureau of Global Public Affairs, which funded travel to a number of countries within Southeast Asia. I am a very strong believer in public education, at home and abroad, and I am grateful to have been selected for this competitive program. Over the course of six months I gave approximately forty lectures in nine Southeast Asian countries plus India, about half of which were sponsored by this program. This facilitated broad exposure I would not otherwise have had to faculty and students, journalists, and think tank experts, as well as government officials. Through these interactions, I experienced many enlightening, and several touching, moments. In each country my activities were facilitated by the cultural affairs and political sections of the US embassies—and I developed deep admiration for the dedicated Foreign Service officers with whom I interacted. In all but one embassy, the American ambassador also kindly hosted a meal on my behalf with local experts and officials.

Third, the Smith Richardson Foundation of Westport, Connecticut, provided a substantial grant that supported further salary, travel in the region, and research materials. This is the fifth of my books that the Smith Richardson Foundation has supported, and its support has been instrumental in the completion of each. I particularly wish to thank Senior Vice President and Director of Programs Marin Strmecki, who has been intellectually engaged with each of the book subjects and pushed me to refine my thinking and draw out the policy implications.

Fourth, I have been the beneficiary of another substantial grant from the Hinrich Foundation of Tempe, Arizona. Merle A. Hinrich—a global business leader, philanthropist, president of the foundation, and longtime resident of Asia—well understood the importance of the topic. I am most grateful to Merle and the foundation's support.

Finally, the China Policy Program at the Elliott School of International Affairs also contributed supplementary funding for the project. Over more than two decades, the China Policy Program has benefited from financial support from many sources—but none more consistent than from Elliott School alumnus Christopher Fussner. Chris has been much more than a financial benefactor, though—as a resident of Singapore and Southeast Asia for more than four decades I have learned a great deal from him over the years.

While this is an original book, I wish to thank the journal *International Security* for permitting me to republish parts of my article "US-China Rivalry in Southeast Asia: Power Shift or Competitive Coexistence?," *International Security* 42, no. 4 (Spring 2018).

I could also not have asked for more in a publisher than Oxford University Press has provided. This is the fourth volume I have published with OUP since 2013 and I cannot be more positive about working with their team. David McBride, Senior Editor for Social Sciences in New York, has a superb understanding of how scholarship benefits policy, and he is a very "hands on" editor who works closely with his authors. Assistant Editor Emily Mackenzie, Project Manager Cheryl Merritt, and copyeditor Timothy DeWerff have also been a joy to work with in flushing out all of the practical details of the production process. Gabriella Baldassin and OUP's international sales team have also been highly professional and proactive in marketing the book worldwide.

I deeply express my appreciation and thank my family—my wife Ingrid and sons Chris and Xander. They provide me daily sustenance, love, and pride. I also wish to thank my brother George, who has been a constant source of love and support throughout my life. Expressions of gratitude would not be complete without mention of our faithful golden retriever Ollie, who has laid next to me for much of the book writing. She epitomizes the aphorism "man's best friend."

Finally, this book has been written in three main locations: at my apartments and ISEAS and RSIS offices in Singapore; at home in Arlington, Virginia; and at our summer cabins in Old Mission, Michigan. All three have proven conducive to thinking and writing.

This book has taken three years to complete. It has been the most difficult book project I have ever undertaken—but also the one I have learned the most from. I hope that readers will also learn from it—but, of course, all errors and omissions are my own.

Notes

Preface

1. *Forest City: An Emerging Futuristic Urban Development—A Prime Model for Future Cities*, brochure. Also see the official website: http://forestcitycgpv.com.
2. See Serina Rahman, *Johor's Forest City Faces Critical Challenges* (Singapore: ISEAS-Yusof Yishak Institute Trends no. 3, 2017); Serina Rahman, "The Socio-Cultural Impacts of Forest City," *Perspective* 42 (2017); Serina Abdul Rahman, "Green Projects Must Also Consider Habitats Lost," *Today* (Singapore), July 25, 2017; Shibani Mahtani, "A Would-Be City in the Malaysian Jungle Is Caught in a Growing Rift between China and Its Neighbors," *Washington Post*, September 10, 2018.
3. See Hannah Beech, "A Rich Melting Pot Centuries Ago, a Globalization Relic Today," *New York Times*, April 12, 2020.
4. "Factbox: Malacca Strait Is a Strategic Chokepoint," Reuters, March 4, 2010, http://in.reuters.com/article/idINIndia-46652220100304. If the Sunda and Lombok Straits are included, half of the world's annual merchant fleet tonnage passes through Southeast Asian waters.
5. See the official website: https://melakagateway.com.

Chapter 1

1. Interview, Singapore, June 19, 2018.
2. Interview, Jakarta, June 25, 2018.
3. Jonathan Stromseth, *Don't Make Us Choose: Southeast Asia in the Throes of US-China Rivalry* (Washington, DC: Brookings Institution, 2019), 2.
4. See Geoff Dyer, *The Contest of the Century: The New Era of Competition with China—and How America Can Win* (New York: Vintage Books, 2014); Michael Pillsbury, *The Hundred Year Marathon: China's Secret Strategy to Replace America as the Global Superpower* (New York: Griffin, 2016); Ashley J. Tellis, Alison Szalwinski, and Michael Wills, eds., *Strategic Asia 2020: U.S.-China Competition for Global Influence* (Seattle and Washington, DC: National Bureau of Asian Research, 2020); Aaron Friedberg, "Competing with China," *Survival* 60, no. 3 (2018): 7–64; Kurt Campbell and Jake Sullivan, "Competition without Catastrophe: How America Can Both Challenge and Coexist with China," *Foreign Affairs* (September/October 2019); David Shambaugh, "Dealing with China: Tough Engagement and Managed Competition," *Asia Policy* 23 (January 2017): 4–12; David Shambaugh, "Towards a 'Smart Competition' Strategy with China," in *The Struggle for Power: U.S.-China Relations in the 21st Century*, eds. Joseph S. Nye, Condoleezza Rice, and Nicholas Burns (Washington, DC: The Aspen Institute, 2020),

141–153; Timothy R. Heath and William R. Thompson, "Avoiding U.S.-China Competition Is Futile: Why the Best Option Is to Manage Strategic Rivalry," *Asia Policy* 13, no. 2 (April 2018): 91–120.

5. For summaries of the evolving debate, see Gilbert Rozman, "The Debate on China Policy Heats Up: Doves, Hawks, Superhawks, and the Viability of the Think Tank Middle Ground," *Asan Forum*, July 16, 2019: http://www.theasanforum.org/the-debate-over-us-policy-toward-china-heats-up-doves-hawks-superhawks-and-the-viability-of-the-think-tank-middle-ground/.

6. See, for example, Pew Research Center, "U.S. Views of China Increasingly Negative Amidst Coronavirus Outbreak," April 21, 2020: https://www.pewresearch.org/global/2020/04/21/u-s-views-of-china-increasingly-negative-amid-coronavirus-outbreak/.

7. See, for example, Friedberg, "Competing with China"; Robert D. Blackwill and Ashley J. Tellis, *Revising U.S. Grand Strategy towards China* (Council on Foreign Relations Special Report No. 72, March 2015): http://carnegieendowment.org/files/Tellis_Blackwill.pdf; Nikki Haley, "How to Win against Beijing: Getting Tough on Trade Is Just the First Step toward Countering China," *Foreign Affairs*, July 18, 2019: https://www.foreignaffairs.com/articles/china/2019-07-18/how-confront-advancing-threat-china.

8. White House, *National Security Strategy of the United States of America*, December 2017: https://www.whitehouse.gov/wp-content/uploads/2017/12/NSS-Final-12-18-2017-0905.pdf; White House, *United States Strategic Approach to the People's Republic of China*, May 2020: https://www.whitehouse.gov/wp-content/uploads/2020/05/U.S.-Strategic-Approach-to-The-Peoples-Republic-of-China-Report-5.20.20.pdf.

9. See Robert Sutter, "The 115th Congress Aligns with the Trump Administration in Targeting China," *PacNet* 62 (August 30, 2018): https://www.pacforum.org/analysis/pacnet-62-115th-congress-aligns-trump-administration-targeting-china; and David Shambaugh, "The New American Bipartisan Consensus on China Policy," *China-US Focus*, September 21, 2018: https://www.chinausfocus.com/foreign-policy/the-new-american-bipartisan-consensus-on-china-policy.

10. https://www.thechicagocouncil.org/publication/public-and-opinion-leaders-views-us-china-trade-war.

11. Campbell and Sullivan, "Competition without Catastrophe," 98.

12. ISEAS-Yusof Ishak Institute, "Survey Report: State of Southeast Asia: 2019," in *ASEAN Focus* (January 2019), 13.

13. See, for example, Michael Yahuda, "Southeast Asia: America's Relative Decline and China's Rise," in Yahuda, *The International Politics of the Asia-Pacific*, 4th ed. (London: Routledge, 2019); Ely Ratner and Samir Kumar, "The United States Is Losing Asia to China," *Foreign Policy*, May 12, 2017; James Guild, "How the US Is Losing to China in Southeast Asia," *The Diplomat*, October 25, 2017.

14. On middle powers mitigating and navigating China's rising influence, an excellent study is Bruce Gilley and Andrew O'Neill, eds., *Middle Powers and the Rise of China* (Washington, DC: Georgetown University Press, 2014).

15. With respect to China, see my book *China Goes Global: The Partial Power* (Oxford and New York: Oxford University Press, 2013).

16. East Timor, which gained its independence in 2002, has yet to join ASEAN as a full member (although it holds observer status).

17. Asian Development Bank Institute, *ASEAN 2030: Toward a Borderless Economic Community* (Tokyo: Asian Development Bank, 2014).

18. Kishore Mahbubani and Jeffery Sng, *The ASEAN Miracle: A Catalyst for Peace* (Singapore: National University of Singapore Press, 2017), chapter 1.

19. "Southeast Asian Economies: OK for Now," *The Economist*, April 14, 2016, https://www.economist.com/news/asia/21697032-region-looking-perkier-most-its-growth-potential-waning-okay-now.

20. Alex Gray, "*The World's 10 Biggest Economies in 2017*" (Cologny, Switzerland: World Economic Forum, March 9, 2017), https://www.weforum.org/agenda/2017/03/worlds-biggest-economies-in-2017/.

21. UMNO lost the election and was turned out of office in May 2018 for the first time in 61 years.

22. See Mahbubani and Sng, *The ASEAN Miracle*.

23. Akhyari Hananto, "Which Military Ranks Southeast Asia's Strongest?" *SEASIA*, January 24, 2017, https://seasia.co/2017/01/24/which-military-ranks-southeast-asia-s-strongest.

24. See Stockholm International Peace Research Institute (SIPRI) Arms Transfers Database, https://www.sipri.org/databases/armstransfers. See also Jonathan D. Caverly and Ethan B. Kapstein, "Who's Arming Asia," *Survival* 58, no. 2 (April/May 2016): 167–184.

25. Donald E. Weatherbee, *International Relations in Southeast Asia: The Struggle for Autonomy*, 2nd ed. (Lanham, MD: Rowman & Littlefield, 2009).

26. Cheng-Chwee Kuik, "How Do Weaker States Hedge? Unpacking ASEAN States' Alignment Behavior towards China," *Journal of Contemporary China* 25, no. 100 (2016): 504. See also Cheng-Chwee Kuik, "Variations on a Hedging Theme: Comparing ASEAN Core States' Alignment Behavior," in *Joint US-Korean Academic Studies*, ed. Gilbert Rozman, Vol. 26 (Washington, DC: Korea Economic Institute of America, 2015), 11–26; and Cheng-Chwee Kuik, "The Essence of Hedging: Malaysia and Singapore's Response to a Rising China," *Contemporary Southeast Asia* 30, no. 2 (August 2008): 159–185.

27. Evelyn Goh, *Meeting the China Challenge: The U.S. in Southeast Asian Regional Security Strategies* (Washington, DC: East-West Center, 2005), 2. See also Evelyn Goh, "Southeast Asian Strategies toward the Great Powers: Still Hedging after All These Years?" *Asan Forum* 4, no. 1 (January/February 2016): 18–37.

28. John D. Ciorciari, *The Limits of Alignment: Southeast Asia and the Great Powers since 1975* (Washington, DC: Georgetown University Press, 2010), especially tables 2.1–3.3.

29. See David B. H. DeNoon, ed., *China, the United States, and the Future of Southeast Asia* (New York: New York University Press, 2017).

30. See in particular Kurt M. Campbell, *The Pivot: The Future of American Statecraft in Asia* (New York: Twelve, 2016); and Hillary Clinton, "America's Pacific Century," *Foreign Policy*, October 11, 2011, https://foreignpolicy.com/2011/10/11/americas-pacific-century/. See

also Robert S. Ross, "The Problem with the Pivot," *Foreign Affairs* 91, no. 6 (November/December 2012): 70–82; and David Shambaugh, "Assessing the U.S. 'Pivot' to Asia," *Strategic Studies Quarterly* 7, no. 2 (Summer 2013): 10–19.

31. See David Shambaugh, "President Obama's Asia Scorecard," *The Wilson Quarterly*, Winter 2016, https://wilsonquarterly.com/quarterly/the-post-obama-world/president-obamas-asia-scorecard/.

32. See Timothy Heath, "Diplomacy Work Forum: Xi Steps Up Efforts to Shape a China-Centered Regional Order," *China Brief*, November 7, 2013, https://jamestown.org/program/diplomacy-work-forum-xi-steps-up-efforts-to-shape-a-china-centered-regional-order/; and Michael D. Swaine, "Chinese Views and Commentary on Peripheral Diplomacy," *China Leadership Monitor*, summer 2014, https://www.hoover.org/sites/default/files/research/docs/clm44ms.pdf.

33. See "Important Speech of Xi Jinping at Peripheral Diplomacy Work Conference" (Beijing: China Council on International Cooperation on Environment and Development, October 30, 2013), http://www.cciced.net/cciceden/NEWSCENTER/LatestEnvironmentalandDevelopmentNews/201310/t20131030_82626.html.

34. See, for example, David Shambaugh, "China Engages Asia: Reshaping the Regional Order," *International Security* 29, no. 3 (Winter 2004/2005): 64–99; and Allen S. Whiting, "ASEAN Eyes China: The Security Dimension," *Asian Survey* 37, no. 4 (April 1997): 299–322.

35. Not all observers agree that China's diplomacy became assertive during this period. See, for example, Alastair Iain Johnston, "How New and Assertive Is China's New Assertiveness?" *International Security* 37, no. 4 (Spring 2013): 7–48; and Michael D. Swaine, "Perceptions of an Assertive China," *China Leadership Monitor*, Spring 2010, https://www.hoover.org/research/perceptions-assertive-china.

36. See discussion in my "China's Long March to Global Power," in David Shambaugh, ed., *China & the World* (New York and Oxford: Oxford University Press, 2020), 17–19.

37. See Zhao Hong, "'One Belt One Road' and China–Southeast Asia Relations," in *Southeast Asia and China: A Contest in Mutual Socialization*, ed. Lowell Dittmer and Ngeow Chow Bing (Singapore: World Scientific, 2017), 211–226.

38. Interview with Hoang The Anh, Deputy Director, Institute of International Studies, Vietnam Academy of Social Sciences, Hanoi, January 22, 2017.

39. Chan Heng Chee, "Southeast Asia at an Inflection Point: An Opinion from ASEAN," in *Advice for the 45th U.S. President: Opinions from Across the Pacific*, ed. Lindsey W. Ford (New York: Asia Society, 2017), 34.

40. Thitinan Pongsudhirak, "A Sino-American Showdown in Southeast Asia?" *Nikkei Asian Review*, January 15, 2017, https://asia.nikkei.com/Viewpoints/Thitinan-Pongsudhirak/A-Sino-American-showdown-in-Southeast-Asia.

41. Interview with senior official, Malaysian Ministry of Foreign Affairs, Putrajaya, Malaysia, April 20, 2017.

42. Ibid.

43. See Richard Wike et al., "U.S. Image Suffers as Publics around World Question Trump's Leadership" (Washington, DC: Pew Research Center, June 26, 2017), http://www.pewglobal.org/2017/06/26/u-s-image-suffers-as-publics-around-world-question-trumps-leadership/.

44. Interview with senior Thai diplomat, Thai Ministry of Foreign Affairs, Bangkok, January 18, 2017.

45. Bilahari Kausikan, *Dealing with an Ambiguous World* (Singapore: World Scientific, 2017), 79.

46. On middle powers in Asia, see Ikenberry, "Between Dragon and Eagle"; and Bruce Gilley and Andrew O'Neil, eds., *Middle Powers and the Rise of China*. On India's role, see Amitav Acharya, *East of India, South of China: Sino-Indian Encounters in Southeast Asia* (New Delhi: Oxford University Press, 2017).

Chapter 2

1. William Seward speech on the floor of the US Senate, July 29, 1852: http://international.loc.gov/cgi-bin/query/r?intldl/mtftext:@field(DOCID+@lit(mtfgc1000_2)).

2. Cited in Mark Borthwick, *Pacific Century*, 2nd ed. (Boulder, CO: Westview Press, 2013), 391.

3. Lyndon Baines Johnson Presidential Library: https://www.youtube.com/watch?v=NSWQztZPMdg.

4. This is also reflected in the various standard histories of the American encounter of [East] Asia, which are dominated by accounts of the US presence in China and Japan. See, for example, Ernest R. May and James C. Thomson Jr., eds., *American-East Asian Relations: A Survey* (Cambridge, MA: Harvard University Press, 1972); Paul H. Clyde and Burton F. Beers, *The Far East: A History of the Western Impact and the Eastern Response, 1830–1965* (Englewood Cliffs, NJ: Prentice Hall, 1966).

5. See Holden Furber, "The Beginnings of American Trade with India, 1784–1812," *New England Quarterly* 11, no. 2 (June 1938): 235–265.

6. United States Information Service, *The Eagle and the Elephant: Thai-American Relations Since 1833* (Bangkok: United States Embassy, 1997), 28-29.

7. See "The Roberts Mission," in *East Asia and the United States: An Encyclopedia of Relations since 1784, Vol. II*, ed. James I. Matray (Westport, CT: Greenwood Press, 2002), 515. Roberts' personal papers are available at the Library of Congress: https://www.loc.gov/item/mm73037960/.

8. Kenton Clymer, "The United States and Southeast Asia," in *Oxford Research Encyclopedia of American History* (Oxford, 2016), 2.

9. John Curtis Perry, *Facing West: Americans and the Opening of the Pacific* (Westport, CT: Prager, 1994), 59.

10. See James C. Thomson Jr., Peter W. Stanley, and John Curtis Perry, *Sentimental Imperialists: The American Experience in East Asia* (New York: Harper & Row, 1981), esp. chapter 4; and Richard W. Van Alstyne, *The United States and East Asia* (London: Thames and Hudson, 1973).

11. Clymer, "The United States and Southeast Asia," 3.

12. Walter G. Sharrow, "William Henry Seward and the Basis for American Empire, 1850–1860," *Pacific Historical Review* 36, no. 3 (April 1967): 339, quoting Seward to the Pacific Railroad Convention, October 1849.

13. Perry, *Facing West*, 64.

14. Quoted in Michael J. Green, *By More Than Providence: Grand Strategy and American Power in the Asia Pacific since 1783* (New York: Columbia University Press, 2017), 91.

15. See Gordon H. Chang, "Asian Immigrant and American Foreign Relations," in *Pacific Passage: The Study of American-East Asian Relations on the Eve of the 21st Century*, ed. Warren I. Cohen (New York: Columbia University Press, 1996), 103–118.

16. Also see Benjamin Armstrong, *Small Boats and Daring Men: Maritime Raiding, Irregular Warfare and the Early American Navy* (Norman: University of Oklahoma Press, 2019), chapter 7 on first Sumatra expedition, 1831–32; chapter 8 on second Sumatra expedition, 1838–1839. These incidents are also recounted in: https://en.wikipedia.org/wiki/Pacific_Squadron; and https://en.wikipedia.org/wiki/Second_Sumatran_expedition.

17. See John H. Schroder, *Matthew Calbraith Perry: Antebellum Sailor and Diplomat* (Annapolis, MD: Naval Institute, 2001).

18. On the Asiatic Squadron during these years see Robert Erwin Johnson, *US Navy in Asian Waters, 1801–1898* (Annapolis, MD: Naval Institute, 1967); John H. Schroder, *Shaping a Maritime Empire: The Commercial and Diplomatic Role of the US Navy, 1829–1861* (Westport, CT: Greenwood, 1985); John H. Schroder, *Shaping a Maritime Empire: The Commercial and Diplomatic Role of the US Navy, 1829–1861* (Westport, CT: Greenwood, 1985); Michael H. Hunt, *The Making of a Special Relationship: The United States and China to 1914* (New York: Columbia University Press, 1983), 16.

19. For a discussion of these debates see Jerald A. Combs, *American Diplomatic History: Two Centuries of Changing Interpretations* (Berkeley: University of California Press, 1983), chapter 6.

20. Quoted in Lockwood, *Southeast Asia in World History*, 115.

21. See Office of the Historian, US Department of State, "Secretary of State John Hay and the Open Door in China, 1899–1900": https://history.state.gov/milestones/1899-1913/hay-and-china.

22. See Jon Tetsuro Sumida, *Inventing Grand Strategy and Teaching Command: The Classic Works of Alfred Thayer Mahan Reconsidered* (Washington, DC: Woodrow Wilson Center; Baltimore: Johns Hopkins University Press, 1997).

23. See William K. Braisted, *The United States Navy in the Pacific, 1898–1909* (Austin: University of Texas, 1958); William K. Braisted, *The United States Navy in the Pacific, 1909–1922* (Austin: University of Texas, 1971).

24. For an excellent discussion of this period, see Green, *By More Than Providence*, chapter 3.

25. Thompson, Stanley, and Perry, *Sentimental Imperialists*, 115; Gary R. Hess, *The United States' Emergence as a Southeast Asian Power, 1940–1950* (New York: Columbia University Press, 1987), 3.

26. See Stephen Kinzer, *The True Flag: Theodore Roosevelt, Mark Twain, and the Birth of the American Empire* (New York: Henry Holt & Co., 2017).

27. Gary Hess, *Vietnam and the United States: Origins and Legacy of War* (New York: Twayne Publishers, 1998), 26; Craig A. Lockwood, *Southeast Asia in World History* (New York: Oxford University Press, 2009), 115.

28. Green, *By More Than Providence*, 91.

29. Gary Hess, *The United States' Emergence as a Southeast Asian Power*, 8.

30. Gerlof D. Homan, "The United States and the Netherlands East Indies: The Evolution of American Anticolonialism," *Pacific Historical Review* 53 (November 1984): 427–428.

31. Hess, *The United States Emergence as a Southeast Asian Power*, 10.

32. Clymer, *The United States and Southeast Asia*, 5.

33. I am grateful to Joseph Liow on this point.

34. Hess, *The United States Emergence as a Southeast Asian Power*, 52.

35. I am indebted to Richard Bush on this point.

36. I am grateful to Joseph Liow on this point.

37. Evelyn Colbert, *Southeast Asia in International Politics, 1941–1956* (Ithaca, NY: Cornell University Press, 1977), 67. Colbert's study of this period is superb.

38. See Michelle Vachon, "How King Sihanouk Brought French Rule to an End," *Cambodia Daily*, November 11, 2013: https://www.cambodiadaily.com/news/how-late-king-norodom-sihanouk-brought-french-rule-to-a-peaceful-end-46825/.

39. Colbert, *Southeast Asia in International Politics*, 86.

40. Paul J. Heer, *Mr. X and the Pacific: George F. Kennan and American Policy in East Asia* (Ithaca, NY: Cornell University Press, 2018).

41. Of the many excellent studies of US-China relations during this period see in particular: Daniel Kurtz-Phelan, *The China Mission: George Marshall's Unfinished War, 1945–1947* (New York: W. W. Norton, 2018); Kevin Perino, *A Force So Swift: Mao, Truman, and the Birth of Modern China, 1949* (New York: Crown Books, 2017); Richard Bernstein, *China 1945: Mao's Revolution and America's Fateful Choice* (New York: Knopf, 2014).

42. Davies' career and perspectives are best captured in his autobiography *China Hand: An Autobiography* (Philadelphia: University of Pennsylvania Press, 1992), and *Dragon by the Tail: American, British, Japanese, and Russian Encounters with China and One Another* (New York: W. W. Norton, 1992).

43. "Review of Current Trends" (PPS-23), February 24, 1948, as cited in Robert M. Blum, *Drawing the Line: The Origin of the American Containment Policy in East Asia* (New York: Norton, 1982), 108.

44. As quoted in Heer, *Mr. X and the Pacific*, 132. I am indebted to Heer's elucidation of the PPS-51 drafting process. Robert Blum's *Drawing the Line* also contains a detailed description of the PPS-51 drafting process, 112–115.

45. For further on US policymaking during the 1948–1949 period, see Andrew J. Rotter, *The Path to Vietnam: Origins of the American Commitment to Southeast Asia* (Ithaca, NY: Cornell University Press, 1987).

46. Quoted in Heer, *Mr. X and the Pacific*, 147.

47. "Memorandum of the Executive Secretary of the National Security Council to the National Security Council: The Position of the United States with Respect to Asia," full text available at: https://history.state.gov/historicaldocuments/frus1949v07p2/d387.

48. See Odd Arne Westad, *The Global Cold War* (Cambridge: Cambridge University Press, 2007).

49. Report to the National Security Council from the Department of State (NSC 64), February 27, 1950: https://history.state.gov/historicaldocuments/frus1950v06/d480.

50. Hess, *Vietnam and the United States*, 52.

51. Ibid., 157.

52. Perhaps the best study remains Stanley Karnow's Pulitzer Prize–winning *Vietnam: A History* (New York: Viking Press, 1983). Also see Hess, *Vietnam and the United States*; Max Hastings, *Vietnam: An Epic Tragedy, 1945–1975* (New York: Harper, 2018); Gareth Porter, ed., *Vietnam: A History in Documents* (New York: Plume–Penguin Books USA, 1981).

53. *Report of the Office of the Secretary of Defense Vietnam Task Force*, National Archives of the United States: https://www.archives.gov/research/pentagon-papers.

54. Quoted in Nicholas Tarling, *Southeast Asia and the Great Powers* (London: Routledge, 2010), 154.

55. Benjamin Zawacki, *Thailand: Shifting Ground between the US and a Rising China* (London: Zed Books, 2017), 37.

56. Among the various studies of the US "secret war in Laos" see Sutayut Osornprasop, "Thailand and the Secret War in Laos," in Malcolm H. Murfett, ed., *Cold War: Southeast Asia* (Singapore: Marshall Cavendish, 2012).

57. For further discussion of SEATO see Colbert, *Southeast Asia in International Politics*, chapter 11; Brian P. Farrell, "Alphabet Soup and Nuclear War: SEATO, China, and the Cold War in Southeast Asia," in Murfett, ed., *Cold War*; and Gary R. Hess, "The American Search for Stability in Southeast Asia: The SEATO Structure of Containment," in Warren Cohen and Akira Iriye, eds., *The Great Powers in East Asia, 1953–1960* (New York: Columbia University Press, 1990).

58. Ang Cheng Guan, *Southeast Asia's Cold War: An Interpretive History* (Honolulu: University of Hawaii Press, 2018), 76.

59. Merle C. Ricklefs, "The Cold War in Hindsight: Local Realities and the Limits of Global Power," in Murfett, ed., *Cold War*, 331. For further discussion of Indonesia during this period see Alan J. Levine, "The Struggle for Indonesia," in *The United States and the Struggle for Southeast Asia, 1945–1975* (Westport, CT: Praeger, 1995).

60. A detailed account of the operation can be found in John Prados, *The Ghosts of Langley: Into the CIA's Heart of Darkness* (New York and London: The New Press, 2017), 99–103.

61. Ibid., 102.

62. Among the many studies, see J. A. C. Mackie, *Konfrontasi: The Indonesia-Malaysia Dispute, 1963–1966* (Oxford: Oxford University Press, 1974).

63. See, in particular, the discussion in Dewi Fortuna Anwar, "Beneficiary of the Cold War: Soeharto and the 'New Order' in Indonesia, 1966–1990," in Murfett, ed., *Cold War: Southeast Asia*.

64. "Sukarno Says US Can Go to Hell with Aid," *Chicago Tribune*, March 26, 1964.

65. Ang Cheng Guan, *Southeast Asia's Cold War*, 120.

66. See Kathy Kedane, "US Officials' Lists Aided Indonesian Bloodbath in '60s," *Washington Post*, May 21, 1999. Also see Ang Cheng Guan's discussion in *Southeast Asia's Cold War*, 122.

67. A 1978 novel by Christopher Koch, 1982 film (starring Mel Gibson, Sigourney Weaver, and Linda Hunt) by this title, and 1982 documentary *The Act of Killing* all depict the time and tensions well.

68. Richard M. Nixon, "Asia after Viet Nam," *Foreign Affairs* 46, no. 1 (October 1967).

69. Ibid.

70. Ronald Spector, "Vietnam War, 1954–1975," *Encyclopedia Britannica*, https://www.britannica.com/event/Vietnam-War.

71. Robert S. McNamara with Brian VanDeMark, *In Retrospect: The Tragedy and Lessons of Vietnam* (New York: Vintage Books, 1995).

72. Ibid., 321–323.

73. By far, the best account of this period is Nayan Chanda, *Brother Enemy: The War after the War, A History of Indochina since the Fall of Saigon* (New York: Macmillan, 1986).

74. "The Cambodian Genocide": http://endgenocide.org/learn/past-genocides/the-cambodian-genocide/.

75. See Odd Arne Westad and Sophie Quinn-Judge, *The Third Indochina War: Conflict between China, Vietnam and Cambodia, 1972–1979* (London: Routledge, 2006); and Chanda, *Brother Enemy*.

76. Chanda, *Brother Enemy*, 288. Chanda's excellent study provides detailed analysis particularly of the Vietnam negotiations as well as internecine bureaucratic battles between the State Department and NSC.

77. Between 1976 and 1981, Indonesia increased its defense spending × 2, Malaysia × 6, the Philippines × 2, Singapore × 1.5, and Thailand × 2.5.

78. Donald E. Weatherbee, ed., *United States–Southeast Asia Relations* (Lanham, MD: Scarecrow Press, 2008), 228.

79. Bush's time in Beijing is recounted well in his *The China Diary of George H. W. Bush: The Making of a Global President* (Princeton, NJ: Princeton University Press, 2008).

80. "The Other Tiananmen Papers," Chinafile, July 8, 2019: http://www.chinafile.com/conversation/other-tiananmen-papers.

81. Joseph Chinyong Liow, *Ambivalent Engagement* (Washington, DC: Brookings Institution, 2017), 51–52.

82. The photo is available at: http://www.petertasker.asia/site/wp-content/uploads/2017/06/IMFired4.jpg. Also see Seth Mydans, "Indonesia Agrees to I.M.F. Tough Medicine," *New York Times*, January 16, 1998: https://www.nytimes.com/1998/01/16/business/indonesia-agrees-to-imf-s-tough-medicine.html.

83. Liow, *Ambivalent Engagement*, 77.

84. See, in particular, Condoleezza Rice, "Campaign 2000: Promoting the National Interest," *Foreign Affairs*, January 1, 2000.

85. Green, *By More Than Providence*, 501.

86. These plots are recounted in Liow, *Ambivalent Engagement*, 88–89.

87. See Diane K. Mauzy and Brian L. Job, "US Policy in Southeast Asia: Limited Re-Engagement after Years of Benign Neglect," *Asian Survey* 47, no. 4 (2007): 22–641; Joseph Chinyong Liow, *Ambivalent Engagement*, 90–109, for an excellent granular country-by-country survey; and Green, *By More Than Providence*, 491–510.

88. Liow, 91.

89. See Natasha Hamilton-Hart, *Hard Interests, Soft Illusions: Southeast Asia and American Power* (Ithaca, NY: Cornell University Press, 2012).

90. Liow, *Ambivalent Engagement*.

Chapter 3

1. The White House, "Remarks by President Obama to the Australian Parliament," November 17, 2011: https://obamawhitehouse.archives.gov/the-press-office/2011/11/17/remarks-president-obama-australian-parliament.

2. The White House, "Remarks by Vice President Pence at the Sixth US-ASEAN Summit," November 14, 2018: https://www.whitehouse.gov/briefings-statements/remarks-vice-president-pence-6th-u-s-asean-summit/.

3. Interview with Singaporean Ambassador-at-Large Tommy Koh, Singapore, April 1, 2017.

4. See Prashanth Parameswaran, "Explaining US Strategic Partnerships in the Asia-Pacific Region: Origins, Developments, and Prospects," *Contemporary Southeast Asia* 36, no. 2 (2014): 262–289.

5. For an excellent review of the Joint Declaration, and the first Obama administration's relations with ASEAN, see Scot Marciel, "A New Era in the Longstanding US-ASEAN Relationship," in *ASEAN-U.S. Relations: What Are the Talking Points?*, ed. Pavin Chachavalpongpun (Singapore: Institute for Southeast Asian Studies, 2012).

6. See Prashanth Parameswaran, "Why the US-ASEAN Sunnylands Summit Matters," *The Diplomat*, February 11, 2016, https://thediplomat.com/2016/02/why-the-us-asean-sunnylands-summit-matters/; and Prashanth Parameswaran, "What Did the US-ASEAN Summit Achieve?" *The Diplomat*, February 18, 2016, https://thediplomat.com/2016/02/what-did-the-us-asean-sunnylands-summit-achieve/.

7. White House, "Joint Statement of the US-ASEAN Special Leaders' Summit: Sunny lands Declaration" (Washington, DC: White House, February 16, 2016): https://obamawhitehouse.archives.gov/the-press-office/2016/02/16/joint-statement-us-asean-special-leaders-summit-sunnylands-declaration. See also Lye Liang Fook, *The First ASEAN-US Standalone Summit: China's Reactions and Implications for China-ASEAN Ties* (Singapore: East Asian Institute Background Brief No. 1118, March 2, 2016).

8. Kurt M. Campbell, *The Pivot: The Future of American Statecraft in Asia* (New York and Boston: Twelve Books, 2016).

9. Ibid., xxi.

10. Hillary Rodham Clinton, *Hard Choices* (New York: Simon & Schuster, 2014), 44.

11. Jeffrey A. Bader, *Obama and China's Rise: An Insider's Account of America's Asia Strategy* (Washington, DC: Brookings Institution Press, 2012), 94, 103.

12. US Mission to ASEAN, "United States–ASEAN: 40th Anniversary Facts" (Jakarta: US Mission to ASEAN, May 8, 2017), https://asean.usmission.gov/united-states-asean-40th-anniversary/.

13. See Ian Storey, *Thailand's Post-Coup Relations with China and America: More Beijing, Less Washington* (Singapore: ISEAS Publishing, 2015).

14. "Plan of Action to Implement the ASEAN-US Strategic Partnership, 2016–2020" (Jakarta: ASEAN Secretariat, November 17, 2015), http://asean.org/wp-content/uploads/images/2015/November/27th-summit/statement/ASEAN-US%20POA%202016-2020_Adopted.pdf.

15. See, for example, Daljit Singh, "Obama's Mixed Legacy in Southeast Asia," *Straits Times*, January 17, 2017; Euan Graham, "Southeast Asia in the US Rebalance: Perceptions from a Divided Region," *Contemporary Southeast Asia* 35, no. 3 (2013): 305–332; and Joseph Chinyong Liow, *Ambivalent Engagement, Ambivalent Engagement: The United States and Regional Security in Southeast Asia after the Cold War* (Washington, DC: Brookings Institution Press, 2017), chapter 6.

16. Liow, *Ambivalent Engagement*.

17. ISEAS-Yusof Ishak Institute, *The State of Southeast Asia: 2019* (Singapore: ASEAN Studies Center of ISEAS-Yusof Ishak Institute, January 2019).

18. Interview, Putrajaya, Malaysia, April 20, 2017.

19. Department of Defense, *Indo-Pacific Strategy Report: Preparedness, Partnerships, and Promoting a Networked Region* (Washington, DC: Department of Defense, 2019), 8.

20. Ibid., 9.

21. Ibid., 8.

22. See, for example, "China Finds New Fans in Southeast Asia as US Turns Inward," *Straits Times*, December 13, 2016; "Asia Draws Closer to China," *Jakarta Post*, May 3, 2017; Winarmo Zain, "As America Pivots Away from Asia, Will China Fill the Void?" *The Nation* (Bangkok), December 10, 2016; Frank Ching, "Beijing Gloats as ASEAN Turns from US," *Asia News Network*, November 9, 2016; Wong Wei Han, "China Waiting in Wings as US Disengages," *Straits Times*, March 28, 2017; Bob Lee, "China Set to Fill Leadership Vacuum as US Turns Inward," *Straits Times*, January 28, 2017; and Bob Savic, "Is US Losing East Asia to China?" *The Diplomat*, December 15, 2016; Ely Ratner and Samir Kumar, "The United States Is Losing Asia to China," *Foreign Policy*, May 12, 2017; James Guild, "How the US Is Losing China in Southeast Asia," *The Diplomat*, October 25, 2017; The Lowy Institute and Council on Foreign Relations, *Southeast Asian Perspectives on US-China Competition* (August 2017), https://cfrd8-files.cfr.org/sites/default/files/report_pdf/Report_Southeast_Asian_Perspectives_Lowy_CFR_OR_0.pdf.

23. See my studies "US-China Rivalry in Southeast Asia: Power Shift or Competitive Coexistence?" *International Security* 42, no. 4 (Spring 2018): 85–127; and *US Relations with Southeast Asia in 2018: More Continuity Than Change*, ISEAS-Yusof Ishak Institute Trends, no. 18 (2018), July 2018. Some sections of this chapter are drawn from these publications.

24. For a listing of Trump's phone calls and meetings with world leaders from January 20 to April 21, 2017, see Malcolm Cook and Ian Storey, "The Trump Administration and Southeast Asia: Limited Engagement Thus Far," *Perspectives* 27 (April 2017), (Singapore: ISEAS–Yusof Ishak Institute), 3. For a series of early evaluations of US policy toward Southeast Asia under the Trump administration, see "Roundtable: The Trump Presidency and Southeast Asia," *Contemporary Southeast Asia* 39, no. 1 (2017): 1–64.

25. Jeevan Vasagar, "US Allies in Asia Dismayed by 'America First,'" *Financial Times*, June 4, 2017; Aaron L. Connelly, "Trump and Southeast Asia: Going through the Motions," *PacNet*, July 6, 2017; and Joshua Kurlantzick, "Southeast Asia in the Age of Trump," *Aspenia Online*, August 6, 2017, http://www.aspeninstitute.it/aspenia-online/contributors/joshua-kurlantzick.

26. "Remarks by the Vice President at ASEAN Secretariat": https://asean.usmission.gov/slide/remarks-vice-president-asean/. Also see Leo Suryadinata and Siwage Dharma Negara, "US Vice President Mike Pence's Visit to Indonesia: A US 'Return' to Southeast Asia?," *Perspective* 32 (May 2017), ISEAS-Yusof Ishak Institute.

27. Goh Sui Noi, "US Remains Committed to Asia-Pacific, Says Defense Secretary James Mattis," *Straits Times*, June 4, 2017: https://www.straitstimes.com/asia/east-asia/us-remains-committed-to-asia-pacific-says-mattis.

28. US Mission to ASEAN, "Readout: Secretary of States Tillerson Meets with the Foreign Ministers of the Association of Southeast Asian Nations," May 4, 2017: https://www.state.gov/r/pa/prs/ps/2017/05/270657.htm.

29. See Thitinan Pongsudhirak, "Trump's Pragmatic Pivot Back to Asia," *Straits Times*, June 6, 2017; Joseph Chinyong Liow, "Is US Engagement Back on Track in East Asia?," *Straits Times*, November 14, 2017; and Storey and Cook, "The Trump Administration and Southeast Asia."

30. See, for example, Sutter, "Trump and China."

31. Alan Chong, "Trump and Southeast Asia: Portents of Transactional Diplomacy," *RSIS Commentary* 207 (November 2, 2017).

32. Chan Xin Ying and David Han, "Najib's United States Visit: What Is Going On?" *RSIS Commentary* 191 (October 11, 2017).

33. Chong, "Trump and Southeast Asia." Also see Pongphisoot Busbarat, "Shopping Diplomacy: The Thai Prime Minister's Visit to the United States and Its Implications for Thai-US Relations," *Commentary* 78 (October 2017), ISEAS-Yusof Ishak Institute.

34. ASEAN Studies Center, ISEAS-Yusof Ishak Institute, "Trump in Southeast Asia," *ASEAN Focus* (December 2017), 4–7; Ian Storey and Malcolm Cook, "The Trump Administration and Southeast Asia: Enhanced Engagement," *Perspective* 87 (November 2017), ISEAS-Yusof Ishak Institute.

35. US Department of Defense, "Remarks by Secretary Mattis at Plenary Session of the 2018 Shangri-la Dialogue": https://www.defense.gov/News/Transcripts/Transcript-View/Article/1538599/remarks-by-secretary-mattis-at-plenary-session-of-the-2018-shangri-la-dialogue/.

36. Ibid., 2.

37. https://www.whitehouse.gov/wp-content/uploads/2017/12/NSS-Final-12-18-2017-0905.pdf; and https://www.defense.gov/Portals/1/Documents/pubs/2018-National-Defense-Strategy-Summary.pdf.

38. *National Defense Strategy*, 2.

39. Randall Schriver, Assistant Secretary of Defense for East Asian and Pacific Security Affairs, Testimony on American Leadership in the Asia-Pacific, May 15, 2018: https://www.foreign.senate.gov/imo/media/doc/051518_Schriver_Testimony.pdf.

40. "Senior State Department Official on East Asian and Pacific Affairs," Office of the Spokesperson, US Department of State, November 15, 2019: https://www.state.gov/senior-state-department-official-on-east-asian-and-pacific-affairs/.

41. US Department of State, *A Free and Open Indo-Pacific: Advancing a Shared Vision*, November 4, 2019: https://www.state.gov/wp-content/uploads/2019/11/Free-and-Open-Indo-Pacific-4Nov2019.pdf.

42. Ibid., 6.

43. Ibid., 10.

44. Ibid., 21.

45. Wu Shicun and Jayanath Colombage, *Indo-Pacific Strategy and China's Response* (Washington, DC: Institute for China-America Studies, October 2019), 8.

46. See, for example, "Diving into the Indo-Pacific," *ASEAN Focus* (ASEAN Studies Center, ISEAS Yusof Ishak Institute, no. 19, December 2017), 8–11; Bilahari Kausikan, "ASEAN: Agnostic on the Free and Open Indo-Pacific," *The Diplomat*, April 27, 2018.

47. See, for example, Amy Searight, "Asia's Diplomatic and Security Structure: Planning US Engagement," written testimony before the House Foreign Affairs Subcommittee on Asia and the Pacific," May 23, 2018. For a 2019 assessment see David Arase, *Free and Open Indo-Pacific Strategy Outlook* (Singapore: ISEAS-Yusof Ishak Institute Trends, no. 12, 2019).

48. John Lee, "The 'Free and Open Indo-Pacific' and Implications for ASEAN," *Trends*, no. 13 (2018), ISEAS-Yusof Ishak Institute.

49. *Indo-Pacific Strategy Report*, 1.

50. Ibid., 4.

51. See, for example, Michael R. Pompeo, Secretary of State, "Remarks at the Lower Mekong Initiative Ministerial," Bangkok, August 1, 2019.

52. As quoted in Tracy Wilkinson and Shashanak Bengali, "Pompeo Seeks to Win Back US Influence in Southeast Asia Amid China's Rise," *Los Angeles Times*, August 1, 2019.

53. Ibid.

54. See Kishore Mahbubani, "ASEAN at 50," Project Syndicate, August 2, 2017: https://www.project-syndicate.org/commentary/asean-50th-anniversary-by-kishore-mahbubani-2017-08?barrier=accesspaylog.

55. https://asean.usmission.gov/our-relationship/policy-history/usasean/.

56. Oddly, this document is on the ASEAN Secretariat website, along with a very useful "Overview of ASEAN-US Dialogue Relations," but neither is available on the US mission to ASEAN website. See: https://asean.org/wp-content/uploads/images/2015/November/27th-summit/statement/ASEAN-US%20POA%202016-2020_Adopted.pdf; https://asean.org/wp-content/uploads/2012/05/2018.06.-Overview-of-ASEAN-US-Dialogue-Relations-shortened-as-of-26June2018.pdf.

57. Interview with Jane Bocklage, chargé d'affaires of US Mission to ASEAN, June 27, 2018, Jakarta.

58. US Mission to ASEAN, "Remarks by Vice President Pence to Sixth US-ASEAN Summit, Singapore, November 16, 2018: https://asean.usmission.gov/remarks-by-vice-president-pence-at-the-6th-u-s-asean-summit/.

59. "The United States and ASEAN: Expanding the Enduring Partnership," November 3, 2019: https://asean.usmission.gov/the-united-states-and-asean-expanding-the-enduring-partnership/.

60. "The United States and ASEAN: An Enduring Partnership," US Department of State, August 2, 2019: https://www.state.gov/the-united-states-and-asean-an-enduring-partnership/.

61. The East-West Center, US-ASEAN Business Council, and ISEAS-Yusof Ishak Institute, *ASEAN Matters for America—America Matters for ASEAN* (Washington, DC: East-West Center, 2019), 24.

62. Ibid., 21. Note: this cumulative figure is at variance with that provided by the US Mission to ASEAN ($271 bn.) in "The United States and ASEAN: Expanding the Enduring Partnership," November 3, 2019: https://asean.usmission.gov/the-united-states-and-asean-expanding-the-enduring-partnership/.

63. Flows of Inward Foreign Investment by Host Country and Source Country (2017): https://data.aseanstats.org/fdi-by-hosts-and-sources.

64. *ASEAN Matters for America—America Matters for ASEAN*, 20.

65. Ibid., 28.

66. https://asean.usmission.gov/connect/.

67. See https://www.usasean.org.

68. *ASEAN Matters for America, America Matters for ASEAN*, 22.

69. Ibid.

70. AMCHAM Singapore, *ASEAN Business Outlook Survey 2018—Fifty to Forward, ASEAN Anniversary Edition* (Singapore: AMCHAM, 2018), 16: https://www.uschamber.com/sites/default/files/abos_2018_final_final_version.pdf.

71. See AMCHAM Singapore, *ASEAN Business Outlook Survey: Fifty to Forward* (Singapore: AMACHAM, 2018). For a good overview of US-ASEAN trade potential, see Peter A. Petri and Michael G. Plummer, *ASEAN Centrality and the ASEAN-US Economic Relationship* (Honolulu: East-West Center Policy Studies No. 69, 2014). Also see US Commercial Service and AMCHAM Singapore, *Crossroads: Doing Business in Singapore and Southeast Asia* (Singapore: AMCHAM, 2018).

72. Shuji Nakayama and Yohei Muramatsu, "China Swoops In as GM Pulls Out of Thailand," *Nikkei Asian Review*, March 2-8, 2020, 20-21.

73. As cited in "Remarks by David R. Stilwell, Assistant Secretary, Bureau of East Asian and Pacific Affairs, at the International Institute of Strategic Studies (ISIS) Malaysia," October 31, 2019: https://my.usembassy.gov/tag/remarks/.

74. Interview with former US ambassador Ralph "Skip" Boyce, Boeing Corporation Director for Southeast Asia, April 18, 2017.

75. American Chamber of Commerce Singapore, *Business Outlook Survey 2018*, 19.

76. Interview, Singapore, June 14, 2018.

77. Interview, Singapore, June 21, 2018.

78. Jon Russell, "Google Report: Southeast Asia's Digital Economy to Triple to $240 Billion by 2025": https://techcrunch.com/2018/11/18/google-report-southeast-asias-digital-economy-to-triple-to-240-billion-by-2025/.

79. See Tristan Chiappini, "Growing Payments in Southeast Asia amid a Dominant Chinese E-Commerce Market," *Mobile Payment Today*, May 3, 2019: https://www.mobilepaymentstoday.com/blogs/growing-payments-in-southeast-asia-amid-a-dominant-chinese-e-commerce-market/.

80. Russell, "Google Report."

81. Hon. Secretary of State Michael R. Pompeo, "On America's Indo-Pacific Economic Vision," Speech to the Indo-Pacific Business Forum/US Chamber of Commerce, Washington, DC, July 30, 2018.

82. Quoted on the PBS News Hour, "China's Massive Belt and Road Initiative Builds Global Infrastructure—and Influence," September 27, 2019: https://www.pbs.org/newshour/show/how-historic-belt-and-road-infrastructure-project-is-building-chinas-global-influence.

83. See "The United States and ASEAN: Expanding the Enduring Partnership," November 3, 2019: https://asean.usmission.gov/the-united-states-and-asean-expanding-the-enduring-partnership/.

84. Interview, Singapore, June 21, 2018.

85. Its European counterpart is the George C. Marshall European Center for Security Studies in Garmisch-Partenkirchen, Germany: http://www.marshallcenter.org/mcpublicweb/en/.

86. ACPSS Mission Statement, available at: https://apcss.org.

87. Information provided during author's visit to APCSS on May 24, 2018.

88. Interview at APCSS, Honolulu, May 24, 2018.

89. See *ASEAN Matters for America, America Matters for ASEAN*, 12.

90. The following figures are taken from "United States Pacific Command" PowerPoint briefing slides (unclassified).

91. "US to Spend $11 Bn. on Military in Asia-Pacific," *Straits Times*, May 9, 2017.

92. "US Pacific Command."

93. Ibid., 18.

94. https://media.defense.gov/2019/May/31/2002139210/-1/-1/1/DOD_INDO_PACIFIC_STRATEGY_REPORT_JUNE_2019.PDF. The following initiatives are drawn from the report, 19.

95. Gordon Lubold, "US Pacific Commander Seeks More Funding to Counter China," *Wall Street Journal*, April 17, 2019.

96. "US to Spend $11 Bn. on Military in Asia-Pacific."

97. Josh Rogin, "To Avoid Conflict, the United States Must Deter Chinese Aggression," *Washington Post*, June 7, 2019.

98. Franz-Stefan Gady, "US Admiral: 'China Seeks Hegemony in East Asia,'" *The Diplomat*, February 25, 2016.

99. "Advance Policy Questions for Admiral Philip Davidson, USN Expected Nominee for Commander, US Pacific Command," to Senate Armed Services Committee, April 17, 2018, available at: https://www.armed-services.senate.gov/imo/media/doc/Davidson_APQs_04-17-18.pdf.

100. INDOPACOM, in conjunction with the Defense Intelligence Agency (DIA), administers the International Intelligence Fellows Program (IIFP), which runs a variety of courses for military intelligence officers from around the region and the world.

101. Mike Ives, "Southeast Asian Nations Join US in Naval Drills," *New York Times*, September 3, 2019.

102. Interview with senior INDOPACOM official, May 24, 2018.

103. *Indo-Pacific Strategy Report*, 36.

104. Donald E. Weatherbee, ed., *United States–Southeast Asia Relations* (Lanham, MD: Scarecrow Press, 2008), 93.

105. For a detailed discussion, see Sheena Chestnut Greitens, "Terrorism in the Philippines and US-Philippines Security Cooperation," Brookings Institution, August 15, 2017: https://www.brookings.edu/opinions/terrorism-in-the-philippines-and-u-s-philippine-security-cooperation/.

106. See Jon Emont, "Philippines to End Pact with US," *Washington Post*, February 12, 2020; Jason Gutierrez, Thomas Gibbons-Neff, and Eric Schmidt, "Over US Objections, the Philippines Plans to Dissolve a Joint Military Pact," *New York Times*, February 12, 2020.

107. For discussion of EDCA see Sheena Chestnut Greitens, "The US Alliance with the Philippines: Opportunities and Challenges," in *Strategic Asia 2014: US Alliances and Partnerships*, ed. Ashley Tellis et al (Seattle: National Bureau of Asian Research, 2014).

108. Interviews, US embassy, Manila, February 16, 2017.

109. Patricia Lourdes Viray, "Duterte: Philippines Will Not Buy Weapons from US," *Philippines Star*, January 11, 2019: https://www.philstar.com/headlines/2019/01/11/1884216/duterte-philippines-will-not-buy-weapons-us.

110. Catharin Dalpino, "The US-Thailand Alliance: Continuity and Change in the 21st Century," in *Strategic Asia, 2014–2015*, ed. Ashely Tellis et al., 153. For another excellent overview see Kavi Chongkittavorn, *The Thailand-US Defense Alliance in the US Indo-Pacific Strategy* (Washington, DC: East-West Center, Asia-Pacific Issues No. 137, March 2019).

111. The text can be found at: https://archive.defense.gov/releases/release.aspx?releaseid=15685.

112. Figure cited in Michael Connors, "Thailand and the United States: Beyond Hegemony?," in *Bush and Asia: America's Evolving Relations with East Asia*, ed. Michael Beeson (London: Routledge, 2006), 142.

113. *Indo-Pacific Strategy Report*, 29.

114. "US, Southeast Asia to Hold First Ever Joint Maritime Drill," *Agence France Presse*, August 26, 2019.

115. See John Blaxland and Greg Raymond, *Tipping the Balance in Southeast Asia?: Thailand, the United States, and China* (Canberra: Australian National University College of the Asia-Pacific Strategic and Defense Studies Center, November 2017), available at: http://bellschool.anu.edu.au/sites/default/files/uploads/2017-11/cog_37.pdf.

116. Ibid., 14.

117. Interview with Thai Vice–Foreign Minister Virasakdi Futrakul, Thai Ministry of Foreign Affairs, Bangkok, January 18, 2017.

118. Interview at ISEAS–Yusof Ishak Institute, Singapore, July 11, 2018.

119. See Benjamin Zawacki, *Thailand: Shifting Ground between the US and a Rising China* (London: Zed Books, 2017), chapter 10.

120. *Indo-Pacific Strategy Report*, 38.

121. Interview, US embassy, Kuala Lumpur, April 21, 2017.

122. Ibid.

123. For an excellent overall assessment of the US-Indonesian relationship see Ann Marie Murphy, "Indonesia's Partnership with the United States: Strategic Imperatives Versus Domestic Obstacles," in *Strategic Asia 2014-2015*, ed. Ashley Tellis et al.

124. *Indo-Pacific Strategy Report*, 37.

125. *Tentara Nasional Indonesia*, literally Indonesian National Military, abbreviated as TNI.

126. Interview, Defense Attaché's Office, US Embassy, Jakarta, June 26, 2018. The following information derives from this interview.

127. For a discussion of Indonesia's parochial strategic outlook see Anne Marie Murphy, "Indonesia's Partnership with the United States: Strategic Imperatives versus Domestic Obstacles," in *Strategic Asia 2014–2015*, ed. Ashley Tellis et al.

128. Interview, US embassy, Hanoi, January 22, 2017.

129. Interview with Nyugen Vinh Quang, Vietnamese Communist Party headquarters, Hanoi, January 22, 2017.

130. Ibid.

131. Prashanth Parameswaran, "US, Singapore Ink New Defense Pact," *The Diplomat*, December 8, 2015.

132. Interview with US Defense Attaché's Office, July 11, 2018. All specific information in this section derives from this interview. I am most grateful to the DAO office for providing me the opportunity and information.

133. Interview with former US ambassador Craig Allen, June 25, 2019.

134. See US Embassy, Vientiane, "United States and Lao PDR Conduct Thirteenth Annual Bilateral Defense Dialogue": https://la.usembassy.gov/united-states-and-lao-pdr-conduct-thirteenth-annual-bilateral-defense-dialogue/.

135. Interview, US Embassy, Yangon, May 26, 2017.

136. International Visitor Leadership Program Fact Sheet, US Department of State, 2017; "Soft Power: The Real Ambassadors," *The Economist*, July 7, 2018, 21.

137. US Mission to ASEAN, "United States–ASEAN: 40th Anniversary Facts" (Jakarta: US Mission to ASEAN, May 8, 2017): https://asean.usmission.gov/united-states-asean-40th-anniversary/.

138. See: https://www.usasean.org/why-asean/educational-exchange. Yet, when compared with China, ASEAN student numbers pale in comparison. In 2015, there were 124,000 students from Southeast Asia studying in Chinese universities. Illustrative of the disparities, according to the IIE, are Cambodian students (2,250 in China, 512 in the United States), Indonesian students (14,714 in China, 8,776 in the United States), Laotian students (9,907 in China, 91 in the United States),

Thai students (23,044 in China, 6,893 in the United States). Source: International Institute of Education, "Open Doors 2016, Regional Fact Sheet: Asia" (New York: International Institute of Education, 2016); China Power Project, CSIS (2018): https://www.csis.org/programs/china-power-project.

139. I had the good fortune to visit @America on June 26, 2018, and was dazzled by the displays, interactive multimedia, state-of-the-art technologies and—above all—the large and excited number of Indonesian visitors. Open 365 days a year and attracting between 3,500–4,000 visitors per *week* (all under 35 years), @American practices "edutainment," according to US Embassy Cultural Attaché Karen Schinnerer. Interview, Jakarta, June 26, 2018.

140. Interview with former VOA executive Jay Henderson, Honolulu, May 26, 2018.

141. Department of State, East Asia and Pacific Bureau, "Strategic Framework for Public Diplomacy EA/P," PowerPoint briefing presentation, May 2018.

142. Ibid.

143. https://www.eastwestcenter.org/education/education-program-overview.

144. https://www.eastwestcenter.org/research/visiting-fellows-and-visiting-scholars.

145. The Asia Foundation, *Six Decades in Asia* (San Francisco: The Asia Foundation, 2014), 11, 24.

146. Drawn from ibid., various pages. I am also particularly grateful to the Asia Foundation's executives Nancy Yuan and John Brandon for providing information about the foundation's work.

147. Interview with former ambassador David Shear, Washington, DC, June 17, 2017.

148. Kishore Mahbubani, *Has China Won? The Chinese Challenge to American Primacy* (New York: Public Affairs, 2020), 246-247. I must admit that, other than these quotations, on balance I do not find Mahbubani's book very persuasive.

Chapter 4

1. Alexander Woodside, *Vietnam and the Chinese Model* (Cambridge, MA: Harvard East Asia Series, 1988), 7

2. G. William Skinner, "Overseas Chinese in Southeast Asia," *Annals of the American Academy of Political and Social Science* 321, no. 138 (1959): 136–147.

3. Wang Gungwu, *China Reconnects: Joining a Deep-Rooted Past to a New World Order* (Singapore: World Scientific, 2019), 124.

4. See Wang Gungwu, "Introduction: China Looking South," in *Imperial China and Its Southern Neighbors*, ed. Victor H. Mair and Liam C. Kelley (Singapore: ISEAS Publishing, 2015), 12.

5. Martin Stuart-Fox, *A Short History of China and Southeast Asia: Tribute, Trade, and Influence* (Crow's Nest, Australia: Allen & Unwin, 2003), 35.

6. Interview with Wang Gungwu, Singapore, June 19, 2018, and email exchanges, July 13–14, 2019.

7. Interview with Professor Nie Dening, Xiamen University, October 24, 2019.

8. Ibid.

9. Wang Gungwu, *The Nanhai Trade* (Singapore: Times Academic Press, 1998).

10. These campaigns are recounted in Wang Gungwu, "Extracts from *The Nanhai Trade*," in *China and Southeast Asia: Volume I*, ed. Geoff Wade (London: Routledge, 2009), 109–111.

11. C. P. Fitzgerald, "Early Chinese Contacts with Southeast Asia," in *China and Southeast Asia: Volume I*, ed. Geoff Wade (London: Routledge, 2009), 39.

12. Ibid., 40, 46.

13. Ibid., 48.

14. Howard W. French, *Everything Under the Heavens: How the Past Helps Shape China's Push for Global Power* (New York: Vintage Books, 2018), 133.

15. Brantly Womack, *China and Vietnam: The Politics of Asymmetry* (Cambridge: Cambridge University Press, 2006).

16. This is a term coined by the late Sinologist Lucian Pye.

17. Brantly Womack, "China, ASEAN, and the Re-centering of Asia," *China's World* 1 (2018): 14.

18. Charles D. Benn, *Daily Life in Traditional China: The Tang Dynasty* (Santa Barbara, CA: ABC-CLIO Greenwood Publishing Group, 2002), 28.

19. Wang Gungwu, "The Nanhai Trade: A Study of the Early History of Chinese Trade in the South China Sea," *Journal of the Malayan Branch of the Royal Asiatic Society* 31, no. 2 (1958): 1, 3–135.

20. Ibid., 31.

21. Ibid., 51.

22. Ibid., 85, 107.

23. Ibid., 113. Also see Wang Gungwu, "Early Ming Relations with Southeast Asia," in *The Chinese World Order*, ed. John K. Fairbank (Cambridge, MA: Harvard University Press, 1968), 47.

24. Interview with Professor Nie Dening, Xiamen University, October 24, 2019.

25. See Louise Levathes, *When China Ruled the Seas: The Treasure Fleet of the Dragon Throne, 1405–1433* (Oxford: Oxford University Press, 1996); Edward Dreyer, *Zheng He: China and the Oceans in the Early Ming, 1405–1433* (New York: Pearson Longman, 2007).

26. Asia for Educators, "The Ming Voyages": http://afe.easia.columbia.edu/special/china_1000ce_mingvoyages.htm.

27. See Dreyer, *Zheng He*.

28. Martin Stuart-Fox, *A Short History of China and Southeast Asia*, 78–79.

29. These are described in Wang, "Early Ming Relations with Southeast Asia," 55–60.

30. Bertil Lintner, *The People's Republic of China and Burma: Not Only Pauk-Phaw* (Arlington, VA: Project 2049 Institute, 2017), 3.

31. For an excellent and extended discussion of this period and these processes, see Michael R. Godley, "The Late Ch'ing Courtship of the Chinese in Southeast Asia," *Journal of Asian Studies* 34, no. 2 (1975): 361–385.

32. Tarling, *Southeast Asia and the Great Powers*, 169–170.

33. G. William Skinner, *Chinese Society in Thailand: An Analytical History* (Ithaca, NY: Cornell University Press, 1957), 72.

34. Cited in Tjio Kayloe, *The Unfinished Revolution: Sun Yat-sen and the Struggle for Modern China* (Tarrytown, NY: Marshall Cavendish, 2017), 143.

35. Ibid., 148.
36. Ibid., 145.
37. Marie-Claire Bergere, *Sun Yat-sen* (Stanford, CA: Stanford University Press, 1994), 194.
38. Kayloe, *The Unfinished Revolution*, 165.
39. Interview with Professor Nie Dening, Xiamen University, October 24, 2019.
40. Stuart-Fox, *A Short History of China and Southeast Asia*, 131.
41. For more on the history of the Comintern, see Julius Braunthal, *History of the International, 1914–1943* (London: Thomas Nelson & Sons, 1967).
42. Ho Chi Minh's time in China, and the CCP-ICP links, are detailed in Stuart-Fox, *A Short History of China & Southeast Asia*, 136–138.
43. See the description of China's role in Ian Storey, *Southeast Asia and the Rise of China: The Search for Security* (London: Routledge, 2011), 56–59.
44. Some of this section is drawn from my "China's Long March to Global Power" in *China & the World*, ed. David Shambaugh (Oxford and New York: Oxford University Press, 2019).
45. This is well recounted in Gregg Brazinsky's superb study *Winning the Third World: Sino-American Rivalry during the Cold War* (Chapel Hill: University of North Carolina Press, 2017).
46. See Harold C. Hinton, *China's Turbulent Quest* (Bloomington: Indiana University Press, 1972), 65; A. Doak Barnett, *Communist China in Asia: A Challenge for American Policy* (New York: Vintage Books, 1960), 304; Zhai Qiang, "China and the Geneva Conference of 1954," *China Quarterly* 129 (March 1992): 103–122.
47. See David Kimche, *The Afro-Asian Movement* (New Brunswick, NJ: Transaction Books, 1972).
48. Mao perceptively first used this term in an August 1946 interview with the American correspondent Anna Louise Strong, to refer to those countries that lay between the emerging Soviet and American camps. See Chen Jian, "Bridging Revolution and Decolonization: The 'Bandung Discourse' in China's Early Cold War Experience," *Chinese Historical Review* 15, no. 2 (Fall 2008): 212.
49. For a Chinese account see Li Qianyu, *Cong Wanlong dao Aerjier: Zhongguo yu Liuci Yafei Guoji Huiyi (1955-1965)* [From Bandung to Algiers: China and Six Asian-African International Conferences, 1955–1965] (Beijing: Shijie zhishi chubanshe, 2016).
50. Agreement between the Republic of India and the People's Republic of China on Trade and Intercourse between the Tibet Region of China and India, April 29, 1954, available at: https://digitalarchive.wilsoncenter.org/document/121558.
51. See David Mozingo, *Chinese Policy towards Indonesia, 1949-1967* (Ithaca, NY: Cornell University Press, 1976), chapters 3–5.
52. I wrote my undergraduate thesis on this subject: David Shambaugh, *China's Dual Policy in the Third World*, George Washington University East Asian Studies, 1977.
53. See J. D. Armstrong, *Revolutionary Diplomacy: Chinese Foreign Policy and the United Front Doctrine* (Berkeley: University of California Press, 1977).
54. See Julia Lovell, *Maoism: A Global History* (New York: Knopf, 2019).

55. See Qiang Zhai, *China and the Vietnam Wars, 1950–1975* (Chapel Hill: University of North Carolina Press, 2000); Womack, *China and Vietnam*, chapter 8.

56. Original source: Li Ke and Hao Shengzhang, *Wenhua Da Geming Zhong de Renmin Jiefangjun* [The People's Liberation Army during the Cultural Revolution] (Beijing: Zhonggong Dangshi Ziliao Chubanshe, 1989), 416, and reproduced in John Garver, *China's Quest: A History of the Foreign Relations of the People's Republic of China* (New York: Oxford University Press, 2016), 239.

57. Chen Jian, "China and the Vietnam War, 1964–1969," *China Quarterly* 142 (June 1995): 378. Chen's article remains the most detailed concerning China's military support for North Vietnam. Also see Allen S. Whiting, *The Chinese Calculus of Deterrence: India and Vietnam* (Ann Arbor: University of Michigan Press, 1975).

58. Garver, *China's Quest*, 213.

59. See William R. Heaton, "China and Southeast Asian Communist Movements: The Decline of Dual Track Diplomacy," *Asian Survey* 22, no. 8 (August 1982): 779–800.

60. See Andrew C. Mertha, *Brothers in Arms: Chinese Aid to the Khmer Rouge, 1975–1979* (Ithaca, NY: Cornell University Press, 2014).

61. Garver, *China's Quest*, 209.

62. Ibid., 225.

63. See the excellent account in Melvin Gurtov, *China and Southeast Asia: The Politics of Survival* (Baltimore: Johns Hopkins University Press, 1975), 101–112.

64. Cited in Garver, *China's Quest*, 221.

65. As quoted in Lovell, *Maoism*, 178–179.

66. As Garver concludes, following an exhaustive examination of the available evidence: "It is virtually certain that CCP and PKI leaders discussed strategy for the Indonesian revolution, and Beijing lauded and encouraged the PKI struggle. Yet there is no evidence that Beijing knew of it, let alone helped plan, the calamitous PKI coup attempt that soon occurred." See Garver, *China's Quest*, 222. Also see Devina Heriyanto, "Was China behind the September 1965 Failed Coup?," *Jakarta Post*, October 20, 2017: https://www.thejakartapost.com/academia/2017/10/20/qa-was-china-behind-the-sept-30-1965-failed-coup.html. This article and other recent scholarship that comes to similar conclusions is based largely on declassified US government documents available through the National Declassification Center and National Security Archive at George Washington University: https://nsarchive.gwu.edu/briefing-book/indonesia/2017-10-17/indonesia-mass-murder-1965-us-embassy-files.

67. The best study of China-Indonesia relations during these years remains Mozingo, *Chinese Policy towards Indonesia*.

68. Heaton, "China and Southeast Asian Communist Movements," 795.

69. Leo Suryadinata, "'Overseas Chinese' in Southeast Asia and China's Foreign Policy: An Interpretive Essay," in *China and Southeast Asia: Volume III*, ed. Geoff Wade (London: Routledge, 2009).

70. Chun-hsi Wu, *Dollars, Dependents, and Dogma: Overseas Chinese Remittances to Communist China* (Stanford, CA: Hoover Institution on War, Revolution, and Peace, 1967), 142, as reprinted in Suryadinata, "Overseas Chinese."

71. Wu Xiao An, *China's Evolving Policy towards the Chinese Diaspora in Southeast Asia (1949–2018)* (Singapore: ISEAS-Yusof Ishak Institute, 2019), 9.

72. Ibid., 1.

73. Fang Fang, "Report on the Current Situation and Overseas Chinese Affairs at the Fourth Plenum of the First Committee of the All-China Federation of Returned Overseas Chinese," *Da Gong Bao* (Hong Kong), December 20, 1959, translated in *Survey of Mainland China Press* (SCMP), no. 2164, December 28, 1959, as cited in Mozingo, *Chinese Policy towards Indonesia*, 171–172.

74. Robert S. Ross, *The Indochina Tangle: China's Vietnam Policy, 1975–1979* (New York: Columbia University Press, 1988).

75. The best studies of China's Vietnam war are Edward C. O'Dowd, *Chinese Military Strategy in the Third Indochina War: The Last Maoist War* (London: Routledge, 2007); Zhang Xiaoming, "China's 1979 War with Vietnam: A Reassessment," *China Quarterly* 184 (December 2005): 851–874; and King V. Chen, *China's War with Vietnam* (Stanford, CA: Hoover Institution, 1987). For excellent studies of the broader deterioration of Sino-Vietnamese relations during this period, see William J. Duiker, *China and Vietnam: The Roots of Conflict* (Berkeley: University of California Press, 1986); Robert S. Ross, *The Indochina Tangle*; and Anne Gilks, *The Breakdown of the Sino-Vietnamese Alliance, 1970–1979* (Berkeley: University of California Press, 1992).

76. Lee Kuan Yew, *From Third World to First: The Singapore Story, 1965–2000* (Singapore: Times Media, 2000), 693.

77. Ibid., chapters 39–40.

78. This process is well chronicled in Alastair Iain Johnston and Robert S. Ross, eds., *Engaging China: The Management of an Emerging Power* (London: Routledge, 1999).

79. Interview with Cui Tiankai, June 11, 2004, Beijing.

80. See the chapters in David Shambaugh, ed., *Power Shift: China and Asia's New Dynamics* (Berkeley: University of California Pres, 2005). Also see Allen S. Whiting, "ASEAN Eyes China: The Security Dimension," *Asian Survey* 37, no. 4 (April 1997): 299–322.

81. I have chronicled and analyzed the first question in my book *China Goes Global*, and China's response to the second and third questions in my book *China's Communist Party: Atrophy and Adaptation*. David Shambaugh, *China Goes Global: The Partial Power* (Oxford and New York: Oxford University Press, 2013); David Shambaugh, *China's Communist Party: Atrophy and Adaptation* (Berkeley and Washington, DC: University of California Press and Woodrow Wilson Center Press, 2008).

82. See Zhang Yunling and Tang Shiping, "China's Regional Strategy," in *Power Shift*, ed. Shambaugh.

83. This process is detailed in the various chapters in Shambaugh, ed., *Power Shift*.

84. See Gilbert Rozman, *China's Strategic Thought towards Asia* (London: Palgrave Macmillan, 2010), esp. chapter 4.

Chapter 5

1. Xi Jinping, "Forging a Strong Partnership to Enhance Prosperity of Asia," 36th Singapore Lecture, ISEAS–Yusof Ishak Institute, November 7, 2015, 10.

2. Statement at ASEAN Post-Ministerial Conference 2010, Hanoi, as quoted in John Pomfret, "US Takes a Tougher Tone with China," *Washington Post*, July 30, 2010. Many diplomats present at the meeting subsequently collaborated Yang's quotation. Yang said it sternly while staring directly at Singaporean Foreign Minister George Yeo.

3. Kishore Mahbubani, "ASEAN Still Critical Catalyst for China's Future," *East Asian Forum Quarterly* (October–December 2016).

4. Sources: "ASEAN-China Relations: Then and Now," *ASEAN Focus* 6 (2018): 12–13; ASEAN-China Center, *25 Years of ASEAN-China Dialogue and Cooperation: Facts and Figures* (Beijing: ASEAN-China Center, 2016); Speech by Ambassador Huang Xilian at the China-ASEAN Belt and Road Business Forum, Jakarta, May 16, 2018; Remarks by Ambassador Huang Xilian at the Roundtable Discussion with Local Think Tanks and Media, February 9, 2018, Jakarta; Ambassador Huang Xilian, "China, ASEAN Enter a New Era Hand-in-Hand," *Jakarta Post*, February 8, 2018.

5. This was also the general conclusion of a state-of-the field volume published in 2007, although the contributors pointed to the potential for further development. Alas, more than a decade later, it cannot be said that the potential has been realized. See Saw Swee-Hock and John Wong, eds., *Southeast Asian Studies in China* (Singapore: ISEAS Publishing, 2007).

6. Interview with Dean Li Yiping, Research School for Southeast Asian Studies, Xiamen University, October 24, 2019.

7. See David Shambaugh, "International Relations Studies in China: History, Trends, and Prospects," *International Relations of the Asia-Pacific* (September 2011).

8. Southeast Asia specialist Jonathan Stromseth of the Brookings Institution reports the exact same observation during his time as Asia Foundation representative in Beijing from 2006 to 2014, but he also notes that the situation began to change markedly toward the end of that period. Says Stromseth: "[In 2006] What I discovered, however, was not just minimal human resource capacity in Southeast Asian studies, but little interest in the region itself. . . . Southeast Asia seemed like a backwater. Now the situation has changed entirely. The study of Southeast Asia is booming not only in Beijing, but across the country where new programs and centers are popping up." Personally, I think Stromseth overstates the current situation, but he nonetheless offers a firsthand perspective. See Jonathan Stromseth, "The Testing Ground: China's Rising Influence in Southeast Asia and Regional Responses," Brookings Institution, November 2019: https://www.brookings.edu/wp-content/uploads/2019/11/FP_20191119_china_se_asia_stromseth.pdf.

9. This is the official English translation used by the journal, although *Research on South [China] Sea Issues* is the literal translation.

10. Wang Shilu, "Southeast Asian Studies in Yunnan," in *Southeast Asian Studies in China*, ed. Saw Swee-Hock and John Wong, 107–108.

11. Zhou Shixin, "ASEAN Centrality in Reginal Cooperation: Status Quo and Challenges," *China International Studies* 1 (January/February 2017): 90–92.

12. Ibid., 94–95.

13. For a comprehensive review of Chinese writings on US-China strategic competition, see Minghao Zhao, "Is a New Cold War Inevitable?: Chinese Perspectives on US-China Strategic Competition," *Chinese Journal of International Politics* 1 (2019): 1–24.

14. See, for example, Wang Jisi, "Dui Zhong-Mei guanxi buwendingxing de fenxi" [The Instability of US-China Relations], *Shijie Jingji yu Zhengzhi* 12 (2010): 29–30;Wang Jisi, "Zhong-Mei jigouxing maodun shangsheng zhanlue jiaoliang nanyi bimian" [US-China Strategic Competition Is Inevitable While the Structural Contradictions between These Two Countries Arise], *Guoji Zhanlue Yanjiu* 47 (2010): 1–4; Zhu Feng, "Zhong-Mei zhanlue jingzheng yu Dong-Ya anquan zhixu de weilai" [Sino-US Strategic Competition and the Future of East Asian Security], *Shijie Jingji yu Zhengzhi* 3 (2013): 9–12; Cui Liru, "Guanli zhanlue jingzheng: Zhong-Mei xin guanxi geju de tiaozhan" [Managing Strategic Competition: Challenges for New US-China Relations], *Meiguo Yanjiu* 2 (2016): 9–12.

15. Xu Jian, "Meiguo duihua zhengce tiaozheng yu Zhong-Mei guanxi de san da fengxian" [The Adjustment of US Policy towards China and Three Major Risks in US-China Relations], *Guoji Wenti Yanjiu* 4 (2018): 14–18; Liu Feng, "Zhong-Mei zhanlue jinzheng yu Dong Ya anquan taishi" [China-US Strategic Competition and East Asian Security], *Xiandai Guoji Guanxi* 8 (2017): 27–28; Zhao Minghao, "Telangpu zhizheng yu Zhong-Mei guanxi de zhanlue zhuanxing" [The Trump Doctrine and the Strategic Transformation of US-China Relations], *Meiguo Yanjiu* 5 (2018): 34–37; Wei Zongyou, "Zhong-Mei zhanlue jingzheng, Meiguo diwei jiaolu, yu Telangpu dui Hua zhanlue tiaozheng" [China-US Strategic Competition, US Status Anxiety, and Trump's Strategic Adjustment towards China], *Meiguo Yanjiu* 4 (2018): 70–73.

16. Chen Yao, "Zhongguo-Dongmeng zhengzhi huxin: Xianzhuang, wenti yu moshi xuanze" [China-ASEAN Political Mutual Trust: Present Situation, Problems and the Model Selection], *Dong Nan Ya Yanjiu* 3 (2014): 34–40.

17. Ibid.

18. Ren Yuanzhe, "Meiguo Dongmeng guanxi de 'san jitao' yu Dong Nan Ya diqu zhixu" [Three Leaps of US-ASEAN Relations and Southeast Asian Regional Order], *Nanyang Wenti Yanjiu* 1 (2017): 23.

19. Chen Xiaoding and Wang Cuimei, "Tiaodong guojia yingdui Zhongguo jueqi de zhanlue xuanze: yizhong jiyu zhiheng nengli he zhiheng yiyuan jieshi" [Strategic Choices of Neighboring States in Responding to China's Rise: An Explanation Based on Balancing Capacity and Balancing Will], *Dangdai Ya Tai* 1 (2019): 157.

20. Lian Bo, "Zhuisui zhanlue de 'huanghun': Jiyu Dong Nan Ya guojia dui Zhong Mei liangguo zhanlue huxiang de fenxi" [The Twilight of Bandwagon Strategy: Strategic Trends in Southeast Asian Countries towards the U.S. and China], *Dangdai Yatai* 1 (2019): 158.

21. Wen Yao, "Dong Nan Ya guojia de dui Hua duichong: yixiang lilun tantao" [Southeast Asian Countries' Hedging Strategies toward China], *Dangdai Ya Tai* 6 (2016): 4–23.

22. Nie Wenjuan, "Dengmeng duihua de shenfen dingwei yu zhanlue fenxi" [An Analysis of ASEAN Views of and Strategies Toward China], *Dangdai Yatai* 1 (2015): 21–37.

23. Quotations are all taken from this article, different pages 21–28.

24. Ibid., 37.

25. See, for example, "Zhongguo zhoubian waijiao de zhengce tiaozheng yu xin linian' [Policy Adjustments and New Concepts in China's Diplomatic Policy towards its Neighbors], *Dangdai Ya Tai* 3 (2014): 4–26.

26. Tao Lianzhou, "2013 nian yilai Zhongguo-Dongmen mingyun gongtongti yanjiu zongshu" [Summary of the China-ASEAN Community of Common Destiny Since 2013], *Dong Nan Ya Zongheng* 3 (2016): 76–80.

27. See Hoang Thi Ha, "ASEAN's Ambivalence towards a 'Common Destiny' with China," *ASEAN Focus* 6 (2018): 10–11.

28. Wang Yuzhu, "Dongmeng jueqi Beijing xia de Zhongguo Dongmeng guanxi: zi wo renzhi bianhua yu duiwai zhanlue tiaozheng" [China-ASEAN Relations in the Context of Rising ASEAN: Its Own Changing Self-Perceptions and Strategic Readjustment], *Nanyang Wenti Yanjiu* 2 (2016): 1–11.

29. Du Lan, "Zhong-Mei zai nanbandao de jingzheng taidu ji hezuo qianjing" [The Situation of Competition and Prospects of Cooperation between China and the US in the Indochina Peninsula], *Nanyang Wenti Yanjiu* 3 (2016): 95–103.

30. For a detailed assessment of US military ties with each of these countries, see Zhao Yi, "Dangqian Meiguo zai Dong Nan Ya de junshi cunzai fenxi" [Analysis of the Current Military Presence of the United States in Southeast Asia], *Dong Nan Ya Yanjiu* 5 (2014): 59–64.

31. Ibid.

32. Zhan Lin and Wu Xueyan, "Meiguo dui Yinni de junshi jiaoyu peixun yuanzhu: neirong, mubiao yu chengxiao" [America's Military Education Training Assistance to Indonesia: Content, Goals and Results], *Nanyang Wenti Yanjiu* 2 (2019): 59–72.

33. Ibid., 60.

34. Wang Boxuan, "Meiguo 'Ya Tai zai pingheng' zhanlue Beijing xia de Zhongguo zhoubian waijiao zhengce" [China's Neighborhood Diplomacy against the Background of the 'Asia-Pacific Rebalance' Strategy of the US], *Dong Nan Ya Zongheng* 3 (2016): 44–48.

35. Wang Xiaoke and Zhang Huizhi, "Daguo jingzheng yu Zhongguo dui Dong Nan Ya de jingji waijiao" [Great Power Competition and China's Economic Diplomacy in Southeast Asia], *Dong Nan Ya Yanjiu* 1 (2015): 27–32.

36. See, for example, Lu Guangsheng and Nie Jiao, "Zhong-mei maoyizhan beijing xia de Zhongguo-Dongmeng guanxi: yingxiang, fengxian yu yindui" [China-ASEAN Relations in the Background of the US-China Trade War: Impacts, Risks, and Countermeasures], *Nanyang Wenti Yanjiu* 1 (2019): 1–10; Bi Shihong, "Quanli zhuanyi beijing xia Dongmeng duobian waijiao zhanlue de yanbian, tedian ji tiaozhan" [The Evolution, Characteristics, and Challenges of ASEAN Multilateral Diplomatic Strategy in the Background of Power Transition], *Nanyang Wenti Yanjiu* 2 (2018): 1–12.

37. See, for example, Yan Sen, "Dong Ya, Dong Nan Ya diqu jingji shouru yu quchengnei maoyi duiqi cujin chengyin de shizheng yanjiu" [An Empirical Study on Economic

Convergence and the Accelerating Effect of Intra-Regional Trade in East and Southeast Asia], *Nanyang Wenti Yanjiu* 1 (2018): 92–104; Lin Mei and Na Wenpeng, "Yinni zaoshu xingqu gongyehua wenti tanxi" [A Study of Indonesia Premature Industrialization], *Nanyang Wenti Yanjiu* 1 (2018): 77–91.

38. See, for example, Zhu Qin, ed., *Dong Nan Ya Diqu Fazhan Baogao: 2017–2018* (Beijing: Shehui kexue wenzhai chubanshe, 2018).

39. See, for example, Qi Huaigao and Li Yanliang, "Jianpuzhai 2017 nian cunxuan qianhou de zhengdang zhengzhi bobian ji songlai zhengju zouxiang" [The Rivalries in Party Politics around Cambodia's 2017 Communal Elections and Its Influence on Cambodia's Future Political Development], *Nanyang Wenti Yanjiu* 1 (2018): 63–76; Peng Hui and Wang Xiaojuan, "Taiguo zhengzhi zhong de 'jiaofu' qunti tanxi" [The Godfathers in Thai Politics], *Nanyang Wenti Yanjiu* 2 (2018): 26–35; Shen Hongfang, "Feilubin duterte zhengfu de zhengzhi jingji gaige yanjiu" [The Philippines Duterte Government's Political and Economic Reforms], *Nanyang Wenti Yanjiu* 3 (2018): 76–85.

40. Interview with Dean Li Yiping, Xiamen Uinveristy, October 24, 2019.

41. Eric Heginbotham, "China's Strategy in Southeast Asia," in *China Steps Out: China's Major Power Engagement with the Developing World*, ed. Joshua Eisenman and Eric Heginbotham (London: Routledge, 2018), 54.

42. Andrew Scobell et al., *At the Dawn of Belt and Road: China in the Developing World* (Santa Monica, CA: The RAND Corporation, 2018), 53.

43. Interview with Minister Counselor Jiang Qin, Chinese Mission to ASEAN, June 17, 2018, Jakarta.

44. Author interview with Richard Horsey, International Crisis Group, Yangon, Myanmar, May 29, 2017.

45. Ronron Calunsod, "China Rises to Become ASEAN's 'Most Important' Dialogue Partner," *Kyoto News*, August 5, 2019.

46. Interview with Minister-Counselor Jiang Qin.

47. These MoUs are all listed in the ASEAN Secretariat Information Paper (July 2019), *Overview of ASEAN-China Dialogue Relations*: https://asean.org/storage/2012/05/Overview-of-ASEAN-China-Relations-Jul-2019_For-Web_Rev.pdf.

48. The 2016–2020 Plan can be found at: https://www.asean.org/storage/images/2015/November/27th-summit/ASEAN-China%20POA%20%202016-2020.pdf.

49. Kavi Chongkittavorn, "Time to Rebuild ASEAN-China Ties for the Next 25 Years," *Straits Times*, June 13, 2016.

50. "Towards a Closer ASEAN-China Strategic Partnership: Joint Statement of the 19th ASEAN-China Summit to Commemorate the 25th Anniversary of ASEAN-China Dialogue Relations," Vientiane, Laos, September 7, 2016: https://asean.org/wp-content/uploads/2016/09/Joint-Statement-of-ASEAN-China-Commemorative-Summit-Final.pdf.

51. Email exchange with ASEAN Secretariat Human Resources Division, September 3, 2019.

52. Interview with ASEAN Secretary-General Dato Lim Jock Hoi, June 27, 2018, ASEAN Secretariat, Jakarta.

53. H. E. Li Keqiang, "Remarks at the 16th ASEAN-China Summit": https://asean.org/wp-content/uploads/2016/09/Joint-Statement-of-ASEAN-China-Commemorative-Summit-Final.pdf. Also see David Arase, *Explaining China's 2+7 Initiative towards ASEAN* (Singapore: ISEAS *Trends in Southeast Asia*, no. 4, 2015).

54. Wang Yi, "Grasping the Historic Opportunity to Promote ASEAN Plus Three Cooperation," August 15, 2016, Kuala Lumpur: https://www.fmprc.gov.cn/mfa_eng/zxxx_662805/t1287933.shtml.

55. Discussion with member of ASEAN Secretariat, June 27, 2018, Jakarta.

56. Interview, Thailand Ministry of Foreign Affairs, Bangkok, January 18, 2017.

57. Kaukisan, *Dealing with an Ambiguous World*, 43.

58. State Council Information Office of the People's Republic of China, "Full Text: China Adheres to Position of Settling through Negotiation the Relevant Disputes between China and the Philippines in the South China Sea," July 13, 2016: http://english.www.gov.cn/state_council/ministries/2016/07/13/content_281475392503075.htm.

59. Declaration of the Conduct of Parties in the South China Sea: https://asean.org/?static_post=declaration-on-the-conduct-of-parties-in-the-south-china-sea-2.

60. See "Ode to Misconduct," *The Economist*, October 5, 2019.

61. One of the best sources to follow the island-building is the Asia Maritime Transparency Initiative: https://amti.csis.org/features/.

62. For further analysis of this complicated issue see Ian Storey and Lin Cheng-yi, eds., *The South China Sea Dispute: Navigating Diplomatic and Strategic Tensions* (Singapore: ISEAS-Yusog Ishak Institute, 2016); Yang Razali Kassim, ed., *The South China Sea Disputes: Flashpoints, Turning Points, and Trajectories* (Singapore: World Scientific: 2017).

63. These include the ASEAN-China Cultural Forum (annual); the Year of China-ASEAN Educational Exchange (2016); the China-ASEAN Cultural Exchange Year (2014); the Double 100,000 Students Plan (intended to send 100,000 students in each direction by 2020—which already was eclipsed in 2016); the China-ASEAN Disability Forum; the ASEAN-China Cultural Industry Forum; the China-ASEAN Youth Association and China-ASEAN Youth Camp; ASEAN-China Young Artists Exchange Camp; the China-ASEAN Expo; the China-ASEAN Information Harbor; the ASEAN-China Center in Beijing; and forums and activities.

64. ASEAN-China Center, *25 Years of ASEAN-China Dialogue and Cooperation: Facts and Figures* (Beijing: ASEAN-China Center, 2016), 23. These activities are also listed in Xu Bu and Yang Fan, "A New Journey for China-ASEAN Relations"; Speech by Ambassador Huang Xilian at the China-ASEAN Belt and Road Business Forum, Jakarta.

65. Ambassador Huang Xilian, "China, ASEAN Enter a New Era Hand-in-Hand," *Jakarta Post*.

66. See Karamjit Kaur, "Southeast Asia Banks on Tourists from China," *Straits Times*, February 26, 2017.

67. "China Whirl: East Asia Has the World's Fastest Growing Tourist Industry," *The Economist*, April 12, 2018.

68. "Tourist Arrivals in ASEAN as of January 2017," ASEAN Statistics: https://asean.org/wp-content/uploads/2015/09/Table-28-checked.pdf; https://asean.org/wp-content/uploads/2015/09/Table-29-checked.pdf.

69. Remarks by Ambassador Huang Xilian at the Roundtable Discussion with Local Think Tanks and Media, February 9, 2018, Jakarta.

70. McKinsey Global Institute, *China and the World: Inside the Dynamics of a Changing Relationship* (Shanghai: McKinsey Global Institute, 2019), figure 38.

71. "China Whirl," *The Economist*.

72. McKinsey Global Institute, *China and the World*.

73. Raul Dancel, "Beaches Are Tops," *Straits Times*, February 26, 2017.

74. "More Tourists from Secondary Chinese Cities," *Straits Times*, February 26, 2017.

75. Sudeshna Sarkar, "An Aligned Vision: ASEAN and Its Ties with China Are Critical to the Revival of Historic Silk Routes," *Beijing Review*, May 25, 2017, 27.

76. For Chinese students in ASEAN see ASEAN-China Center, *1991–2016: 25 Years of ASEAN-China Dialogue and Cooperation—Facts and Figures* (Beijing: ASEAN-China Center, 2016), 23; for ASEAN students in China see Ministry of Foreign Affairs of the People's Republic of China, "Table of Overseas Students Accepted by China (2016)," *China's Foreign Affairs 2017* (Beijing: Shijie zhishi chubanshe, 2017), 575–576.

77. "Why More Southeast Asian Students Are Choosing China for Higher Education," Channel News Asia (Singapore), March 18, 2018: https://www.channelnewsasia.com/news/asia/why-more-southeast-asian-students-are-choosing-china-for-higher-10042118.

78. Based on personal discussions with Indonesian and Filipino students.

79. Mo Jingxi, "Scholarships Boost China-ASEAN Relations," *China Daily* (North American edition), December 19, 2018, 5.

80. Ibid.

81. Xiamen University Malaysia: http://www.xmu.edu.my.

82. "Why Southeast Asian Students Are Choosing China for Higher Education."

83. "Southeast Asian Students Are Flocking to Thai Universities," January 17, 2019: https://www.scmp.com/print/news/asia/southeast-asia/article/2182542/chinese-students-are-flocking-thai-universities-drawn.

84. Ibid.

85. See David Shambaugh, "External Propaganda Work: Missions, Messengers, and Mediums," *Party Watch Annual Report 2018*, available at: https://docs.wixstatic.com/ugd/183fcc_e21fe3b7d14447bfaba30d3b6d6e3ac0.pdf.

86. See Eva O'Dea, "Chinese Language Media in Australia Almost Completely Dominated by the PRC," *Lowy Interpreter*, January 18, 2016; James Glenday, "China's Influence over Chinese Language Media Outlets Growing," ABC News, October 15, 2014: https://www.abc.net.au/news/2014-10-16/chinas-influence-over-australia-media-growing-analysts-say/5816922; Larry Diamond and Orville Schell, eds., *China's Influence and American Interests: Promoting Constructive Vigilance* (Stanford, CA: Hoover Institution Press, 2019), Appendices II and III; Sarah Cook, *The Implications for Democracy of China's Globalizing Media Influence* (Washington, DC: Freedom House, 2019): https://freedomhouse.org/report/freedom-media/freedom-media-2019#china-essay; Sarah Cook, "The Long Shadow of Chinese Censorship: How the Communist Party's Media Restrictions Affect News Outlets around the World," Center for International Media Assistance, October 22, 2013, http://www.cima.ned.org/wp-content/uploads/2015/02/CIMA-China_Sarah%20Cook.pdf; Emily Feng, "China and the World: How Beijing

Spreads the Message," *Financial Times*, July 12, 2018, https://www.ft.com/content/f5d00a86-3296-11e8-b5bf-23cb17fd1498; Louisa Lim and Julia Bergin, "Inside China's Audacious Global Propaganda Campaign," *The Guardian*, December 7, 2018, https://www.theguardian.com/news/2018/dec/07/china-plan-for-global-media-dominance-propaganda-xi-jinping; and David Shambaugh, "China's Soft Power Push—The Search for Respect," *Foreign Affairs* (July/August 2015).

87. Wang Fengjuan, "Dubbed with Popularity: Chinese Films and Television Are Welcomed in Southeast Asia," *Beijing Review*, April 21, 2016, 18–19.

88. See Tyler Roney, "Chinese Propaganda Finds a Thai Audience," *Foreign Policy*, August 28, 2019: https://foreignpolicy.com/2019/08/28/chinese-propaganda-finds-a-thai-audience/.

89. For a fuller discussion of Xinhua's global reach see David Shambaugh, *China Goes Global: The Partial Power* (Oxford and New York: Oxford University Press, 2013), 228–230.

90. Steven Jiang, "China Has a New Propaganda Weapon: Voice of China," CNN Business, March 21, 2018: https://money.cnn.com/2018/03/21/media/voice-of-china-propaganda-broadcaster/index.html.

91. Samantha Custer et al., *Influencing the Narrative: How the Chinese Government Mobilizes Students and Media to Burnish Its Image* (Williamsburg, VA: AIDDATA, College of William and Mary, December 2019), 14.

92. See Diamond and Schell, eds., *China's Influence and American Interests*; Ann-Marie Brady, "Magic Weapons: Chinese Political Influence Activities under Xi Jinping," Woodrow Wilson Center, June 2017: https://www.wilsoncenter.org/sites/default/files/for_website_magicweaponsanne-mariesbradyseptember2017.pdf; Anne-Marie Brady, "Exploit Every Rift: United Front Work Goes Global," *Party Watch Annual Report 2018*, available at: https://docs.wixstatic.com/ugd/183fcc_5dfb4a9b2dde492db4002f4aa90f4a25.pdf; Alexander Bowe, "China's Overseas United Front Work," US-China Economic and Security Review Commission, August 24, 2018: https://www.uscc.gov/sites/default/files/Research/China%27s%20Overseas%20United%20Front%20Work%20-%20Background%20and%20Implications%20for%20US_final_0.pdf; Jonas Parello-Plesner, "The Chinese Communist Party's Foreign Interference Operations: How the US and Other Democracies Should Respond," Hudson Institute, June 2018: https://s3.amazonaws.com/media.hudson.org/files/publications/JonasFINAL.pdf; Juan Pablo Cardinal et al., *Sharp Power: Rising Authoritarian Influence* (Washington, DC: National Endowment for Democracy, 2017): https://www.ned.org/wp-content/uploads/2017/12/Sharp-Power-Rising-Authoritarian-Influence-Full-Report.pdf; and Project ChinfluenCE: Chinese Influence in Central Europe (https://www.chinfluence.eu).

93. The only studies that the author is aware of are the section on "Singapore and ASEAN" in Appendix II in Diamond and Schell, eds., *China's Influence and American Interests*; Amy E. Searight, "Chinese Influence Activities with US Allies and Partners in Southeast Asia," testimony before the US-China Economic and Security Review Commission, April 5, 2019; Russell Hsiao, "A Preliminary Survey of CCP Influence Operations in Singapore," *China Brief* 19, no. 13 (2019): https://jamestown.org/program/a-preliminary-survey-of-ccp-influence-operations-in-singapore/.

94. The CCP-ID Chinese website with a list of its activities, overseas visitors, and delegations can be found at: http://www.idcpc.org.cn.

95. The CCP United Front Work Department Chinese website with a list of its activities can be found at: http://www.zytzb.gov.cn/html/index.html. Activities concerning overseas Chinese can be found at: http://www.zytzb.gov.cn/hwhs/index.jhtml.

96. The Overseas Chinese Affairs Office of the State Council Chinese website can be found at: http://www.gqb.gov.cn.

97. The CPIFFC Chinese website with a list of its activities, overseas visitors, and delegations can be found at: http://www.cpaffc.org.cn.

98. The CPIFA homepage can be found in English at: http://www.cpifa.org/en/.

99. See David Shambaugh, "China's 'Quiet Diplomacy': The International Department of the Chinese Communist Party," *China: An International Journal* 5, no. 1 (March 2007); Julia Bowie, "International Liaison Work for the New Era: Generating Global Consensus?" *Party Watch Annual Report 2018*, available at: https://docs.wixstatic.com/ugd/183fcc_687cd757272e461885069b3e3365f46d.pdf.

100. These can be found at: http://www.idcpc.org.cn/jwdt/index_1.html.

101. Activities concerning overseas Chinese can be found at: http://www.zytzb.gov.cn/hwhs/index.jhtml.

102. See: http://en.cpaffc.org.cn/friendly/index.html.

103. Author interview with knowledgeable scholar in Yangon, Myanmar, May 27, 2017.

104. Khin Khin Kyaw Kyee, *China's Multilayered Engagement Strategy and Myanmar's Realities: The Best Fit for Beijing Policy Preferences* (Yangon: Institute for Strategy and Policy, 2018), 14–15.

105. State Council of the People's Republic of China, *China's Foreign Aid (2014)*, 11: http://english.www.gov.cn/archive/white_paper/2014/08/23/content_281474982986592.htm. For a full description of China's foreign aid projects in Southeast Asia see Bai Yunzhen et al., *Zhongguo duiwai yuanzhu de zhizhu yu zhanlue* [China's Foreign Aid Foundation and Strategy] (Beijing: Shishi chubanshe, 2016), 202–222.

106. Samantha Custer et al., *Ties That Bind: Quantifying China's Public Diplomacy and Its "Good Neighbor" Effect* (Williamsburg, VA: AidData, 2018): http://docs.aiddata.org/ad4/pdfs/Ties_That_Bind—Full_Report.pdf.

107. Ibid., 2.

108. Hanban website: https://english.hanban.org.

109. See Li Mingjiang and Kwa Chong Guan, eds., *China-ASEAN Sub-Regional Cooperation: Progress, Problems, and Prospects* (Singapore: World Scientific, 2011); and Chong Koh Ping, "Fujian Gears Up to Boost Trade Links with Southeast Asia," *Straits Times*, May 12, 2017.

110. ISEAS-Yusof Ishak Institute, *The State of Southeast Asia 2019 Survey Report*: https://www.iseas.edu.sg/images/pdf/ASEANFocus%20FINAL_Jan19.pdf.

111. "International Publics Divided on China," Pew Research Center, October 1, 2018: https://www.pewresearch.org/global/2018/10/01/international-publics-divided-on-china/.

112. "How People in the Asia-Pacific View China," Pew Research Center, October 16, 2017: https://www.pewresearch.org/fact-tank/2017/10/16/how-people-in-asia-pacific-view-china/.

113. Wu Xiao An, *China's Evolving Policy Towards the Chinese Diaspora in Southeast Asia (1949–2018)* (Singapore: ISEAS-Yusof Ishak Institute, *Trends*, no. 14, 2019), 19.

114. Ibid.

115. Ibid.

116. Leo Suryadinata, *The Rise of China and Chinese Overseas: A Study of Beijing's Changing Policy in Southeast Asia and Beyond* (Singapore: ISEAS-Yusof Ishak Institute, 2017), 25. This figure is based on Taiwan's Overseas Chinese Affairs Council, *2011 Statistical Yearbook of Overseas Chinese Affairs Council* (Taipei: Overseas Chinese Affairs Council, 2011), 11.

117. As cited in "High Wire Act," *The Economist*, May 30, 2020, 54.

118. Suryadinata, *The Rise of China and Chinese Overseas*, 114.

119. Cheong Suk-Wai, "China's 'One Big Family' Policy Raises Concerns," *Straits Times*, April 30, 2017.

120. "The Nationality Law of the People's Republic of China," adopted at the Third Session of the Fifth National People's Congress, September 10, 1980, Appendix 1 in Suryadinata, *The Rise of China and Chinese Overseas*.

121. Liu Hong, *Haiwai Huaqiao Huaren yu Zhongguo de Gonggong Waijiao* (Guangzhou: Jinan Daxue chubanshe, 2015), chapter 3.

122. Suryadinata, *The Rise of China and Chinese Overseas*, 236.

123. See Alex Joske, "Reorganizing the United Front Work Department: New Structures for a New Era of Diaspora and Religious Affairs Work," *China Brief* 19, no. 9, May 9, 2019: https://jamestown.org/program/reorganizing-the-united-front-work-department-new-structures-for-a-new-era-of-diaspora-and-religious-affairs-work/.

124. The Chinese website and description of activities can be found at: http://www.zhongguotongcuhui.org.cn.

125. For a list of the branches and national associations see: http://www.zhongguotongcuhui.org.cn/hnwtch/yz/. Also see John Dotson, "The United Front Work Department in Action Abroad: A Profile of the Council for the Promotion of the Peaceful Reunification of China," *China Brief* 18, no. 2, February 13, 2018: https://jamestown.org/program/united-front-work-department-action-abroad-profile-council-promotion-peaceful-reunification-china/; John Dotson, "The United Front Work Department Goes Global: The Worldwide Expansion of the Council for the Promotion of the Peaceful Reunification of China," *China Brief*, March 9, 2019: https://jamestown.org/program/the-united-front-work-department-goes-global-the-worldwide-expansion-of-the-council-for-the-promotion-of-the-peaceful-reunification-of-china/.

126. For a report on the June 2019 conference see: http://www.gqb.gov.cn/news/2019/0624/46424.shtml.

127. See Deng Yingwen, "Dong Nan Ya diqu de Zhongguo shanghui yanjiu" [A Study of the Chinese Chambers of Commerce in Southeast Asia], *Dong Nan Ya Yanjiu* [Southeast Asian Studies] 6 (2014): 74–83.

128. Ibid., 78–79.

129. See "Appendix 2: Singapore and ASEAN," in Diamond and Schell, eds., *China's Influence & American Interests: Promoting Constructive Vigilance*, 195–201; Russell Hsiao, "A Preliminary Survey of Chinese Influence Operations in

Singapore," Jamestown Foundation *China Brief*: https://jamestown.org/program/a-preliminary-survey-of-ccp-influence-operations-in-singapore/.

130. S. S. Teo, "Singapore Well-Placed to Tap Belt and Road Opportunities," *Straits Times*, May 25, 2017.

131. "China-ASEAN Trade Hits Record High," Xinhua, March 13, 2019: http://www.xinhuanet.com/english/2019-03/13/c_137892383.htm.

132. Sarah Y. Tong and Wen Xin Lim, "China-ASEAN Economic Relations," in Dittmer and Ngeow, *Southeast Asia and China*, 172.

133. Issaku Harada, "US Overtaken by Southeast Asia as China's No. 2 Trade Partner," *Nikkei Asian Review*, July 13, 2019.

134. https://www.ceicdata.com/en.

135. CEIC Database as cited in Malcolm Cook, "Divergence and Displacement: Southeast Asia-China Trade, 2013–2018," *Perspective* 88 (October 2019): 5: https://www.iseas.edu.sg/images/pdf/ISEAS_Perspective_2019_88.pdf.

136. Malcolm Cook, "Divergence and Displacement"; also see Sanchita Basu Das, "Southeast Asia Worries Over Growing Economic Dependence on China," *Perspective* 81 (November 2017), published by ISEAS-Yusof Ishak Institute, 8 (table 2).

137. Ibid.

138. China National Bureau of Statistics figure as of 2014 is $47.6 billion. See *2014 Statistical Bulletin of China's Outward Foreign Direct Investment*: http://oversea.cnki.net/kns55/oldNavi/n_item.aspx?NaviID=4&BaseID=YDZTZ&NaviLink=中国对外直接投资统计公报. Adding to this the ASEAN figures of $6.8 bn. in 2015, $6.5 bn. in 2016, $13.7 billion in 2017, and $10.1 billion in 2018 (https://data.aseanstats.org/fdi-by-hosts-and-sources), one arrives at a total of $84.7 billion at the end of 2018.

139. Sanchita Basu Das, "Southeast Asia Worries over Growing Economic Dependence on China," *Perspective* 81 (November 2017), ISEAS–Yusof Ishak Institute, 10 (table 5a). For useful individual country studies, see John Lee, *China's Economic Engagement with Southeast Asia: Thailand* (Singapore: ISEAS Publishing, 2013); John Lee, *China's Economic Engagement with Southeast Asia: Indonesia* (Singapore: ISEAS Publishing, 2013); Nyiri Pal, *New Chinese Migration and Capital in Cambodia* (Singapore: ISEAS Publishing, 2014); Danielle Tan, *Chinese Engagement in Laos: Past, Present, and Uncertain Future* (Singapore: ISEAS Publishing, 2015); and US-China Economic and Security Review Commission, *China's Economic Ties with ASEAN*, March 17, 2015.

140. "ASEAN-China Relations: Then and Now," *ASEAN Focus* 6 (2018): 13.

141. Guanie Lim, "China's 'Going Out' Strategy in Southeast Asia," *China: An International Journal* 15, no. 4 (November 2017): 167.

142. See: https://data.aseanstats.org/fdi-by-hosts-and-sources. Also see John Reed and Valentina Romei, "Who Dominates the Economies of Southeast Asia?" *Financial Times*, April 30, 2018.

143. https://data.aseanstats.org/fdi-by-hosts-and-sources.

144. Ma Tieying, "Understanding China: BRI in Southeast Asia—Beyond Infrastructure," DBS Group Research, August 20, 2018, 5.

145. Among the many studies and media reports, see Chien-peng Chung and Thomas J. Voon, "China's Maritime Silk Road Initiative: Political-Economic Calculations of Southeast Asian States," *Asian Survey* 57, no. 3 (May/June 2017): 416–449.

146. Sources for the following list include Chris Leung, "Understanding China: BRI Tactics for Southeast Asia," DBS Group Research, March 26, 2018; Lance Nobel and Tom Miller, "Assets and Albatrosses on the Maritime Silk Road," Gavekal Dragonomics, August 8, 2018; Kelvin Tay et al., "The Belt and Road Initiative: Ancient Ideas in the Modern World," UBS Research, September 2017; Sanchita Basu Das, "Do the Economic Ties between ASEAN and China Affect Their Strategic Partnership?" *Perspective* 32 (2018); Chris Devonshire Ellis, *China's New Economic Silk Road: The Great Eurasian Game and the Strong of Pearls* (N.p.: Asia Briefing Ltd., 2015); Bob Teoh and Ong Juat Heng, *The Dragon Stirs: The New Silk Road* (Kuala Lumpur: Kanyin Publications, 2018); and Will Doig, *High-Speed Empire: Chinese Expansion and the Future of Southeast Asia* (New York: Columbia Global Reports, 2018).

147. Dylan Loh, "Vietnam and Indonesia Stand Out as Belt and Road Bets," *Nikkei Asian Review*, August 18, 2019; Ching Koh Ping, "Belt and Road Investment in Southeast Asia Jumps: Report," *Straits Times*, August 14, 2019.

148. Michelle Jamrisko, "China No Match for Japan in Southeast Asia Infrastructure Race," Bloomberg, June 22, 2019: https://www.bloomberg.com/news/articles/2019-06-23/china-no-match-for-japan-in-southeast-asia-infrastructure-race. Data cited in this article come from Fitch Solutions.

149. US dollar amounts for each of these projects come from Bhavan Jaipragas, "11 Projects That Show China's Influence over Malaysia—and Could Influence Its Election," *South China Morning Post*, October 11, 2017.

150. Author discussion with Malaysian scholar, Kuala Lumpur, April 21, 2017.

151. Interview with senior Malaysian Foreign Ministry official, Kuala Lumpur, July 9, 2018.

152. "Speed and Scale of Chinese Contractors Ignite Fear in Malaysia," *Straits Times*, May 7, 2017.

153. Shannon Teoh, "Jitters over China Project with Axing of Bandar Malaysia Deal," *Straits Times*, May 5, 2017; Shannon Teoh and Trinna Leong, "Chinese Deals in Malaysia under Scrutiny," *Straits Times*, May 7, 2017; Ushar Daniele, "Sour Deal Complicates Najib's Trip to Beijing," *South China Morning Post*, May 10, 2017; and Bradley Hope and Tom Wright, "1MDB Deal Falls Apart," *Asian Wall Street Journal*, May 4, 2017.

154. Johan Nylander, "Chinese Taking Over Malaysia in Twenty Years, Politician Warns," *Asia Times*, May 6, 2017; Wan Saiful Wan Jan, "Malaysian's Response to Big China Presence Shows Concerns," *Straits Times*, April 27, 2017; FMT Reporters, "Sri Lanka: Debt Woes with China a Warning to Malaysia," *Free Malaysia Today*, July 31, 2017: http://www.freemalaysiatoday.com/category/nation/2017/07/31/report-sri-lankas-debt-woes-with-china-a-warning/.

155. See Wan Saiful Wan Jan, "Malaysians' Response to Big China Presence Shows Concerns," *Straits Times*, April 27, 2017; also see Tham Siew Yean, "Chinese

Investment in Malaysia: Five Years into the BRI," *Perspective* 11 (2018), ISEAS–Yusof Ishak Institute.

156. Reme Ahmad, "Mahathir Takes Aim at China Investments in Key Party Speech," *Straits Times*, January 15, 2017.

157. PBS News Hour, "China's Massive Belt & Road Initiative Builds Infrastructure—and Influence," September 27, 2019: https://www.pbs.org/newshour/show/how-historic-belt-and-road-infrastructure-project-is-building-chinas-global-influence.

158. N.A., "Malaysia's Belt and Road Railway Project Suspended," *Straits Times*, July 5, 2018; Amanda Erickson, "Malaysia Cancels Two Big Chinese Projects, Fearing They Will Bankrupt the Country," *Washington Post*, August 21, 2018.

159. N.A., "Mahathir Axes Rail Link with Singapore," *South China Morning Post*, May 28, 2018.

160. N.A., "KL Probes China-Backed Projects' Links to 1MDB," *Straits Times*, July 6, 2018.

161. Adam Schreck, "Malaysia's Mahathir Aims to Scrap China Deals," AP News, August 13, 2018: https://www.apnews.com/27dd8af785214660b29cbb917161b47e.

162. N.A., "Mahathir Axes Rail Link with Singapore."

163. Quoted in Hannah Beech, "'We Cannot Afford This': Malaysia Pushes Back against China's Vision," *New York Times*, August 20, 2018.

164. Ibid.

165. Among various reports see Bhavan Jaipragas, "Malaysia to Go Ahead with China-backed East Coast Rail Link," *South China Morning Post*, April 12, 2019; Chun Han Wong and Yantoultra, "China Cuts Price on Malaysian Railway," *Wall Street Journal*, April 13–14, 2019.

166. See Zachary Abuza, "Malaysia: Navigating between the United States and China," *Asia Policy* 15, no. 2 (April 2020), 118-120.

167. Asian Development Bank, "Meeting Asia's Infrastructure Needs": https://www.adb.org/publications/asia-infrastructure-needs.

168. Michelle Jamrisko, "China No Match for Japan in Southeast Asia Infrastructure Race," Bloomberg, June 22, 2019: https://www.bloomberg.com/news/articles/2019-06-23/china-no-match-for-japan-in-southeast-asia-infrastructure-race.

169. Pichamon Yeophantong, "Is China a Rogue Investor?," *East Asia Forum Quarterly* 11, no. 4 (October–December 2019): 36.

170. Mingjiang Li and Xue Gong, "China's Belt and Road Initiative: How May It Change the Regional Order in Southeast Asia?," in *China's Belt and Road Initiative: Understanding the Dynamics of a Global Transformation*, ed. Yue Wah Chay, Thomas Menkhoff, and Linda Low (Singapore: World Scientific, 2019), 151–176.

171. For an overview see Prashanth Parameswaran, *Managing the Rise of China's Security Partnerships in Southeast Asia* (Washington, DC: Woodrow Wilson Center, July 2019).

172. Aude Fleurant et al., "Trends in International Arms Transfers, 2016" (Stockholm: SIPRI, February 2017), https://www.sipri.org/sites/default/files/Trends-in-international-arms-transfers-2016.pdf. See also Ron Matthews, "The Endgame of China's Arms Export Strategy," *East Asia Forum*, September 27, 2017,

http://www.eastasiaforum.org/2017/09/27/the-end-game-of-chinas-arms-export-strategy/.

173. Panu Wongchaum, "Thailand Plans Joint Arms Factory with China," *Reuters*, November 16, 2017.

174. "Malaysia, China Set Up High-Level Defense Cooperation Committee," *Channel News Asia*: http://www.channelnewsasia.com/news/asiapacific/malaysia-china-set-up-high-level-defence-cooperation-committee-8785226.

175. Jeffrey Becker, "What Is the PLA's Role in Promoting China-Cambodia Relations?," *The Diplomat*, April 29, 2017, http://thediplomat.com/2017/04/what-is-the-plas-role-in-promoting-china-cambodia-relations/; and Bhavan Jaipragas, "How China Is Helping Malaysia's Military Narrow the Gap with Singapore, Indonesia," *South China Morning Post*, August 20, 2017, http://www.scmp.com/week-asia/geopolitics/article/2107408/how-china-helping-malaysias-military-narrow-gap-singapore.

176. Kristin Huang, "Weapons Sales Making China a Big Gun in Southeast Asia," *South China Morning Post*, October 7, 2017.

177. Author interview with Philippines official, Manila, February 16, 2017.

178. Yang Razali Kassim, "Is Malaysia Tilting towards China?" (Singapore: S. Rajaratnam School of International Studies, December 30, 2016).

179. See Zheng Xianwu, "Dongmen anquan gongtongti jianshe yu Dong Nan Ya duobian fangwu waijiao zhuanxing" [ASEAN Security Community-Building and Transformation of Defense Diplomacy in Southeast Asia], *Nanyang Wenti Yanjiu* 175, no. 3 (2018): 31–46.

180. Prashanth Parameswaran, "China to Hold First Meeting with ASEAN Defense Ministers in Beijing," *The Diplomat*, June 3, 2015.

181. Sarah Zheng, "China and ASEAN to Go Ahead with First Joint Naval Exercise," *South China Morning Post*, October 24, 2017.

182. Lim Min Zhang, "China, ASEAN Kick Off Inaugural Maritime Field Training Exercise in Zhanjiang, Guangdong," *Straits Times*, October 22, 2018.

183. Minnie Chan, "China Begins Joint Naval Drills with Six Southeast Asian Nations," *South China Morning Post*, April 26, 2019.

184. "63rd Joint Patrol Starts on Mekong River," *China Daily*, October 27, 2017.

185. Ma Jianguang, Li Mingfu, and Long Chaowei, "Zhongguo yu Dongmeng Junshi Waijiao: xianzhuang, Beijing ji lujing" [China and ASEAN Military Diplomacy: Status Quo, Background, and Methods], *Nanyang Wenti Yanjiu* 3 (2018): 55.

186. Xinhua, "Full Text: China's Policies on Asia-Pacific Security Cooperation," available at: http://www.xinhuanet.com//english/china/2017-01/11/c_135973695.htm.

187. Keynote Address by H. E. Li Keqiang, Premier of the State Council of the People's Republic of China at the ASEAN Secretariat, May 7, 2018, Jakarta.

Chapter 6

1. Interview with D'ato Lim Jock Hoi, ASEAN Secretariat, Jakarta, June 27, 2018.

2. Interview with Madame Jiang Qin, Chinese Mission to ASEAN, Jakarta, June 27, 2018.

3. Rizal Sukma, "Indonesia, ASEAN, and the Shaping of the Indo-Pacific Idea," *East Asia Forum Quarterly* 11, no. 4 (October–December 2019): 11.

4. I have visited this institute twice and was quite impressed by the researchers' knowledge of domestic Chinese affairs, although not so much concerning foreign affairs and national security. See: http://en.vass.gov.vn/noidung/gioithieu/cocautochuc/Pages/thong-tin-don-vi.aspx?ItemID=124&PostID=69.

5. See Howard W. French, *Everything Under the Heavens: How the Past Helps Shape China's Push for Global Power* (New York: Alfred A. Knopf, 2017).

6. Bilahari Kausikan, *Dealing with an Ambiguous World* (Singapore: World Scientific Publishing, 2017), 41.

7. Ibid., 69.

8. See Thitinan Pongsudhirak, "Geopolitical Outcomes Beyond COVID-19," *Bangkok Post*, May 15, 2020; Ian Storey and Malcolm Cook, "Same Game, No Winners: COVID-19, US-China Rivalry, and Southeast Asian Geopolitics," *Asia Pacific Bulletin* (East-West Center), May 13, 2020.

9. See Hoang Thi Ha, "Understanding China's Proposal for an ASEAN-China Community of Common Destiny and ASEAN's Ambivalent Response," *Contemporary Southeast Asia* 41, no. 2 (2019): 223–254.

10. Thitinan Pongsudhirak, "Trump, Southeast Asia, and Thailand," *Bangkok Post*, January 20, 2017.

11. Xi Jinping, "Forging a Strong Partnership to Enhance Prosperity of Asia," speech at ISEAS–Yusof Ishak Institute, November 7, 2015, 13.

12. Xu Bu and Yang Fan, "A New Journey for China-ASEAN Relations," *China International Studies* (January/February 2016): 71–72.

13. See, for example, Zhang Yunling, "China's Neighborhood: New Situation and Consideration," *China International Studies* (January/February 2015): 41–55; Wen Yao, "Dong Nan Ya guojia de duihua duichong: Yixiang lilun tantao" [Southeast Asian States' Hedging toward China: A Theoretical Examination], *Dangdai Yatai* 2 (2016): 4–32; and Nie Wenjuan, "Dongmeng dui Hua de shenfen dingwei yu zhanlue fenxi" [An Analysis of ASEAN Views and Strategies toward China], *Dangdai Yatai* 1 (2015): 21–37. For a useful assessment of Chinese analyses of China's role in the region, see Michael A. Glosny, "Chinese Assessments of China's Influence in Developing Asia," in *Rising China's Influence in Developing Asia*, ed. Evelyn Goh (Oxford: Oxford University Press, 2016), 24–54.

14. See David Hutt, "Why China Gets It Wrong in SE Asia," *Asia Times*, November 1, 2019: https://www.asiatimes.com/2019/11/article/why-china-gets-it-wrong-in-se-asia/.

15. Evelyn Goh, "Will China Get What It Wants in East Asia?," *East Asia Forum Quarterly* (July–September 2016): 17–19.

16. Gregg Brazinsky, *Winning the Third World: Sino-American Rivalry during the Cold War* (Chapel Hill: University of North Carolina Press, 2017).

17. See David Shambaugh, *Power Shift: China & Asia's New Dynamics* (Berkeley and London: University of California Press, 2006).

18. Joseph Chinyong Liow, *Ambivalent Engagement: The United States and Regional Security in Southeast Asia after the Cold War* (Washington, DC: Brookings Institution Press, 2017).

19. For a good overview of Thai foreign policy activism, see Pongphisoot Busbarat, "Thailand's Foreign Policy: The Struggle for Regional Leadership in Southeast Asia," in *Globalization, Development, and Security in Asia, Vol. 1*, ed. Zhiqun Zhu and Benny Teh Cheng Guan (Singapore: World Scientific, 2013).

20. John Blaxland and Greg Raymond, "Learning to Trust: Lessons from Thailand, the US, and China," *The Lowy Interpreter*, December 11, 2017.

21. This is the main argument of Benjamin Zawacki, *Thailand: Shifting Ground between the US and a Rising China*, 2/e (London: Zed Books, 2020).

22. Pongphisoot Busbarat, "Thai-US Relations in the Post–Cold War Era: Untying the Special Relationship," *Asian Security* 13, no. 3 (2017): 257.

23. Interview with former Thai national security official, Singapore, July 6, 2018.

24. https://en.wikipedia.org/wiki/Thailand–United_States_relations.

25. Interview with former Thai national security official, Singapore, July 6, 2018.

26. Busbarat, "Thai-US Relations in the Post–Cold War Era."

27. Brian Harding, Deputy Director of the Southeast Asia Program at CSIS in Washington, "Moving the US-Thai Alliance Forward," *Commentary*, August 7, 2018: https://www.csis.org/analysis/moving-us-thailand-alliance-forward.

28. Congressional Research Service, *Thailand: Background and US-Thailand Relations*, December 13, 2018: https://fas.org/sgp/crs/row/IF10253.pdf.

29. Interview with Pete Haymond, US Embassy, Bangkok, January 1, 2017.

30. Murray Hiebert, "Prayuth's White House Visit Expected to Kick-Start Normalization of Thai-US Relations," CSIS Commentary, September 29, 2017: https://www.csis.org/analysis/prayuths-white-house-visit-expected-kick-start-normalization-thai-us-relations.

31. Pongphisoot Busbarat, "Shopping Diplomacy: The Thai Prime Minister's Visit to the United States and Its Implications for Thai-US Relations," *Perspective* 78 (2017): 5

32. Marwaan Macam-Marker, "Thailand Mends Military Ties after Post-Coup Tilt to China," *Nikkei Weekly*, July 30, 2018.

33. Email exchange, May 21, 2019.

34. Kavi Chongkittavorn, *The Thailand-US Defense Alliance in the US Indo-Pacific Strategy* (Washington, DC: East-West Center Asia-Pacific Issues, No. 137, March 2019), 4.

35. US Department of State Bureau of East Asian & Pacific Affairs, "U.S. Relations with Thailand: Fact Sheet," January 24, 2017.

36. Ibid.

37. Busbarat, "Thai-US Relations in the Post-Cold War Era," 259.

38. Ibid., 257.

39. Titipol Phakdeewanich, "Pryut's Trip to Washington Confirms US Non-Interventionist Foreign Policy," *The Nation* (Bangkok), October 3, 2017.

40. Quoted in Kerry Gershaneck, "Military Exchanges—A Chance to Revitalize," *Bangkok Post*, February 10, 2017.

41. Zachary Abuza, "America Should Be Realistic about Its Alliance with Thailand," *War on the Rocks*, January 2, 2020, 15: https://warontherocks.com/2020/01/america-should-be-realistic-about-its-alliance-with-thailand/.

42. Ian Storey, *Thailand's Post-Coup Relations with China and America: More Beijing, Less Washington* (Singapore: ISEAS-Yusof Ishak Institute, Trends in Southeast Asia, no. 20, 2015), 17.

43. Benjamin Zawacki, *Thailand: Shifting Ground between the US and a Rising China*.

44. Benjamin Zawacki, "West Must Act Firmly to Stem Rise of 'China Model' in Thailand," *Nikkei Asian Review*, May 20, 2019: https://asia.nikkei.com/Opinion/West-must-act-firmly-to-stem-rise-of-China-model-in-Thailand.

45. https://en.wikipedia.org/wiki/Thai_Chinese.

46. Patrick Jory, "Enter the Dragon: Thailand Gets Closer to China," *The Lowy Interpreter*, July 7, 2017.

47. "High Wire Act," *The Economist*, May 30, 2020.

48. Xinhua, "Chinese Visitors to Thailand Hit 10 Million for First Time," December 20, 2018: http://www.xinhuanet.com/english/2018-12/20/c_137686283.htm.

49. Ministry of Foreign Affairs, "Thailand," in *China's Foreign Affairs 2017* (Beijing: Shijie zhishi chubanshe, 2018), 287.

50. Busbarat, "Thai-US Relations in the Post–Cold War Era," 270.

51. Ron Corben, "Thailand Facing Dilemma over Fate of Ethnic Uighurs," VOA News, July 14, 2017: https://www.voanews.com/east-asia-pacific/thailand-facing-dilemma-over-fate-ethnic-uighurs.

52. Ed Wong and Poypiti Amatatham, "Ignoring Protests, Thailand Deports about 100 Uighurs back to China," *New York Times*, July 9, 2015.

53. Storey, *Thailand's Post-Coup Relations with China and America*, 14–15.

54. Ernest Z. Bower and Alexandra Sander, "Expanding Military to Military Engagement: China and Thailand," CSIS cogitASIA blog, November 14, 2012, 3: https://www.cogitasia.com/expanding-military-to-military-engagement-china-and-thailand/.

55. Ian Storey, "Thailand's Military Relations with China: Moving from Strength to Strength," *Perspective*, May 27, 2019; table 2 details each and every one of these exercises.

56. Interview with Thai scholar, Bangkok, January 18, 2017.

57. Storey, "Thailand's Military Relations with China."

58. John Blaxland and Greg Raymond, *Tipping the Balance in Southeast Asia?: Thailand, the United States, and China* (Canberra: Strategic & Defense Studies Center, November 2017), 15.

59. Ibid.

60. Abuza, "America Should Be Realistic about Its Alliance with Thailand," 7.

61. US-China Economic and Security Review Commission, *2017 Report to Congress* (Washington, DC: US Government Printing Office, 2017), 313.

62. Storey, "Thailand's Military Relations with China," table 1; N.A., "Thai Junta Gives Nod to Buy Chinese Submarines," *Straits Times*, January 26, 2017.

63. Abuza, "America Should Be Realistic about Its Alliance with China."

64. Prashanth Parameswaran, "Thailand Will Buy 10 More Tanks from China," *The Diplomat*, April 4, 2017; Patpicha Tanakasempipat, "Thailand Approves Purchase of Chinese Tanks to Replace Old US Model," *Reuters*, July 22, 2017; N.A., "Cabinet Approves Bt2 Bn. Deal for 10 Tanks from China," *The Nation*, April 5, 2017.

65. Kristin Huang, "China Gets Rolling on Military Vehicle Delivery to Thailand," *South China Morning Post*, November 19, 2019: https://www.scmp.com/news/china/military/article/3038445/china-gets-rolling-military-vehicle-delivery-thailand.

66. Interview with Major General Zhang Li, March 1, 2020, Washington DC.

67. See, for example, Cao Xiaoyang, "Zhong-Tai anquan hezuo de jichu, xianzhuang ji qushi," *Dong Nan Ya Yanjiu* 6 (2014): 67–73.

68. Amy Sawitta Lefevre, "After Delays, Ground Broken for Thailand-China Railway Project," *Reuters*, December 21, 2017.

69. Interview with Thai Vice Foreign Minister Virasakdi Futrakul, January 18, 2017, Bangkok.

70. Wichit Chaitrong, "China's Loan Terms Rejected," *The Nation*, August 14, 2017.

71. Interview with Thai Vice Foreign Minister Virasakdi Futrakul, January 18, 2017, Bangkok.

72. Interview with Thai Foreign Ministry official, Ministry of Foreign Affairs, January 18, 2017, Bangkok.

73. See Bertil Lintner, *The Rise and Fall of the Communist Party of Burma* (Ithaca, NY: Cornell Southeast Asia Program, 1990).

74. Interview with former US ambassador Derek Mitchell, December 20, 2019.

75. Department of State Bureau of East Asian and Pacific Affairs, "US Relations with Burma: Fact Sheet," January 27, 2017.

76. For a firsthand account of the visit, see Kurt M. Campbell, *The Pivot: The Future of American Statecraft in Asia* (New York: Twelve Books, 2016), 340–344.

77. See Jurgen Haacke, *Myanmar's Foreign Policy under President U Thein Sein: Non-Aligned and Diversified* (Singapore: ISEAS-Yusof Ishak Institute, no. 4, 2016).

78. Interview with US embassy officer, Yangon, May 27, 2017.

79. See Hunter Marston, "Has the US Lost Myanmar to China?," *The Diplomat*, January 20, 2020: https://thediplomat.com/2020/01/has-the-us-lost-myanmar-to-china/.

80. Interviews with US embassy officer, Yangon, May 27, 2017.

81. Jürgen Haacke, *Myanmar and the United States: Prospects for a Limited Security Partnership* (Sydney: United States Studies Center, University of Sydney, 2015).

82. Melvin Gurtov, *China and Southeast Asia: The Politics of Survival* (Lexington, MA: Lexington Books, 1971), 90.

83. Bertil Lintner, *The People's Republic of China and Burma* (Arlington, VA: Project 2049 Institute, 2017), 4.

84. Burma Press Summary, *Working People's Daily* (Rangoon) Vol. III, no. 10 (October 1989), 17, as quoted in Lintner, *The People's Republic of China and Burma*, 19.

85. Interview with Ye Htut, June 1, 2017, Singapore.

86. Lintner, *The People's Republic of China and Burma*, 20.

87. See J. Mohan Malik, "Myanmar's Role in China's Maritime Silk Road," *Journal of Contemporary China* 27, no. 111 (2017): 362–378.

88. John Liu Htoo Thant, "Xi's Myanmar Visit to Move Ahead China-Backed Port," *Myanmar Times*, January 10, 2020; Thompson Chau, "China & Myanmar Tighten Their Belt & Road Ties," *Asia Times*, January 21, 2020.

89. Chan Mya Htwe, "SEAOP Says Safety Measures in Place for Oil Tankers," *Myanmar Times*, May 26, 2017.

90. See Gregory B. Poling, "Kyaukpyu: Connecting China to the Indian Ocean" (Washington, DC: CSIS Briefs, March 2018).

91. Haacke, *Myanmar and the United States*, 11.

92. US-China Economic and Security Review Commission, *2017 Report to Congress* (Washington, DC: US Government Printing Office, 2017), 304.

93. See Su-Ann Oh and Philip Andrews-Speed, *Chinese Investment and Myanmar's Shifting Political Landscape* (Singapore: ISEAS Trends in Southeast Asia, no. 16, 2015).

94. David I. Steinberg, "Undulating Waves of Myanmar-Chinese Foreign Relations," unpublished paper presented at the US Institute of Peace, September 17, 2018.

95. See, for example, Tan Hui Yee, "China's Deepening Imprint on Myanmar in Mandalay," *Straits Times*, May 16, 2017; "Chinese Influx Transforming Myanmar's Quintessential City," *Associated Press*, May 1, 2018. This period and the growing Burmese frustrations with China are covered particularly well in Ian Storey, *Southeast Asia and the Rise of China: The Search for Security* (London: Routledge, 2011), 150–164.

96. N.A., "Viva Laos Vegas," *The Economist*, February 1, 2020.

97. Interview with foreign diplomat, May 26, 2017, Yangon.

98. See Liu Dehui, "Mei-Mian guanxi de gaishan ji dui Zhongguo de yingxiang" [The Impact on China of the Improvement in US-Myanmar Relations], *Dong Nan Ya Yanjiu* 1 (2014): 39–46.

99. Initiatives undertaken by China in these spheres are well documented in Khin Khin Kyaw Kyee, *China's Multilayered Engagement Strategy and Myanmar's Reality: The Best Fit for Beijing's Preferences* (Yangon: Institute for Strategy and Policy-Myanmar, Working Paper No. 1, February 2018).

100. Interview with Richard Horsey of the International Crisis Group, May 29, 2017, Yangon.

101. Kyee, *China's Multilayered Engagement Strategy and Myanmar's Reality*, 14–16.

102. Interview with scholar, May 27, 2019, Yangon.

103. Kyee, *China's Multilayered Engagement Strategy and Myanmar's Reality: The Best Fit for Beijing's Preferences*, op cit, p. 18.

104. See David Shulman, ed., *Chinese Malign Influence and the Corrosion of Democracy: An Assessment of Chinese Interference in Thirteen Countries* (Washington, DC: International Republican Institute, 2019), 51–54.

105. Ibid., 38.

106. Jane Perlez, "China Is Drawing Myanmar Closer as the World Turns Away," *New York Times*, December 1, 2017; Jane Perlez, "China Showers Myanmar with Attention, as Trump Looks Elsewhere," *New York Times*, July 19, 2017.

107. See The Transnational Institute, *China's Engagement in Myanmar: From Malacca Dilemma to Transition Dilemma* (Amsterdam, July 2016).

108. Shibani Mahtani and Cape Diamond, "Xi Seeks Renewed Influence in Myanmar amid Western Retreat," *Washington Post*, January 18, 2020.

109. For an excellent study of this issue see US Institute of Peace Senior Study Group, *China's Role in Myanmar's Internal Conflicts* (Washington, DC: USIP, 2018).

110. Officially the Lao People's Democratic Republic.

111. Angela Savada, *Laos: A Country Study* (Washington, DC: Library of Congress, 1995), 271.

112. Angaindrankumar Gnanasagaran, "Lao PDR's Geopolitical Advantage in Southeast Asia," *ASEAN Post*, May 18, 2018: https://theaseanpost.com/article/lao-pdrs-geopolitical-advantage-southeast-asia.

113. See, for example, Marius Zaharia, "As Obama Heads to Laos, Signs of a Tilt away from China," Reuters, August 27, 2016: https://www.reuters.com/article/us-laos-china-vietnam-idUSKCN11300Z; "Laos Signals a Tilt away from China," *Today* (Singapore), August 29, 2016.

114. The White House, *Joint Declaration between the United States of America and the Lao People's Democratic Republic*, September 6, 2016: https://obamawhitehouse.archives.gov/the-press-office/2016/09/06/joint-declaration-between-united-states-america-and-lao-peoples.

115. Lower Mekong Initiative: https://www.lowermekong.org/about/lower-mekong-initiative-lmi.

116. US Department of State, "Relations with Laos": https://www.state.gov/u-s-relations-with-laos/.

117. Florence Rossetti, "The Chinese in Laos: Rebirth of the Laotian Chinese Community as Peace Returns to Indochina," *China Perspectives* 13 (1997): 26–39.

118. See Danielle Tan, *Chinese Engagement in Laos: Past, Present, and Uncertain Future* (Singapore: ISEAS Trends in Southeast Asia, no. 7, 2015), 9.

119. "Torrent to a Trickle," *The Economist*, May 16, 2020.

120. Prashanth Parameswaran, "What's behind Laos' Banana Ban?" *The Diplomat*, April 14, 2017.

121. Brenda Goh and Andrew R. C. Marshall, "Chinese-Led Banana Boom in Laos Is a Blessing and a Curse," *Myanmar Business Today*, May 25–31, 2017, 13.

122. Lauren Hilgers, "Laos Vegas: A Chinese Entrepreneur Crosses the Border to Build His Gambling Empire," *Good*, March 14, 2012, as cited in Tan, *Chinese Engagement in Laos*, 22.

123. Ibid., 23.

124. Chris Horton, "Capital of Laos Seeks Stronger Ties to China," *New York Times*, September 25, 2018.

125. "China, Laos Ink Deal on Business Development," Xinhua, May 28, 2019: http://www.xinhuanet.com/english/2019-05/28/c_138096780.htm.

126. Ministry of Foreign Affairs of the People's Republic of China, "Laos," in *China's Foreign Affairs 2017* (Beijing: Shijie zhishi chubanshe), 208.

127. See David M. Lampton, Selina Ho, and Cheng-Chwee Kuik, *Rivers of Iron: Railroads and Chinese Power in Southeast Asia* (Berkeley: University of California Press, 2020).

128. See Marimi Kishimoto, "Laos Merely a Bystander as China Pushes Belt and Road Ambitions," *Nikkei Asian Review*, October 6, 2017; David Hutt, "Laos Is Key Link for China's OBOR Ambitions," *Asia Times*, July 15, 2017.

129. Marwaan Macan-Markar, "China's Belt and Road Rail Project Stirs Discontent in Laos," *Nikkei Asian Review*, March 15, 2018.

130. Edgar Pang, "'Same-Same but Different': Laos and Cambodia's Political Embrace of China," *Perspective* 66 (2017), ISEAS-Yusof Ishak Institute, September 5, 2017.

131. Congressional Research Service, *Cambodia: Background and US Relations*, January 28, 2019, 8: https://fas.org/sgp/crs/row/R44037.pdf; US Department of State, "Factsheet: Relations with Cambodia," February 12, 2016, 1.

132. See Sek Sophal, "US-Cambodia Relations: Growing Strategic Mistrust?," *PacNet* 43 (July 26, 2019).

133. Chansambath Bong, "Making US-Cambodia Relations Great Again," *East Asia Forum*, December 14, 2019.

134. Ian Storey provides a particularly detailed and insightful description of this complex period in *Southeast Asia and the Rise of China*, 178–188.

135. David Shulman, ed., *Chinese Malign Influence and the Corrosion of Democracy*, 12.

136. US-China Economic and Security Review Commission, *2017 Annual Report* (Washington, DC: U.S. Government Printing Office), 305.

137. Ibid., 306.

138. Congressional Research Service, *Cambodia: Background and US Relations*.

139. N.A., "Cambodia-China Trade Volume Jumps to $5.8 bn. USD Last Year: Minister," *Xinhua*, June 21, 2018: http://www.xinhuanet.com/english/2018-06/21/c_137270877.htm.

140. Among the many studies of Chinese investments in Cambodia see Carlyle A. Thayer, "Cambodia: Impact of Chinese Investment Assessed" (Thayer Consultancy Background Briefing, February 13, 2018); Shahar Hameiri, "Chinese Aid and Investment in Cambodia," *East Asia Forum Quarterly* (April–June 2019); James Kynge et al., "How China Bought Its Way into Cambodia," *Financial Times*, September 8, 2016; Terence Chong, "The Politics behind Cambodia's Embrace of China," *Perspective* 59 (2017); Vannarith Chheang, "Cambodia Embraces China's Belt & Road Initiative," *Perspective* 48 (2017); Vannarith Chheang, *The Political Economy of Chinese Investment in Cambodia* (Singapore: ISEAS-Yusof Ishak Institute, Trends in Southeast Asia, no. 16, 2017); Nyiri Pal, *New Chinese Migration and Capital in Cambodia* (Singapore: ISEAS-Yusof Ishak Institute, Trends in Southeast Asia, no. 3, 2014); Michael Verver, *"Old" and "New" Chinese Business in Cambodia's Capital* (Singapore: ISEAS–Yusof Ishak Institute, Trends in Southeast Asia, no. 17, 2019).

141. Quoted in Hannah Ellis-Petersen, "'No Cambodia Left': How Chinese Money Is Changing Sihanoukville," *The Guardian*, July 31, 2018: https://www.theguardian.com/cities/2018/jul/31/no-cambodia-left-chinese-money-changing-sihanoukville; Anna Fifield, "This Cambodian City Is Turning into a Chinese Enclave, and Not Everyone is Happy," *New York Times*, March 29, 2018.

142. Sheith Khidhir, "Sihanoukville Has Become a Dangerous Playground," *ASEAN Post*, January 14, 2020: https://theaseanpost.com/article/sihanoukville-has-become-dangerous-playground.

143. N.A., "How China Changed Sihanoukville," *ASEAN Post*, December 29, 2019: https://theaseanpost.com/article/how-china-changed-sihanoukville.

144. Pamela Victor, "What Does China Mean to Cambodia?," *ASEAN Post*, February 13, 2018: https://theaseanpost.com/article/what-does-china-mean-cambodia.

145. N.A., "Cambodian PM Hun Sen Welcomes Extra US $600 Million in Aid during Visit to Beijing," *South China Morning Post*, January 22, 2019.

146. This incident is well recounted in Ang Cheng Guan, *Southeast Asia after the Cold War: A Contemporary History* (Singapore: National University of Singapore Press, 2019), 170–175.

147. US-China Economic & Security Review Commission, *2017 Annual Report* (Washington, DC: US Government Printing Office), 306.

148. Mech Dara, "Banh Inks Sino-Cambodian Military Deal on China Trip," *Phnom Penh Post*, October 21, 2019.

149. Jeremy Page, Gordon Lubold, and Rob Taylor, "Deal for Naval Outpost in Cambodia Furthers China's Quest for Military Network," *Wall Street Journal*, July 22, 2019.

150. See Hannah Beech, "China Builds Airstrip, and Toehold, in Cambodia," *New York Times*, December 23, 2019.

151. Emanuele Scimia, "Cambodia Is the US-China's Rivalry's Latest Front, as Talk of Base Access Alarms Washington," *South China Morning Post*, August 5, 2019.

152. Beech, "China Builds Airstrip, and Toehold, in Cambodia."

153. Lu Liya, "Cambodian Military Adamant There Is No Secret China Deal," VOA News, September 21, 2019.

154. Shaun Turton, "China's Belt & Road Ports Raise Red Flags over Military Plans," *Nikkei Asian Review*, July 23, 2019.

155. See Kenji Kawase, "The 'Chinaization' of Cambodia," *Nikkei Asian Review*, March 16, 2017; George Wright, "Anti-Chinese Sentiment on the Rise in Cambodia," *The Diplomat*, November 7, 2018; Dominic Fauldner and Kenji Kawase, "Cambodians Wary as Chinese Investment Transforms Their Country," *Nikkei Asian Review*, July 18, 2018; and Simon Denyer, "The Push and Pull of China's Orbit," *Washington Post*, September 6, 2015.

156. Quoted in Hannah Beech, "Embracing China, Facebook and Himself: Cambodia's Ruler Digs In," *New York Times*, March 17, 2018.

157. See, for example, Toru Takahashi, "Hun Sen Gently Adjusts Cambodia's Intimacy with China," *Nikkei Asian Review*, July 13, 2019.

158. Discussion with Jim Laurie, December 16, 2019, Washington, DC.

159. For a good survey of Vietnamese foreign relations since the 1980s, see Carlyle Thayer, "The Evolution of Vietnamese Diplomacy, 1986–2016," in *Vietnam's Foreign Policy under Doi Moi*, ed. Le Hong Hiep and Anton Tsvetov (Singapore: ISEAS-Yusof Ishak Institute, 2018).

160. See Hannah Beech, "Vietnam, in a Bind, Tries to Chart a Path between US and China," *New York Times*, November 11, 2017.

161. Interview with Nguyen Vinh Quang, Director-General, External Relations Department of the Vietnamese Communist Party, Hanoi, February 22, 2017.

162. Interview with Trinh Duc Hai, Deputy Director, National Boundary Commission, Vietnam Ministry of Foreign Affairs, Hanoi, February 23, 2017.

163. See Brantly Womack, *China and Vietnam: The Politics of Asymmetry* (New York: Cambridge University Press, 2006).

164. Ibid., 5.

165. Le Hong Hiep, *Living Next to the Giant: The Political Economy of Vietnam's Relations with China under Doi Moi* (Singapore: ISEAS–Yusof Ishak Institute, 2017), 153. Also see his article "Vietnam's Hedging Strategy against China since Normalization," *Contemporary Southeast Asia* 35, no. 3 (2013): 333–368.

166. Pew Research Center, "How People in the Asia-Pacific View China," October 16, 2017: https://www.pewresearch.org/fact-tank/2017/10/16/how-people-in-asia-pacific-view-china/.

167. Nguyen Xuan Cuong and Nguyen Thi Phuong Hoa, "Vietnam-China Relations: Review of Period from 1991 to Now and Forecasts of Future Prospects," unpublished paper, March 2017. Both authors of the study are with the Vietnam Academy of Social Sciences Institute of Chinese Studies.

168. China Ministry of Foreign Affairs, "Vietnam," in *China's Foreign Affairs 2017* (Beijing: Shijie zhishi chubanshe, 2018), 310.

169. N.A., "Chinese Navy to Hold Joint Patrol with Vietnam," Xinhua, November 30, 2017.

170. A list of these can be found in Hiep, *Living Next to the Giant*, 168.

171. Xi Jinping, "For a New Vista in China-Vietnam Friendship," Xinhua, November 9, 2017.

172. Le Hong Hiep, "Pull and Push: Sino-Vietnamese Relations and President Xi's Hanoi Visit," *Perspective* 92 (2017): 3.

173. Lam Thanh Hai, "Chinese FDI in Vietnam: Trends, Status, and Challenges," *Perspective* 34 (2019): 3.

174. Wilfred Tan Kwang Shean, "Challenges for the Belt and Road Initiative in Vietnam," *ASEAN Post*, May 2, 2018; Le Hong Hiep, "The Belt and Road Initiative in Vietnam: Challenges and Prospects," *Perspective* 18 (2018).

175. See John Lee, *Reforms Will Determine Degree of Vietnam's Dependence on China* (Singapore: ISEAS–Yusof Ishak Institute, Trends in Southeast Asia, no. 4, 2014).

176. See Lam Thanh Ha and Nguyen Duc Phuc, "The US-China Trade War: Impact on Vietnam," *Perspective* 102 (2019).

177. Le Hong Hiep and Anton Tsvetov, eds., *Vietnam's Foreign Policy under Doi Moi* (Singapore: ISEAS–Yusof Ishak Institute, 2018), 88.

178. Do Thanh Hai, "Vietnam Confronts China in the South China Sea," *East Asia Forum* (December 2019).

179. Ministry of National Defense, Socialist Republic of Vietnam, *2019 Vietnam National Defense* (Hanoi: National Political Publishing House, 2019), 16.

180. See Bill Hayton, *Vietnam and the United States: An Emerging Security Partnership* (Sydney: United States Study Center, University of Sydney, 2015).

181. Interview, US Embassy, Hanoi, February 22, 2017.

182. Interview, US Embassy, Hanoi, February 22, 2017

183. Quoted in Keegan Elmer, "Vietnam Uses US-China Trade War to Rebalance Its Economic and Security Relationships," *South China Morning Post*, December 12, 2018.

184. Interview, US Embassy, Hanoi, February 22, 2017. For a description of the range of US-Vietnam military exchanges, see Nguyen Manh Hung, *The Politics of the*

United States–China–Vietnam Triangle in the 21st Century (Singapore: ISEAS–Yusof Ishak Institute, Trends in Southeast Asia, no. 21, 2015), 15–16; and Prashanth Parameswaran, "US-Vietnam Defense Relations: Problems and Prospects," *The Diplomat*, May 27, 2016.

185. Xuan Loc Doan, "Vietnam-US Relations Flourishing under Trump," *Perspective* 63 (2019): 3.

186. Office of the US Trade Representative, "Vietnam": https://ustr.gov/countries-regions/southeast-asia-pacific/vietnam.

187. The full interview can be accessed at: https://www.youtube.com/watch?v=XL_AMOnnV5o.

188. US Department of State, "US Relations with Malaysia": https://www.state.gov/u-s-relations-with-malaysia/.

189. Ibid.

190. Ibid.

191. Interviews, US Embassy, Kuala Lumpur, April 21, 2017.

192. For an in-depth account of the 1MDB scandal, see Tom Wright and Bradley Hope, *Billion Dollar Whale* (New York and Boston: Hachette Books, 2018).

193. See Tom Wright and Simon Clark, "Investigators Believe Money Flowed to Malaysian Leader Najib's Accounts amid 1MDB Probe," *Wall Street Journal*, July 3, 2015: https://www.wsj.com/articles/SB10130211234592774869404581083700187014570.

194. Mergawati Zulfakar, "Najib: China-Malaysia Ties at Their Best Now," *Star Online*, November 17, 2016, https://www.thestar.com.my/news/nation/2015/11/17/malaysia-china-bilateral-ties-at-its-best/.

195. Hannah Ellis-Petersen, "1MDB Scandal Explained: A Tale of Malaysia's Missing Millions," *The Guardian*, October 25, 2018: https://www.theguardian.com/world/2018/oct/25/1mdb-scandal-explained-a-tale-of-malaysias-missing-billions; Bahvan Jaipragas, "Rosmah Mansor, Wife of Disgraced Malaysian Ex-PM Najib Razak, Is Arrested," *South China Morning Post*, October 3, 2018: https://www.scmp.com/week-asia/politics/article/2166812/rosmah-mansor-wife-disgraced-malaysian-leader-najib-razak.

196. See Hannah Beech, "Malaysia's Prime Minister Ousted by King, or So It Seems," *New York Times*, March 1, 2020.

197. See "Muhyiddin's Mess," *The Economist*, May 23, 2020; Richard C. Paddock, "Democracy Fades in Malaysia as Old Guard Is Restored Without a Vote," *New York Times*, May 24, 2020.

198. See Lye Liang Fook, "China-Malaysia Relations Back on Track?" *Perspective* 38 (2019).

199. Interview with Dato' Abdul Majid Ahmad Khan, Kuala Lumpur, April 21, 2017.

200. N.A., "Xi, Mahathir Boost Relations," *Global Times*, August 20, 2018.

201. See Ngeow Chow Bing, "Barisan Nasional and the Chinese Communist Party: A Case Study in China's Party-Based Diplomacy," *China Review* 17, no. 1 (February 2017): 53–82. This is a detailed and excellent case study that reveals the surprising extent of CCP penetration into Malaysia.

202. Ibid., 76.

203. These activities are detailed in the excellent survey by Ngeow Chow Bing, "Comprehensive Strategic Partners but Prosaic Military Ties: The Development of Malaysia-China Defense Relations, 1991–2015," *Contemporary Southeast Asia* 37, no. 2 (2015): 269–304.

204. A. Kadir Jasin, "Dr. M's China Visit to Remove Kinks in the Relationship," *Star Online*, August 15, 2018.

205. Quoted in "Malaysia and China Laud Strong Ties, Signal Greater Cooperation," *Reuters* republished in *Today* (Singapore), July 31, 2018.

206. Cheng-Chwee Kuik, "Malaysia between the United States and China: What Do Weaker States Hedge Against?" *Asian Politics & Policy* 8, no. 1 (2016): 169. Also see Cheng-Chwee Kuik, "The Essence of Hedging: Malaysia and Singapore's Response to a Rising China," *Contemporary Southeast Asia* 30, no. 2 (2008): 159–185; Ayame Suzuki and Lee Poh Ping, "Malaysia's Hedging Strategy, a Rising China, and the Changing Strategic Situation in East Asia," in *Southeast Asia and China: A Contest in Mutual Socialization*, ed. Lowell Dittmer and Ngeow Chow Bing (Singapore: World Scientific, 2017).

207. Interview with former ambassador Craig Allen, Washington, DC, January 27, 2020.

208. US Department of Commerce, "Brunei: Defense Equipment," July 12, 2019: https://www.export.gov/article?id=Brunei-Defense-Equipment.

209. N.A., "Brunei Bets on China's Silk Road in Hard Times," *Straits Times*, March 6, 2018.

210. Michael Hart, "Brunei Abandons South China Sea Claim for Chinese Finance," *Geopolitical Monitor*, April 4, 2018: https://www.geopoliticalmonitor.com/brunei-abandons-south-china-sea-claim-for-chinese-finance/.

211. Interview with official, Brunei Ministry of Foreign Affairs, Bandar Seri Begawan, February 13, 2017.

212. Interview with Director-General, Brunei Ministry of Foreign Affairs, Bandar Seri Begawan, February 13, 2017.

213. This is chronicled in his trilogy Lee Kuan Yew, *The Singapore Story: Memoirs of Lee Kuan Yew* (New York: Prentice Hall, 1998), *From Third World to First: The Singapore Story, 1965–2000* (Singapore: Times Publishing Group, 2000), and *Hard Truths: To Keep Singapore Going* (Singapore: Straits Times Press, 2011).

214. See, for example, Graham Allison, Robert D. Blackwill, and Ali Wyne, eds., *Lee Kuan Yew: The Grand Master's Insights on China, the United States and the World* (Cambridge, MA: MIT Press, 2013).

215. See Amitav Acharya, *Singapore's Foreign Policy: The Search for Regional Order* (Singapore: World Scientific, 2008).

216. N.A., "Our Unity, Resolve Will Be Tested," *Straits Times*, March 4, 2017.

217. See Zhang Feng, *Assessing China's Changing Attitudes towards Singapore* (Singapore: East Asian Institute Background Brief No. 1241, April 2017); Han Fook Kwang, "What's Behind Singapore's Latest Run-Ins with Beijing?," *Straits Times*, December 17, 2016.

218. Michael Tan and Ngee Tiong, "Time for Singapore to Move Away from Uncle Sam's Embrace?," *Straits Times*, January 7, 2017.

219. Ibid.

220. See Charles Clover and Gloria Cheung, "Beijing Steps Up Pressure on Singapore over Taiwan Links," *Financial Times, January* 10, 2017; N.A., "SAF's Terrex Vehicles Will Be Returned to Singapore," *Straits Times*, January 25, 2017.

221. See Pei Shing Huei, "West Is Best: Chongqing Wins Bid for Singapore Business Park as Xi Promotes Development of Western China," *South China Morning Post*, November 7, 2015; Lim Tai Wei, *The Singapore-Chongqing Government-to-Government Project* (Singapore: East Asia Institute Background Brief No. 1111, February 2016).

222. Interview with retired senior Singapore official, July 11, 2018.

223. Interview with Singaporean diplomat, January 29, 2020, Washington, DC.

224. Ching Koh Ping, "Sino-S'pore Ties on the Mend," *Straits Times*, March 1, 2017; Chua Mui Hoong, "Three Myths about S'pore-China Ties," *Straits Times*, May 21, 2017; Goh Sui Noi, "Normal Singapore-China Ties Can Also Be Strong and Beneficial," *Straits Times*, June 16, 2017.

225. Lecture by Bilahari Kaukisan, "Navigating Power Shifts: A Rising China and President Trump's America," Singapore, January 25, 2017.

226. David Shambaugh, "The Coming Chinese Crackup," *Wall Street Journal*, March 6, 2015.

227. "Full Text: Joint Statement between Chinese, Singaporean Governments," Xinhua, November 15, 2018: http://www.xinhuanet.com/english/2018-11/15/c_129994460.htm. Also see Zheng Yongnian and Lye Liang Fook, eds., *Singapore-China Relations: 50 Years* (Singapore: World Scientific, 2016).

228. See the Special Symposium "The 'Singapore Model' and China's Neo-Authoritarian Dream," *China Quarterly* 236 (December 2018): 930–1032.

229. As cited in Tommy Koh, "Singapore's Friendship with China," *Straits Times*, May 2, 2017: https://www.straitstimes.com/opinion/singapores-friendship-with-china.

230. US Department of State, "US Relations with Singapore": https://www.state.gov/u-s-relations-with-singapore/.

231. "In Full: PM Lee Hsien Loong's Speech at the 2019 Shangri-la Dialogue," Channel News Asia, May 31, 2019: https://www.channelnewsasia.com/news/singapore/lee-hsien-loong-speech-2019-shangri-la-dialogue-11585954.

232. Lee Hsien Loong, "The Endangered Asian Century," *Foreign Affairs*, June 4, 2020: https://www.foreignaffairs.com/articles/asia/2020-06-04/lee-hsien-loong-endangered-asian-century.

233. Bilahari Kausikan, "No Sweet Spot for Singapore in US-China Tensions," *Straits Times*, May 29, 2019.

234. Lee Kuan Yew, *One Man's View of the World* (Singapore: Straits Times Press, 2018), 34, 70–71.

235. Allison, Blackwill, and Wyne, eds., *Lee Kuan Yew*, 6–7.

236. Interview with Ambassador Joseph Donovan, US Embassy, Jakarta, June 26, 2018.

237. Interview with US Embassy Public Affairs and Cultural Attaché Karen Schinnerer, Jakarta, June 26, 2018.

238. See: https://id.usembassy.gov/education-culture/fulbright-program/.

239. Interview with US Embassy Public Affairs and Cultural Attaché Karen Schinnerer, Jakarta, June 26, 2018.

240. These activities include a Bilateral Defense Dialogue; US-Indonesia Security Dialogue; Secretary of Defense and other high-level DoD exchanges; Individual Annual Service talks (ASTs) between Army, Navy/Marines, Air Force; Joint exercises (CARAT, Komodo, Pacific Partnership, RIMPAC, Garuda Shield, Keris Marir, COPEWEST; Maritime Domain Awareness (MDA) training; Subject Matter Expert exchanges; Counterterrorism cooperation and intelligence sharing; IMET and E-IMET professional military education exchange; Exchanges with US War College, National Defense University, and Ranger School; and Foreign Military Sales (FMS) of $1.6 bn. and Foreign Military Financing (FMF) of $2.4 million in FY 2018. Interview with Office of Defense Cooperation, US Embassy, Jakarta, June 26, 2018.

241. https://www.defense.gov/Newsroom/Releases/Release/Article/1863375/joint-statement-between-the-ministry-of-defense-of-the-republic-of-indonesia-an/.

242. See Joshua Kurlantzick, *Keeping the US-Indonesia Relationship Moving Forward* (New York: Council on Foreign Relations, 2018); Natasha Hamilton-Hart and Dave McRae, *Indonesia: Balancing the United States and China, Aiming for Independence* (Sydney: United States Studies Center, 2015).

243. Statement at conference on "New Dimensions of China's Influence in Southeast Asia: Implications for Singapore, Indonesia, and Malaysia," Singapore Management University, February 6, 2017.

244. Interview with Jusuf Wanandi, Singapore, April 14, 2017.

245. Interview with University of Indonesia scholar, Jakarta, May 4, 2017.

246. Ibid.

247. Statement by Natalia Soebagyo, Chair of the Center for Chinese Studies, Jakarta, June 26, 2018.

248. Statement by unnamed scholar, Center for Chinese Studies, Jakarta, June 26, 2018.

249. See "Full Text of China-Indonesia Joint Statement," Xinhua, May 7, 2018: http://www.xinhuanet.com/english/2018-05/08/c_137163660.htm. Also see N.A., "Courting China," *Jakarta Post*, January 24, 2017.

250. https://oec.world/en/profile/country/idn/.

251. Leo Suryadinata, *The Growing "Strategic Partnership" between Indonesia and China Faces Difficult Challenges* (Singapore: ISEAS–Yusuf Ishak Institute, Trends in Southeast Asia, no. 15, 2017), 6.

252. Tassia Sipahutar, "More Tourists Visited Indonesia Last Year Than Ever Before," *Bloomberg*, February 1, 2019: https://www.bloomberg.com/news/articles/2019-02-01/malaysians-chinese-lead-record-influx-of-tourists-to-indonesia.

253. N.A., "Indonesia, China Cooperate to Boost Tourist Arrivals," *Jakarta Post*, March 11, 2017.

254. Liza Yosephine, "China Boosts Scholarships for Indonesians," *Jakarta Post*, March 15, 2017.

255. Interview at Al-Azhar University, Jakarta, May 3, 2017.

256. Rika Theo and Maggi W. H. Leung, "China's Confucius Institutes in Indonesia: Mobility, Frictions, and Local Surprises," *Sustainability* 10 (2018): 12.

257. These military ties are well described in Hamilton-Hart and McRae, *Indonesia*, 8–9.

258. Jon Emont, "China Campaign Mutes Criticism of Uighur Camps: Effort in Indonesia Pays Off as Muslim Groups Accept Beijing's Policies in Xinjiang," *Wall Street Journal*, December 12, 2019.

259. See, for example, John McBeth, "How Indonesia Stared Down China in South China Sea," *Asia Times*, January 17, 2020; Niharika Mandhana, "Indonesia Tries to Gently Repel China," *Wall Street Journal*, January 18–19, 2020; Arlina Aeshad, "Jokowi Plays Down Stand-Off with China in the Natunas," *Straits Times*, January 10, 2020.

260. Estimate from Zuraidah Ibrahim and Phila Siu, "Widodo Wants Chinese to Keep Coming—as Investors, Not Workers," *South China Morning Post*, April 28, 2017. For a detailed assessment of the Chinese labor issue, see "Labor on the Loose: Chinese Workers Flood Industry and Infrastructure Projects," *Tempo*, September 6, 2015.

261. See, for example, John McBeth, "Indonesia's Mega Fast-Rail Project Runs into Trouble," *Asia Times*, December 21, 2017.

262. The best single study of BRI in Indonesia is Siwage Dharma Negara and Leo Suryadinata, *Indonesia and China's Belt and Road Initiatives: Perspectives, Issues, and Prospects* (Singapore: ISEAS–Yusuf Ishak Institute, Trends in Southeast Asia, no. 11, 2018).

263. "China Invests in Indonesia's Newest Province, North Kalimantan," *Koran Tempo*, September 6, 2017.

264. N.A., "Indonesia to Propose Projects Worth $91 Billion for China's Belt and Road," *Straits Times* (from *Jakarta Post*), March 20, 2019: https://www.straitstimes.com/asia/se-asia/indonesia-to-propose-projects-worth-us91-bilion-for-chinas-belt-and-road. Also see discussion in Jonathan Stromseth, *Don't Make Us Choose: Southeast Asia in the Throes of US-China Rivalry* (Washington, DC: Brookings Institution, 2019), 9–10.

265. N.A., "Indonesia Polls Bring Battle over China's Belt and Road Push," *Star Online*, April 15, 2019: https://www.thestar.com.my/news/regional/2019/04/15/indonesia-polls-bring-battle-over-belt-and-road-push.

266. See Diego Fossati, Hui Yew-Foong, and Siwage Dharma Negara, *The Indonesian National Survey Project: Economy, Society, and Politics* (Singapore: ISEAS–Yusuf Ishak Institute, Trends in Southeast Asia, no. 10, 2017), 40, 44.

267. See Johanes Herlijanto, "How the Indonesian Elite Regards Relations with China," *Perspective*, February 10, 2017; Daniel Novotny, *Torn between America and China: Elite Perceptions and Indonesian Foreign Policy* (Singapore: ISEAS Publishing, 2010).

268. Interview with Professor Lin Mei, Xiamen University, October 24, 2019.

269. Interview with Minister of Maritime Affairs Luhut Pandjaitan, Jakarta, June 26, 2018.

270. Ibid.

271. Interview, Center for Strategic and International Studies, Jakarta, May 3, 2017.

272. Quoted in Catherine Wong, "Philippines Not Married to US, Can Pursue China, Says Manila's Top Diplomat," *South China Morning Post*, July 4, 2017.

273. See, for example, Richard Heydarian, "Philippine Military Still Sees US as Country's Main Ally," *South China Morning Post*, October 21, 2019.

274. Michael R. Pompeo, "Remarks with Foreign Secretary Teodoro Locsin Jr.," March 1, 2019: https://ph.usembassy.gov/category/us-secretary-of-state/.

275. Quoted in Catherine S. Valente, "Duterte Confronts US over S. China Sea," *Manila Times*, March 30, 2017.

276. See Jon Emont, "Philippines to End Pact with US," *Washington Post*, February 12, 2020; Jason Gutierrez, Thomas Gibbons-Neff, and Eric Schmidt, "Over US Objections, the Philippines Plans to Dissolve a Joint Military Pact," *New York Times*, February 12, 2020; Richard Heydarian, "Duterte's Rash Action Threatens Security," *Nikkei Asian Review*, March 2-8, 2020, 48-49.

277. See Reuters and Chen Weihua, "Philippine Leader 'Separates' from US" *China Daily*, October 21–23, 2016; Barbara Demick and Tracy Wilkinson, "Philippines President Duterte: 'I Announce My Separation from the United States'": https://www.latimes.com/world/asia/la-fg-philippines-us-20161020-snap-story.html.

278. Interview with Chito Romana, Manila, February 16, 2017.

279. Interviews with scholars and journalists, Manila, February 16–18, 2017.

280. Interview, Manila, February 17, 2017.

281. "Full Text of China-Philippines Joint Statement," *China Daily*, November 22, 2018: https://www.chinadaily.com.cn/a/201811/22/WS5bf6125ca310eff30328a5c2.html.

282. For a useful overview and evaluation of Xi's visit see Malcolm Cook, "China-Philippine Relations and Xi Jinping's State Visit: Context, Significance, and Challenges," *Perspective*, December 14, 2018.

283. Erin Cook, "Duterte's Fifth China Visit: Heavy on Promise, Light on Results," *The Diplomat*, September 5, 2019: https://thediplomat.com/2019/09/dutertes-fifth-china-visit-heavy-on-promise-light-on-results/.

284. See Alvin Camba, "What Happened to the Billions China Pledged to the Philippines?," *South China Morning Post*, August 5, 2018: https://www.scmp.com/week-asia/business/article/2158237/what-happened-billions-china-pledged-philippines-not-what-you.

285. See, for example, Richard Heydarian, "What Has Duterte Gained from His China-Friendly Policy?" *Straits Times*, July 12, 2018; and interviews with US Embassy officers, Manila, February 16, 2017.

Chapter 7

1. Quoted in Seow Bei Yi, "ASEAN Has to Work with the World as It Is: PM Lee Hsien Loong," *Straits Times*, November 15, 2018.

2. Quoted in Eileen Ng, "Pompeo Says US Not Asking Asian Nations to Take Sides in Rivalry with China," *Associated Press*, August 1, 2019.

3. Quoted on PBS News Hour, "China: Power and Prosperity," September 27, 2019: https://www.youtube.com/watch?v=xl_kw3mNazY.

4. See, for example, Ashley Tellis, Alison Szalwinski, and Michael Wills, eds., *Strategic Asia 2020: US-China Competition for Global Influence* (Seattle and Washington, DC: National Bureau of Asian Research, 2020); Aaron L. Friedberg, "Competing with China," *Survival* 60, no. 3 (June–July 2018): 7–64; Timothy R. Heath and William R. Thompson, "Avoiding US-China Competition Is Futile: Why the Best Option Is to Manage Strategic Rivalry," *Asia Policy* 13, no. 2 (April 2018): 91–120; David Shambaugh, "Towards a 'Smart Competition' Strategy for US China Policy," in *The Struggle for Power: US-China Relations in the 21st Century*, eds. Joseph S. Nye, Condolleeza Rice, and Nicholas Burns (Washington, DC: The Aspen Institute, 2020).

5. *The National Security Strategy of the United States of America* (Washington, DC: White House, December 2017), 25: https://www.whitehouse.gov/wp-content/uploads/2017/12/NSS-Final-12-18-2017-0905.pdf.

6. See, for example, Michael D. Swaine et al., *Creating a Stable Asia: An Agenda for a US-China Balance of Power* (Washington, DC: Carnegie Endowment for International Peace, 2016): https:/carnegieendowment.org/files/CEIP_Swaine_U.S.-Asia_Final.pdf.

7. Cheng-Chwee Kuik, "How Do Weaker States Hedge?: Unpacking ASEAN States' Alignment Behavior towards China," *Journal of Contemporary China* 25, no. 100 (2016); "Variations on a Hedging Theme: Comparing ASEAN Core States' Alignment Behavior," in *Joint US-Korean Academic Studies*, ed. Gilbert Rozman, Vol. 26 (Washington, DC: Korea Economic Institute of America, 2015), 11–26; Evelyn Goh, "Southeast Asian Strategies toward the Great Powers: Still Hedging after All These Years?," *The Asan Forum* 4, no. 1 (January/February 2016): 18–37; and John D. Ciorciari, *The Limits of Alignment: Southeast Asia and the Great Powers since 1975* (Washington, DC: Georgetown University Press, 2010).

8. Joseph Chinyong Liow, "Southeast Asia and Sino-US Competition: Between a Rock and a Hard Place," in *Strategic Asia 2020: US-China Competition for Global Influence*, ed. Ashley Tellis et al., 227.

9. Ibid., 223.

10. ASEAN Studies Center, ISEAS–Yusof Ishak Institute, *The State of Southeast Asia: 2020 Survey Report* (Singapore: ISEAS–Yusof Ishak Institute, 2020), 17.

11. Author discussion with Singapore Ambassador-at-Large Tommy Koh, December 21, 2017.

12. ASEAN Studies Center, ISEAS–Yusof Ishak Institute, *The State of Southeast Asia 2020*, 17.

13. See Ja Ian Chong, "Shifting Winds in Southeast Asia: Chinese Prominence and the Future of Regional Order," in *Strategic Asia 2019: China's Expanding Strategic Ambitions*, ed. Ashley Tellis, Alison Szalwinski, and Michael Wills (Seattle and Washington, DC: National Bureau of Asian Research, 2019).

14. See David Hutt, "Why China Gets It Wrong in Southeast Asia," *Asia Times*, November 1, 2019.

15. See Mark J. Valencia, "The US Needs a 'Smarter' Policy in Southeast Asia," *Global Asia* 14, no. 4 (2019).

16. See Daljit Singh, *How Will Shifts in American Foreign Policy Affect Southeast Asia?* (Singapore: ISEAS–Yusof Ishak Institute, Trends in Southeast Asia, no. 15, 2019).

17. See Jonathan Stromseth, *Don't Make Us Choose: Southeast Asia in the Throes of US-China Rivalry* (Washington, DC: Brookings Institution, 2019).

18. Interview with senior Malaysian official, Putrajaya, Malaysia, April 20, 2017.

19. See Satu Limaye, "Despite Stumbles, America's Engagement Runs Deep," *Global Asia* 14, no. 4 (2019).

Index